Databases:
an introduction

David M. Rothwell

McGRAW-HILL BOOK COMPANY

London · New York · St Louis · San Francisco · Auckland · Bogotá
Caracas · Hamburg · Lisbon · Madrid · Mexico · Milan · Montreal
New Delhi · Panama · Paris · San Juan · São Paulo · Singapore
Sydney · Tokyo · Toronto

Published by
McGRAW-HILL Book Company Europe
Shoppenhangers Road, Maidenhead, Berkshire, SL6 2QL, England
Telephone (0628) 23432
Fax (0628) 770224

British Library Cataloguing in Publication Data

Rothwell, David M.
  Databases: Introduction
  I. Title
  005.74

ISBN 0-07-7077703-2

Library of Congress Cataloging-in-Publication Data

Rothwell, David M.
  Databases : an introduction / David Rothwell.
    p.   cm.
  Includes bibliographical references and index.
  ISBN 0-07-707703-2
    1. Data base management. I. Title.
  QA76.9.D3R778 1992
  005.74 – dc 20   92–28123 CIP

1234   CUP   9543

Typeset by Computape (Pickering) Limited, North Yorkshire
and printed and bound at the University Press, Cambridge

With pleasure and thanks I would like to dedicate this book to my mother, my wife and a galaxy of Gilsons.

Contents

Acknowledgements

Since the whole of this book was written in a Norfolk village, its writing involved little academic consultation with or help from other people. I am, however, pleased to thank Robert Bunning and Peter Adcock for the help that they provided in the writing of the final chapter of this book. The two reviewers that McGraw-Hill asked to vet the first draft of this book were also very helpful and I was able to make a number of valuable alterations because of their comments. I thank them for this time and care.

None the less, although I incurred few academic debts in the writing of this book, my dedication does encapsulate a number of very important personal debts. For moral support, financial assistance and a touching faith in the worthiness of my endeavours, I can only thank my mother (obviously a Rothwell), my wife (who was a Gilson), and all the other Gilsons, my parents-in-law (who are much nicer than music hall tradition would lead you to expect), my sister-in-law and my brother-in-law. I only hope that, in dedicating this book to these six people, they will realize how grateful I am to them all. Thank you also to my editor and his assistant, both of whom were helpful, efficient and pleasant.

Acknowledgements

PART ONE

Laying the foundations

1
The object of the exercise

Edward Yourdon, in the preface to his *Modern Structured Analysis* (Yourdon, 1989) commences as follows:

> Let me begin by addressing a very obvious question: *does the world really need another book on systems analysis?*

Before this book was even started, and continuously during its writing, I too asked myself if the world really needed another book on databases, particularly since I have gained the impression that books on databases are even more numerous than books on systems analysis. However, since you are currently holding the book in your hand, I clearly decided that the world *did* need yet another book on databases. I want, in this short opening chapter, to explain the *raison d'être* of this book, and at what sort of reader it is aimed.

This book is aimed at three potential types of reader. Let me categorize them in turn:

1. The first is that well-known mythical beast, the educated general reader. Most writers believe in this quaint creature. He or she is a librarian or a civil servant. With a moderately informed interest in the arts, a daily perusal of a quality newspaper, and a passion for ornithology (or numismatics or whatever), this person knows that information technology (IT) is the most significant socio-economic change since the Industrial Revolution. This person also knows that databases are at the centre of IT, and he or she has a genuine (though peripheral) interest in discovering what databases in particular and the computer revolution in general are all about.

2. The second type of person who is pining for this book is someone who works in a company which has a database. Constantly he or she hears staff making remarks like: 'Well, if the data isn't normalized, you are not going to get effective mapping are you?' Not only is our company employee irritated by not being able to understand the jargon of his or her peers, but this person

3

also realizes that some knowledge of database construction and handling could be very useful indeed in the promotion stakes. Hence personal pride and ambition means that this person would welcome a book explaining the database world.

3. The third type of person is the IT student at university or college. Having opted for a course in computer applications, database design, or whatever, the student desperately seeks a book that is not written by a computer scientist for other computer scientists to read, but by a teacher for the uninformed to read. This type of student and their need for an introductory book on databases will increase, since a greater number of college courses are intended for students with no previous background in IT. Even so, someone who has done advanced-level computer science will have learnt remarkably little about databases, and is still likely to find many of the books devoted to databases intimidating.

You will have perceived then that this book is designed as a genuine introduction to databases. In our increasingly computerized world, more and more people are going to have to understand something about databases. This book is designed to give such an understanding. None the less, I must return to my original question. Since there already is a large number of books devoted to the topic of databases, what possible use can there be for another one?

I am very conscious of the remark that people who live in glass houses should not throw stones. Despite the very large number of books that already exists on the subject of databases, I do not believe that there is a single book which performs the function which I have outlined. If I were to survey here all the books which have been written about databases, the result would be tedious and not very meaningful. It is not a very profitable enterprise just to read about scores of books of which you have previously never heard. None the less, it is dishonest not to give the intending reader some survey of existing sources. *All* of the books which are cited in the bibliography at the end of this book have contributed, in some way or other, to my own understanding of the database world. Some of those books would be excellent ones to move on to after reading this book. Hence, I have attempted to give some guidance as to the nature of most of the books contained in that bibliography. Given that this is the case, let me, therefore, merely categorize general texts on databases in two ways.

First of all, and most numerous, are those books on databases which, even though they often contain the word 'introduction' in their title, are really aimed at the reader who already has at least an undergraduate understanding of databases and their place in the realm of computer science. Most books on databases do, at least, assume that you know what a database is. The majority also assume that you know the difference between files and databases. They tend too to take for granted terms like 'byte', 'processor', 'tuple' and sundry other computer science terms. As a result, such books, often admirable on their own terms, fail to be very meaningful to the genuine beginner.

There are, however, other books which do claim to be real introductions. Yet even such books invariably assume an understanding of elementary computer principles. It does seem to have been impossible for previous writers to write about databases in such a way that the real beginner can follow the exposition without confusion or bafflement. My realization that this was the case was a consequence of writing my first book. That book was concerned with a particular database called INGRES (Rothwell, 1992). In writing it, I had to provide some elementary theory so as to indicate the way in which INGRES in particular coped with such issues. A friend who works in a British polytechnic told me that he was going to use that book with his students, not because they were working with INGRES, but because he felt that the INGRES book gave them more of the database background than any other book that he knew. I had independently come to realize that a general book on databases for the beginner did not exist. While my INGRES book did provide some of that background, it inevitably did so in a partial and incomplete fashion. Hence this book. If, despite the number of times in which I have already used the word, you do not know what a database is, you will do so by the end of this chapter and even more fully by the end of Chapter 2.

Let me not, however, mislead. While this book is designed for the uninformed, it will require some study. A very conscious effort has been made to avoid the mindless jargon that so often clutters the pages of computer books, but databases are complex entities. They are less formidable than they are often made to appear, but they do demand concentration. Let me, therefore, lay out the menu.

I shall assume that you do not know the meaning of the words 'data' and 'database' or, indeed, any other vaguely technical terms commonly used by computer scientists. Nor are you expected to be conversant with the concepts that concern database designers or information technologists. None the less, if you are to understand anything about data and databases, you do need to have a nodding acquaintanceship with the basic concepts and vocabulary of computer science. Like any significant subject, IT comprises a wide range of topics. As in any other subject, people tend to specialize in one or two of those topics, simply because it is impossible to become an expert over the entire field. As you know, this book is about databases. It is not, therefore, concerned with programming, computer arithmetic or systems analysis. Yet, because IT is a genuine and coherent subject in its own right, just like biology, history or theology, you will require at least a basic understanding of the whole before you can begin to understand one specific section. Indeed, in the pages which follow, there are references to programming, computer arithmetic and quite a substantial section on systems analysis. There is, in IT, no such entity as a self-contained aspect. Every aspect depends upon or interacts with many other aspects. This, indeed, is why so many books on databases are incomprehensible to the newcomer; they use an in-house vocabulary that has become second nature to fellow computer scientists but is meaningless to others. Computer scientists are no more perverse than anyone else in this respect. If you are a research biologist investigating the breeding habits of bison, you will still understand when a fellow biologist refers to *Drosophila*, because you did lab experiments with *Drosophila* (the fruit fly) when you were an undergraduate. If you are an historian writing a book about Nicholas I (1825–55), you will still know what is meant when a colleague refers to the Whig interpretation, even though the phrase refers to an out-moded approach to English history. Indeed, in the two examples that I have cited, it would be impossible (or, at least, difficult) for our biologist and historian to do their work without this background. Although the biologist is now concerned with bison, much biological understanding of breeding habits has come from lab work with *Drosophila*. Our historian, researching into the reign of Nicholas I, needs to be aware of the pernicious temptations held out by the concept of progress, temptations that the so-called Whig historians failed to resist. If you had been a computer scientist in the early 1960s, you would not have been interested in databases because they did not then exist. Peter Bishop, in his A-level text *Computing Science* (Bishop, 1981), begins his chapter on databases by writing: 'This chapter introduces a relatively new, but rapidly developing area of computing, ... ' S. M. Deen, in the General Introduction to *Practical Database Techniques* (Deen, 1990), a collection of 12 essays which he edited (and four of which he wrote), points out that the word 'database' did not gain general currency until the late seventies. Hence databases are an aspect of computer science that developed out of the first 20 years or so of IT. Not unnaturally, books on databases have tended to take as read the developments of the first couple of decades of IT, but in so doing, have made life difficult for those approaching databases without this preceding information. Consequently, Chapter 2 tries to provide all the background material that you need in order to place databases within their overall context. Inevitably that chapter is rather skeletal, though I have tried to make some useful suggestions within it as to where fuller (and readable) expansions can be found of the topics that are covered. Indeed, this book as a whole is littered with references to other books, a reflection of my original training in the humanities. It can never be true that confining yourself to one book on a subject is a good idea. Books inevitably reflect their author's interests, attitudes, prejudices and ignorance. Only by reading widely can you gain a full and mature understanding of a subject. The title, author(s), publisher and date of publication of any book to which I refer may be found in the References or Bibliography. You may not want to refer to that book, but if you do, I have given the data which will aid you in its acquisition. I must also underline a prejudice which I have already revealed. I do believe that computer science or IT is a coherent and structured subject in its own right. As a consequence of this, I do not believe that aspects of computer science can be separated. But, of course, they must be. An excellent general introduction to information technology as a whole is provided in *Computer Science* (French, 1986), yet the 773 pages of that book contain only nine pages on databases. The 227 pages of *Mastering Computers*

(Wright, 1984) contains only two pages on databases. Yet if a database is the collection of facts used by an organization or enterprise, and a database management system is the set of programs devoted to accessing those facts, then a database is the core of every establishment. So it is. It therefore follows that all the topics dealt with by French in the other 764 pages of his book or by Wright in the remaining 225 pages of his, are bound to impinge in some way or other upon your understanding of a database. The particular type of machines that are used in a computer system will affect the nature of its database. The particular languages that are used in programming will interact with the database. The sort of operating system that a computer uses will have reper-cussions upon its database. Hence it is impossible (or, at least, grossly mislead-ing) to look at databases in any sort of isolation.

This first chapter and the second are of a very introductory nature. They try to provide the overall context into which an understanding of databases needs to be placed. They therefore comprise the first section of this book. The remainder of the book tries to follow, explain and expand upon the issues superficially glanced at in this first part.

The second part, simply entitled 'Data', concentrates, as its title indicates, upon the core of computer science, the data that computers process. Thus Chapter 3 looks at how to decide what range of data you require for an effective database. The fourth chapter examines methods of collecting data, the next chapter shows the techniques necessary for presenting data in a computer-compatible fashion, and Part Two concludes by looking at some of the data storage alternatives that are available.

Part Three looks at ways of managing the data that you have collected and refined. In other words, it looks at (and is entitled) 'The database management system'. I explain briefly what these are in Chapter 2. Understandably, they are crucial to any understanding of databases at all, which is why they have an entire part devoted to them.

The fourth part is devoted to communicating with a database. A database is just a lump of data, a mass of unthinking facts. A database management system will manage that data in all sorts of interesting and ingenious ways, but it will only do so if it is told what to do. Part Four looks at ways of instructing a database management system—of holding a conversation with it.

The fifth part is devoted to looking after a database; how we can protect it against damage or misuse; how we can make it even more suitable for our users; and how, above all, we can make it the hub of our business or organization.

The sixth part is concerned with distributed databases and developments in devising still more efficient database structures. Entitled 'Current developments and future progress', it tries to sketch out the ways in which thinking and technology are currently moving. Every computer book is out of date the moment it appears on the shelves. The principles that this book outlines will not become out of date, but the hardware and software embodying those principles will be replaced by other machines and programs which embody those same principles in a different (and possibly better) way. It would have been misleading not to have included a section that looked onwards.

Finally, the seventh part looks at a real database. Since the bulk of this book is devoted to providing a theoretical understanding of the database world, it seemed appropriate to see how that theory is translated into practice.

These seven parts should take you from a state of total ignorance to a state of conceptual understanding that is adequate for any company or any first degree in computer science. Note, however, that this book will only provide a conceptual understanding. It cannot provide a practical expertise. There are a considerable number of database management systems. It would be impossible to provide a user guide to them all. Even if one is only concerned with one database management system, as I was in my last book, that system is likely to exist in so many differing versions and implementations as to make a user guide difficult to provide. Furthermore, much of the rationale of this book stems from a belief in the primacy of the conceptual understanding. If you are a student at university, the specific database upon which you are working will almost certainly be very different from the database that you operate when you take up your first job. If you are already employed within a company that uses a database, you can guarantee that when you change employment and move to another company, they will use an entirely different system.

I have indicated that this book is aimed at the totally uninformed. This book is not going to present anything remotely original about databases. My own understanding of databases stems entirely from knowledge gained from the books mentioned in the References or Bibliography, from working on databases myself, and from conversations with colleagues. This is an introductory textbook, not a pioneer work designed to extend the frontiers of computer science. Hopefully, however, it will put you into the position of being able to understand more advanced work on databases, possibly even to begin doing such work yourself. Clearly that will depend to a considerable degree upon the clarity and accuracy of this book, but, even more importantly, it will depend upon you. Databases do demand study. Each part of this book consequently ends with a series of questions for you to answer. It is important from your own point of view that you do try to answer each set of questions before moving on to the next part. I have been considerably irritated with other books that provide questions but do not then provide the answers. Even Malcolm Bull, in his *Students' Guide to Databases* (Bull, 1990), though he does provide answers to the questions he sets, nullifies this by failing to provide any guidance for the activities that he so plentifully sets out. This book does provide the answers to all the questions that are set. Thus, if you get a question wrong, you can see immediately that it is wrong and perceive the nature of the mistake that you made.

There is also a glossary at the end of this book. This is not designed as a ruse for simply filling more pages. It has already been hinted in the course of this chapter that terminology is a significant obstacle to understanding almost any aspect of computer science. While every attempt has been made in the course of this book to define objects clearly and accurately, it will be an unusual reader who retains all those definitions. Hence circumstances will arise when a reader needs to remind him or herself as to what exactly a conceptual model is, or a string, or a Boolean operator, or a variable. It is clearly more convenient to have a glossary as the arbiter of such puzzles rather than put the reader to the trouble of searching the index, and then the text, in order to find the necessary information. None the less, even the fullest of glossaries cannot put into context every item that it defines. Hence the glossary at the end of this book will, apart from defining the object concerned, also provide page references which will enable the reader to revise that particular topic in more depth should they need so to do. This again seems to me to be a useful support to the student, and a number of other authors take the same path, though less extensively than I have here.

Welcome, then, to the world of databases, I hope that you come to find them as fascinating (and infuriating) as I do.

References

Bishop, P. *Computing Science*, Nelson, 1981.
Bull, M. *Students' Guide to Databases*, Heinemann Newnes, 1990.
Deen, S. M. (ed.) *Practical Database Techniques*, Pitman, 1990.
French, C. S. *Computer Science*, 2nd edn, DP Publications, 1986.
Rothwell, D. M. *Ingres and Relational Databases*, McGraw-Hill, 1992.
Wright, G. G. L. *Mastering Computers*, 2nd edn, Macmillan, 1984.
Yourdon, E. *Modern Structured Analysis*, Prentice-Hall, 1989.

2
Data and databases in the computer context

2.1 Definitions

According to *The Oxford English Dictionary*, 'data' is the plural of 'datum'. A datum is a thing given or granted, something known or assumed as a fact, and made the basis of reasoning or calculation. The *OED* extends the definition to a datum being an assumption or premise from which inferences are drawn.

Dictionaries, however, even ones as magisterial as the *OED*, are not legislative tomes. They are descriptive books; they describe the way in which words are used. Most of us are well aware that words change their meaning over the years. The word 'nice', which may now be said to be virtually devoid of any meaning whatsoever, used to mean meticulous, fastidious, refined. 'Uninterested' and 'disinterested' used to have very distinct meanings from each other; today they seem to be synonymous. Hence, despite the *OED*, it is only realistic to begin this chapter with a recognition of the fact that 'data', a plural noun, has now assumed the status, especially in the computer world, of a word like 'sheep' which can be singular and plural. The matter is not one needing or deserving much time spending on it, but, for the sake of accuracy and clarity, it is a point that needs making.

Data, then, is facts or assumed facts. A *database* is a collection of those facts.

The first chapter of this book was so brief as to barely deserve the title of being a chapter. Since this chapter is entitled 'Data and databases' and both have now been defined, you might wonder why on earth this chapter proceeds for another 16 pages. Could not Chapter 2 turn out to be even briefer than Chapter 1?

This hypothetical question has been posed with a purpose. The primary purpose of this book is to introduce databases to people who, while they are people with a reasonable degree of intelligence and a reasonably enquiring mind, none the less know nothing whatsoever about data and databases. It is consequently imperative that such an audience should master the basics of this subject, and those basics are remarkably straight forward. Data is facts, a database is a collection of facts.

Of course it is not quite as simple as this, but the complications are few and undemanding. Indeed, there are only two criteria that we need to add to the basic definitions provided so far:

1. Each item of data needs to be *single-valued*.
2. A database needs to consist of related facts.

Let me just explain what these two criteria mean, and the definition of data and databases will be complete.

To describe an item of data as 'single-valued' means that it cannot be broken down into anything simpler while retaining any useful meaning. Clearly, you can break down the name 'Stanley Broadhurst' into two parts, the forename 'Stanley' and the surname 'Broadhurst', but it is the combination of both names which provides an identifying label, though even then not a unique one; there are probably dozens of Stanley Broadhurst's in the world. Equally one can break the formula H_2SO_4 into three elements, hydrogen, oxygen and sulphur, but if you do, you are not then left with sulphuric acid which is the entity in which you are interested. Hence, in calling an item of data single-valued, one means that it is an indivisible entity. The line of an address—32 Cemetery Road—comprises three distinct elements, but it is the joining of those three that creates an indivisible entity. The number '32' by itself would signify nothing. The combination of '32' and 'Cemetery' might suggest 32 Cemetery Road, but might equally well be 32 Cemetery Walk, 32 Cemetery Row or whatever. Hence, while it is not always self-evident as to what a single-valued item of data ought to be, most of the time simple common sense will indicate.

The second criterion is virtually self-evident. Here is an extract from a database:

Robert Simpson	String Quartet No. 7	1977
French Defence	P–K4	P–K3
Lord Liverpool	1812	1827
Nupe	Nigeria	Niger–Congo
denken	denkend	gedacht

The first line names a composer, one of his works and the year in which it was composed. The second line gives the name of an opening in chess and its first two moves. The third names a prime minister and gives the dates of his tenure of office. The fourth line names a language, the country in which it is spoken and the family of languages to which it belongs. The final line gives the infinitive, present participle and part participle of a German verb.

Such a database would be less than useful. A database needs to contain within it data devoted to one subject. It would be perfectly feasible to have a database devoted to the music of Robert Simpson. Equally one could have a database of chess openings, British prime ministers, languages of the world or German verbs. One cannot, however, usefully have a single database devoted to them all. The database would become too big. It would run very slowly. It would pose major problems in indexing. Nor would it be useful. One is, after all, somewhat unlikely to want to know about the music of Robert Simpson while writing an article about Lord Liverpool, an article that referred to the Nupe language, the German verb 'to think' and a chess defence.

Hence we can slightly extend our original definitions. Data is single-valued facts or assumed facts. A database is a collection of interrelated data.

Therefore, using the definitions given so far, the following would be a reasonable extract from a database:

Piano Sonata No. 1	F minor	Op. 2, No. 1
Piano Sonata No. 2	A major	Op. 2, No. 2
Piano Sonata No. 3	C major	Op. 2, No. 3
Piano Sonata No. 4	E flat major	Op. 7
Piano Sonata No. 5	C minor	Op. 10, No. 1
Piano Sonata No. 6	F major	Op. 10, No. 2
Piano Sonata No. 7	D major	Op. 10, No. 3

As it happens, and as we shall eventually discover, there are still some deficiencies in such a database, but it will serve us for the moment. As some of you will have already realized, it is a database of the music of Beethoven. The extract given merely lists his first seven piano sonatas, giving in turn its title, key and opus number, each of them being an individual data item. Hence, with these basic definitions behind us, let us move on to look at the process of designing an actual database.

2.2 Designing a database

There is, of course, a massive impertinence in dealing with the design of database simply as a short section within a chapter. There are, for instance, a number of excellent books totally devoted to the problems of designing a database. None the less, it is possible to give an outline of the major aspects in this process. In so doing, we shall extend still further the basic definitions provided in the preceding section.

The major question that confronts anyone designing a database is the purpose of that database. Why do you want it? The answer is almost always the same: you want a database in order to ease your work. If, every week, you have a pay a workforce of 450 people a wage, it is convenient to be able to do so quickly and accurately. Imagine that you are a wages clerk working for the firm Scrooge & Co. You possess a list of workers. The first member appearing upon that list is Samuel Applestone. Accordingly you seize a wage slip and write Samuel Applestone alongside the 'name' heading upon that wage slip, together with the relevant date. Your staff list informs you that Samuel is a storekeeper, that he works 40 hours per week at a rate of £3.50 per hour. You next turn to the 'staff absences' list produced each week. Samuel does not appear upon it. Consequently you work out how much 40 hours at £3.50 per hour comes to.

You then write the total, £140, alongside the 'total earnings' heading on the wage slip. Next, however, you have to work out deductions from that gross salary. Is Samuel Applestone a member of the company pension scheme? Accordingly you look up the pension list, discover that he is, and consequently enter £2.50 as a pension deduction. Then you enter his income tax and his national insurance contribution, subtract them and the pension contribution from his gross pay, and enter his net pay. Needless to say, of course, all of this takes time. It is also, of course, dependent upon the total accuracy of the wages clerk, and we all know that total accuracy is not a common attribute of human beings. The resulting wage slip looks something like this:

Name: Samuel Applestone		Date: 7 Feb. 1990	
Gross pay: 140	Deductions:	Absences	
		Pension	2.50
		Income tax	30.46
		Nat. insur.	3.25
Net pay: 103.79			

Each wage slip takes about five minutes to fill out. With 450 staff, it consequently takes the wages clerk over 37 hours to do all the wage slips. If, however, it was possible to computerize this operation, so that the computer worked out and printed all 450 wage slips, Scrooge & Co. could save a great deal of time and, in all probability, dispense with the services of a wages clerk completely. There would, then, seem to be good reasons for Scrooge & Co. to develop a payroll database.

The above scenario seems delightfully strategic straightforward. The argument for computerizing the payroll seems indisputable, and there would seem to be no major problems. If the staff of Scrooge & Co. clocked in at work every morning and clocked out again each night, and if the clock fed its data to the computer system, then the computer would have all the necessary data about absences. Provided that the database had the employee number, employee name, hourly rate of pay, pension contribution, tax and insurance rate, then the computer could work out each employee's weekly wage and print the results upon standardized wage slips. Instead of taking 37 hours, the whole thing could be done on a Friday afternoon.

This idyllic picture could, indeed, be a realistic one. This is, after all, the primary purpose of databases: to save time and money. And this is all that you have to do to design them: work out whether or not having a database is worth it in the first place, and then, if it is, work out exactly what sort of data you need in order to construct the database. In the example given above, the operation was not difficult. It was decided to give each employee a unique employee number. As it happens, there were no name repetitions working for Scrooge & Co.—two John Smiths or three Ann Jones—but there could be in the future. Hence Samuel Applestone was given the employee number 0001, and so on down the list. The employee number thus became a unique identifying element.

Next to the number came the name of the employee. There was thus a unique one-to-one relationship between employee number and employee name. It was impossible for Samuel Applestone to be other than employee number 0001. He could not, at the same time, be employee number 0169. Nor could anyone else be 0001. The clock system fed in the number of hours per week that Samuel worked, his rate of pay formed part of the database, as did his tax code, his national insurance rate and his membership or otherwise of the Scrooge Pension scheme. Thus, conceptually, the database comprised 450 entries all of which looked very like this one:

Employee number: 0317   Employee name: Margaret Simpson
Hours worked: 40   Hourly rate: £2.75
Pension scheme: £1.50   Tax rate: 25%
NI: £3.25

Thus, without a great deal of thought or effort, we have managed to design a database for Scrooge & Co. which has ensured that all their employees get paid on time, get paid the correct amount, and with virtually no human intervention. True, it cost £76,000 to install the new computer system, but that will soon be recouped in the savings made in the salary of the wages clerk who, upon being sacked, immediately managed to get a new job as a census enumerator. Here we can see the benefits of databases in a classically trouble-free case.

Unfortunately, this idyllic picture only lasted for about one week. It was then that certain discoveries were made. First of all, a surprisingly large number of the workforce belonged to the Scrooge & Co. social club. To be a member of this club cost an annual subscription of only £5 and it had been the custom that anyone who did join the social club would, instead of paying the £5 as a lump sum, pay an initial subscription of 30p and, from then on, have his or her weekly wage decreased by 9p. Unfortunately this item had been forgotten during the construction of the database, and 298 employees now seemed to be enjoying free membership. Secondly, those who belonged to the pension fund had been used to having their pension contribution deducted at source before tax had been taken. Consequently, an employee who earned £182 per week but who paid £5 per week into the pension fund would only be taxed on earnings of £177. It made little difference, but the work staff were irritated by that difference and resentful of it. Finally, having installed the payroll system, other departments of Scrooge & Co. began to think that something similar would be useful to them. Thus the ordering manager felt that a database of suppliers and products would be handy. The accountant thought that the payroll database could become merely a part of an entire accounting scheme. The production manager felt that the rates of pay of employees would be useful to him in deciding upon production priorities. But, of course, there was no rapid or easy way of satisfying such new-found desires. The payroll database had been designed as an entity on its own, not as a component in a broader database.

The payroll database was rapidly found to be inadequate, and for two quite different reasons. First of all, it was inadequate within its own terms of reference. The old manual system was time consuming and expensive, but it had worked. The new system did not even do everything that the old system had accomplished. Secondly, because the payroll database was designed in terms of payroll priorities rather than in terms of the company as a whole, it was quite inadequate in adapting itself to other needs. Very quickly the glee felt by Ebenezer Scrooge and his partners at the introduction of a computer system turned to regret.

The inadequacies of the Scrooge payroll system stemmed from two parallel mistakes. The reason that the payroll system did not even operate properly on its own terms was because not enough thought went into determining what sort of data was necessary for its construction. The process of identifying the data needed for a computer system is vital. Indeed, Perkinson (1984) states that: 'The data-oriented approach to data base design . . . is the heart and soul of the data analysis methodology.' In other words, and it is, after all, self-evident, unless you give your computer system accurate and complete data, it will not produce for you accurate and complete results. Hence an essential element of designing a system lies not in design at all but in collecting and analysing the data necessary for the system to be designed. Now Scrooge & Co. did not even manage to collect and analyse the data necessary for an accurate and complete payroll system. The question as to whether or not that payroll system could be merely one section of a broader computer system never seems to have occurred to them at all.

You will by this time doubtless be a little irritated by Scrooge & Co., or, more probably, by me for inventing them. No one, least of all you, would be so foolish as to design a database system as thoughtlessly as Scrooge & Co. did. Unfortunately, the facts would indicate otherwise. It is easy to design a database in your study. When, however, that system comes to be installed, problems always present themselves. It is usual for a company to spend much more money on maintaining a computer system than it cost them to buy it in the first place. Howe (1989) begins by inventing a manufacturing company, Torg Ltd, who have decided to begin their computerization by devising a catalogue system to facilitate the printing of an up-to-date catalogue of products each month. Their catalogue system works admirably, but when they try to introduce a new stock control system as well, the problems begin to multiply. Howe entertainingly charts their progress from catastrophe to catastrophe. Whitten *et al.* (1986) began virtually every chapter with a minicase, each example highlighting a common problem commonly experienced in business or industry. Behling (1986) reprints numerous extracts from journals showing how real organizations coped with the unexpected problems that computerization brought. Lucas (1985) scatters throughout his text specimen problems frequently encountered during the incubation period of a computer system. Here is one from Lucas' fifth chapter.

The president of Farway Manufacturing Company was pondering the firm's recent disastrous attempt to develop a computer-based system for factory-floor data collection. The company wished to improve scheduling and control over work-in-process inventories. A consultant was hired who recommended the development of a computer-based production control system.

The recommendations of the consultant were accepted, and he was hired to design the system. It turned out that the consultant had designed a similar system for another manufacturing company and proposed to transfer it to Farway. This approach seemed very economical, so the president quickly agreed.

The consultant set about his task with zeal; within 6 months the necessary programming changes had been made, and the system was ready to begin operation. Over one weekend, terminals were installed in all departments and on Monday morning, workers were supposed to begin using the new system to report production. The workers are paid on piece rate and are unionized.

For reasons not completely understood by the president, the system failed completely. No one provided input, and the few data collected were all erroneous. What happened? Why did the systems development effort fail so miserably?

It seems to me to be unfortunate that Lucas does not provide solutions for his systems problems. In the one quoted above, it is fairly obvious that the consultant concerned did not appreciate that all companies are unique. It is rarely possible to transport one system which works well for company A over to another company, and for it then to work satisfactorily. Nor in the systems problem just quoted does any time seem to have been allowed for easing the staff of Farway into the new procedures, or indeed on consulting them before-hand. The best computer system in the world will not work unless there are people to work it, and a bloody-minded staff can ensure that state-of-the-art equipment is less useful than a wastepaper bin. Indeed, Scrooge & Co. them-selves were also far too limited and blinkered in their thinking. Ebenezer and his partners thought exclusively in terms of saving the salary of their redundant wages clerk; they gave no attention to the fact that databases and computer systems do need people to look after them.

However, we have strayed away from the topic of database design. This, of course, is both necessary and inevitable. As was pointed out in the opening chapter, IT is a seamless robe. Since it incorporates so many different aspects, it has to be divided into manageable sections. Those sections, all given suitable labels like 'systems analysis', 'database design', 'Boolean algebra' and so on, are not independent and self-contained sections. Each section depends upon or interacts with one or more other sections. You can only specialize in one or two of those sections, but it is distressing when a computer scientist is unable to place his own specialism within the overall framework of IT. It negates the very *raison d'être* of *information* technology.

Clearly, I cannot attempt here to give any rigorous examination of database design. I shall be returning to the topic more fully later. All that I was concerned with was to emphasize the primacy of data in the design process, and just to glance at some of the problems that data can present. None the less, central thought data is to any database system, it is not the only important element. It is at other components in the data/database matrix that we must now look.

2.3   Hardware

Once upon a time, almost every educated person would have at least a nodding acquaintanceship with the poetry of Virgil and the prose of Caesar. No longer is this the case. Today almost every educated person knows the difference between hardware and software. Hardware is the actual machines and implements used in and by a computer system. Software is the programs used by the machines and implements. Thus a database is software. There is obviously, however, no point in having the most marvellously designed database unless you have hardware upon which to run it. Hence it is far from irrelevant in this setting-the-scene chapter to glance at the hardware options available.

Only three things happen with a computer system:

1. *Input*
2. *Processing*
3. *Output*

In other words, you ask the computer for some information or you give it some new data. In either case, you input something to the computer. The computer will then react to your input. If you have asked for some information, the computer will scurry away and find it. If you have given the database some fresh data, then the computer will store that data for you. In other words, the computer will process your input. Then, nine times out of ten, you, the user, want some output from the computer. If you have asked a question, you want the answer. If you have added new data to the database, you want some acknowledgement that the data has been received and correctly stored. In every computer and every computer system, ranging in price from £200 to £2,000,000, that is all that ever happens: input, processing and output. But to do it, you need hardware.

The most common mode of inputting data or requests to a computer system is to type that data upon a keyboard very much like a typewriter. Suppose you type an item of data:

D. H. Lawrence

Each time you press a key, a series of electrical impulses travels from the keyboard to the central processing unit of the computer, where it is interpreted and acted upon, i.e. processed. Then you are likely to receive some output upon the screen which is almost certainly in front of you. The screen may simply echo your input—D. H. Lawrence—thereby providing you with some assurance that the correct message has been received. Alternatively, the screen may announce that data has been input, but not give any clue as to the nature of that data. Whatever the format of the screen output, it will give you some assurance that the data has been satisfactorily processed.

This, of course, is the simplest configuration that one can have, though none of the alternatives alter this basic threefold division: input, processing, output. You can input data by selecting an option from a menu that is presented to you on the screen. You can input data by punching a keypunch machine. In many shops, data is input by passing a bar code printed on the product over a bar code reader. The symbols printed at the bottom of cheques can be data input for a magnetic-ink character recognition machine. One can even input data in some circumstances by merely touching the screen which is displaying the available options. A beginning has also been made on using speech as an input medium.

There is also a variety of modes for outputting data. Apart from being displayed upon a screen, data can also be displayed as printed output, and there are a wide variety of printers that can be so used: dot matrix, daisywheel, laser, inkjet, and so on. Microfilm and microfiche are also common output media.

In between the input and the output comes the processing. Each computer possesses a *central processing unit* (CPU). Broadly speaking, what happens is that each input is examined by the *control unit* of the CPU. The control unit identifies the type of data that has been input and decides what to do with it. If the data just needs storing for future use, then the control unit sends it along to the memory section. If, however, the data needs to be involved in some mathematical or logical operation, then the control unit sends it along to the *arithmetic/logic unit* (ALU) to be processed. The processed data will then be stored in memory or output (or both).

All this sounds reasonably simple, and basically, of course, it is. Unfortunately, a computer does not have the mental flexibility of you and I. If I mention Maine Road football ground, there is a fair chance that you will immediately think of Manchester City football club. If I mention *Pride and Prejudice*, there is a likelihood that you will think of Jane Austen. In the case of a computer, nothing of the kind will happen. A computer only possesses knowledge that you or I give it. A computer only performs logical actions, such as sending a multiplication problem to the ALU and then working it out, if it has already been told exactly how to do this. Of course, strictly speaking, the same is true for human beings also. If your interest in football is nil, you may never have heard of Maine Road. If you have given every waking moment to the study of geology, you might never have heard of Jane Austen. None the less, by the time you come to the stage of reading a book about databases, your mind has enjoyed (or suffered) 20 years or so of constant bombardment. As a result, your brain is stocked with a vast array of facts, procedures and prejudices. It therefore requires an imaginative leap to remember that a computer does not take anything for granted and has no experience to draw on. Hence, while we understand the necessary connections between input, processing and output, the computer does not.

Imagine you are standing in your local branch of W. H. Smith. You see the latest issue of *The Bell Ringer's Gazette*. You note that it costs £1.75. You next examine the contents of your pockets, and discover that you only have 63p. Consequently you decide to buy a copy of the *Daily Mirror*. Notice that you have experienced input, processed the input, and produced an output:

Input	Price of *The Bell Ringer's Gazette*	1.75
Processing	Can I afford it?	
	Check cash available	
Input	Cash available	0.63
Processing	Cannot afford *The Bell Ringer's Gazette*	
	Would I like something else that I can afford?	
Output	Buy copy of *Daily Mirror*	

As you can see, this was a fairly complicated procedure, requiring at least two separate input operations, sophisticated processing activities and a call upon your internal memory for you to be able to know that you could afford the *Daily Mirror*. It is exactly this sort of operation that the hardware of a computer system performs. It accepts the input, analyses it, processes it and then gives the necessary output. Let us just have a look at exactly how the payroll program of Scrooge & Co. actually operated.

It had been decided that, in order to set the payroll program in action, one simply had to type, at the keyboard, the single word 'Pay'. This acted as a preset instruction to the central processing unit (hereafter known as the CPU). The control unit then fetched, from the internal memory, the instruction on how to work out the gross pay of the workforce. The control unit then decoded that instruction so that the computer could execute it. This decoded processing instruction, always known as the *op code*, is then placed into a tiny section of the hardware known as the *instruction register* so that it is ready to begin the processing. The control unit then looks for the whereabouts of the data that needs to be processed. Obviously this data includes the employee numbers, name, rates of pay, pension contributions, national insurance, and absences of each member of the Scrooge workforce. The control unit is not interested in fetching this data at the moment. All it wants to know is where the data can be found and where the results of the processed data should be placed. These two pieces of information are known as the *operands*, and they are placed in a tiny section known as the *address register*. This process is summarized in Fig. 2.1.

Once all this has been accomplished, often referred to as *instruction time*, the processing of the data can begin. The first set of data, that pertaining to Samuel

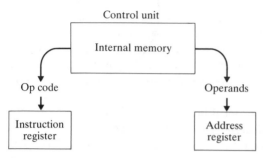

Figure 2.1

Applestone, is taken out of memory and sent along to the ALU. Using the op code, the control unit instructs the ALU to work out gross pay.

Of course, I have oversimplified. To begin with, there is much more than just gross pay to work out. Income tax, national insurance and possible pension contributions also have to be deducted in order to arrive at net pay. These arithmetic results have to be printed onto a standard wage slip. If you want a somewhat fuller explanation of what is called the 'machine cycle' then most textbooks on computer science will provide it. French (1986) devotes Chapter 16 to the topic. The fourth chapter of Kalicharan (1988) provides a clear outline. Wright (1984) packs a remarkable amount of technical information into his third chapter. Perhaps best of all in my experience is the third chapter of Carter (1989).

Once you have the tripartite nature of IT fully understood—input, processing, output—and the three pieces of hardware necessary to perform that triple process—keyboard, CPU, screen—clear in your mind, then you have made a significant step towards computer literacy. Even so, one more element does need some further comment. The CPU is normally thought of as comprising three elements: control unit, arithmetic and logic unit, and *memory*. Unfortunately, the memory within the CPU is normally relatively small. It is certainly far too small for an entire database to be stored within it. Hence memory in a computer system consists of two types: *internal memory* (i.e. that which is attached to the CPU) and *external memory*. External memory will today comprise a disk or set of disks which are connected to the computer but which are not immediately or instantly on-line to the computer. Upon that disk or disks, your database will reside. Hence, when the CPU needs a section of the database, it has to send a message to the disk concerned to recall that section and place it within the internal memory so that it can be processed.

One of the most important things that you need to remember about IT concerns nomenclature. To refer to a compound consisting of equal proportions of sodium and chlorine, a chemist will talk about sodium chloride. To refer to a chess piece that only moves diagonally across the board, a chess player will talk about a bishop. However, to refer to something specific the computer scientist could select from about half a dozen alternatives. Thus to mention internal memory a computer scientist could in fact refer to primary storage, main memory, semiconductor storage, on-line memory, immediate access store or any remotely viable combination of those terms. External memory is commonly referred to as secondary storage, off-line memory, or backing storage. When I was talking a few paragraphs back about a screen being a common output device, I was not using the most usual term. The television-type screen upon which computer scientists view their input and output is more frequently termed a monitor or a visual display unit (VDU) or a cathode ray tube (CRT). This polysyllabic plethora can be a major handicap. If you want to discover what John Smith has to say about memory in his recently issued (though mythical) textbook *Computers for Numismatists*, you will sensibly enough look for memory in the index. When you do not find it, you may conclude that Smith does not even mention memory in his entire book. In fact he does, but always calls it storage, which is where you will find it in the index. It is in part because of this terminological excess that this book has a glossary. In that glossary, an attempt has been made to include all the synonyms that you are likely to encounter.

Anyway, very tersely, this concludes our glance at the hardware of which you need to be aware. A database (which is software) is likely to reside on a disk pack (a collection of disks stored one above the other). You can add to your database (input) or request some information from your database (output). In either case, the input data or the request for output has to be processed, the job of the CPU. Yet in order to handle even simple actions like these, two more items of software are required. These two software elements are so important that they need a section to themselves.

2.4 System software and database management

We have glanced at the CPU which directs the processing of a computer. In order to do so, however, it rests upon an underlying software system which is called the *operating system*.

We looked briefly at what a database is, but a database by itself is merely an inert collection of data. In order to do anything useful with a database, it needs to have a software program to manage it.

Both these software elements are vital. Every computer needs an operating system. In a sense, it is the conductor of the computer orchestra. Every database needs a *database manager*. Without it, the database would be dead.

An operating system falls under the general heading of *system software*, in other words, software which defines and creates the environment within which operations are conducted. Thus all operating systems regulate the way in which programs are stored upon a disk. If you are using a small *microcomputer*, that is virtually all that the operating system will control. On larger computers, called *minis* or *mainframes*, an operating system will enable a number of micros to be linked together and to share facilities such as disks and printers. Some operating systems will enable the computer to do several things simultaneously, a facility known as *multitasking*. For our purposes in connection with databases, you do not need to know very much about operating systems. Indeed, one of the *raisons d'être* of an operating system is that it should perform its functions in an entirely unobtrusive fashion. That is why calling an operating system the conductor of the computer is very appropriate. If you are listening to Mahler's fourth symphony and are conscious only of how marvellous that symphony is, then you can guarantee that the orchestra has a good conductor. If, however, you are conscious of interpretive nuances, then the conductor is interposing himself or herself between you and Mahler. So it is with an operating system. Fundamental though the operating system is, it should operate just like MI5, silently and secretly.

None the less it does have to be borne in mind that not all operating systems can cope with databases. Deitel (1984) claims that in the personal computing field: 'the CP/M operating system has become a de facto standard'. Yet CP/M can only cope with disk management, and so rapid is the rate of computer technological advance, that personal computers (PCs) are now able to cope with databases. As a consequence, of course, CP/M is no longer a de facto standard, though even so, a PC using CP/M can now handle at least fairly simple databases, as Morris (1986) demonstrates.

This question is unlikely to concern you unless you are establishing an entirely new computer system and database system, but it is a question of which you ought to be at least aware. Two popular operating systems, MS–DOS and its derivatives and UNIX and its derivatives, are the operating systems that you are most likely to encounter, though VMS for the VAX series of computers is also common. All can cope with the full functions of a database.

However, as has been pointed out already, a database itself is nothing more than an inert mass of data. The operating system will control the hardware context for the database, but we need something to control or handle the database itself. Such an entity is called a *database management system*. Yet, to some extent, this is an oversimplification. The database itself will, in its creation, be conditioned by the database management system that is going to handle it. Database management systems (hereafter called DBMSs) vary in the range of their facilities. It is no use building a database with its data arranged in a specific structure if the DBMS concerned cannot handle that particular type of structure. Hence, when people in general talk about a database, they are almost invariably talking about a database *and* its DBMS. It is rather like the British usage of the word 'tea'. If someone invites you to tea, you know perfectly well that you are not going to be given just a cup of tea. Just as 'tea' tends to mean a sandwich, cake and drink, so 'database' includes the database itself and its management system. The truncation is understandable, since the two are inseparable. Naturally, in a book like this, one needs to pay considerable attention to the DBMS, which is why Part Three is devoted to the topic.

2.5 The computer combination

We have looked, briefly, at databases, hardware, software and other such mysteries of IT. You can, of course, operate a computer, use software packages, and even build a database without knowing anything about what actually happens at a technical level. However, the matter is of considerable interest, does provide a fuller and essential vocabulary, and also increases your comprehension of computer and database capabilities and problems. Hence we shall conclude this panoramic view of the computer-world by glancing at the lowest, most basic level of them all.

When, in 1962, Arnold Wesker wrote a play entitled *Chips with Everything*, he was making a comment about the dietary conservatism of the British public. Were someone to write a play with that title today, he or she would more likely be referring to the omnipresence of computer chips. I cannot believe that anyone reading this book, no matter how ignorant of IT they may be, has not heard of a silicon chip. Chips are tiny objects consisting of layers of silicon neatly packaged in a thin container which has a dozen or so electrical contact pins. On the silicon itself are etched thousands and thousands of electric circuits.

To simplify very considerably (though not to falsify), the silicon layers themselves and the arrangement of the etched-in circuits ensure that, at this basic technical level, there are only two possible states: on/off, true/false, yes/no. Obviously the whole concern is performed by impulses of electricity. Either there is an impulse detected, or there is not. The absence of an impulse we signify by the symbol '0'. The presence of an impulse we signify by the symbol '1.' Hence a computer operates with a binary system of arithmetic, there being only two numbers, 0 and 1. Of course, for the computer itelf, there are no numbers; there are either pulses of electricity or the absence of such pulses. Clearly, though, it is convenient for us humans to think in terms of numbers rather than in terms of the presence or absence of electrical pulses.

If a chip of silicon receives an electrical impulse, the silicon becomes magnetized in one direction. The absence of an impulse (or the presence of a very weak one), means that the magnetic spot is slanted in the opposite direction. Hence, one direction represents 1, the opposite direction is 0.

This might, at first glance, seem less than helpful. How on earth can you make any sort of sense of a mass of mutually opposed polarities? Needless to say, of course, human beings have devised codes for the combinations. Each spot, whatever its direction of magnetism, represents a binary digit (always abbreviated to a *bit*). A well-known coding scheme called the American standard code for information interchange (and always abbreviated to ASCII— pronounced 'As key') groups bits into sequences of seven or eight bits at a time, depending upon the hardware that will be using it. Another coding system known as the extended binary-coded decimal interchange code (EBCDIC for short, and pronounced 'Eb see dik') always uses eight bits (known as a *byte*).

Each system represents all the numerical digits, letters of the alphabet and signs of punctuation by a specific sequence of bits. A selection of ASCII and EBCDIC codes is given in Table 2.1

Table 2.1

Character	ASCII	EBCDIC
A	1000001	11000001
B	1000010	11000010
C	1000011	11000011
D	1000100	11000100

Of course, if you want to look up the payroll details of Alana Pooplehurst, it will be less than useful to be presented with rows of 1s and 0s across the screen. Fortunately the operating system will translate all those 0s and 1s into the alphanumeric characters that we recognize.

Even so, while it is comprehensible that information is stored in bits of magnetized or unmagnetized silicon, it is still not clear how a computer can make decisions or process in any significant way the data with which it has been presented. One may understand that a computer can read 10111100 and place on the screen the symbol '<' as a consequence, but how does a computer perform logical operations? The answer lies in gates. The reason for the electric circuits etched onto a chip is to enable the computer to make choices and decisions. Let me explain.

Data is data. Rows and rows of magnetized and non-magnetized spots, while meaningless to you and me, enable the computer to print out all the names of the payroll for Scrooge & Co. But how does the computer work out how much Abel Munster or Samantha Pringlegrot need to be paid? This is done by using logical operators called *gates*. There are three basic types of gate, an *AND gate*, an *OR gate* and a *NOT gate*. If we look at each in turn, the mysteries of computer operation will become clear.

An AND gate examines two electrical impulses. Obviously there are four possible states for these two inputs:

- Both could be positive, i.e. on.
- The first could be positive and the second negative.
- The first could be negative and the second positive.
- Both could be negative.

Representing these four different states by means of binary digits, we can consequently show them as follows:

- 11
- 10
- 01
- 00

Now an AND gate is so arranged as to only give a positive result—a yes, on, true answer—when it receives two positive inputs. Any other combination will provide a negative result—a false, no, off answer. This state of affairs is represented by drawing up what is called a *truth table* for the AND gate. If the two inputs are *A* and *B* then the truth table looks like Table 2.2.

Table 2.2

A	B	A and B
0	0	0
0	1	0
1	0	0
1	1	1

Let us, therefore, assume that you want some action taken when two things are true, but that you do not want any action taken if one or both items are untrue. You would use an AND gate to process this for you. Thus you programmed your computer to order a carton of champagne if

- The English cricket team were all fit,

and

- The West Indian cricket team were all suffering from influenza.

Only if both these conditions were met could you be certain of an English victory (though even then, one wonders).

An OR gate, on the other hand, will return a positive or true output if either of the two inputs is true. Table 2.3 illustrates the situation.

Table 2.3

A	B	A or B
0	0	0
0	1	1
1	0	1
1	1	1

Hence you would use an OR gate if you wanted a positive result in a situation like the following:

- If it is raining, I shall practise the piano.
- If the library is closed, I shall practise the piano.
- If it is not raining and the library is open, I shall not practise the piano.

The NOT gate only needs one input because all that it does is to reverse the value that it has received. It is so constructed that it makes a circuit when no current is applied to it, but breaks the circuit when there is a current. The truth table for a NOT gate is boringly obvious (Table 2.4).

Table 2.4

A	NOT A
1	0
0	1

However, a NOT gate can be attached to an AND gate to create a *NAND gate*, or to an OR gate to create a *NOR gate*. By such means, combinations of gates can cope with any possible logical situation or complex of situations.

A microprocessor or logic chip, consequently, performs arithmetic or any other operation that can be reduced to a yes or no situation or set of situations. It is a microprocessor (or group of such processors) that forms the CPU of a computer. By and large, the power of a computer is measured by the power of its microprocessor. There is a variety of these, all with instantly memorable and eye-catching names like 6502, 80386 or 68020. Some microprocessors like the 6502 can only deal with eight bits (one byte) at a time. Its *word length* is thus said to be a byte. Others like the 8086 or the 80286 can handle 16 bits at a time. The 68000 and 68020 chips can cope with 32 bits at a time. Obviously the larger the number of bits that a computer can handle at any one time, the faster its rate of processing. Since all processing operations take place at about the speed of light, a modern computer can make a million or more decisions per second. But note that these decisions are in themselves extremely simple, involving a true or false response, a yes or no answer. Computers have changed many, many aspects of work and business and are likely to continue so to do. They can solve a complicated tax problem in less time than it takes you or I to comb our hair. But they do so only because of three previously given elements:

1. The hardware itself;
2. The operating system that controls that hardware;
3. The database and DBMS that provide and handle the data needed.

It is with the last of this trinity that we are concerned, but it would have been absurd, and even demeaning, to look at databases and their management systems without laying the foundations for doing so. The pages of this chapter have been superficial in the extreme, but they have given us some form of context in which to begin our prime study. None the less, introductory though this first part has been, do ensure that you have understood it by doing the questions on the following page. And don't cheat by looking at the answers. The questions are, I hope, both simple and interesting enough not to be counted as a weariness of the flesh.

References

Behling, R. *Computers and Information Processing*, Kent Publishing Co., 1986.

Carter, R. *Student's Guide to Information Technology*, Heinemann Newnes, 1989.

Deitel, H. M. *An Introduction to Operating Systems*, Addison-Wesley, 1984.

French, C. S. *Computer Studies*, 2nd edn, DP Publications, 1986.

Howe, D. *Data Analysis for Data Base Design*, 2nd edn, Edward Arnold, 1989.

Kalicharan, N. *Computer Studies for GCSE*, Cambridge University Press, 1988.

Lucas, H. C. *The Analysis, Design and Implementation of Information Systems*, 3rd edn, McGraw-Hill, 1985.

Morris, S. *Using Databases on the Amstrad PCW8256 and PCW8512*, Glentop, 1986.

Perkinson, R. C. *Data Analysis: The Key to Data Base Design*, QED, 1984.

Whitten, J. L., Bentley, L. D. and Ho, T. I. M. *Systems Analysis and Design Methods*, Times Mirror/Mosby College Publishing, 1986.

Wright, G. G. L. *Mastering Computers*, 2nd edn, Macmillan, 1984.

Questions on Part One

1. A word that was used without explanation in Chapter 2 was the word 'entity'. What did you take the word entity to mean?
2. You have entered as an item of data the following:

   Charles Dickens, *Great Expectations*

   What error have you made?
3. In performing one simple transaction, the machine cycle is divided into instruction time and execution time. Distinguish between the two and explain what happens in each operation.
4. What do the following abbreviations stand for?

   (a) IT   (b) CPU   (c) ALU   (d) VDU   (e) PC
   (f) DBMS   (g) bit   (h) CRT   (i) ASCII   (j) EBCDIC

5. Four operating systems were mentioned in Chapter 2. How many of them can you name?
6. What is the function of a database management system?
7. Define binary arithmetic.
8. What is a truth table? Construct a truth table for an AND gate and an OR gate.
9. What is a microprocessor?
10. Within a computer system, which would you regard as the more important, the hardware or the software?

Answers

1. An entity is an object, physical or conceptual, in which we are interested and about which we need to store data. Thus employee could be an entity, as could supplier, salary, town and countless other things. As Date (1990) wearily remarks 'the term "entity" is widely used in database circles

to mean any distinguishable object that is to be represented in the database'.

2. You are trying to enter as one item of data something which is really two items, the name of the author and the title of the book.

3. The machine cycle refers to the interaction of the CPU elements in carrying out a single machine operation.

    (a) The instruction time is when the CPU fetches an instruction, works out what it means, and then places the op code and the operands in their respective registers.

    (b) The execution time is the period during which the data is retrieved from primary storage and the ALU performs upon that date the relevant operation.

4. (a) Information technology; (b) central processing unit; (c) arithmetic and logic unit; (d) visual display unit; (e) personal computer; (f) database management system; (g) binary digit; (h) cathode ray tube; (i) American standard code for information interchange; (j) extended binary-coded decimal interchange code.

    Don't worry if you didn't manage the last two; I always have to look them up too, and no one ever refers to them in full anyway. In addition, to put in the word 'bit' was a bit unfair (sorry—about the pun, not the unfairness). No one today thinks of the word 'bus' as an abbreviation for the word 'omnibus'. So it is with 'bit'. It has become a proper word on its own.

5. The four operating systems mentioned in Chapter 2 were (a) CP/M; (b) MS–DOS; (c) UNIX; (d) VMS. If you know the names of other operating systems like MVS, Pick, XDS–940 or OS/2, deduct several marks from your score as a penalty for being too well-informed.

6. The function of a database management system is to enable the user to handle a database. It will provide facilities for storing data in the database, retrieving data, defining data and communicating with physically separate stores of data.

7. Binary arithmetic is arithmetic performed with a number base of two. In other words, there are only the numbers 0 and 1 in the binary system. Hence decimal numbers like 2 or 7 are represented as 10 and 111 respectively.

8. A truth table is a table which shows the possible inputs to a gate and the resulting output. Both AND and OR gates show two inputs and produce one output.

AND			OR		
0	0	0	0	0	0
0	1	0	0	1	1
1	0	0	1	0	1
1	1	1	1	1	1

9. A microprocessor is a silicon chip upon which are etched all the gates and circuits to enable it to act as the CPU for a microcomputer.

10. Clearly there is no hard-and-fast answer to this question. A computer system needs both hardware and software, so both of them are essential. None the less, there are good reasons for saying that software is more important than hardware. It is the software which is going to process your data in the way that you desire. That processing could be done on a considerable variety of hardware options, but, no matter how superb your hardware may be, your database system is only going to be effective if you have got the software correct. If your database itself is incomplete or inaccurate, chaos will result. If your DBMS is too limited in its functions, then you will not be able to manage your data in the most effective fashion. If your operating system is limited, then your DBMS may not be able to access all its facilities. Thus it is software, more than hardware, which determines the range of options which you can perform.

PART TWO

Data

3
What sort of data is needed?

Scrape and Blow had been the premier music shop of East Anglia for decades. Founded in 1873 by Theodore Scrape and Benjamin Blow, the firm was still a family concern. The current partnership of Franklin Scrape and Tiberius Blow was harmonious enough, and, through its near monopoly position, the firm still made handsome profits. None the less, Tiberius in particular was becoming concerned.

It was the habit of Franklin and Tiberius, both of whom worked very hard, to spend 30 or 40 minutes at the end of each day relaxing in the comfortable lounge of *The Quavering Crochet*, a pleasant pub in the market square of East Dereham. It was on a Wednesday last May that Tiberius voiced his concerns: 'You know, Franklin, I've been thinking.'

This was not an activity with which Franklin Scrape was particularly familiar. He had inherited the partnership and its practices from his father, and it had never occurred to him that his function was other than to maintain the time-hallowed procedures. Such cerebral activities as did exercise Franklin Scrape tended to be confined to practising the euphonium for East Dereham Brass Band. Accordingly he raised a somewhat perturbed eyebrow at Tiberius.

'What about?' he suspiciously enquired.

'Hetty,' came the reply.

'Good Lord, Tibby, I have often marvelled at your overactive mind, but I don't see how even you could spend much mental power on the topic of Hetty Freezer. She's a superb administrator for us, but she has the sort of face that would sink a thousand ships, and a voice that resembles a tuba with asthma.'

As you will have gathered, Franklin's aethestic soul did not thrill at the thought of Hetty Freezer, yet she was Scrape and Blow's database. This was a point that Tiberius went on to make.

'All right, Frank, I will accept that the thought of being marooned on a desert island with Hetty is enough to make one's mind turn to thoughts of suicide, but you will admit that, in real terms, it is she who runs this company, not us.'

Franklin, gave a grudging nod.

'Well,' Tiberius continued, 'do you know how old dynamo Hetty is?'

'One hundred and three,' Franklin muttered.

'Not quite,' Tiberius replied, 'but she will be sixty-three next month. In other words, she is already past retiring age. Like it or not, we must face the fact that Scrape and Blow cannot expect to retain Miss Freezer's services for much longer. Now, have you thought what that will mean?.'

The vacuity of Franklin's face provided the answer.

'Who orders all our scores and sheet music?' Tiberius queried. 'Who finds out what new instruments the local schools require? Who orders special books to mark musical anniversaries? Who monitors the costs of metronomes, music stands, mutes *et al*?'

There was an uncomfortable pause.

'Well, who does?' Tiberius repeated.

'Hetty,' replied Franklin.

'Exactly,' responded Tiberius. 'And how does she do it? Would you know how many violins there were in Wayland's orchestra? What are sales like on the scores of Bruckner's symphonies? Where is the best place from which to order new cello strings?' We are the directors of this company, but neither of us has the slightest idea as to how to run it. Sure, you do the accounts very well, and I cope perfectly well with customer correspondence, but we only have accounts and customers because of Hetty. Honestly, Franklin, for the last decade or so, we have been cushioned from reality by Hetty Freezer. I think we ought to give some thought to life post-Hetty.'

The justice of Tiberius' remarks was too evident for even Franklin to quibble. Indeed, the starkness of life without Hetty spurred him to unprecedented action.

'By gum, Tibby. I think we need another pint. This needs thinking about.'

Two more pints of Abbot's bitter were brought to the table, and the two directors gazed at each other with somewhat furrowed brows.

'You two are looking peculiarly sphinx-like this evening,' interposed the friendly baritone voice of Graham Wrexham, deputy head of Southgate High School.

'Oh hello, Graham,' Franklin exclaimed. 'I don't know about sphinx-like, but Tibby here has been painting dire pictures.'

'Dire pictures!' Graham exclaimed. 'you don't mean someone's lost the magic flute.'

Messrs Scrape and Blow favoured Graham's quip with a wintry smile. Tiberius did, however, explain the subject of their concern.

'Well, there isn't really a problem is there?' Graham comforted. 'The satanic Hetty may be infallibility personified at the moment, but she can be replaced easily enough.'

'Oh yes, and by whom?' Franklin indignantly enquired. 'She's been with us for decades. No one else knows how the system works. Indeed, she is the system.'

'No doubt,' Graham replied, 'but she could explain that system to someone else, couldn't she?'

'One doubts even that,' Tiberius muttered. 'Hetty's extremely competent, but most of the system exists in her head, not on paper. No one would ever remember everything, even if Hetty could declaim it all. And anyway, without maligning Hetty, no one ever does explain a system very well. They are so used to it themselves that they take it as second nature. You, Graham, if asked to explain the organization of Southgate High School, would doubtless mention the option system in the fourth year, but it would never occur to you to explain what an option system was. You would assume that everybody knew. Frank assumes that everyone knows what a flugelhorn is. I assume that everyone knows what a Köchel number is. So Hetty would make masses of assumptions, and the newcomer would get, at best, an incomplete and distorted picture. As a result, everything would go wrong, the Hetty replacement would resign, and the next newcomer would have to devise a new system from scratch. Meanwhile, all our customers would have become so cheesed-off with out incompetence that they transferred their custom to Godfreys in Norwich or to Steins in Kings Lynn. Scrape and Blow would just expire.'

'Well, well, well,' Graham muttered. 'I see the cause of your furrowed brows. Even so, you misunderstand me. I wasn't thinking of your ever replacing Hetty.'

'You mean that she really is immortal,' Franklin exclaimed.

'No,' Graham snorted. 'Not even the omniscient Hetty has yet attained eternal life. I was thinking that you could transfer the Hetty system to a computer system. Then you'd have no fears about Hetty's departure or her replacement.'

'A computer system!' Franklin bellowed, as if Graham had just played a piece of music in the wrong key. 'What on earth would we do with a computer system?'

'The question is,' Graham mildly responded, 'What could a computer system do for you? The answer almost certainly is, quite a lot.'

'What do you mean, Graham?' Tiberius asked. 'We are not a multinational company employing thousands of staff and shifting tons of stock per week. We may be big in East Anglia, but even then only within a small and specialist section of the market. People don't buy Steinway grands the way they buy potatoes.'

'Granted,' Graham replied, 'but you do have an extensive and complex business. The headquarters of your business is here in Dereham, but you have stores in Norwich, Newmarket, Bury St Edmunds and Ipswich. In the whole of East Anglia, a sizeable area, you are the prime suppliers of musical instruments from organs to recorders, virtually the only suppliers of musical scores, the established source for music stands, manuscript paper, batons, metronomes, etc. to every school, college and music society in the region. The whole thing is crying out to be computerized.'

'Why do you say it is crying out?' Tiberius enquired.

'You've virtually admitted it yourself,' Graham replied. 'If Hetty left to-morrow, you would be up the blue Danube without a Strauss. With a computer system, you could keep track of all the suppliers from whom you buy your goods, you could monitor the sales of every one of your shops, you could carry data about every school to whom you supplied material. All this information could be instantly accessible day or night, it would consume no paper and require no filing cabinets, and above all, it could be an eternal Hetty, never forgetting, never leaving, never being ill, and not even wanting a salary.'

'The never wanting a salary sounds good, but how much would it cost to buy this paragon of efficiency?' Franklin enquired. 'Any anyway, how do we teach it all of Hetty's system?'

'Well,' Graham replied, 'it would certainly cost quite a lot, but you could justify its expense by the subsequent savings that it would bring. As for teaching it Hetty's system, you really ought to get a systems analyst.'

'A systems what?' Tiberius grunted.

'A systems analyst,' responded Graham. 'That's a man or woman or a group of them who examine your business in order to discover what information needs it has, and who then recommend the type of computer equipment that would fulfil those needs. They would come along, discover what your business currently did and how it did it, make recommendations as to how your business could be streamlined or improved, and suggest the type of system that you needed to implement those requirements.'

'So not only would we have to buy computer equipment,' Franklin commented, 'but we'd have first of all to employ this analyst team to find out what sort of equipment we needed.'

'Strictly speaking,' Graham replied, 'it is even more basic than that. A systems analyst would be able to tell you whether or not you even needed a computer system at all. It isn't his job to peddle databases or spreadsheets, it's his job to determine what sort of system would best serve your needs. In theory, it need not be a computer system, though frankly it is almost bound to be. Computers can store and process data so massively more effectively than the old filing cabinets and secretaries ever could.'

'Look,' Tiberius interposed, 'this seems as if it might be developing into a serious conversation. Shall I get us all another drink, and then we can really quiz you, Graham?'

'I'm not so sure about the quizzing,' Graham said, 'but I rarely refuse another drink.'

'We've already had two, you know,' Franklin complained.

'Just pretend it's band practice night,' Tiberius unsympathetically replied. 'You get through a pint for every piece you practise, and you normally practise half a dozen.'

Franklin pulled a face of mock outrage, but ceased his mutterings. Tiberius procured three more pints of bitter from Rod, the publican, bore them to the table and resumed his seat. With an expression of rare intensity, Tiberius turned to Graham and asked for more information about the work of a systems analyst. Graham made the usual apologies about not being an expert on the subject, but the moment he started to explain, the pedagog within him warmed to the task.

'Basically a systems analyst just analyses your system,' Graham began. 'He looks at what data enters your organization, what happens to that data, and what output your system requires. He tries to see whether or not your current system is fulfilling the real needs of your company, and, where there are deficiencies, how those deficiencies can be best remedied. Since today computers handle data so much more effectively than we humans can, he is likely, at the end of his investigations, to recommend some form of computer system.'

'But how does he carry out his initial survey?' Franklin asked. 'Surely while he's around, the company concerned can't get on with any work.'

'On the contrary,' Graham replied, 'it is very important for a systems analyst that the company concerned does carry on its normal activities. Unless it did, he would stand no chance of observing its strengths and weaknesses. In your case, for instance, a systems analyst, would want to interview you and Tibby to find out your objectives for the company, and he would clearly need to interview Hetty, probably at some length. Most of the time, however, he would just be observing. He'd want to visit every one of your stores and see how they operated. He'd want to talk to some of your suppliers, to see how they coped with orders from Scrape and Blow. He'd want to talk to some of your customers to see how satisfactory they found your service. He'd want to do some timing, to see how long an order from, say, Southgate High School took to be processed and completed. In other words, an efficient systems analyst would build up a very full picture of your company, its present mode of operation, its failings and its strengths.'

'Good Lord,' Franklin exclaimed, 'he'd end up knowing more about Scrape and Blow than we do.'

'Yes, in one sense he would,' Graham answered. 'Or at least he'd know more about the pure mechanics of the system than you. That, of course, is all he needs, the mechanics. Then, when he has examined your current system, accessed how fully your current system fulfils your needs, and analysed what sort of system would most effectively replace Hetty, then his job is done.'

'And how long would this operation take?' Tiberius asked. 'It all sounds very professional, but at the end of it all, we have presumably consumed some days or weeks, paid doubtless large sums of money to this analyst fellow, but not actually got anything concrete to show for it.'

'Very true,' Graham smiled. 'And by the time you'd paid the analyst, you might not have any money left to pay a systems designer to design your new system, let alone the money to buy the hardware and software for the new system.'

'Wonderful,' Franklin interjected. 'We spend time and money for an intellectual exercise. It's not what I would call sound professional practice.'

'Then you'd be wrong,' Graham snapped back, a touch of asperity entering his tone. 'Companies waste more time and lose more money through trying to cope and amend inadequate systems than they could conceivably do if they had got the system right in the first place. And anyway, what alternative do you have? You both recognize that Hetty can have, at the outside, only a couple of years left of her working life. You both also seem to agree that finding a human replacement for Hetty would not be easy, and that even if you did, it would only postpone the problem. Unless you solve this problem, Scrape and Blow will cease to exist. There are other music firms in East Anglia. The moment Scrape and Blow begin to appear less than competent, then these other companies will swoop like vultures.'

Franklin and Tiberius looked as if someone has just destroyed all of Schubert's music. Graham emptied his glass. The sight of their woebegone faces amused him, but also made him feel somewhat compassionate for these nineteenth-century businessmen adrift in the sea of high technology.

'Look,' he said, 'think it over. If you decide I'm right, give me a ring at school. Then I can let you have some phone numbers of firms who might be able to help you.'

'Thanks Graham,' they said in unison.

'Fine. Anything to help. See you.' Graham strolled from the pub, leaving a somewhat bemused Scrape and Blow. Slowly Franklin and Tiberius finished their own pints, replaced the tankards on the bar, and left. They felt not unlike Emperor Honorius confronted by Alaric the Goth.

The above narration may well indicate why I have never won the Booker prize, but, more relevantly from our point of view, it does illustrate the sort of context in which a data processing system might be considered and the kind of issues that need bearing in mind during such a consideration. The rest of this chapter will consider these issues more formally.

Before constructing a database, you need to know what sort of data must appear in that database. Indeed, even more fundamentally, you need to know whether or not you really need a computerized database at all. As Graham Wrexham explained to Franklin, and Tiberius, this is the province of the systems analyst, and it is to that we first turn.

3.1   The systems analysis life cycle

This is a somewhat pretentious label, though its common usage virtually demands that we adopt it rather than inventing another title. All it signifies is that the operation or process of systems analysis goes through separate stages. Most things in life have a life cycle. When you are doing the washing, there is a life cycle involved. You first of all sort out which clothes go into the washing machine first, you then load the machine with them, set the machine to the required program, and then, when the machine has finished its operation, you remove the clothes from the machine and place them in the tumble dryer or hang them out to dry. You then repeat the process until all the clothes have been washed. Fortunately, however, you never actually refer to this activity as the washing-day life cycle. Computer scientists, however, being more self-important and grandiose than normal people, are always referring to the systems analysis life cycle. All they mean is that a systems analyst has to go through various stages in order to do a complete and effective job. There are methodological reasons too for being somewhat self-conscious, or at least aware, about this life cycle. Yourdon (1989) itemized them thus:

1. To define the activities to be carried out in a system development project.
2. To introduce consistency among many systems development projects in the same organization.
3. To provide checkpoints for management control for go/no-go decisions.

The above points seem self-explanatory enough, and it should also be fairly obvious that they are important points. Only by defining your activities can you secure an adequate sense of direction. In a large systems analysis exercise, it is clearly imperative that analyst *A* uses the same procedures and nomenclature as analyst *B*. Disparity in techniques and vocabulary would rapidly ensure chaos. Finally, if a process is divided into separate stages, each of those stages provides an opportunity for assessment and consideration, giving the chance for change, revision or even abandonment. Thus the systems analysis life cycle is the conceptualization of the entire software system development. If you are thinking of having a database, it is the systems analysis life cycle which will carry that thought from vague wonderings to defined procedures and eventually a working system. Wright (1984) compares the work of a systems analyst to the work of an architect. The analogy is a good one. It highlights how correct Graham Wrexham was in urging a proper systems analysis upon his music business friends. Let us then look at this systems analysis life cycle.

It is useful to begin with one element of clarification. In considering the topic of systems analysis, we should never forget that it is bound to contain four vital elements:

1. An *organization*—you are, after all, doing the systems analysis for an organization, be it Scrooge & Co, Scrape and Blow, or a massive multinational company.
2. *People*—they are going to run, or wreck, the brilliant analysis that you perform. If you forget the people who are going to run the new system, the odds are that they will wreck it.
3. *Data*—you need facts about the organization and the people who work in it.
4. *Technology*—your system will require programs and machines to run those programs.

Hence, although Part Two of this book is dedicated to only one of the above, data, it is vital not to forget the other three components. Whatever methodology you adopt, type of data structure you choose, and implementation arrangement you opt for, the entire enterprise will fail unless you succeed in balancing the differing requirements of these four elements.

The systems life cycle is likely to begin with a management decision. When the managers of a company come to see that their current system is in some respects inadequate, they are likely then to make soundings as to the advisability of replacing that system with another. If they call in a systems analyst to assess the situation, he or she is likely to begin with what is called a *feasibility study*. Its title indicates what sort of survey this is. The analyst, before beginning any full-scale analysis, wants to gain an overall view as to the practicability and desirability of that analysis. Are the problems of the company concerned sufficiently grave as to warrant the complete replacement of their current, manual system with an embracing computer system? Can their current deficiencies be remedied by some relatively minor amendments of the existing system? Would the replacement of the existing system with a completely new one be within the financial abilities of the company? Let us assume that the upshot of this feasibility study is a recommendation that an entirely new system be adopted. The analyst then starts collecting data; data about the existing system, what it does, how effectively or ineffectively it does it, how wasteful (or economic) it is in terms of time and manpower, and how the employees of the company concerned react to the existing system and respond to the idea of a new one. Once all the relevant facts have been collected, the analyst can then start on the core of the job, the actual detailed analysis itself. Of course, analysis has already played an important part in the life cycle so far. To begin with, there was the strategic analysis of the managers in coming to the conclusion that the existing system did not fulfil adequately the overall company objectives. Then came the analysis necessary in the feasibility study, and the provisional costings such a study would entail. The detailed analysis that now follows is concerned with providing all the material that is going to be needed to design a new system. Not until the detailed analysis is done, in part at least, can anyone start designing such a new system. Strictly speaking, systems analysis and systems design are two quite disparate activities, but it is far from uncommon for the analyst to be involved, perhaps totally, in the design of the new system that the analysis has demonstrated to be necessary.

Then, when the new system has been designed, it has to be implemented. In other words, the new hardware (if any) has to be bought and installed, the new software (if any) has to be bought, or created, and installed, and the two, hardware and software, have to be configured or set up in such a way so as to ensure their harmonious and effective cooperation and activity. Even then, the systems analysis life cycle is not quite complete. No matter how rigorous the analysis and design operations have been, the company will change, and its system will need modifying in order to accommodate such changes. Hence, even when a completely new system has been implemented, it will still be necessary to review and maintain its operations for all the years of its life. Eventually, of course, the company will change so much that the new system becomes as inadequate as the old one was, and the whole process starts all over again.

Curt though this outline of the systems analysis life cycle is, it provides a framework which is comprehensible. Needless to say, there are considerable differences of emphasis among systems analysts. Lying behind the outline just given was an important assumption. Without being stated, it was assumed that the purpose of the systems analysis was to discover what the real functions of the company concerned were and to design a system which would enable those functions to be fulfilled. Jackson (1983) begins his first chapter by highlighting this assumption:

> Traditionally, the starting point in system development is the functional requirement. The developer begins by establishing the system's function, determining what the system is to do and what outputs it is to produce. The essential content of the system specification is the statement of system function.

Yet Jackson has only highlighted the assumption in order to argue that is is a mistaken procedure, and he goes on to outline an analytical procedure where functions become an explicit addition later in the life cycle rather than an implicit assumption from the beginning. He expresses himself as follows:

> JSD (Jackson System Development) relegates consideration of system function to a later step in development, and promotes in its place the activity of modelling the real world. The developer begins by creating a model of the reality with which the system is concerned, the reality which furnishes its subject matter, about which it computes.

This is not designed as a textbook on systems analysis, but it would be misleading to suggest that there was only one viable approach.

The systems analysis life cycle outline provided in this chapter may also have given the impression of being a technical system, a system that had behavioural and social consequences but that was primarily, if you like, an engineering activity. Yet Wood-Harper *et al.* (1985) argue that this is a misguided attitude. Instead of seeing information systems as technical systems, they claim that they 'are better seen as social systems which rely to an increasing extent on information technology.' Indeed, the whole 'soft systems methodology' (SSM), as it has been labelled, was pioneered by Peter Checkland in the 1970s at Lancaster University, and a most readable book by him and Jim Scholes (Checkland and Scholes, 1990), presents a most persuasive argument.

It would be easy to extend this catalogue of divergences. There are systems analysts who believe that prototyping is the most effective approach, that is, a system of rapidly constructing an outline system and testing that before moving on to refine it. There are those who emphasize top-down analysis, a method in which one begins with an overall, global structure, analyses the directional or commanding elements within that structure and slowly move downwards until one reaches the shop floor level. Others place their faith in the bottom-up approach which, as you might imagine, is the converse of top-down. Here one begins at the shop floor and slowly follows the lines of communication and command until one reaches the Board of Directors. In the house of systems analysis, there are many mansions, though to echo the New Testament in this fashion is perhaps a mistake; in systems analysis, there are fewer mansions than prefabs. In an IFIP working conference on the Comparative Review of Information Systems Design Methodologies held in 1984, T. W. Olle was frank in admitting the conceptual confusion:

> It was agreed at the first meeting of the Review Committee that the aim of the review process was not to select the 'seven best metholodogies' for the simple reason that it was not clear how it would be possible to define what 'best' meant.

Perhaps in no other area of IT is there such methodological disparity, and this is understandable. Systems analysis is, in part at least, an interpretive and evaluative operation. There are no clear right or wrong approaches. It is irritating, though, that systems analysts themselves rarely discuss varying methodologies. D. E. Avison and G. Fitzgerald's book (Avison and Fitzgerald 1988) is the most recent one of which I am aware. From our point of view, however, this methodological confusion is not seminal. The seven-point procedure that was outlined earlier, and cribbed, in fact, from C. S. French's *Computer Science* (1989), will be a perfectly adequate basis upon which to begin. Let me just cite French's tabular outline of the system life cycle:

1. Preliminary survey/study
2. Feasibility study
3. Investigation and fact finding
4. Analysis
5. Design
6. Implementation
7. Maintenance and review

It must not, though, ever be thought that the systems analysis life cycle is a straightforward sequential process with one thing following another in a predetermined order. Part of the system can be implemented while analysis of another part is still in operation. The design of one aspect can be under way while the feasibility of some elements is still being examined. Also, as French, whose seven-stage outline I have borrowed, comments: '"Systems Analysis" takes places at all stages in the life cycle not just the analysis stage.'

However, complex and disparate though systems analysis may be, there are some generally agreed tools and techniques. If we examine those, it will cast some light on information systems generally and databases in particular.

3.2 The tools and techniques of data modelling

Data, as we have seen, is the foundation upon which information technology rests. Without data, there is nothing. Yet, as we have also seen, data alone is quite useless. It is only when data is placed in a meaningful context that it becomes useful. Then it becomes not data, but information. Yet it only does so because the data item, an entity, is placed in a relationship with another entity or entities. This entity–relationship (E–R) construct is a high-level conceptual data model. 'High-level' means that it is far removed from thoughts of computer implementation. The process of systems analysis should not be concerned with how a system will ultimately be expressed for computer management. The important thing is to arrive at a full and meaningful expression of the data involved within the system and the relationships between that data. Until such a model has been created, you stand little chance of even knowing what sort of database management system would be most suitable for implementing the model. Coates and Parkin (1977) discuss the entire concept of the model, computer or otherwise, and its necessary omnipresence in 'matters such as truth and explanation'. Let us, therefore, look closely at this entire entity–relationship concept.

A moment's thought will reveal that there are three possible types of relationship between entities, and all textbooks on systems analysis particularize them. The examples provided by Atre (1980) seem to me to be as clear and sensible as you can find, and so I borrow them.

1. There can be a one-to-one relationship between two entities. Hence, in a typical British or American hospital, there will be a one-to-one relationship between a hospital patient and a hospital bed. In other words, there will be one patient, and only one, sleeping in a bed, and that bed will be, during the patient's stay in hospital, the only bed which he or she will normally use. Diagrammatically, we can express this entity–relationship model as shown in Fig. 3.1. Note the single-headed arrow line.

Figure 3.1

2. There can be a one-to-many relationship between entities. Our same, long-suffering patient will be placed in a room or ward of a hospital, but there will normally be many patients in the same room or ward. Thus, while there is only *one* ward in which a patient will be placed, there will be *many* patients within that ward, as shown in Fig. 3.2 Note that the double/single-headed arrow line does indicate that we are expressing many patients in one ward.

Figure 3.2

3. Finally, of course, there can be a many-to-many relationship between entities. Atre suggests the patient/surgeon relationship as being applicable here. I hope that it is not a common occurrence where a patient is operated upon by many surgeons, but it clearly could happen over successive visits to hospital, and it is obvious that any one surgeon will operate on a number of different patients. The diagrammatic representation is consequently obvious (Fig. 3.3). The doubled-headed format at both ends of the line represents the many-to-many relationship.

Figure 3.3

There are, of course, alternative methods of signifying such relationship types. Frequently, in such E–R diagrams, a one-to-one relationship is simply expressed by an unbroken line, while the 'many' symbol is a three-pronged terminus. You can also write the nature of the relationship alongside the arrow linking the entities. This is the format adopted by McDermid (1990) as Fig. 3.4 illustrates.

Figure 3.4 (a) One-to-one relationships (1 : 1)

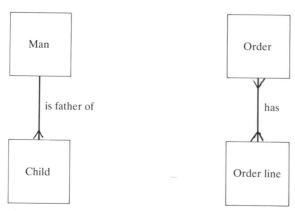

(b) One-to-many relationships (1 : n)   (c) Many-to-many relationships (m : n)

You can also (Elmasri and Navathe, 1989) represent the nature of the relationship in a special diamond-shaped box (Fig. 3.5) as does Oxborrow (1989).

As you can see, Fig. 3.5 illustrates that one employee manages one department. However, whatever the precise type of representation may be, the underlying intention is clear: for any information of whatever nature to be adequately shown in a data model, the relevant entities concerned must be depicted in the correct relationship with fellow entities. However, you cannot limit yourself to relationships between two entities, as has been done so far in this chapter. You will need to depict the entire matrix of entities and relationships with which you are concerned. Elmasri and Navathe entitle the third chapter of their book 'Data modeling using the entity–relationship model', and deal with the matter reasonably fully, providing an E–R diagram of a company, showing the entities Employee, Department, Project and Dependent and the relationships Works for, Controls, Manages, Works on and Dependents of. McDermid, in his third chapter, also shows with considerable clarity why it is a good idea to eliminate many-to-many relationships, and how to deal with recursive relationships, i.e. relationships where an entity has a relationship with itself. More fully still, Howe (1989) devotes Part Three of his book to E–R modelling and introduces such delights as chasm traps and flexing by splitting. Certainly there is more to E–R models than it would be reasonable to deal with here. However, before we leave the E–R model, one more piece of terminology needs to be introduced.

Figure 3.5

Each entity clearly possesses qualities of its own. If the entity concerned is a person, then that person possesses a name, an age, a sex, an address, and so on. If the entity concerned is a car, then that car will possess bodywork, a chassis, an engine, wheels and so on. These qualities or components of an entity are usually termed *attributes*. Thro (1990) defines the word 'attribute' as being the 'Distinguishing characteristic or quality applied to, inherent in, or symbolic of a person or thing.' Of course, what attributes of an entity you decide to represent in a database are, to some extent, a matter of personal choice. Most databases, for instance, are likely to contain the entity Employee. The following columns show the differing attributes that two different companies chose to represent:

Employee	*Employee*
Name	Colour of eyes
Address	Favourite food
Age	Height
Home tel. number	Political attitude

You may feel, with a certain amount of justification, that one of these columns is a great deal more sensible than the other, but you will, I hope, take the point. There are no such things as automatic attributes. It could be, in some contexts, that colour of eyes is a significant attribute to have concerning an employee as in, for instance, the staff list of a Hollywood studio. It does, though, follow that, if the attributes of an entity are themselves important (and they normally are), then those attributes will need to be represented upon an E–R diagram. Hence we draw up a construct something like Fig. 3.6.

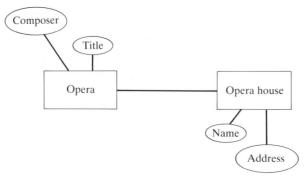

Figure 3.6

Thus, the two entities, 'Opera' and 'Opera House', both have two attributes each. If we put specific values to those attribute labels, then we could, for example, draw Fig. 3.7.

Figure 3.7

In such a fashion, by identifying relevant entities, perceiving the relationship between entities, and by selecting appropriate attributes for those entities, you can build up a data model that is an accurate reflection of reality. Rock-Evans (1987) makes a useful distinction between basic attributes and derived attributes. Basic or primary attributes are those that are inherent in the entity. Thus if you have the entity 'Person', then that entity is going to have a sex, a date of birth, and so on. However, if, in a hospital database, one has the entity 'Patient', then that entity is also going to have the basic or primary attributes of sex, date of birth, and so on. Yet this entity is also going to have some derived attributes, attributes that are not an inherent property. 'Drugs prescribed' or 'Date of operation' would be instances. Thus a skilfully and carefully constructed E–R diagram can do an excellent modelling job. It is an important technique, so let me summarize it in a formal fashion.

TOP-DOWN ANALYSIS – THE ENTITY–RELATIONSHIP APPROACH

The principal objectives are to identify first the entity types, and then the relationships between them in the system which is being studied.

Entities, relationships and roles   The ideal objective of data analysis is to build a model of the data which supports present needs for formal messages together with all future formal message needs of the organization.

An *entity type* (or *entity set*) is a class of object, person, event, place, operation, or other feature which exists in the object system and which is to be the concern of a formal message, for example:

CUSTOMER (NAME, ADDRESS)

'The analyst's most important tasks are the definition and identification of entity types.' (Rock-Evans, 1987). Rock-Evans classifies entity types under a number of headings:

1. Events and actions.
2. Classifications, i.e. the 'classification' entity type classifies another entity type, e.g. job type_____job.
3. Collectives, e.g. jury, committee.
4. Time and time periods.
5. Decision tables—particularly useful for recording rules and regulations.
6. Expert system knowledge bases.
7. Unstructured data—sound, image and text.
8. Intersection entity types, i.e. entity types which exist only because other entity types exist, e.g. 'job history' which exists only because the entities 'job', 'person' and 'date' already exist.

NB: a basic entity type exists in its own right; a derived entity type exists and has been created by using the attribute values from other entity types. Thus 'person's pay' is derived from 'hours worked', 'rate per hour', etc.

An *entity* or *entity occurrence* is an instance of an entity type, for example:

A. Jones & Son, High Street, Newtown.

A *relationship type* (or *relationship set*) is a class of event, place, operation, transaction or other feature of the object system which connects two or more entities and which is to be the concern of a formal message, for example:

CUSTOMER ORDERS PRODUCT

A *relationship occurrence* is an instance of a relationship type.

It is possible for two entities to enjoy more than one relationship type between them, representing different roles.

Attributes and values   The third principal component of the data structure is the set of attributes for the entities: these two can be deduced readily from the system description, being the properties of the entities. An attribute is a class of number, name, value, quantity, place, time, or other feature of an entity type or relationship type, whose value is to be contained in (or is otherwise some determinant of) a formal message. For example, a Customer entity type may have the attributes Customer-no, Customer-name, Customer-address, Customer-credit-limit, etc.

The *values* of an attribute are the specific instances of Customer-no, Customer-name, etc. An attribute value may be null, that is not yet known or not applicable, Rock-Evans calls them *permitted values*.

None the less, an E–R model is inevitably a somewhat static construct. It gives a picture of an organization or a situation at a particular moment in time. If the entities and relationships have been skilfully chosen, that picture will remain valid for some time to come, but, despite its validity, it is irreducibly static. But situations change. Organizations alter. Firms conduct business. In other words, in the real world, activity is the norm. E–R diagrams do not depict activity, though they may imply it. However, for modelling the activity of a company or an enterprise, one can have recourse to a modelling tool that has been used since the 1950s, the *dataflow diagram*.

The dataflow diagram (and its inevitable acronymn DFD) consists of four elements. First of all, there is the data flow itself which represents entities moving from one state or process to another. Thus, if you were a customer wishing to reserve a library book, the dataflow might look like Fig. 3.8.

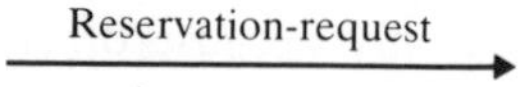

Reservation-request

────────────────────────────────────▶

Figure 3.8

Obviously, however, a dataflow has to originate from a source. Thus the request to reserve a library book will come from a borrower. A source tends to be depicted by a circle, as shown in Fig. 3.9.

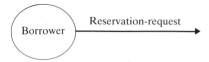

Figure 3.9

Once a dataflow has originated from a source, it has to undergo some form of process. Almost invariably, the process element is shown by a rectangle (see Fig. 3.10). There are a number of variations that can be encountered for the other DFD elements—see Wright (1984, p. 118) as an example—but the process operation seems to have been universally depicted as an oblong.

In the example shown in Fig. 3.11, the borrower's name needs to be checked to ensure that he or she is a valid borrower, and hence entitled to request books.

Figure 3.10

The requested book itself has to be checked so that relevant data—author, title, publisher, date of publication, ISBN—can be collected. Such data comes from a data store, represented by a rectangle minus its right-hand side.

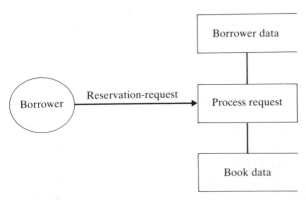

Figure 3.11

Ultimately, of course, when the book reserved is returned to the library concerned, the borrower is informed that the book is now awaiting collection, something that can be shown in a DFD with an arrow leading from the Process rectangle to the Borrower source. Deitel and Deitel (1985) give a brief breakdown of DFDs. The seventh chapter by Whitten *et al.* (1986) gives a fuller and extremely clear account, while Donald McDermid (1990) gives a more academic approach. Indeed, most books on what is called software engineering—the development of software under the guidance of engineering principles rather than individual idiosyncrasies—devote some space to the DFD. Whitten *et al.* conclude that

> A data flow diagram has no peer in its ability to document all aspects of a system including data, information, data storage, knowledge workers, methods and procedures, and computer equipment and programs. Additionally, data flow diagrams can effectively model all transaction processing, management reporting, and decision support functions in a system.

With the E–R diagram and the DFD, we have examined two extremely useful ways of modelling data. Both can be important tools and techniques for the systems analyst. Nor are they confined to one stage of the systems life cycle. The good analyst will refine and extend them as the work of discovery and analysis continues. Note how they complement each other. The E–R diagram describes the stored data layout of a system at a high level of abstraction; the DFD models the functions performed by a system. Together, they go far in providing a rounded picture.

There are, of course, other modelling tools. Yourdon (1989) devotes a whole chapter to state-transition diagrams, which highlight the time-dependent behaviour of a system. There are also HIPO diagrams, structure charts, and a wealth of variations on flow charts, all admirably surveyed. None the less, with E–R diagrams and dataflow diagrams we have selected the two most significant data modelling tools. There is, however, one more tool at which it is well worth looking. Called a *decision table*, there is a wonderful tool for clearing the mind. It indicates actions to be taken under various conditions. Let me explain.

It so happens that you are an ardent supporter of Hinstock Rovers football club. When the conditions are right, you bet on their success. You have drawn up three conditions that are almost certain to result in Hinstock's success:

1. They are playing at home.
2. It is not raining.
3. The Hinstock second team does not have a match at the same time.

When playing at home, Hinstock is encouraged by the vocal support of their entire fan club. With a reasonably dry, firm ground, the ball control skills of their forwards can be seen at its best. If the second team is not playing simultaneously, the Hinstock Rovers manager has a larger pool from which to select his team. Consequently, when all the above conditions are true, you bet on a victory by Hinstock Rovers.

From the information given above, it is now possible to draw up a decision table. It comprises three sections:

1. Condition stubs, which set out the respective conditions.
2. Action stubs, which set out the conceivable decisions.
3. Rules, which indicate which actions are to be taken under what conditions.

Your decision table for Hinstock Rovers would consequently look like Fig. 3.12. I hope that the general idea of decision tables is clear from this frivolous example.

	Hinstock is playing at home	Y	Y	Y	Y	N	N	N	N
	It is a dry day	Y	Y	N	N	Y	N	Y	N
Condition	The second team is not playing	Y	N	N	Y	Y	Y	N	N
	Place bet on Hinstock Rovers	X							
	Do not bet on Hinstock Rovers		X	X	X	X	X	X	X

Figure 3.12

It should not be difficult to see that it is possible (and useful) to build decision tables in order to formalize, clarify or even create business policy. You first of all, identify all the possible conditions and the respective values attached to those conditions. The respective values do not have to be a simple yes or no, as they were in the Hinstock Rovers example. Let us imagine that one of the conditions is the state of your personal bank account. The value given in response to that condition will determine whether or not the bank is prepared to cash your cheque. It could be decided that your cheque would be cashed if you were either in credit or only overdrawn by less than £100 (Fig. 3.13).

	In credit	O/D < £100	O/D > £100
Current state of account			

Figure 3.13

Having identified the various conditions (and the data item that each condition tests and the values that these data items can assume), you next establish the number of rules that are necessary in order to cover every eventuality. Fortunately there is a simple mathematical rule for so doing. Let us return to your money-winning scheme connected with Hinstock Rovers. You take the first condition—are they playing at home?—and work out how many alternatives there are to that condition. Clearly there are only two: they are either playing at home or they are playing away. If they are not playing at all, you would have no need to consult the decision table. You next look at the second condition and discover how many alternatives there are. Again there are only two. You now multiply the first number of alternatives—two—with the second, also two. This gives a total of four. You now examine the third and final condition—is there a second team match occurring at the same time?—and discover that there are again only two possible alternatives. You now multiply the four that you already have by the final two, producing a total set of possibilities. As you can see from the decision table that we did set out, there is a matrix of eight possibilities shown. Hence eight is our maximum (and minimum) number of rules.

What follows is virtually self-evident. You identify the possible actions, enter all the possible rules and then define the actions for each rule. Indeed, Yourdon (1989) provides a useful checklist for decision tables. He summarizes the steps necessary to create a decision table for a process specification as follows:

1. Identify all the conditions, or variables, in the specification. Identify all the values that each variable can take.

2. Calculate the number of combinations of conditions. If all the conditions are binary, then there are 2^N combinations of N variables.
3. Identify each possible action that is called for in the specification.
4. Create an 'empty' decision table by listing all the conditions and actions along the left side and numbering the combinations of conditions along the top of the table.
5. List all the combinations of conditions, one for each vertical column in the table.
6. Examine each vertical column (known as a rule) and identify the appropriate action(s) to be taken.
7. Identify any omissions, contradictions, or ambiguities in the specification (e.g. rules in the decision table for which the specification does not indicate that actions should be taken).
8. Discuss the omissions, contradictions and ambiguities with the user.

The resulting decision table is easy to read, easy to explain to your client, and very useful for clarifying the range of options available.

To return to our main thread of argument, you will have noticed that an E–R diagram does not really provide you with any extra information. It merely clarifies the situation with which you are presented. It is, of course, exactly the same with the DFD and with decision tables. They are modelling tools. You have already collected the necessary information. These tools are simply methods of confirming that information and making it more accessible to your own mind and that of your client.

Central to both the E–R diagram and the DFD (and all the other modelling techniques) is the existence of relevant data. No data modelling can be done until the data itself has been collected. It is to that topic that the next chapter is devoted.

References

Atre, S. *Data Base: Structured Techniques for Design, Performance and Management*, John Wiley, 1980.

Avison, D. E. and Fitzgerald, G. *Information Systems Development: Methodologies, Techniques and Tools*, Blackwell, 1988.

Coates, R. B. and Parkin, A. *Computer Models in the Social Sciences*, Arnold, 1977.

Checkland, P. and Scholes, J. *Soft Systems Methodology in Action*, John Wiley, 1990.

Deitel, H. M. and Deitel, B. *Computers and Data Processing*, Academic Press, 1985.

Elmasri, R. and Navathe, S. *Fundamentals of Database Systems*, Benjamin Cummings, 1989.

French, C. S. *Computer Science*, 3rd edn, DP Publications, 1989.

Howe, D. *Data Analysis for Data Base Design*, 2nd edn, Edward Arnold, 1989.

Jackson, M. *System Development*, Prentice-Hall, 1983.

McDermid, D. C. *Software Engineering for Information Systems*, Blackwell, 1990.

Oxborrow, E. *Databases and Database Systems*, 2nd edn, Chartwell-Bratt, 1989.

Rock-Evans, R. *Analysis within the Systems Development Lifecycle*, Pergamon, 1987.

Thro, E. *The Database Dictionary*, Microtrend, 1990.

Whitten, J. L., Bentley, L. D. and Ho, T. I. M. *Systems Analysis and Design Methods*, Times Mirror/Mosby College Publishing, 1986.

Wood-Harper, A. T., Antill, L. and Avison, D. E. *Information Systems Definition: The Multiview Approach*, Publisher, 1985.

Wright, G. G. L. *Mastering Computers*, 2nd edn, Macmillan, 1984.

Yourdon, E. *Modern Structured Analysis*, Prentice-Hall, 1989.

4
Collecting data

It might have been just a fraction more logical to have transposed this chapter with the preceding one. We cannot, after all, do any systems analysis and data modelling without having collected that data in the first place. But the two operations are parallel, not sequential. If you walk into a school, you know that some of the entities in their computer system are going to be *staff*, *pupils*, and *subjects*. If you talk for only three minutes with Messrs Scrape and Blow, you will be aware that *scores*, *instruments* and *sales* are going to be components of their database. Hence the construction of data models goes hand-in-hand with the identification and collection of that data.

While this may be the case, you still might wonder why an entire chapter is devoted to the task of collecting data. The data needed by a database is self-evident anyway; imagine having a database for a zoo which did not include any animals, or a database for a railway company that did not list any stations or trains. The method of collection is equally obvious. If you are collecting data for a college database, you go to the relevant deputy head for the timetable, to the head of PE for a list of fixtures, to the caretaker for a building plan, and to the head for local authority inputs and outputs. Perhaps it is all so obvious, yet the occasions on which it is done properly do seem remarkably rare. Hence, in a section devoted to data, it seems not unreasonable to discuss the collection of that data.

4.1 Preparing for collection

Before you can collect data, you need to make suitable preparations for the activity. I am conscious that much of this book will sound like an advertisement for the Boy Scout movement—*be prepared!*—but it is an inescapable fact that few things can be done adequately and completely without a thorough preparation beforehand. The task of collecting data may sound like a very straightforward activity, but it will be fruitless without prior preparation. Let me begin by just highlighting some aspects of this preparation.

4.1.1   IDENTIFYING THE FACTS

You cannot collect data until you are aware of the sort of data that you need. Professor Andrew Parkin, in his book on systems analysis, expresses this with his customary succinct clarity:

> What facts to find is a more important topic than the techniques used to find them. The analyst who understands what decisions he can or should ask for from the users, and what objective or quantified data he should accumulate, is in a strong position to make progress.

Hence the analyst can operate with a threefold strategy in order to discover specific operational alternatives:

1. Perform an external search for equivalent systems, i.e. try to find a similar situation elsewhere;
2. Model underlying processes of the specific system, rather like drawing a sketch map of the locality;
3. Perform a local search in and around the existing system so you become familiar with the environment.

It is important to remember that our object is to determine and link four entities:

- Business objectives
- Business tactics
- System objectives
- System tactics

Kozar (1989) expresses this strategy in one long sentence:

> A problem or opportunity creates a need to avoid some business costs or increase some revenues (business objectives) which require changed user behaviour (business tactics) which is supported by different information system achievements (system objectives) which require changed system behaviour (system tactics).

Clearly, unless you constantly bear the objectives in mind, you are not going to prepare meaningfully for the collection of your data.

4.1.2   SEARCHING FOR EQUIVALENT SYSTEMS

It is highly likely that the system upon which the analyst is working will have a close parallel which has already been studied. It is, therefore, worth looking at this earlier example to

- Provide prompts for the analyst's fact-finding questions.
- Suggest alternatives.
- Avoid pitfalls.

Sources which will aid such tracking down include:

- Computer manufacturer's representative
- Computer users' groups
- Packages
- Trade or industry association
- Government department
- Literature

4.1.3 MODELLING THE OBJECT SYSTEM

Unless analysts have a good picture of the business they are analysing, they will be unable to evaluate what they are told by users of the business. Hence they need to build up a model—by map, drawing, block diagrams, precedence networks, etc. Such a model will show the outputs of the business, the inputs used to produce them and the transformations by which the outputs are derived from the inputs.

4.1.4 LOCAL SEARCH IN THE EXISTING MESSAGE SYSTEM

Although conceiving or observing the object system can be a cost-effective means of fact-finding and can lead to original ideas for data processing systems, examination of the existing message system is essential too in most cases. The analyst must ask the following questions:

1. What is the purpose of this data, information or report? (Maybe it has none; it served an old need and is not required in a new system.)
2. What new information or reports are desirable to improve the system? (Maybe these can be prepared using data already present in the system.)

However, although I believe that everything that I have written so far is both true and useful, it is all at a somewhat theoretical level. What do we actually do in order to prepare ourselves for the effective collection of data? It is clearly impossible to provide a vade-mecum to cover all data collection contingencies. Oliver and Chapman (1979) try to cover data collection and controls in two pages. The result is abbreviated beyond comprehension. Indeed, so various and numerous are the conceivable contexts for data processing that a multivolumed book could not cover every possibility. There would seem, though, to be four basic tasks to be completed in the process of preparation. These we have already either identified or implied:

1. We must establish the range of our operation, discover what 'areas' come within our purview;

2. We must identify and record the sources of data that are available;
3. From those sources, we must select the best;
4. Finally, we must decide what method of collection would be the most appropriate for the data source or sources that we have chosen.

Each one of these demands at least a brief explanatory comment.

The first item is undoubtedly the most taxing. We are, after all, establishing a boundary for our area of study, and it is never easy so to do. Obviously too, much will depend upon which school of systems analysis we follow. A supporter of the multiview position taken by Wood-Harper *et al.* will have a much broader range of relevance than James Martin and his school. Bearing in mind the disparities that such interpretational differences are likely to bring, it seems a safe enough generalization to state that the first task of preparation is to relate the scope of our concern to specific areas of study: to systems, locations and organizational units. Hence if our scope is stock control, we are likely to find that inventory control, purchase ledger and the commodity statistics system all impinge upon our concerns. If we were doing a systems analysis for an investment house, we would need to identify sources of information, both factual and speculative, as to share prices, building society interest rates, Treasury forecasts, financial press opinion, and so on. This, of course, is a conceptual demarcation. We also need to identify the physical, 'real-world' entities that fall within the scope. Thus, in stock control, we are likely to encounter 'warehouses' as a very tangible entity. In investment we encounter real businesses rising or falling on the stock exchange, and real stockbrokers advising real clients. Wilkes (1991) rightly points out that establishing one's purview is bound to define the nature of its impact upon the organization concerned. He lays out five crucial factors that have to be considered:

1. The organization's relationship to its environment.
2. Embracing the organization as a whole as the unit of analysis.
3. Gaining inputs from a variety of functional areas.
4. Providing direction for and constraints on administrative and operational activities.
5. Being important to the overall success of the enterprise.

Hence establishing the scope of our enquiry, the demarcations of our analysis, is a seminal activity. Yet this is an area that is frequently neglected, to the ultimate peril of the entire operation.

Having established our boundaries, we next need to identify all conceivable sources of input data. What or who is going to give us the data that we need? To find out, we are going to need to examine all the users of the system, the preceding analysts and designers, and all current documentation about the system. Having been as exhaustive as we can be, we then take the long list of available sources on the inputs and eliminate, on criteria of practicality, reliability, accessibility, availability and quality, those which are inadequate. These five criteria are important, and should not be passed over lightly.

1. *Practicality* in part implies simply a willingness to accept that the ideal is probably not going to be possible. If the person who designed the existing system has now left the company and taken up a post as an anthropologist in the Brazilian jungle, then it is not going to be practical to contact him or her. If some significant users or participants within the system happen to be a set of inarticulate buffoons, then it may not be practical to extract information from them. If a company needs a distributed system but the managing director insists upon a centralized one, there is little that you can do about it. Practicality also entails an awareness of various constraints, of which the budget limitations are likely to be the most obvious and constricting. A superbly designed database system costing £825,000 is not wildly relevant to a company that can barely afford a word processor.
2. *Reliability* is a judgement that one makes with respect to the data source. It can be a character judgement: Mrs Peacock is too scatter-brained to be an accurate source, Tom Annison slants his information to favour his prejudices, Dr Grimes is so wrapped up in research that her awareness of what goes on around her is minimal, and so on. It can be a quasi-objective assessment of tangible evidence: those reports were drawn up too long after the meetings to which they refer, there seem to be excellent checks to ensure the validity of the sales figures, and so on.
3. *Accessibility* refers to the relative ease or otherwise with which you can approach a source. Mr Taylor is on site, but gives information so grudgingly that you are constrained in your elicitation. Budgets for the first 10 years of the company are available, but they are kept by our accountants 30 miles away.
4. *Availability* is even more fundamental. You may wish to consult with the sales director, but he happens to be in Lima. When a source of data is available but not very accessible, it is unfortunate but soluble. When a source is not available at all, there is nothing that you can do.
5. *Quality* is the icing on the cake. When a source of data is practical, reliable, available and accessible, then you can start trying to assess its quality. How significant is this source for the analysis that you are doing? Clearly this is a question of judgement, dependent to a considerable degree upon the boundaries that have already been defined as forming the scope of your analysis. The work and thought necessary before you have even begun collecting any data to analyse is considerable.

Once you have completed your preparation, you have merely to collect the data that you have spent so long in identifying and assessing. The 'merely' in the last sentence was ironic; there is such a range of collective methods that you may be almost overwhelmed.

4.2 Collecting

Getting ready to collect data can take some time; actually collecting it can happily take a century or so. This, however, is not the sort of time scale that most businesses (or systems analysts) are prepared to contemplate. Hence they construct a compromise practicality using a selection of the following methods.

4.2.1 INTERVIEWS

One of the most obvious and popular means of eliciting information is by means of interview. If you wish to analyse how a company works and what its major inputs and outputs are, then it does not take a massive amount of perception to realize that interviewing members of the company concerned could be a quick and effective method of gaining the information required. Equally you could interview others who came into professional contact with the company concerned: suppliers, customers, etc. It is consequently not surprising to see that interviewing gains considerable attention from writers in this field. Clifton (1983) gives more space to interviewing than to any other information-gathering procedure. Interviewing is virtually the only data-gathering technique that Yourdon (1989) looks at at all. Daniels and Yeates claim that: 'Interviewing is probably the most productive fact-finding activity for an analyst' (p. 13), a view that seems to be shared by Mittra who devotes about four pages to interviewing technique. (pp. 36–40).

Yet, if this recognizes that interviewing is the most important and most frequently used fact-finding technique, no myths should be upheld about its difficulties. There are major advantages in conducting interviews. Above all, perhaps, an interview gives a member of the company concerned, from managing director to shopfloor worker, an active sense of involvement. The interviewee can feel that they are actively contributing to the systems project, and can thus be more committed to the new computerized regime when it becomes operative. Interviews, particularly through observation of body movements and facial expressions, can provide much more than objective facts; they can provide the analyst with a feel for attitudes and tensions that are unconsciously revealed. Furthermore, an interview allows the interviewer to explore avenues that he or she only becomes aware of at all during the interview itself. There is no opportunity for this sort of feedback in a written questionnaire. Yet, despite such patent advantages, there are considerable pitfalls in the interviewer's path. It is all too easy to ask loaded questions, that is, questions which, in their phrasing, reveal the analyst's personal opinion on the subject. As a consequence, the interviewee will respond, not to the content of the question, but to the interviewer. If the interviewee likes the interviewer, the answer given will correspond to the interviewer's own stance, or vice versa. Somewhat similar are leading questions, ones which positively invite a set response: 'You won't put an engineer in charge of that, will you?' stridently requests the answer: 'Of course not.' Nor is it unknown for interviewers to provide the answers to their own questions: 'How many hours will this operation take? I would have thought seven would be the maximum.' Obviously, too, the whole approach and manner of the interviewer is of prime importance. Managing directors tend to dislike being treated as store cleaners. Store cleaners themselves dislike being patronized, or, at the other extreme, baffled by over-complex questions.

On top of the difficulties of personal relations that interviews can present, there are some objective and unavoidable disadvantages. It is a very time-consuming operation, and consequently costly. There can also be considerable difficulties in arranging for interviews to take place. It is not always possible to do them during the employee's working day, but alternatives can present problems of willingness, timing and location. There can be no doubt that interviews do have a number of important advantages, but their disadvantages and difficulties are equally striking. I suspect that the popularity of interviews stems in part from factors unconnected with their effectiveness. First of all, very few systems analysts are ever going to think that they are weak at handling interviews. Indeed, the very nature of the systems analyst's job is likely to attract people who are highly likely to possess considerable self-confidence. They are consequently even less likely to doubt their own interviewing technique, deplorable though in fact it might be. Secondly, interviews are a visible way of occupying one's time. Passing round questionnaires or simply observing a working context does not score any brownie points for commitment, activity and involvement. Hence the systems analyst is, unconsciously perhaps, almost bound to plump for interviews. Andrew Parkin provides a useful checklist for the conduct of the successful interview:

Did the interviewer:
   make a prior appointment, state expected duration;
   try to get a sensible time and place;
   introduce himself/herself agreeably;
   state his/her purpose in a way you understood;
   state what he/she believed your role to be;
   appear to have planned the discussion, state the agenda;
   ask questions appropriate to your knowledge and status;
   listen to your answers and opinions;
   quiz you on uncertain terminology or vague answers;
   ask for sets of documents and completed specimens;
   make notes;
   check back his/her facts or understanding before leaving;
   depart agreeably, leaving the door open for a return visit?

Did he/she:
   arrive late;
   stick unduly to his/her plan;
   annoy you through mannerisms, excessive jocularity, etc.;
   interrupt your answer and prevent you from completing your point;
   allow you too much rein with opinion or side-tracks;
   confuse you with technicalities;
   argue with you or criticize your suggestions;

dominate when you should have been given more freedom;
anticipate your answers or jump to conclusions;
part with missing detail or understanding?

Error can also be minimized if the interviewer prepares a report of the interview which is then sent to the interviewee for confirmation. Clifton (1983) provides some guidelines:

1. Obtain a manager's consent before interviewing the staff.
2. Arrange the time, place and subject of the interview well beforehand.
3. The interviewer should brief himself/herself on the position and general duties of the interviewee.
4. Provide a quiet, interruption-free environment.
5. Listen more than talk.
6. Interview only one person at a time.
7. Minimize digressions, separating opinions from facts, and not allowing generalizations to obscure the true situation.
8. Do not attempt to cover too much ground.
9. Conclude with a brief résumé.

4.2.2 QUESTIONNAIRES

As an information-gathering technique, questionnaires have not aroused much enthusiasm. Clifton (1983) comments sourly that: 'A questionnaire should be utilized only when no other method of fact-finding is practicable.' I am less averse to their use. A questionnaire does not intimidate its recipient; an interview often can. A questionnaire does not hurry its recipients; an interview often can. Clearly, on matters of unambiguous factual content, a questionnaire is quicker and a great deal cheaper than conducting interviews. In certain situations, where there is, for instance, considerable distance between the systems analyst and the desired respondents, a questionnaire may be the only practicable method anyway. Certainly, if sufficient care is taken to ensure that the questions in the questionnaire are both neutrally phrased and un-ambiguous, there should be considerable value in its use. The one apparently unavoidable drawback is that one never gains a 100 per cent response from questionnaires.

Anyway, having indicated the benefits of questionnaires, let me now summarize their failings:

1. Low response may mean an unrepresentative sample.
2. Reliability is often untested or untestable.
3. Validity (does the question elicit the intended information) is often untestable.
4. The limitations of written questioning may lead to a shallow answer.
5. People may be prejudiced against questionnaires.

For Clifton (1983), questionnaires are best suited to the following situations:

1. Where the systems analyst is located at a considerable distance from the staff to be questioned.
2. Where there are too many people to make interviewing viable.
3. As a means of verifying information found by other methods.
4. Where the questions are simple and factual.
5. Where a full set of replies is not necessary in order to determine the facts.

4.2.3   OBSERVING

For someone whose ambition has always been to become a fly on the wall, observing is an ideal technique. The object of the exercise is that the analyst just merges into the background and watches the company at its work. Unfortunately, merging into the background is not easy; much of the time it is downright impossible. Employees resent strangers peering at them. Any attempts to time activities are almost bound to produce vagrant results: employees will deliberately dawdle or, at the other extreme, pretend they are training for an Olympic 100 metres. The only way in which one can be a really effective observer is to hang around observing for so long that, eventually, employees do forget that you are there. This, however, would make observing even more time consuming than interviewing.

4.2.4   PARTICIPATION

One way of escaping from the penalties of observing is to become a genuine participant in the company. In other words, to join the workforce. Other workers will then accept you with no suspicion. The drawback, of course, is that you are then limited in your effective observation to the area such workers would occupy, and it is likely to negate the purpose of the operation if you turned up one week as a welder, next week as a salesman, next week as a caretaker, and so on.

4.2.5   READING

Virtually all companies and organizations have reams of reading material in the form of reports, regulations, surveys, accounts, and public relations material. Some of it might be useful. The trouble is, you rarely know whether or not something will be useful until you have finished reading it, and, in most companies, you could easily spend several months in just reading. None the less, documents carry useful information about the data elements and terminology used in the existing system and the analyst should aim to collect a completed specimen (or photocopy) of each relevant document. Documents worth perusing include:

1. Reports of previous surveys and investigations
2. Company instructions

3. Sales literature and company information booklets
4. Job descriptions

4.2.6 OTHER TECHNIQUES

Rock-Evans suggests a number of other methods of gaining information:

Phone calls can be cheap and time saving, but lack face-to-face contact and can be inconvenient for the person phoned.

Meetings can be effective, good for the morale of users and can eliminate the users' tendency to push personal goals, but they are often difficult to arrange, can merely expose personality clashes and power struggles, and are a poor way of extracting detailed information.

Teleconferencing has the advantages of a meeting but is expensive and complicated to set up and has all the disadvantages of a meeting except the difficulty of getting people together.

Cooption removes time constraints and increases commitment but can produce bias.

Experimentation can simulate events which are rare, allow more accurate control and new approaches, and can be repeated, but can also be costly, need considerable prior knowledge and can produce false results because everyone knows that it is not 'real life'.

The above techniques, or some judicious combination of them, are the ways in which a systems analyst would gather information. That data is used in a database, and that database is going to make the company, organization or person concerned more efficient, effective and economic. It will, however, only do so if the data is presented to the computer in an acceptable fashion. A database, after all, is a collection of structured and formatted data. It would be unfortunate to spend weeks collecting data, only to waste it by storing it in an unacceptable fashion. Hence preparing data for the computer forms the subject of the next chapter.

References

Clifton, H. D. *Business Data Systems*, 2nd edn, Prentice-Hall, 1983.

Kozar, A. K. *Humanized Information Systems Analysis and Design*, McGraw-Hill, 1989.

Oliver, E. C. and Chapman, R. J. *Data Processing*, 4th edn, DP Publications, 1979.

Wilkes, R. B. 'Draining the Swamp: Defining strategic use of the information systems resource' in *Information and Management: The International Journal of Information Systems Applications*, January 1991.

Yourdon, E. *Modern Structured Analysis*, Prentice-Hall, 1989.

5
Preparing data for the computer

You have been approached by the Mozart Appreciation Sabian Society to construct a database for them. First of all, a word or two about the society itself. After 1991, the 200th anniversary of Mozart's death, few people in Western society could have escaped coming into contact with at least Mozart's name, if not his music. The Mozart Appreciation Sabian Society was founded in Ercallalorum Parva in mid-Mercia in order to act as a permanent research organization into Mozart's life and works. Its somewhat odd name stems from the fact that 'Sabian' refers to a religious sect mentioned in the Koran, a sect associated with star worship. Since Simeon Grumblethitch, the founder of the society, regarded Mozart as the star of stars, Sabian seemed to him to be appropriate. Furthermore, when the society was founded in late 1990, the United States of America and her allies had begun a disagreement with Iraq that was to lead to war. Simeon felt that using a word from the Koran would help to heal Islamic/Christian tensions. The inevitable acronym for the society (MASS) gave, Simeon felt, a feeling of catholicity to the society. As you might also have gathered, Simeon Grumblethitch was entirely mad.

Apart from his wayward mind, Simeon was blessed with vast amounts of money and a passion for Mozart (normally a sign of total sanity!). He also had the eclecticism often associated with intellectual disorder. Hence, in May 1991 he was reading Arthur Hutchings' *A Companion to Mozart's Piano Concertos*, and Khalid Azis's *So You Think Your Business Needs a Computer?* (Aziz, 1986). It was from the latter that he encountered the following sentence: 'A database is the computer name for a very grand filing cabinet which, on top of its huge storage capacity, has the ability to sort through vast amounts of data and present it to you in a simple, straightforward way.' All of a sudden, illumination flooded Simeon's mind. He had a huge library of books about Mozart. He had an even larger record and tape collection of Mozart's works. What he needed was a database.

Seized by this inspiration, Grumblethitch recalled that, somewhat earlier in the book, Khalid Aziz had written about employing a consultant. It was at this point that he contacted you. Your brief was straightforward. Simeon wanted a database to store his books and records. He then wanted to be able to use that database in a number of ways. Should he need to know what books about Mozart had been written by H. C. Robbins Landon, the database must be capable of telling him. Should anyone need to know the K-number of Symphony no. 36, the database should tell him. Were there any Mozart operas starring Maria Callas? Where and when did *La Clemenza di Tito* receive its first performance? Which piano sonatas were written in C major? In other words, Simeon wanted the database to be all-knowing and capable of giving answers to a wide variety of questions. This is a matter which concerns the database management system employed, the topic of Part Three, and we shall return to Simeon Grumblethitch's desires then. But, on top of these demands, Simeon also demanded to be able to add new data to the computer once the database had been set up. This was, after all, a perfectly reasonable request. There is not a lot of point in having a database constructed if you cannot then add new items to that database. Accordingly you have set aside a Friday afternoon for instructing Simeon in how to enter data into a database in such a way that the database can handle that data subsequently. What follows is what you should tell him.

First of all, you explain to Simeon that a computer wants to deal with data one item at a time. You state that, if requested to deal with two or three items simultaneously, the database begins to develop indigestion. Consequently you have designed records or entries into the database that are split into single-valued elements. To illustrate what you mean, you show Simeon his own record catalogue of Mozart works. This is a folder in which entries are listed as follows:

1. Symphony no. 25 in G minor, K.183 played by the London Symphony Orchestra under Sir G. Solti on Decca Eclipse ECS 591.
2. *The Marriage of Figaro* with the Glyndebourne Festival Chorus and Orchestra conducted by K. Busch and starring Aulikki Rautavaara, Audrey Mildmay, Roy Henderson, Willi Domgraf-Fassbaender, Heddle Nash and Italo Tajo on Classics for Pleasure CFP 117/8.
3. Symphony no. 28 in C major, K.200 played by the English Chamber Orchestra under Colin Davis on Oiseau-Lyre SOL 266.
4. Clarinet Concerto in A major, K.622 played by John McCaw with the New Philharmonia Orchestra under R. Leppard on Unicorn UNS 239.
5. String Quartet no. 1 in G major, K.80 played by the Heutling Quartet on HMV HQS 1226.

And so it goes on, page after page of neatly written entries, compiled more or less as Simeon acquired the records concerned. As a database, it does not exist. There is no order to it. It is impossible to discover whether or not Simeon possesses a record of Walter Klein playing the 16th Piano Sonata in B flat major, K.570 without reading through the entire catalogue, entry after entry, until you either reach the desired entry or arrive at the end of the catalogue. Nor, of course, is it possible to divide each entry easily into its component parts of single-valued items. You point out to Simeon that a database is a structured collection of data. His massive catalogue needs some structure imposed upon it. Accordingly you indicate that the works of Mozart should first be divided into convenient categories: symphonies, concertos, string quartets, operas, and so on. Then for each category, a series of columns should be devised so that each column contains a single item of data pertaining to the work in question. For the category 'Symphony' for instance, a table could be constructed that looks like Table 5.1. Such a table would cope with all the symphonies of Mozart, since, unlike Beethoven, Mahler, Vaughan Williams and others, Mozart never wrote a symphony which also contained the human voice. Hence each row within the above table would uniquely identify each performance of each Mozart symphony that Simeon and/or the Mozart Appreciation Sabian Society possessed.

Table 5.1

Record no.	Symphony no.	Köchel no.	Key	Orchestra	Conductor

Up to this point, Simeon Grumblethitch nods calmly, feeling that constructing a database is a great deal easier than analysing a Mozart symphony. Consequently you feel able to launch into the topic of functional dependence. Fortunately this is not a difficult concept.

You point out that there are, in the table that has so far been set up, three unique data items. To illustrate your point, you fill in the table with three entries (Table 5.2). By talking to Simeon, you get him to point out that Key cannot be a unique item. Even in the three items above, there are two G minors, and in the full catalogue of symphonies there will be lots of C majors, B flat majors, and so on. Nor can Orchestra be a unique item. The Vienna Philharmonic has doubtless recorded many Mozart symphonies. Equally, Conductor cannot be unique. Sir Georg Solti must have recorded a dozen or more Mozart symphonies. Hence, in the completed table for the Grumblethitch collection of Mozart symphonies, the Vienna Philharmonic, the key C major, and the conductor Solti will doubtless appear many times, though not, of course, necessarily in the same row.

By this time it will be obvious to Simeon that the remaining three columns have to contain unique data items. There is only one record labelled SDD233 or, more accurately, the hundreds of records with the number SDD233 are all

Table 5.2

Record no.	Symphony no.	Köchel no.	Key	Orchestra	Conductor
SDD233	40	550	G minor	Vienna Phil.	Karajan
ECS591	25	183	G minor	London SO	Solti
VICS1529	36	425	C major	Boston SO	Leinsdorf

completely identical. Certainly there is only one Symphony no. 40 and it is
indissolubly linked to the Köchel number 550. (For those who do not know,
Köchel numbers are a classification system for Mozart's music devised by
Ludwig von Köchel (1800–77) and revised by Alfred Einstein in 1937.) Hence
we come to the concept of functional dependence. If we see a particular Köchel
number, we know—or can find out—what work is being referred to. There is
only one K.581 and, if you are a fanatic about Mozart like Simeon Grumblethitch, then you will know that the work in question must be the clarinet quintet
in A major. From this it follows that the title of a Mozart work and its Köchel
number are functionally dependent upon each other. If you are given the
K-number, you can find out the name of the work in question; if you are given
the name of the work, you can find out the K-number; each item *functionally
determines* the other. The particular key that a work is in only displays
functional dependence in one direction. If you are talking about the oboe
quartet, K.370, then you know that the key must be F major. The key is
functionally dependent upon both the title and the K-number. They both
functionally determine the key. If, however, you mention the key F major, you
are not functionally determining anything. It could be the Divertimento no. 10
for two horns and string quartet, the Piano Concerto no. 15, the String Quartet
no. 5, the second piano sonata or a whole range of other alternatives.

It is relatively easy to see that the title of a work or its K-number are mutually
functionally dependent, and that either or both functionally determine the key
signature. Simeon Grumblethitch is likely to follow this without too much
difficulty, and even to enjoy himself naming dozens of works that are in F
major. One difficulty, however, now begins to present itself. If you mention
Mozart's Symphony no. 38 to Simeon Grumblethitch, he is going to know
immediately that you are referring to the Symphony in D major, K.504. He is
not, though, going to know necessarily which orchestra is playing it or which
conductor is conducting it. It could, after all, be any one of a number of
combinations. It could be the London Symphony Orchestra under Solti, the
Philharmonia under Karajan, the English Chamber Orchestra under Davis, or,
for all that you and I are likely to know, the Scunthorpe Band under Fred
Bloggs. Simeon, however, wildly eccentric though he may be, is not stupid. He
is likely to point out that there is another unique data item in our table: the
Record no. The Record no. will itself functionally determine all the other
elements. If you cite Record no. ST1032, you can only be talking about the

World Record Club issue of the Philharmonia under Karajan playing K.504. If you have the Record no. ECS591, you can only be referring to the playing of K.504 by the LSO under Solti on the Decca Eclipse label. Simeon is constantly going to announce triumphantly that the Record no. is a unique data item that functionally determines all the others. Through your expert tuition, you have persuaded Simeon Grumblethitch to apprehend fully the concept of functional dependence.

Unfortunately there are still some problems remaining. Simeon may, at the moment, be congratulating himself on mastering the arcane practices of systems analysis. He may well be unamused to discover that there is more to come. Your tactics here are likely to depend upon your assessment of Simeon. You may feel that the remaining steps are well within his comprehension (as, indeed, they are), and decide to plough ever onwards. Alternatively, you may decide that functional dependence is enough for one day, and arrange with Simeon to see him again next Wednesday. Whatever your decision, the following points are going to have to be made:

1. The Record no. does not simply determine that Symphony no. 38 in D major, K.504 is being played; it also determines that another work is also being played. Hence, while Record no. ST1032 does indicate that K.504 is being performed, it also indicates that Symphony no. 29 in A major, K.201 is being played. Hence there is not a one-to-one relationship between ST!032 and anything else. There is a one-to-one relationship between Symphony no. 38 and the Köchel number 504. There is a one-to-one relationship between Symphony no. 38 and the key of D major. But the Record no. ST1032 has a relationship with two very different works. As it happens in this instance, it has a relationship with two different orchestras as well, since K.504 is played by the Philharmonia and K.201 is played by the Berlin Philharmonic. In both cases the conductor is Karajan, but clearly this need not have been the case. Not infrequently one encounters records which contain a number of works performed by a number of different ensembles and conducted by a number of different conductors.

2. There is also an intellectual disparity involved here. The data items of Title (Symphony no. 38) and Köchel number (K.504) and Key (D major) are all intimately connected. They all refer to a musical work by Mozart. The Record no. ST1032, however, does not have this intimate relationship with Mozart. It is merely an arbitrary label given to a manufacture which, in this case, does happen to be concerned with Mozart. Records, however, are deleted. They can then be reissued on a different label and with a different number. It is also conceivable that another record—let us say of Neville Marriner conducting the Mozart *Jupiter Symphony*—appears with the Record no. ST1032. That would not be any problem for the record company since the original ST1032 had long since been deleted, but it would be a problem for the Mozart Appreciation Sabian Society since their database

could then have two identical data items referring to two very different entities.

By this time, there is a fair chance that Simeon will be intrigued. Perhaps this database business does have some perplexities, he feels. It may even be that Simeon suggests the next move himself. It is, after all, not too difficult to see that, if the Mozart symphony table is currently too complex or too fragmented, the situation might be solved if two tables were created instead of one. There could be a table devoted to the music, and another table devoted to the records. Something like Tables 5.3 and 5.3 might be suggested.

Table 5.3 Mozart symphony

Symphony no.	K-no.	Key
No. 34	338	C major

Table 5.4 Mozart symphony records

Record no.	Symphony	Orchestra	Conductor
CPR117	34	Bamberg SO	Leinsdorf

At this point, you can congratulate Simeon. He now has two tables, each with one data item in common so the two tables could be linked if necessary, but each devoted to a distinct entity, the first to the music, the second to the records.

Alas, there are still problems. We know that Record no. CPR117 has upon it a performance of Mozart's 34th symphony, but we do not yet know what other work or works is/are also included upon that record. In most cases, this is not a real problem. You just repeat the primary key data item, CPR117, and list the remaining work, as shown in Table 5.5.

Table 5.5

Record no.	Symphony	Orchestra	Conductor
CPR117	34	Bamberg SO	Leinsdorf
CPR117	36	Bamberg SO	Leinsdorf

It does mean, however, that Record no. can no longer act as a primary key because it is not a unique identifier. The same 'key' could be used for two or more rows in the database. Indeed, not a single item in Table 5.5 could be a primary key. There might be dozens of recordings of Symphony no. 34, so that could not be the primary key. One sees the distinction between this table and the earlier one: there is only one Symphony no. 34, so, in a table of Mozart's symphonies, the 34th would only appear once. One could possess, however, several entirely different recordings of that symphony. The same argument applies to Orchestra and Conductor too. Hence, for Table 5.5 to have a primary key that will never be repeated, you are going to have to give the table an identifying field of its own, as shown in Table 5.6.

Table 5.6

Item no.	Record no.	Symhony	Orchestra	Conductor

There is also a problem if a particular record does not contain music entirely by Mozart. It is not particularly uncommon for a record to contain two symphonies by two different composers. If the record number CPR117 (which I have invented) carried Mozart's 34th symphony and Schubert's 5th, then there is no way in which the existing table could reveal this fact. This might be perfectly in order for Simeon Grumblethitch. He might only want the works by Mozart indicated. If, though, he did want a full and accurate listing of what music his records and tapes did contain, then you would need to put another column into the table, a column indicating the composer concerned.

The problems with Simeon Grumblethitch and the MASS were designed as an introduction to the basic topic of this chapter: *normalization*. We are well aware of the fundamental question:

Given that you have a substantial amount of data which you wish to arrange and store in a database, what is the most sensible and convenient way of structuring that data so as to create a logical database structure?

The answer to this question is that you normalize your data. Words like 'normalization' and phrases like 'normalizing your data' will, at the moment, be entirely meaningless, but there is no cause for concern. Normalization is merely the process of creating a logical database structure. To normalize data, you take it through different stages until you have reached the level of normalization that you require. These different stages are termed *forms*: first normal form, second normal form, and so on. Data that has been organized so that it is in fifth normal form (the highest level) is data that should give absolutely no trouble when managing the database. In fact, for most practical purposes, data that is in third normal form will normally be quite adequate. Let me give an analogy. Imagine that you are standing in your bedroom totally naked. You are in zero normal form. You now put on your fetchingly styled pink underwear and your delightful emerald green vest. You are now in first normal form. Next you put on that attractive yellow top and your beautifully pressed skirt or trousers. You are now in second normal form. You next put on your socks or stockings, shoes and jacket. You are now fully dressed and equipped for most social occasions. This is third normal form. Should circumstances demand it, you might next put on your overcoat. This we will call fourth normal form. Finally, in somewhat extreme circumstances, you might decide to wrap a scarf round your neck and put on your Cossack-type fur hat. This would be fifth normal form.

In this section of the chapter we shall proceed through these five normal forms. There are only two concepts that are crucial in the understanding of normalization: functional dependence and keys. Since we have already encountered both those concepts, normalization itself should pose no problems.

Although we have not yet reached the topic of database management, it is worth mentioning here that it is commonly regarded as comprising three basic types:

- Hierarchical
- Network
- Relational

It has often been argued that normalization is only an operation that has any relevance to relational database management contexts. Revel (in Deen, (ed.) 1990) raises this issue, and roundly declares that: 'a normalized data model is the starting point for the design of any type of database system'. Indeed, as Revel admits, it does not even have to be a database system at all. Normalization is an invaluable technique in virtually any data-orientated situation. As such, it is vital to learn it. Consequently, although we have already met the important concepts, this section of the chapter will introduce the technical in-house vocabulary that is adopted by computer scientists. Perkinson (1984) even begins his chapter on normalization by defining 15 terms that are commonly encountered in dealing with this topic. Some of those terms—entity, data item, key, relationship—we have already met. The others will be explained as we need them.

We already know that it is convenient to place data into a table structure, each table naturally consisting of rows and columns. Such a table is frequently termed a *relation*. This name stems from mathematics, and I shall always refer to a table rather than a relation. It will be useful, though, for you to know that the two terms, in this context, are synonymous.

We shall now look at a table that is not in any normal form at all. It will be your job to work out why this table can be said to be completely unnormalized. Personally, when reading books packed with tedious tables, I tend to skim over the tables at the rate of about 0.0001 second per table. This is a deplorable habit, tribute only to my undisciplined mind. I can only ask you not to copy me. Do really look at the tables that appear from now on in this chapter. Only by so doing can you be certain of understanding normalization. Anyway, the first of them is Table 5.7.

The reason that this table is not in any normalized form at all is that it contains what is called a *repeating group*. You will recall that it has already been indicated that in a database table, each space (or *field*, as they are called) should be filled by a single-valued item of data. In Table 5.7, the column devoted to Cast has five data elements for each so-called entry. Hence the table is unnormalized.

It is quite easy (though very tedious) to turn an unnormalized table into one that is at least in first normal form. You must eliminate the repeating group or groups, though this will, almost inevitably, involve some repetition. Hence, if we were to eliminate the repeating groups in Table 5.7, it would be done like

Table 5.7   Plays put on at the Cock Theatre

Author	Title	Cast
T. Kyd	*The Spanish Tragedy*	Colin Baker Angela Down Meg Soper Michael Sharpe Peter Jackson
T. Dekker	*The Shoemaker's Holiday*	Simon Rogers Margaret Gilson Jeremy Erskine Ruth Gomme Colin Poledark
C. Marlowe	*Edward II*	Colin Baker Margaret Gilson Richard Browne Christopher Hale David Simcox

this, though I confine myself to only one example, not the three that were in the table:

C. Marlowe	Edward II	Colin Baker
C. Marlowe	Edward II	Margaret Gilson
C. Marlowe	Edward II	Richard Browne
C. Marlowe	Edward II	Christopher Hale
C. Marlowe	Edward II	David Simcox

And there we have a group that is certainly in first normal form, the repeating group having been removed. The fact that the author and title of the play are now repeated five times is wasteful of space, but that is a fault that is much less worrying than the presence of a repeating group.

A table may be in first normal form but still have problems associated with it. We need now to concentrate on the concept of key. Each row of a table should have a primary key upon which all the items within that row are fully dependent. Have a look at Table 5.8.

What on earth is the primary key here? Clearly Dept no. does functionally define the Dept name, but it does not functionally define the remaining three

Table 5.8   Employee

Dept no.	Dept name	Employee no.	Employee name	Address
10	Bedding	183	S. A. Brown	14 Toftwood Road
11	Fruit and veg.	184	M. P. Evans	74 Hanson Close
13	Audio	239	R. W. Simpson	36 Felix Street
10	Bedding	114	T. D. Wright	3 The Broadway
12	Coats	265	L. Throstle	21 Ely Way

elements at all. They, on the other hand, are congruent with each other. The employee number 183 does functionally define the employee S. A. Brown, and the Employee name does, in turn, functionally define the given Address. Hence, while the table above is in first normal form—it contains no repeating groups—it is not in second normal form in that not all its elements are dependent upon one primary key. The answer, of course, is to split the table into two separate ones, each one having an unambiguous primary key. The situation, as you can see, is very similar to the problem encountered with Simeon's records and tapes of Mozart's music where again it was not easy to see which was the primary key of the original table. Anyway, Tables 5.9 and 5.10 are in second normal form.

Table 5.9 Department

Dept no.	Dept name
10	Bedding

Table 5.10 Employee

Employee no.	Employee name	Address
13	R. W. Simpson	36 Felix Street

Of course, by doing this, we then lose the information about the department in which each employee works, but we could always add an extra field onto Table 5.10 since, for instance, Employee no. 13 does determine in which department the employee concerned works. Table 5.10 would then have four fields instead of three, and there would be some repetition of data in that Dept no. now appeared in two tables. Both tables, however, would be in second normal form.

To be sure that we have a table that is in third normal form, we have to look again at the concept of dependency. As it happens, Tables 5.9 and 5.10 are both in third normal form. In order to see why, let us look at another table that is certainly in second normal form, but is not in third normal form. Can you see the qualitative difference between Table 5.11 and Tables 5.9 and 5.10.

Table 5.11 is concerned with some projects undertaken by the pupils of Southgate High School. This is obviously in first normal form; there are no repeating groups. Furthermore, if we assume that the key to each row is Pupil

Table 5.11

Pupil name	Project	Date due
Steven Bowles	Feminism in Hackney	12.6.92
Mary Charman	Islington Music	25.6.92
Roger Giddings	Arts in Herne Hill	18.6.92
Samantha Said	Feminism in Hackney	12.6.92
Peter Knowles	Acton Parking Policy	30.6.92
Sarah Soper	Arts in Herne Hill	18.6.92

name, then it is second normal form, since the other two data elements are dependent upon that name. If you are Steven Bowles, then your project is due on 12 June 1992 and its title is Feminism in Hackney. None the less, there is a problem. The date that a pupil's project is due to be handed in is dependent not only upon the pupil's name, but also on the title of the project itself. If you happen to be engaged in the project on the Arts in Herne Hill, then it is due to be handed in on 18 June 1992 no matter what the name of the pupil or pupils engaged upon it may be. Hence the data item Date due is not an independent element; it is indissolubly tied to the project title. It is consequently said to be *transitively dependent* upon the primary key of the table, Pupil name. A table is only in third normal form if there are no transitive keys in the rows of the table.

You can doubtless see that, once again, the solution to the problem is to split the table into two. In Table 5.12 the primary key, Pupil name, functionally determines the project. In Table 5.13 the primary key, Project, functionally determines the Date due. There are no repeating groups, therefore it is in first normal form. There are no data items that are not fully dependent upon the

Table 5.12

Pupil name	Project
Stephen Bowles	Feminism in Hackney

Table 5.13

Project	Date due
Feminism in Hackney	12.6.92

primary key, so it is consequently in second normal form. Nor are there any nonkey data items that are also directly related to each other in such a way that the changing of the one would also necessitate the changing of the other. In fact, of course, with there only being two fields per table, such a circumstance would be impossible anyway. However, let us extend both of these tables so that we can familiarize ourselves with the nature of third normal form tables. If Table 5.12, with Pupil name as its primary key, were to be extended as shown in Table 5.14, would it still be in third normal form?

The entry in Table 5.14 is clearly in third normal form. The key to the row is the pupil's name. All the other elements in the row are fully functionally dependent upon that key. 4S is the only form or class of which Belinda is a member. She was born only on 3 July 1976, and the only project on which she is engaged is the one concerning Database Usage in the NHS. There are no repeating groups and no transitive dependents; every data item is independent.

Table 5.14

Pupil name	Form	Date of birth	Project
Belinda Dewar	4S	3.7.76	Database Usage in the NHS

How about Table 5.15? In order to understand it you need to know that although the projects concerned are the overall responsibility of the sociology department, each project is supervised by a member of the school whose subject is related to the sociological research. I hope that you can see that in the new Project table there is now a transitive dependency. While it is true that anyone doing a project on Numeracy for Infants will be supervised by someone from the Maths department, it is also true that the field 'Maths' in the first row of our abbreviated table is dependent upon T. W. Goodwin, since Mr Goodwin is a member of the Maths department. The same argument, of course, is true for the second and final row of the table.

Table 5.15

Pupil name	Project	Supervisor	Dept
Trevor Blake	Numeracy for Infants	T. W. Goodwin	Maths
Megan Worksup	Visual Arts in Camden	G. R. Huntley	Art

For the vast majority of normal purposes, third normal form is as far as anyone need concern themselves. Indeed, most rows that are in third normal form are also in fourth and fifth normal form, as we shall shortly see. Let us, however, be entirely clear as to what kind of data is contained in a table in third normal form. Each row of such a table has a number of qualities. First of all, every data item in that row is single-valued. It does not comprise a group of entities, nor can it be broken down meaningfully to anything simpler. The computer jargon for such a data item is to describe it as *atomic*. One of those data items, normally the first, acts as a key to all the other items in the row. Normally called the *primary key*, it follows that all the other items in the row are fully functionally dependent upon that key. You can have occasions when a row of data contains more than one possible primary key. Nor unnaturally, you will select one as the primary key; the other possibility or possibilities are called *candidate keys* or *alternate keys*, though as we have already seen, when looking at Simeon Grumblethitch's problems, candidate keys are not desirable within a row. Finally, each data item within a row must be *independent*. That means, if you need to change the value of one of the data items within a row, you need only change one of them because there are no other data items within that row which are dependent upon the one that you have to change (other than the primary key, of course, upon which all the other items are dependent). Take as an example the following row:

Name	Address	Occupation	Date of birth
Roy Smithfield	12 The Byre, Newton	Postman	30.11.49

Now, if Roy Smithfield changes his address to 47 Broad Street, Cowsby you will only have to change one item of data, his address. The fact that he has moved has no effect upon his occupation or his date of birth. All three nonkey elements in that row of data are mutually independent. If, however, you had the following row of data, the situation would be very different:

Form teacher	Form	Number in form
John Chapman	2W	27

As I am sure you have immediately spotted, the data item 'Number in form' is functionally dependent, not on the primary key, John Chapman, but on the preceding data item, 'Form'. Hence the two nonkey attributes in this row are not mutually independent. The row consequently cannot be in third normal form. Note, however, that attributes within a row can be so totally dependent upon the primary key that they cannot be changed if the primary key itself is to be retained. Take the following example:

Title of work	K-number	Date of composition
Symphony no. 36	425	1783

Assuming that the first item is the primary key, then you cannot change any of the others because they are all dependent upon that primary key to such an extent that to change either of them would result in a musical or historical inaccuracy. The concept of attribute independence only applies to nonkey elements, but this independence can be difficult or impossible if there are other candidate keys within a row of data.

Before moving onto any further developments, I am uncomfortably aware that there may well be some vocabulary queries that have arisen because, in explaining the first three normal forms, a number of synonyms have been used without being previously defined or identified as synonyms. The most obvious instance here is the name given to each data item in a row. I have, so far, tended to refer to them as data items. Hence the row immediately below has five data items within it:

Author	Title	Publisher	Year	ISBN
G.B.A.M. Finlayson	England in the 1830s	Arnold	1969	7131 5485 3

However, data items within a row are also called *data elements, fields* or *attributes*. I have, in fact, used all of these terms in this chapter. I trust that the context always made it clear as to what was being meant. However, since we have now reached third normal form, let us have a terminological breakdown:

1. Data in a database is stored in a series of *tables*, each table being devoted to a particular aspect of the individual, company or organization concerned. These tables are also referred to as *relations*, and you will also encounter the word *file*, though there are good reasons for not using this word in a database context, as we shall eventually discover.
2. Each table is naturally divided into rows and columns. The rows are often referred to as *tuples* (to rhyme with couples), though there has never seemed to me to be any reason for using this word.

3. Each row has a *primary key* which determines all the attributes within that row. In other words, each data item in the row is functionally dependent upon the primary key. It can happen that the primary key is a combination of two or more attributes, in which case the primary key may be referred to as a *composite key*.
4. Every row within a database (or any other normalized structure) must be unique. It is not possible for there to be two (or more) identical rows within a table.

With the material so far covered, we have dealt with most of the problems encountered in creating relations. Gane and Sarson (1977) refer to normalization as 'inspired common sense', and there is certainly no reason why normalization should be the province of the professional systems analyst or the company systems designer. I shall, however, be brief in dealing with the two remaining normal forms.

We have already encountered the problem that led to the development of fourth normal form. You recall the column 'Cast' in Table 5.7 led to what are called *multivalued dependencies*. In other words, for any one production, we had to enter the author of the play and the title of the play into the table a number of times in order to accommodate the names of the cast of that play. Clearly this resulted in considerable redundancy. Having to store the name T. Kyd and the title of his play *The Spanish Tragedy* half a dozen times wasted a great deal of space. There was exactly the same problem with Simeon Grumblethitch's record catalogue when we came to an opera with six or seven members of the cast who had to be listed. The solution to this dilemma is simple enough. We create a separate table for the cast. This reduces the redundant attributes in the original table and also gives us the opportunity of adding further useful information in that we can now ally each member of the cast to the character they depict. As a result, we might obtain, for example, Table 5.16.

Table 5.16 Cast of *Edward II* by C. Marlowe

Character	Actor
Edward II	Colin Baker
Q. Isabella	Margaret Gilson
Prince Edward	Richard Browne
Gaveston	Christopher Hale
Mortimer	David Simcox

Most tables that are in third normal form are also in fourth normal form. Only when the problem of multivalued attributes manifests itself is there any need consciously to convert a set of data to fourth normal form.

The need for fifth normal form is very rare, and I shall not go into details here. We have, however, seen that it is frequently necessary, in order to produce third normal form or fourth normal form, to split an existing table into two separate ones. Clearly it is vital, when this is done, not to lose any information. The two tables formed from splitting one previous table must carry at least as much information as the original had done. In our examples, this has always been accomplished. Very occasionally, however, the situation arises that, when splitting one table into two, some information is inevitably lost, or, to be more precise, some element of the relationship between attributes of those tables is lost. When this is the case, the problem can be solved by splitting the original table into three or more tables instead of the normal two. When this is necessary, the resulting tables are said to be in fifth normal form. In the vast majority of occasions, a third normal form table is also in both fourth and fifth normal forms.

In addition to skating over fifth normal form, one extension to third normal form has also been omitted. This is called the Boyce–Codd rule, named after the two people who expounded it. Indeed, the whole formalization of the normalization process was originally propounded by E. F. Codd in a paper that he published in 1971. However, the explanation of normalization that has been given in this chapter has virtually incorporated the Boyce–Codd rule anyway, so it does not require separate treatment.

We can now, however, come close to concluding. Two things remain to be done, and the first of them is almost self-evident. Having laboured through several pages devoted to normalization, you are entitled to ask, 'Is normalization really important?' Date (1986) points out that normalization is a useful aid in the process of database design, but adds that 'it is not a panacea'. None the less Date had earlier stated (p. 244) that there was at least one reason for insisting that all relations should be normalized, so, while admitting that the process is not a panacea for anything, it is none the less extremely important. I might even differ from Date and claim that normalization is vital. It seems fitting, therefore, to itemize some of the benefits of well-normalized tables.

1. A normalized table indicates more clearly than any other format the dependencies within the data and the constraints under which those data items may be placed.
2. A normalized table has an extremely simple structure which produces a high degree of data independence. This means, among other things, that it is not tied in any way to the manner in which the data is physically arranged on the disk or disks.
3. Normalization eliminates data anomalies. As a result, the data is consistent throughout the database.
4. Normalization helps to identify and remove redundancies from a database.
5. As a consequence of these aspects, all additions, modifications or deletions to the data can be accomplished in a virtually problem-free context.

Yet, 'inspired common sense', though normalization may be, it is not, for someone entirely new to the concept, the easiest subject to grasp. An attempt has been made in this chapter to explain it as clearly as possible, but, in my experience, it is frequently an advantage to look at other people's explanations too.

We have so far, in this Part Two, looked at why you might need a database system, at how to collect data, and how to prepare that data for input into a database system. Data processing, however, is a large topic, and a database is far from being the only way of storing and handling data. It seems sensible, therefore, to conclude this section devoted to 'Data' by looking at various data contexts. It is to this topic that the next chapter is devoted.

Further Reading

There are many books that also deal with normalization, including, indeed, those that have been referred to elsewhere in this book. The ones listed just happen be the ones on my shelves, and I know only too well that you can waste a considerable amount of time in searching for books. It is hoped, therefore, that the list will short-circuit your own attempts to find further material on this topic, should you wish to do so. As I have indicated, it always seems to me an excellent idea to see how other writers express or explain a matter.

S. Atre, 1980, *Data Base: Structured Techniques for Design, Performance, and Management* John Wiley, pp. 131–48.
I like Atre's book which is clear and nonpatronizing.
D. S. Bowers, 1988, *From Data to Database* Van Nostrand Reinhold, Chapter 5.
Makes some excellent points, though the prose is sometimes rather indigestible.
C. J. Date, 1986, *An Introduction to Database Systems*, Vol. I, 4th ed. Addison-Wesley, Chapter 17.
Very good. Rather forbidding for the newcomer to the subject, but should be well within your grasp now.
Ramez Elmasri and Shamkant B. Navathe, *Fundamentals of Database Systems* (Benamin/Cummings 1989), pp. 371–82.
Very good but very demanding.
Mark L. Gillenson, *Database Step-by-Step* (John Wiley 2nd ed. 1990), pp. 275–80.
Since the word 'normalization' does not appear in the index or the table of contents, you have to read the first 274 pages before you discover the topic at all. The treatment is then very brief, but it could prove a useful revision summary.
D. R. Howe, *Data Analysis for Data Base Design* (Arnold 2nd ed. 1989), Part 2, Chapters 3 to 7.
An excellent and intelligent treatment, though it does demand both intelligence and concentration to absorb it. If, however, this chapter has proved

perfectly trouble-free, I cannot think of a better extension to it than Dr Howe's treatment.

Donald C. McDermid, *Software Engineering for Information Systems* (Blackwell 1990), Chapter 5.
A clear and methodical treatment.

Elizabeth Oxborrow, *Databases and Database Systems* (Chartwell-Bratt 2nd ed. 1989), pp. 37–48.
While I disagree with the author who sees normalization as an alternative method to top-down analysis, her summary is interesting and useful.

M. Tamer Ozsu and Patrick Valduriez, *Principles of Distributed Database Systems*, (Prentice Hall 1991), pp. 19–25.
Little more than a summary and one written in technical jargon, but a useful revision guide.

Richard C. Perkinson, *Data Analysis: The Key to Data Base Design* (QED 1984), Chapter 3.
Clear, intelligent and interesting.

Philip J. Pratt and Joseph J. Adamski, *Database Systems: Management and Design*, (Boyd & Fraser 1987), Chapter 4.
Good and well illustrated with table examples.

Peter D. Smith and G. Michael Barnes, *Files & Databases* (Addison-Wesley 1987), Chapter 9.
Requires concentration in order to absorb it, but a sound professional treatment.

Gottfried Vossen, *Data Models, Database Languages and Database Management Systems* (Addison-Wesley 1990), pp. 217–38.
A book written for mathematically competent computer scientists, Mr Vossen's treatment of normalization would not be comprehensible even if you had fully understood everything in this chapter.

References

Aziz, K. *So You Think Your Business Needs a Computer?*, Kogan Page, 1986
Date, C. J. *Introduction to Database Systems*, 4th edn, Addison-Wesley, 1986.
Gane, Christopher and Sarson, Trish *Structured Systems Analysis: Tools and Techniques*, IST Data Books, 1977.
Perkinson, R. C. *Data Analysis: The Key to Data Base Design*, QED, 1984.
Revel, N. in (ed.) Deen, S. M. *Practical Database Techniques*, Pitman, 1990.

6
To database or not to database

The preceding three chapters have operated under the assumption that it is a database for which we have been planning, collecting and preparing data. Almost every other chapter in this book will also be proceeding under this assumption. None the less, it is useful to look briefly at some of the alternatives to databases that exist. After all, if you are a newcomer to the world of IT, it is instructive to become aware of other types of data storage and data application, particularly since a business or organization might want to undergo some computerization and might, indeed, ask for a database, but that it transpires that a database is not, in fact, their best option. Secondly, although this book is concerned almost entirely with databases, many of the things that are necessary to learn about databases (like the information contained in Chapters 3, 4 and 5) are also relevant for many of the database alternatives. It would, consequently, be a shame to learn all this material and not realize that it had a wider relevance than databases alone. Thirdly, it has already been indicated that semantics or terminology can be a difficulty in IT: one thing being referred to by any one of half a dozen synonyms or even there being a genuine imprecision in existing vocabulary. This is, indeed, the situation in the database field. Ask anyone to distinguish between a database, a management information system and a knowledge-based system, and you are likely to enter a semantic quagmire. It is hoped that this chapter will provide guidance on all three of these aspects. Indeed, as the title of this chapter indicates, we hope to resolve one of the most famous questions in the whole of English literature:

To database or not to database: that is the question:
Whether 'tis nobler in the mind to suffer
The slings and arrows of unnormalized data,
Or to take arms against a sea of troubles,
And by computers end them.

We shall begin by looking at the two most common types of application program, a word processor and a spreadsheet, and then move on to consider in turn some of the entities that are even more sophisticated or advanced than a database.

6.1   Applications

It would be generally agreed that all software is divided into one of three broad categories:

1. System software, like the operating system;
2. Programming languages, like BASIC, C, Pascal or FORTRAN;
3. Applications software that allows you to perform a specific task or series of tasks like playing chess or designing a poster.

While I am anxious to leave no confusion, it would be impossible to look in any sort of detail at these three types of software. The first type, system software, is a class of software that most users of computers can often ignore. System software is normally 'invisible'. It is the software tucked away inside the computer and which provides the facilities and system within which the user is operating. If you go and see a film this evening, you will not know (or care) what sort of cameras were used to shoot that film. Clearly those cameras are an essential ingredient of the film that you will see, but they are an ingredient which you can afford to ignore. So, for most of the time, is system software. It simply establishes the context within which you operate, and, if your computing requirements are relatively simple and straightforward, there is no need for you even to be aware of the system software at all.

Equally, unless you are a programmer, you do not need to know about programming languages. The system software that you unconsciously use is written in a particular computer language. The program that you are using, a word processor, a spreadsheet, or a game, is also written in a computer language, but it need not concern you as to what language is involved. When you play bowls with your friends, you know perfectly well that the bowling green is mown by a lawnmower, but it probably never occurs to you to worry about what type or make of lawnmower is employed. Equally, when you are playing chess on your computer or writing a letter to a friend, it is a matter of indifference as to the language in which the chess program or the word processor is written.

However, from all this you will deduce that a database itself is an example of applications software. Applications software is simply software which performs an application. A spreadsheet performs an application; it enables you to handle financial, accounting and other numerical operations. A word processor is an application; it enables you to write letters, reports, articles and books. A computer game is an application; they enable you to capture the dragon, shoot down the enemy, play backgammon or whatever. But databases, expert systems and some of the other objects at which we look in this chapter are such complex examples of application software that they tend to be exalted into categories of their own. Two types of application, spreadsheets and word processors, are now so common that no one concerned with IT can afford to be ignorant of them, and sophisticated spreadsheets and word processors are now so versatile that, for an individual or a small business, they could well be adequate in place of a database. We shall, therefore, glance at them both.

6.1.1 WORDPROCESSORS

At its simplest level, the word processor is the replacement of the typewriter. You sit at the keyboard and type merrily away. Your text, instead of being transferred onto paper as in a typewriter, appears on the screen of the VDU in front of you. Then, when you have finished the document in question, you issue a simple command at the keyboard, and the writing can be printed onto paper of your choice.

At just this simple level, the word processor has major advantages over the typewriter. If, when typing, you make a mistake and type a word incorrectly, then you simply take the screen cursor back to the word in question and correct your mistake. No more is your life dogged with Tipp-Ex. In addition, you can, almost instantly, add various embellishments. It is simple to <u>underline</u> a word or words. *It is equally easy to type a sentence in italics.* Most adequate word processors will allow you to cope with a variety of alphabets so that you can write words like Flüße or letters like ь, π and з. You do not have to worry about whether or not a particular word will fit onto the end of a line. If it doesn't quite fit, a facility known as 'wordwrap' will automatically transpose it onto the next line. Equally easily you can change the size of the print from very small indeed to quite large or even to double width. Such facilities make the word processor an extremely versatile typewriter, but hardly a rival to a database. There are, however, more extensive word processor facilities.

First of all, a word processor allows you to play around with the positioning of text. If, for instance, you are preparing a pamphlet on international trade and have written a couple of paragraphs about 'Tariffs', you might later decide that you want that section on 'Tariffs' to be placed before the section on 'Competition in international trade' instead of after. A word processor will allow this with ease. You just mark out on the screen the passage that you wish to move, press the appropriate command keys on your keyboard, place the cursor at the point where you have decided to insert 'Tariffs', again press the appropriate command key or keys, and the transference has been done. There is no way in which a typewriter could accomplish this.

Secondly, you can instruct your word processor to store, let us say, your own address. Then, when you come to write a letter to a customer, a supplier of a friend, you can just press one key and the entire address is loaded onto the screen. Such 'programmable' keys or 'macro features' as they are sometimes called can save an enormous amount of time. Indeed, you could save a number of typical paragraphs from business letters and insert them whenever needed.

It almost follows from what has already been said that, if you were preparing a report on some topic and wished to include in this report an extract from an earlier one, then a word processor would allow you to transfer text from one document to another, while still leaving the original document unaltered.

Finally, virtually everything that the word processor does depends upon the fact that it possesses a memory. As a consequence, reports, minutes, letters, agendas and so on can all be stored on disk to be recalled whenever the need arises. In this sense, a word processor can be a minidatabase. A man sitting at home writing a book about databases doesn't need a database himself; he only needs a word processor. A company devoted to being a clearing house for emigré Bulgarians could probably manage quite adequately with a word processor. The secretary of the parish council could almost certainly cope with only a word processor. (Many of them seem to cope with a battered biro.) Let me conclude with a real life example. Clark (1987) provides a short case study. It reads as follows:

> Nottingham City Council uses word processing for the preparation of agendas and minutes for Council meetings. Some of the items on the agenda are the same from month to month, such as confirmation of the minutes of the previous meeting and Question Time. Because of this, these items do not have to be retyped.
>
> The papers and reports which are submitted for discussion use standard headings and are often concluded with a formally worded resolution which authorises the spending of money. These motions are in a standard form, which again can be word processed.
>
> When the minutes of the meeting are being prepared for approval at the next meeting, the agenda papers can be used with the supporting detail erased, but the formal motion copied as a record of the business. Again, this is done with no retyping of text.
>
> If a list of all members voting for and against a motion is to be included, this can often be copied and adapted from a previous occasion, as the lists are similar each time, with voting on party lines.

A word processor is not a rival to a database, but, if you need a database, you almost certainly want a word processor too. If you don't need a database, you still probably need a word processor.

6.1.2 SPREADSHEETS

An electronic spreadsheet provides rows and columns into which figures and text can be entered. The junction of each row and column is called a cell. A small spreadsheet will have 60 columns and 250 rows, giving you a sum total of 15 000 cells. Some current spreadsheets have several hundred columns and 8500 rows. Clearly you can only see a small fraction of the total spreadsheet on the screen at any one time.

The purpose of a spreadsheet is to do accounts. You put in the figures and the spreadsheet adds them up. But it will also do a great deal more than that. Quite apart from the basic arithmetic processes like addition, subtraction, multiplication and division, the spreadsheet will also handle exponentiation, cope with formulae, format data into a tabular presentation, or express results by means of a graph or pie chart. Operations used in one part of a complex calculation can be replicated in another. Forecasts based on statistical likelihoods can be prepared. A recalculation in one area that has repercussions in other areas is dealt with automatically by the spreadsheet.

I could, in fact, wax lyrical about the facilities of a spreadsheet, and it was, interestingly enough, the invention of the electronic spreadsheet that led to the computer revolution. However, I shall restrain myself here from telling that story. Glossbrenner (1984) tells it well in Chapter 15 of his book. The spread of spreadsheets has, of course, been so extensive that no accountant today could cope without one. And it may be all that he does need. If an individual, company or organization is primarily concerned with the accounting function, then a spreadsheet could be a great deal more useful than a database. You can, of course, save the data on disk, and print it well and clearly formatted in page after page of financial analysis. Provided you input the correct figures in the first place, the spreadsheet will process those figures in virtually any conceivable way that you desire.

As Morris (1988) points out, the spreadsheet is rarely the main reason for buying a computer. It is frequently just an element within a wider accounts system, a system that will include programs on sales ledger, payroll, purchase ledger and so on. None the less, it is often the most commonly used element within the entire accounts package.

These two common application entities, a word processor and a spreadsheet, are now regarded as essentials by most businesses. They are the workhorses of the IT revolution. In our fervour for databases, we should not forget them. They are a great deal more limited than a database, but either or both could be adequate for many people. It would be a poor systems analyst who recommend a database to a company when all they needed was a spreadsheet.

6.2 Expert systems

From the basic, bread-and-butter level of IT, we move to a much more rarefied aspect. A word processor and a spreadsheet, examples of applications software, both do things that you and I can do; they just do them much more quickly. An expert system, however, also an example of applications software, can do things that almost no human being can achieve. So, what is an expert system? An expert system uses a database, but is more sophisticated (and, at the same time, more limited) than a database alone. Hence you cannot understand expert systems without knowing something about databases. It is, though, worthwhile having a brief glance at expert systems so that we can see the distinction between them and databases.

Most of us know the occasional expert. A friend of mine is an expert on the poetry of Tennyson. Another friend seems to diagnose the ailments of cars with an uncanny accuracy. We have all met those bizarre individuals who can do *The Times* crossword in about two minutes. Many of us have children who are supreme masters at finding excuses. So what is it that makes an expert? Clearly, knowledge is an important element. Someone who thinks that a big end is a reference to the next-door neighbour's posterior is unlikely to be an expert car mechanic. Clearly, then, an expert system is going to comprise a corpus of knowledge about the subject to which it is devoted. Let us presuppose that we have an expert system devoted to Christian religious sects. Such an expert system would rely upon a database packed with factual information. It would tell you that there were 16 830 practising Seventh-Day Adventists in Canada in 1966. It would relate the founding of the Jehovah Witnesses by Charles Taze Russell. It would explain what Christadelphians mean by the word 'ecclesia'. It would chart the success of the Pentecostalists in Chile. It would account for the introversion of the Rappites. It would show how the Plymouth Brethren split in the 1840s from the Exclusive Brethren. It would be, as you can imagine, a very large database. But we all know that it is not simply knowledge that makes an expert. The real expert internalizes his or her knowledge in such a way as to be able to solve problems and even to predict consequences. It is this high-level expertise that marks the expert. We would, therefore, expect our religious sect expert system to explain why the Spiritualists attracted more support in the 1990s than the Christadelphians. We would expect it to assess the strength of millennial thinking across the whole range of Christian sects. It would be the ability to perform this sort of intellectualized activity that would distinguish it from simply a database. Consequently, as well as a body of facts, an expert system needs a set of rules for dealing with those facts and a set of reasoning procedures in order to handle the combination of rules and facts. This set of reasoning procedures is generally known as the *inference engine*.

It is obvious from this brief outline that expert systems are highly complex entities. In order to build one it is necessary to acquire a real human expert on the subject in question, a computer analyst (often called a knowledge engineer) who can organize the expert's knowledge so that it can be handled by a computer, and, of course, a series of programmers to input the data, rules and reasoning techniques. Waterman (1986) shows how PROSPECTOR, an expert system designed to aid exploration geologists in their search for ore deposits, took more than 30 person-years to produce, and involved nine different mineral experts as well as knowledge engineers and programmers. None the less, PROSPECTOR appears to work. So do others. There are now successful expert systems from agriculture to space technology. There are scores of them in different branches of medicine. It is not entirely fanciful to imagine that a visit to the doctor in the year 2050 will simply involve answering some questions posed by a computer.

Since the core of an expert system rests in a body of facts, it is clear that a database plays an important role in expert systems. There is some disagreement among computer scientists as to whether that database should be tightly coupled to the expert system so that they act an an integrated system or loosely coupled so that each can perform more efficiently than when operating as a unit. Fortunately, this is not an argument in which we need to become involved here.

6.3 Knowledge-based systems

We are reasonably clear as to what we mean when we refer to a database. We can also distinguish a database from an expert system since the former lacks the range of rules and reasoning procedures of the latter. Yet they are both surely knowledge-based systems. Indeed, for that matter, a spreadsheet or word processor are both knowledge-based systems, as are the pocket calculators that most schoolchildren carry with them these days. How, then, can we defend a separate heading for knowledge-based systems if this chapter has been doing nothing so far but talk about them?

Frost (1986) admits that there is no widely accepted definition of the term 'knowledge base', and comments that 'the term is used by different people to mean different things'. Frost does go on to make some distinctions between a database, an expert system and a knowledge-based system, but his distinctions are not very precise and some of them have been invalidated by developments in databases since he wrote. Broadly speaking, Frost argues that knowledge-based systems are objects which have more inferential powers than a database but a wider sphere than an expert system. Elmasri and Navathe (1989) also grapple with the terminology, but have such difficulties in defining the work 'knowledge' that they come close to parody.

Rather than resolve the entire dilemma with some supremely perceptive insight, I shall muddy the waters even more. There are objects known respectively as management information systems (MIS) and decision-support systems (DSS). Hicks (1986) talks about them extensively. Insofar as I can understand Hicks, an MIS seems to me to be virtually identical to a database, while a DSS seems very like Frost's description of a knowledge-based system. I admit that I am not entirely sure. It is unfortunate that, in order to enter the world of databases, you ideally need a Ph.D. in linguistic philosophy, an M.Litt. in semantics and a D.Phil. in logic. Failing these, you have to make do with an element of realism, a little common sense and a sense of humour. From our point of view, all this about word processors, spreadsheets, expert systems and knowledge-based systems has been an extended digression. They are all probably terms which you have already encountered in everyday life, and I wanted to place them in some sort of overall context.

Having glanced at some alternatives to databases, it seems only fitting to conclude this chapter (and the entire section devoted to data) by returning to databases themselves. We have looked at how you can estimate your need for a database. We have learnt how to collect data for a database and how to prepare that data for entry into the database. What then are the real advantages of a database? Is having a database worth taking all this trouble? To database or not to database: that is the question.

It is not a question that will delay us long. Expert systems and knowledge-based systems depend upon a database. The majority of organizations, however, are perfectly content with an unadorned database itself. What are its virtues?

1. A database contains data which the database management system (DBMS) can transform into information. This information is then accessible to all who are authorized to access it. A database thus provides an economy of scale: one large facility open to all.
2. Since a database can be shared among a variety of users, it can happen that several users require, in their differing contexts, the same piece of data at the same time. This is perfectly viable for a database. Furthermore, if one user has to amend that piece of data, the emendation can then be immediately perceived by all other users.
3. Because the database is a unity, it can therefore ensure that nomenclature, definitions and formulae are consistent throughout the database.
4. Again as a consequence of its uniqueness (i.e. it is the *only* repository of data), a database can ensure that there is no redundant data present in the system.
5. A database has the flexibility to respond to different requests in differing ways, being able to process disparate data from different tables in a variety of ways.
6. It is possible to safeguard data in a database from unauthorized access.
7. A database can ensure that users are forced to input data in the prescribed manner, thus preserving the integrity of the database.
8. A database can be modified in various ways without this having any impact upon the programs using the database.
9. The existence of a database can increase the ease by which other application programs are developed very considerably.

Of course, how well and how easily a database can display the above benefits depends almost entirely upon the DBMS that is controlling the database. It is with this factor that Part Three is concerned.

References

Clark, A. *Small Business Computer Systems*, Hodder & Stoughton, 1987.
Elmasri, R. and Navathe, S. *Fundamentals of Database Systems*, Benjamin Cummings, 1989.

Frost, R. A. *Introduction to Knowledge Base Systems*, Collins, 1986.
Glossbrenner, A. *How to Buy Software*, Macmillan, 1984.
Hicks, J. O. *Information Systems in Business: An Introduction*, West, 1986.
Morris, S. *The Automated Office*, Heinemann, 1988.
Waterman, D. A. *A Guide to Expert Systems*, Addison-Wesley, 1986.

Questions on Part Two

1. What is a feasibility study and why is it carried out?
2. What skills are important for a systems analyst to possess in order to perform his (or her) function successfully?
3. Many writers on systems analysis suggest that you need to begin your work by gaining a clear and detailed understanding of the current system. Only when you appreciate the context of the existing business and the employees in that business, they argue, can you have any hope of designing a new system that will meet the requirements of the company and its workers. Others systems analysts, however, claim that the objective is to provide the best possible system for the company concerned. In order to do so, you only need to understand the logical requirements of the company. Once you have fully understood what the company really needs, you can then design an ideal system for achieving that. To look in detail at the existing state of affairs is both unnecessary and probably ill-advised, since your mind will then be cluttered with irrelevant facts and prejudices. What is your view on this matter?
4. How far is it true to say that the dataflow diagram and the entity–relationship diagram model *different* aspects of the same system?
5. You have been told that a patient can only have one doctor, but that a doctor can have many patients. Draw an E–R diagram showing this situation.
6. You are conducting a systems analysis for a particular company. You have arranged an interview with the managing director in order to gain some information. The interview goes like this:

    YOU: Well, Mr Carstairs—or shall I call you Fred?—clearly this company is pretty prehistoric in its data processing. I'm going to have to have extensive powers if I'm to succeed in dragging it into the twentieth century.

MD: What do you mean? We are, after all, the foremost company in the UK for breeding tropical fish.

YOU: Yes, but that is only because your customers are as wet as the fish themselves. After all, just look at your way of processing customer orders!

MD: What is wrong with that? We get the right fish to the right customer within four days of receiving the order. That hardly seems inefficient to me.

YOU: Maybe not to you, but you can hardly pretend to know anything about information technology, can you?

MD: I probably know as much about IT as you know about tropical fish breeding.

YOU: Ah! That's the problem! I don't need to know about fish breeding, but sure as hell, you need a crash course in IT.

Perhaps you would like to comment upon the success or otherwise of this interview. Identify its merits and faults.

7. If you were collecting information about company *A*, why might it be a good idea to visit company *B*?

8. Below is a collection of entities and instances of attributes. Place them into two columns under the correct heading:

   student, Mary Rhodes, employee, 14 High Street, 83%, piano sonata, address, blue, G major, department

9. You are to normalize the Order entity within a company. You have the following data items:

   Order number, Customer number, Order date, Customer name, Product number, Product name, Product price, Product quantity.

   Produce a table or tables in fully normalized format.

10. The secretary of the local cricket club has approached you asking for advice on keeping a record of their results. He wishes to preserve the following data:

    Date of the match; Name of the opposing team; Scores of both teams; Result, i.e. lost by five wickets or won by 29 runs.

    What would you advise him to purchase: a word processor, a spreadsheet, a database, a knowledge-based system or an expert system?

Answers

1. A feasibility study is an initial survey in order to discover whether or not it is viable to computerize some organization or activity. It would clearly be extremely foolish (and expensive) to establish a new computerized system if such a system produced only marginal benefits or if such a system turned

out to be noncost effective. A feasibility study could be an entirely paper exercise aimed at estimating probable benefits and costs, or it could entail the construction of an experimental or prototype system.

2. Clearly there is no cut-and-dried answer to a question like this one. A systems analyst needs to: have a clear and logical mind; be able to relate well to people; have a secure command of various technical skills like drawing data flow diagrams and normalizing data. It will greatly help if the analyst approaches each task without any preconceptions, but allows the evidence discovered during the analysis to be the only conditioning factor. By and large, it is safe to say that a systems analyst needs the methodological grasp of a supreme administrator, the conceptual insight of Einstein, the creative genius of Mozart, the determination of Scott of the Antarctic and the human compassion of Mother Theresa.

3. Both sides here make sensible points. The decision you take is almost certainly, in part at least, a reflection of your own character. Yet surely the best answer has to be that you do try to do both. It is no use designing a superbly logical new system if the workers of the company concerned dislike it so much that they refuse to operate it properly. Nor is there much point in designing a new system which is better but, because it entails scrapping all the existing procedures and equipment, is too expensive to implement. A major difficulty of the systems analyst's work is compromising between the ideal and the practical.

4. Very true. The DFD models the functions performed by a system. The E–R diagram reveals the data used within a system and the relationships between those items of data. The E–R diagram is thus at a higher level of abstraction than the DFD.

5. There are, in fact, various modelling options available. It could be shown as either of the following:

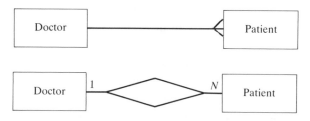

6. Such an interview has no merits. You were overfamiliar, impolite and not concerned with learning anything at all. You presented a set of unflattering presuppositions, patronized the managing director, and had an arrogant belief in your own importance. Politicians apparently believe that they can act in this fashion; systems analysts can't.

7. It would be a good idea to visit company B if it was engaged in the same type of activity as company A. You could then gain some impression as to how a competitor organized itself and performed its data processing. This

could alert you to possible dangers and/or suggest viable approaches for company *A*. Alternatively, you might want to visit company *B* because it was a customer of company *A*. You possibly thought of other viable instances for yourself.

8. It is not always possible, out of context, to determine what is an entity and what is an attribute instance. The instances given in this question, however, were all fairly obvious. The columns should be as follows:

Entities	Attributes
student	Mary Rhodes
employee	14 High Street
piano sonata	83%
address	blue
department	G major

9. Because of problems with repeating groups and transitive dependence, the attributes listed should be placed into four separate tables:

   (a) Order
        Order number, Customer number, Order date
   (b) Customer
        Customer number, Customer name
   (c) Items
        Order number, Product number, Product quantity
   (d) Product
        Product number, Produce name, Product price

   In fact, of course, one would also need other attributes, like Customer address, in order to make the above into fully meaningful tables.

10. A pen and an exercise book.

PART THREE

The database management system

7

The functions of the DBMS

While this topic has already been glanced at, it is clearly a matter of some significance. Indeed, while we already know that it is a major function of a DBMS to store, update and retrieve data in a database, we do not know very much about its other functions. Yet, in 1982, E. F. Codd wrote an article, published in *Communications of the ACM*, in which he listed eight services that should be performed by any self-respecting DBMS. It is important to look at the Codd catalogue (and at some suggested additions to it) because databases, like everything else in the IT world, have suffered from overkill. All software packages that make any pretence at handling data will these days be referred to as a database, even though to do so is rather like calling a penny-farthing bicycle jet-propelled. Of the three basic ways of managing a database—hierarchical, network and relational—it is generally agreed that the relational method is the most effective. Consequently, any software package put up for sale today is almost bound to describe itself as relational, even though it has fewer facilities than the average abacus. This book will not reform the linguistic laxness of the IT world, but at least we can observe some semantic propriety within its pages. Before we look at the three major methods of managing a database then, let us define a DBMS by looking at the functions that it needs to be able to perform to be regarded as a genuine DBMS.

7.1 DBMS functions

Function 1 A DBMS must have the ability to store, retrieve and updata data in the database

Although this is the fundamental function of a DBMS, it needs little expansion. Obviously, unless a DBMS can perform these three interrelated functions, it has no viability whatsoever. Every product that calls itself a database will be able to do at least three things. Only two qualifying comments are needed.

First, although these functions are performed by the DBMS, they are only done at the request of the user. The DBMS cannot read your mind, so you have to tell it what it is that you want to store, retrieve or update. Secondly, the person using a database system should not need to know or at any point be aware of how the DBMS actually does perform these functions. As we will see in the succeeding chapters of Part Three, the structure of a database and the methods employed for manipulating those structures can differ widely. Such techniques should remain invisible to the user.

Function 2   A DBMS must ensure that, when you are performing an update operation, either the entire operation is carried out successfully or that none of it is done.

This doubtless does require some explication. Let us imagine that you are changing a customer record in your database. Rowland Spinks has a banker's order by which means £50 each month is credited to his account with your company. It is simple enough to credit Rowland's current balance by this additional £50. It does, however, mean that not only does his current balance change, but also his credit limit is increased. If, in the course of the operation, Rowland's current balance is altered but his credit limit remains unchanged, then the database will have become inconsistent. It follows, therefore, that, if after altering the current balance, some defect occurs which prevents the credit limit from being changed, then the DMBS should ensure that the alteration to his current balance is then negated. The database will then be out of date, but at least it will retain its internal consistency. Since the system will inform you that the transaction had not been accomplished, you can then take steps to ensure that it is repeated, but at least you won't have to worry about how much of it has been done and how much remains still to do. 'All or nothing' should be the standard of the DBMS. In jargon terms, the database must have the ability to *roll back* until all the partial changes made during this aborted update have been negated.

Function 3   A DBMS must ensure that updates are handled correctly even though many users may be updating the database simultaneously

The problem here is fairly obvious. If a dozen cartons of Nuits-Saint-Georges are delivered to the Skidmore Wine Store, then the database will be changed to show this fact. If, at the same time, Scrape and Blow Ltd order ten bottles of Nuits-Saint-Georges for their Christmas celebration, then the database will be changed to show this fact. Imagine, however, that the database is just being updated to show the arrival of the dozen new cartons when someone in the shop indicates that 10 bottles have just been sold. The 10 bottles are then subtracted from the original stock. Meanwhile, the 12 new cartons are added, also to the original stock. In other words, the two operations have no awareness of each other's existence. Consequently, at the end of both operations, the database will be left in an incorrect state. If the Skidmore Wine Store had 40 bottles of Nuits-Saint-Georges in its cellar, the subtraction of another 10 for Scrape and Blow would have left 30 bottles remaining. The new delivery has added another 144 bottles to the cellar. The database, however, has added those 144 to the original 40 bottles, giving a total of 184. In fact, of course, the real new total is 174. Simultaneous access has resulted in an error. It is precisely this sort of accident that a DBMS must prevent.

Function 4   A DBMS, if damaged by an accident, must have the means of preserving the database in an unblemished state.

There are clearly a number of acts of God that can afflict a database and its management system. A power failure is probably the most common, though disks seem quaintly prone to catch some crippling disease just as you are completing a massive series of inputs. Whatever the event may be, the DBMS must have methods of recovery from such catastrophes or allow the user to safeguard against them.

Function 5   A DBMS must allow its users to access communications software.

Few users of a DBMS actually communicate directly with it. Normally the user is seated at his or her own terminal, while the database itself is residing on a hard disk housed in another machine. The DBMS must ensure safe, secure and easy communication between the user's terminal and the database itself.

Function 6   A DBMS should provide a dictionary or catalogue which lists all the data items accessible to the users.

If you are using a database, it is obviously more than convenient to have the means of seeing what fields are contained in the current database, to see what relationships are expressed in the database, to check on what restrictions are imposed within the database, and so on. This aspect, normally called the data dictionary, is so important that a much fuller description is given in Chapter 12.

Function 7   A DBMS must ensure that only authorized users can access the database.

This implies, of course, that the DBMS will have means of insisting that safeguards are imposed so that only authorized users can access the database. It will mean that measures will be imposed so that it is very difficult for an unauthorized person to enter the database in the first place. In addition, if an unauthorized person does enter the database, there will need to be some means of preventing him or her accessing the data within it.

Function 8   A DBMS must insist that inputs of data and changes to such data both follow certain constraints so as to ensure the integrity of the database.

For instance, if a regular customer of Scrape and Blow's moved from East Anglia to northern Scotland, then it would be quite reasonable for Scrape and Blow to delete that customer's record from the database. If, however, that customer still had an outstanding order, it would not be reasonable to carry out such a deletion. The DBMS needs to safeguard against such eventualities.

These are the eight services itemized by Dr Codd in his article. Pratt and Adamski (1987) go on to suggest two further necessary functions.

Function 9   A DBMS must be able through the actual structure of the database to support the independence of programs.

The concept of data independence is a major one in the database world. Almost all database systems provide some degree of data independence, and Codd himself was well aware of its importance. I look at the issue more closely later on in this chapter. For the moment it is sufficient to say that data independence implies the ability to alter the structure of the database without any changes being necessary for the programs that use that database.

Function 10   A DBMS should provide a set of utility services.

Pratt and Adamski include this as the second of their additional functions. They do not, however, explain very fully what sort of utilities they have in mind. They mention that it would be useful if the DBMS had the ability to examine the database for any internal imperfections. They also suggest that it would be useful if the DBMS could provide statistics on patterns of database usage. Even so, it may be felt that Pratt and Adamski have 'invented' the tenth function as an umbrella to cover all desired improvements to databases. And, of course, there are always going to be some desired improvements. Su (1988) has a section entitled 'The need for more powerful database management systems'. In an appendix Oxborrow (1989) discusses DBMS limitations. And so it will always be. It is not in the nature of human beings to rest content with any existing technology; there is always a better one just round the corner. Indeed, I look at the end of this book at some of the directions in which database technology is now moving. For our purposes at the moment, however, we can rest content with the first nine of the functions listed as being perfectly adequate for defining a database.

To define necessary functions is not, in itself, a difficult task. It becomes more taxing trying to explain how these actual functions are implemented in a database, and yet this is a necessary task. In deciding that a database must have rollback facilities, we need also to describe how such facilities can be provided. All serious databases, be they hierarchical, network or relational, need to provide the integrity of updates. Hence by looking at such questions, we come to understand databases in general. In so doing, we are also enlarging our knowledge of computer jargon. This may not be at the top of any sane person's priorities, but it does help in understanding the computer press and in impressing the neighbours. Hence, having outlined the functions that an adequate DBMS should possess, the second part of this chapter looks at how those functions can be implemented. It does so by looking, not at individual functions, but at broader issues that create the context for the effective implementation of such functions. Since all such issues are important, they have been placed in alphabetical order. The desirable elements of a DBMS are considered under the following headings:

- Accessing data
- Communications
- Data dictionary
- Date independence
- Integrity
- Recovery
- Security
- Sharing data
- Update completion

7.1.1   ACCESSING DATA

To access data, whether to retrieve, amend or delete, is clearly the fundamental function of a DBMS. Equally clearly, the way in which such accession is performed will depend upon the nature of the DBMS itself, and three common types of DBMS are the subjects of the remaining chapters of Part Three. None the less, some introductory comments here are apposite because they will broaden our understanding of the context.

Data can be stored in a number of different ways, and the method of storage dictates the available methods of accession. This is something we all know from everyday life. My daughter stores things upon the floor of her bedroom. Her methods of accession consequently entail random kicking, frantic crawling, puzzled reflections and anguished squeals. My wife stores things in filing cabinets. Her mode of access is quicker and less frenetic than our daughter's. These homely examples may not yet seem relevant, yet there are computerized ways of storing data that bear a strong resemblance to my daughter's system. Let us look at the two basic storage methods and the accession imperatives that they impose.

First of all, data can be stored more or less in the order in which it arrives. Imagine that you are entering the names and addresses of students who enrol for the new academic year at the Moribund Matriculation College. The first student to arrive is Gustav Minklebrot. You accordingly enter his name and address. Next comes Rubella Sprat. Her data is entered. At the end of registration week you have a sum total of 850 students, of whom Gustav Minklebrot was the first and Janet Grimes happened to be the last. There is no order, other than the accident of arrival for registration, in your student list at all. It has, however, taken no effort to compile. Such an organization, in computer jargon, is known as a *heap* or *pile* system, and such random nonsequential files are the easiest to create. Some database systems—INGRES, for instance—provide heap organization by default, and certainly there are advantages. To make additions to the database is effortless. They do, however, pose a problem of access. Single relation retrievals require the entire file to be searched. How do you find the record for William Prendergast when you have no idea where-abouts in the student list it is to be found? There seems to be no alternative to a sequential search. You start at the beginning of the list, and examine every row of data until you arrive at the row that you want. Of course, you won't have to examine the entire row of data each time—a glance at the primary key will suffice—but even so it is a time-consuming process, as the layout of Fig. 7.1 indicates. Would you really want to do this every time? There are ways of short-circuiting a sequential search, but if your data happens to be stored on tape, instead of disk, then a sequential search is virtually the only option available.

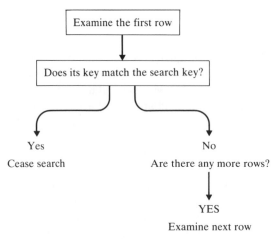

Figure 7.1

If you can store data in a nonsequential list, you can clearly also store data in a sequential one. The sequence can be alphabetical or numerical. It can be based on the primary key of the row of data concerned or upon some other field. Whatever the precise mode of sequence, it is easy to see how that data can be retrived. Sequential files, though, can produce problems. Databases are subject to constant alteration. Rows of data are added and deleted. If you delete data, this creates gaps in the physical storage of the file. If you want to make additions, there may be no room to insert a new row of data at the point where it ought, logically, to go. Yet, ironically, for a computer, it does not matter in the least whether or not data is arranged sequentially or not. Why is this?

All remotely acceptable database systems operate what are called *indexing* procedures. Strictly speaking, that is not entirely true. Some computer systems operate what is called *hashing*. Whether one uses hashing or indexing, the object is the same: to speed up data access.

If a system employs hashing, all that happens is that the DBMS takes a particular field of the row (normally the primary key), and uses that field to generate an address. What normally happens is that the primary key value is converted (if necessary) to a numeric value. This number is then passed through a hashing algorithm which then returns a value—the hash key—which corresponds to the physical address at which the items of data will be stored. To retrieve that particular row on a later occasion, the DBMS is given the primary key, generates an address in the same way, and then fetches the row in question. There are a number of ways of hashing—techniques like division remainder, digit analysis, folding, and other enigmatic titles—but for them all it involves turning a word into a number, and it is thus turns out that it is perfectly possible for one data item to generate an identical address to another data item. It is not possible to store two attributes at the same address, and so methods have to be devised to cope with such *collisions*. As a consequence, hashing is less common than indexing, though it is a useful technique, particularly with relatively stable collections of data. The two relational databases, INGRES and Rapport, both incorporate a hashing mechanism.

While by the hashing method rows of data can be scattered all over the disk concerned with no contiguous arrangement at all, indexing—and again there are a number of methods—tends to organize the data concerned physically in contiguous locations. Obviously, keeping an index of data takes up more space, but it does enable data to be retrieved almost instantly. Basically speaking, what happens is that as the database itself is created, the DBMS simultaneously creates an index to that database. Let us imagine that it is indexing an Employee table, and is using the Surname field as its key. The index will doubtless store each surname, often in a shortened form so as to save space, and attached to each surname will be the 'address' of the entire row. Of course, you might well want an index maintained of other fields in the same row as well. This too is perfectly easy to arrange, but it can result in the index to a database ending up as bigger than the database itself.

However, for effective access to a database, either hashing or indexing is an essential. Perfection on this issue is rarely possible. Instant access, which is desirable, conflicts with economy, which is also desirable. Compromise is therefore essential. We shall look at indexing techniques a little more closely later. For the moment, it is important to see that they are a vital element for the DBMS to handle.

7.1.2 COMMUNICATIONS

While a DBMS must clearly have the ability to link the database with the separate terminals that are using the database, the topic of communications is deferred until we come to look at distributed databases, where the question of communications is of paramount importance.

7.1.3 DATA DICTIONARY

A data dictionary is the catalogue that a DBMS should compile about all the entities, indexes and relationships contained within the database. It is an invaluable tool, but detailed discussion of it is deferred until Part Four.

7.1.4 DATA INDEPENDENCE

It has already been observed that data independence is an extremely desirable element. Vossen (1990) goes so far as to claim that: 'the introduction of a database system within or into a given enterprise is always connected to the goal of achieving data independence'. Data in a database only exists in order to be used by a whole series of different programs. If the database itself is changed in any way, it is clearly desirable for the programs using that database to remain unaffected (and, indeed, unaware) of such changes. If this is not the case, then any physical or logical change to the database might well necessitate changes to all the programs using that database. The resulting maintenance required would be an insupportable burden.

Let us first of all distinguish between physical and logical changes. The physical organization is the way that data is actually stored in a storage device. For instance, is that data encrypted? Are the fields of data fixed or variable, i.e. are all surnames stored in a 15-bit field or can a name like Smith be stored in a 5-bit field, Rothwell in an 8-bit field and so on? Is numerical data stored as fixed or floating-point numbers, i.e. is the decimal point always in the same position or does it vary depending upon how many numbers there are before and/or after the decimal point? Such concerns are the business of how data is represented upon the disk or disks.

Logical organization is the way the user sees the data. Should we add another field to our wine table by including the shipping company that transported the wine to England? Should we merge the two fields, Title of work and Köchel number, into one? By doing either, or both, of those, we change the way in which we, the users, apprehend the table or tables of data in question.

If physical or logical changes are made, the existing programs ought to be able to carry on operating totally unperturbed. Obviously, though, this is going to be difficult to ensure. Virtually no DBMS can currently provide total data independence. Nonrelational systems are less adept than relational ones in coping with this issue, and a nonrelational DBMS finds it virtually impossible to cope with changes in relationships without also requiring some alterations to the programs themselves. Data independence, though a highly desirable element, cannot be taken yet as the norm

7.1.5 INTEGRITY

Perhaps a synonym for integrity would be consistency. Imagine that an organization decided to have as a primary key for its Employee table an Employee number. New employees are entered into the database by the manager of the department that employed the employee. The manager of the advertising department prefixed all employee numbers with the letters AD. The manager of the sales department prefixed all his employee numbers with 0 followed by a decimal point. And so it went on. As a result, there was no uniformity whatsoever. A DBMS should be able to prevent such idiosyncracies by imposing what are called *integrity restraints*. These can be of a very varied nature. The DBMS may prevent you deleting a customer's record if that customer still owes money. A DBMS should be able to prevent a salesperson being awarded a commission of 45 per cent. The DBMS must be able to ensure that all the employee numbers are of an identical type. Hence integrity constraints both prevent certain types of invalid updates from being entered and dictate that a certain type of processing must (or must not) be implemented.

Obviously, integrity constraints could be imposed by the users of the database, but this would be highly undesirable. Inconsistency might result. Users might forget. The result in both cases would be a lack of integrity in the database. It is clearly a great deal better for this aspect to be a DBMS responsibility.

7.1.6 RECOVERY

It is clearly vital that a database should have the ability to recover from whatever catastrophe may befall it. The simplest method, of course, is for there to be a duplicate copy of the database that can be used to replace the damaged database. All remotely sensible companies make a copy of their current database (normally on tape) at the end of every day. Thus, should catastrophe strike the following day, they then have a reasonably up-to-date backup.

In order to keep a track of activities undertaken during the day, the DBMS should keep a *log* or *journal* of all updates. Then, should a crash occur, there will be a record available of modifications made during the day of the crash.

7.1.7 SECURITY

While a DBMS should allow a number of methods of protecting the database from human error or malice, the imposition of such security procedures is very much the responsibility of the database administrator (DBA). Consideration of security methods is consequently deferred until we look at the role of the DBA.

At least two of the ten functions listed earlier implied that the DBMS should be a multiuser tool. In most companies, this is an essential. A database is needed that can be accessed by the advertising agent, the salespeople, the managing director, the account and so on. For this to be possible, the DBMS must include *concurrency control* software to ensure that several users trying to update the same data at the same time do so in a controlled and accurate manner.

You will recall the problem outlined earlier concerning cartons of Nuits-Saint-Georges. The fact that a delivery occurred at the same time as a sale meant that the database was left in an inaccurate state. There are, however, two ways of dealing with such eventualities. First of all, they can be completely avoided. During the day, users are allowed to retrieve any items of data that they wish. Should they, however, wish to update that data, they may do so, but the update so accomplished is not immediately transferred to the database. Instead it is placed in a new and separate table (or file). Then, at the end of the day, all the updates of that day are processed and transferred to the relevant table. Where there are updates to the same field (or data item), they can then be reconciled so that the resulting state of the table concerned is up to date and accurate. The problem of simultaneous access is thus completely avoided. None the less, a moment's thought will indicate that, while one problem is solved, another one is conceivably created. Imagine that, during the day, a customer's account is overdrawn to such an extent that no further drawings from that account are permitted. Unfortunately, this fact is not going to be evident in the database itself until the end of the day. Meanwhile, that particular customer makes yet another purchase which further increases the overdraft. This should not be possible, but, because the true state of affairs is not yet manifest in the database itself, such an eventuality could occur. Hence avoidance of the entire problem in this fashion might not be by any means the ideal solution.

Fortunately there is a way of preventing this situation. It is called *locking*. If a person wishes to update an item of data, he or she may do so. While their update is being processed, however, no one else is allowed to modify that data item in any way. The field or fields are locked. Obviously this prevents the sharing of data, but it only does so for the presumably short period of time taken by the transaction in question. Even so, there still remain conceivable problems. Imagine that field A has been updated. While it was being updated, it was locked. That meant that another update to that field could not be accomplished. However, as soon as field A had been updated by transaction X, it can be further updated by transaction Z. Unfortunately, transaction X, although it accomplished the update to field A perfectly satisfactorily, had still not completed all its work. As it was doing so, some problem or other led to its abortion. Consequently, the entire operation of transaction X was rolled back, including, of course, its update to field A. Meanwhile, however, transaction Z had also modified field A while transaction X was attempting to accomplish its post field A updates. When transaction X aborted, the resulting rollback put field A back into the position that it was in before transaction X had begun. As a result, the update performed on field A by transaction Z is lost. In other words, transaction X had relinquished its lock on field A too early. As you might imagine though, this possibility is not difficult to avoid. The DBMS is simply instructed not to release a lock until an entire transaction has been accomplished, not just the part of a transaction involving a specific field. Obviously this extends the length of time that a field or fields could be in a locked position, thus preventing any sharing of data, but it is better that a user or users be forced to wait a little before carrying out an update than allowing the database to become corrupt.

There is, however, one further problem connected with the sharing of data. Known as *deadlock* or the *deadly embrace*, it is as unpleasant as its name might suggest. Fred is busy making a series of updates. As his transaction approaches the respective fields requiring these updates, those fields are locked and will remain locked until his entire transaction has been completed. Everything is going well. The updates to the first five data items were completed successfully, and those data items are currently in a locked position. As Fred's transaction approaches the sixth and final field to which it needs to make an update, it discovers that it cannot enter that particular field because it has been locked. The problem is that Bob, who also needs to perform a series of interrelated updates, began his transaction at the same time that Fred began his. Unfortunately, the first data item that Bob's transaction needed to modify happened to be the sixth data item needed by Fred's transaction. Hence, when Fred's transaction tried to approach this field to lock it, it discovered that it was already locked. Now Bob's transactions will not release the lock on this field until the entire transaction has been completed. As luck would have it, one of the data items that Bob needs to update happens to be the first data item that Fred's transaction used. As a result, this field is now locked. Hence, when Bob's transaction gets round to this particular field, it cannot access it. Thus Fred is waiting for a data item locked by Bob, and Bob is waiting for a data item locked by Fred. Such a situation, though rare, could clearly happen. It would furthermore appear that no resolution for such a situation is likely until either Fred or Bob commits suicide in despair or until one of them retires.

Fortunately the situation is not quite so dire. There are two possibilities. First of all, Fred could lock all the relevant fields *before* beginning any updates at all. If, in so doing, he encounters any already existing locks, then he would relinquish *all* his own locks, and try again in a few moments. In this way, a deadlock would be prevented. It does, however, depend upon Fred knowing exactly what fields are going to be modified in the operation he is about to undertake. This is not always possible. Consequently it is just not a viable option to prevent all conceivable deadlocks. As a result, if a deadlock does occur, the DBMS must select one of the users and abort that transaction. The remaining user can then complete a transaction in the normal way. Once that has been done, the other user can be reinstated.

As you can see from this, the sharing of data, while perfectly viable for the vast majority of occasions, will have to be suspended occasionally. Fortunately, computers perform their operations with such speed that the delay to users is normally slight.

7.1.9   UPDATE COMPLETION

It has been pointed out already that an important function of the DBMS is to ensure that either an update is completed in full or that it is not performed at all. Either every aspect of a particular update is processed in full, or no alteration at all is accomplished. This all-or-nothing ruling is essential if internal coherence is to be maintained within the database.

There are obviously real difficulties here. After all, one single update might be only part of an entire series of updates. It could be the case that a single deficiency within one update could invalidate the entire series of related updates too. Obviously, though, a DBMS is not going to know whether or not this is the case. A DBMS may be highly efficient, but it is not going to possess any real mental awareness of the operations that it carries out. Hence, if a series of updates is grouped together to constitute a unity, the DBMS has to be informed of this. Thus, in both cases, that of a single update operation or that of a series of related updates, the DBMS has to be told about the parameters to be observed. Let us take each instance in turn.

Imagine that a new order has to be added to the database. This is a single update, but it will entail modification to the Customer table so that the order can be added to that table, to the Sales representative table so that a member of the sales staff can be associated with that order, and to the Order table itself. For one simple update, three tables need modification. The DBMS has to be capable either of 'knowing' as a matter of course that one Order entails three operations, or of being informed in each instance that this is the case. Obviously the former is the more effective and efficient mode of operation, and a good DBMS will have the ability for so linking separate steps into an indivisible whole. Should any one of the steps not be taken, the DBMS will cancel or delete the others so that the entire transaction is nullified.

Where a whole series of updates is involved, each one possible entailing two or three distinct operations, then the DBMS can be instructed to 'begin transaction' and, at the end of the entire series, be instructed to 'end trans-action'. Not until the DBMS receives the 'end transaction' instruction will it commit the alterations made to the database itself. Should an error occur during the series of modifications, the whole will be *rolled back*, and no program or table will see the results of any of the updates that were accomplished before the error occurred. It is unfortunate that such a safeguard seems to be impossible in other aspects of life. Hence, when I pour salt into the rice pudding instead of sugar, the error is not normally discovered until the happy family is eating the rice pudding. They then cease being a happy family. Hence, as a career option, I would recommend database manager in preference to chef.

We have looked at the facilities that a DBMS ought to be able to perform. It is clear from this glance that certain so-called databases do not really merit being known as such. I mentioned in passing in Chapter 2 Morris (1986), yet the majority of the products that Morris examines are only called databases as an act of imprecise generosity. The Matchbox Electronic Filing System from Quest Automation plc will not allow any alteration to a table once that table has been created and confirmed. Nor can you transfer data from one table or file to another. There is no means of sorting a file; if you want rows of data to appear in a certain order, then they must be entered in that order. Cardbox, published by Caxton Software Ltd, is more sophisticated than Matchbox, but it does not distinguish between different types of field (they are all treated as text), and it too has no sorting facility. AtLast 1, from Rational Solutions, does allow you to sort data, but it is the operating system that has to do the normal DBMS activities. Not until Morris reaches the package called Sagesoft Retrieve is he really looking at anything that could realistically be called a database package at all, and then you discover that the package is too complex to be run on a single-disk Amstrad PCW8256. This book is not designed as a consumer's guide to the best database, but it is as well to be warned that not everything that calls itself a database is justified in so doing.

7.2 Terminology

I want, however, to end this chapter by at last facing another of these terminological dilemmas that constantly confront us. This concerns the word 'file'. I have tried to avoid using the word very much, but it is a convenient synonym for words like 'table' or 'record'. While I have avoided using the word 'record' (except when referring to black, circular objects that produce music), I have not always escaped using the word 'file'. It is, after all, one of the most frequently used words in the field of computer science. Whitten et al. (1986) devote their twelfth chapter to the question of designing computer files, and define a file as being 'the data set of all occurrences of a logical record (or physical record, which is a superset of the logical record)'. Gillenson (1990) defines a file in his glossary as being 'a collection of like-structured records'. Samson (1990) refers throughout to files. And so I could go on. Yet there are problems. Howe (1989) never refers to files at all, always using the word 'tables' instead. Smith and Barnes (1987) do use the word 'files', but distinguish between files and databases, and state in their preface that 'studying DBMS principles helps illuminate the limitations of files'. Oxborrow

(1989) has a section entitled 'The traditional file approach versus the database approach'. What, then, is the reality?

As you might expect, there is no real problem. Indeed, the only problem that does exist arises as a consequence of people not defining their terms with sufficient clarity. A database system does consist of a collection of related files. If Scrape and Blow were to develop a database, they would doubtless have files on suppliers, customers, payroll and so on. If Simeon Grumblethitch and MASS were to have a database, they would doubtless have files on symphonies, concertos, operas and so on. However, what is important about a database system is that the user is not conscious of there being any files at all. The database exists as a unified whole. Hence, if you want to compare or contrast two items, and those two items happen to be physically in two different files, then you, the user, need neither know nor care about this. The DBMS will produce the two items for you wherever you may reside. As Burstein (1986) comments:

> A business that uses a database rather than files can save time and money in developing its application programs, can lower data maintenance costs and store requirements since the same centralized data are now acessible to all, and can exploit its data more efficiently since they are easier to get at.'

Exactly how well a business can do all of this will depend largely upon the type of DBMS it possesses. It is at these that we next look.

References

Burstein, J. S. *Computers and Information Systems*, Holt, Reinhart & Winston, 1986.
Gillenson, M. L. *Database Step-by-Step*, 2nd edn, John Wiley, 1990.
Howe, D. *Data Analysis for Data Base Design*, 2nd edn, Arnold, 1989.
Morris, S. *Using Databases on the Amstrad PCW8256 and PCW8512*, Glentop, 1986.
Oxborrow, E. *Databases and Database Systems*, 2nd edn, Chartwell-Bratt, 1989.
Pratt, P. J. and Adamski, J. J. *Database Systems: Management and Design*, Boyd & Fraser, 1987.
Samson, W. B. *Practical Database Techniques*, Pitman, 1990.
Smith, P. and Barnes, M. *Files and Databases*, Addison-Wesley, 1987.
Su, S. Y. W. *Database Computers*, McGraw-Hill, 1988.
Vossen, G. *Data Models, Database Languages and Database Management Systems*, Addison-Wesley, 1990.
Whitten, J. L., Bentley, L D. and Ho, T. I. M. *Systems Analysis and Design Methods*, Times Mirror/Mosby College Publishing, 1986.

8
The hierarchical database model

It so happens that you are fascinated by the English royal family who ruled over England in the sixteenth century, the Tudors. (To be accurate, the Tudors began their occupancy of the English throne in the late fifteenth century, 1485, and ended it in the very early seventeenth century, 1603.) Not unnaturally, in the course of your investigations into the Tudors, you draw up a family tree. It looks like Fig. 8.1. (Since I do not want any historians writing to me complaining that I have given a remarkably oversimplified family tree, let me acknowledge this fact from the outset. I know that Margaret married James IV of Scotland and that from that line there developed the Stuart royal family. I know too that Henry VII's daughter Mary married and eventually became the grandmother of the shortest reigning monarch in British history, Jane Grey. I also know that Henry VIII had more than three wives, so historical scholars will be good enough to accept that the family tree below has just been provided in order to illustrate the nature of a hierarchical data model.)

You will have already assumed that a hierarchical data model is organized

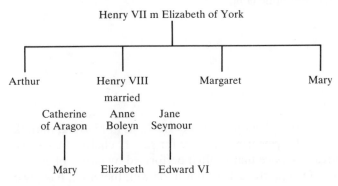

Figure 8.1

exactly like a family tree. At the top, in direct contradiction to the way real trees are organized, is the *root*. From that root, a series of *nodes* are developed, connected to the root by *branches*. Most of the nodes will be *parents*, having one or more children. Nodes at the end of a particular branch with no children of their own are sometimes called *leaf nodes*.

Quite apart from family trees, we are all of us accustomed to this hierarchical arrangement. Some of us work in schools or colleges which have a head (the root), followed by heads of department (parent nodes), each of whom is responsible for certain members of staff. Businesses tend to have a managing director (the root), directors of departments (parent nodes), and shopfloor staff. As a result of the fact that many of our lives are organized around a pecking-order structure, the hierarchical data model turns out to be a convenient and readily understandable construct. It is not, therefore, surprising to learn that it was the hierarchical model which was the first to appear in the database world. In 1968 IBM released an Information Management System (IMS) which has virtually dominated the hierarchical market ever since, though other hierarchical systems like System Development Corporation's Time-shared Data Management System (TDMS), and MRI's System-2000 were other early examples. The chapter on the hierarchical model in Date (1986) is devoted entirely to an examination of IMS, as are the equivalent chapters in the books by Bowers (1988), Pratt and Adamski (1987), Gillenson (1990) and Perkinson (1984). This is a perfectly proper way of dealing with hierarchical models, though I want here to confine myself purely to a theoretical understanding, not to any one specific implementation. A consideration of IMS is deferred until Chapter 11.

Theory, however, is unhelpful unless it is linked to some practical exemplification of that theory. Let us, therefore, return to considering the chain of East Anglian music shops run by Scrape and Blow. If you recall, the administrative centre of this mythical concern was based in East Dereham, and it seems logical to have as the root of their envisaged database the Headquarters presided over by Franklin Scrape and Tiberius Blow, but effectively run by Hetty Freezer. This then would be our root node (Fig. 8.2).

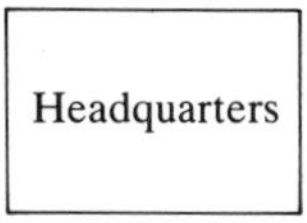

Figure 8.2

This Headquarters is responsible for a number of shops in Norfolk, Suffolk and Essex. Headquarters also performs a service for sundry choirs, orchestras, schools, etc., in the area, a service that is often performed by means of correspondence to and from Headquarters. The root node will, therefore, have two children (Fig. 8.3).

Figure 8.3

Each of these nodes will itself have a number of children:

Shops	*Postal business*
Staff	Schools
Salaries	Choirs
Stock	Town bands
Suppliers	Musical societies

Hence our tree will look like Fig. 8.4. Each one of the nodes is represented by a series of data rows, a table, each row having a primary key.

As can be seen from the tree in Fig. 8.4, this is not intended to be a full representation of Scrape and Blow's thriving business—do the shops have no

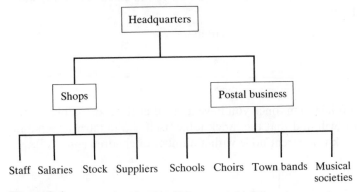

Figure 8.4

accounts, for instance? – but each node shown would be represented by a table (or relation) somewhat along the following lines:

Shops: Shop number; Address; Tel. no.; Manager
   Staff:
      Name; Address; Tel. no.; Position
   Salaries:
      Name; Salary; National Insurance; Tax rate
   Stock:
      Product number; Description; Number in stock; Reorder level
   Suppliers:
      Supplier number; Name; Address; Tel. no.; Speciality

Postal business: Client; State of account
  Schools:
    Name; Address; Tel. no.; Headmaster
  Choirs:
    Name; Address; Tel. no.; Choirmaster
  Town bands:
    Name; Address; Tel. no.; Secretary
  Musical societies:
    Name; Address; Tel. no.; Secretary

Such an arrangement may be very incomplete, as our family tree of the Tudors was, but certain elements are fairly obvious. Each node can only have one parent, but that limitation works perfectly well here. If Headquarters, the root node, wants to write to Thetford Gilbert and Sullivan Society, it will enter the Postal business table, locate the society in that table, and from there enter the Musical societies table. There it will locate the Thetford Gilbert and Sullivan Society, note the address of the society and the name of their secretary, and then exit. The situation will be equally easy if Headquarters should want to know if the Ipswich shop happens to have a bassoon in stock. The downward path is clear and quick:

Of course, in the full system, once you have arrived at the Stock table for the Ipswich shop, you will find that the Stock table itself is a number of separate tables, so that Stock is a parent node with a number of children (Fig. 8.5).

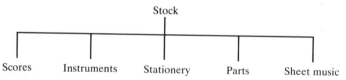

Figure 8.5

Each of those children could also be a parent. Thus the Instruments table might merely give you the option of choosing yet another table; Strings, Woodwind, Brass and Percussion. The Parts table could be similarly divided, so that if you wanted a new string for a violin, you entered the Strings node, if you wanted a new mute for a trumpet, you entered the Brass node. The Scores table could be subdivided into Symphonies, Concertos, Operas and so on. It is obvious, though, that the whole operation is clear and uncomplicated. It is not surprising that the hierarchical type of DBMS has been operating successfully for over 20 years, which, in IT terms, is equivalent to a century.

It should also be clear that the data content of each table is straightforward and easy to normalize. The Shops table, for instance, will look like Table 8.1, though only four of Scrape and Blow's stores are shown.

Table 8.1 Shop

Shop no.	Address	Tel. no.	Manager
001	13 Croft Way, Norwich	191–371622	W. R. Skiffle
002	26 Midden Road, Bury	0284–98831	P. C. Plood
003	7 The Triangle, Ipswich	0473–55482	V. K. Creston
004	35 Brook Street, Newmarket	0638–14473	L. H. Wraggston

The primary key for each row is the unique shop number allocated to each of the Scrape and Blow stores. If Tiberius wanted to examine the Stock situation at the Bury St Edmunds store, he would simply place the cursor on 002 field, press the Return key on the keyboard, and be presented with the options Staff, Payroll, Stock and Suppliers. Moving the cursor to Stock and again pressing Return would give him the Stock table of the Bury store.

You will have noticed that we have been perfectly able to employ the vocabulary—field, primary key, row, table—that was introduced in Chapter 5. Indeed, such a vocabulary is appropriate for all computerized implementations. Unfortunately different database products from different IT manufacturers are prone to using their own terminology. IBM's IMS, for instance, calls a table of data (or even a row within such a table) a *segment*, while most writers call it a *record*. The word 'record' strikes me as being inherently ambiguous because of its numerous different meanings (ten, according to the *Shorter Oxford English Dictionary*). 'Segment' seems to me to be just as bad. It is given seven different meanings in the dictionary, and each one of those meanings is in flat contradiction to this database usage. A segment is a small portion of something. You can eat the segment of an orange. The spinal cord is divided into segments. A leaf is divided into segments by long clefts or incisions. But a row of data is a collection of attributes which, together, describe an entire entity. Hence to describe it as a segment is to fly in the fact of linguistic sanity. In addition, the IMS database can call each particular field in a row a *sequence field* if that field is arranged in a particular order. Hence when a *coup d'état* installs me in power, you can be assured that the vocabulary that I have employed in this book will become mandatory. You might, therefore, be well advised always to use it yourself if only to safeguard your future.

Let us now itemize the knowledge that we have so far gained about the hierarchical data model.

1. The model always starts with a root node. It is the only node in the tree that does not have a parent.
2. Every node consists of a number of attributes describing the entity which is

exemplified at that node. Thus the Shop node in our example above comprises four attributes.
3. Each node, excluding the root node, can have only one parent, but each
parent node can have many children.
4. Each node is reached or retrieved by passing though all the preceding nodes.

From these rules, a number of conclusions can be made:

1. Since each node can only have one parent, it is virtually impossible to
represent a many-to-many relationship in a hierarchical database. As far as
Scrape and Blow are concerned, this is no real handicap, but it can be a
considerable disadvantage for many applications. Sundry bells and whistles
have been added to hierarchical data models in order to circumvent this
obstacle, but such tinkering is clumsy and slows down processing.
2. It is also slow and tiresome to compare and contrast differing entities within
a hierarchical database. If, for instance, Diss High School wanted to order a
new trombone, and Hetty wanted to see if the Norwich store had a trombone
in stock, it would mean moving from the Order table (a child node of Diss
High School) up to the root node via Postal business and then down to the
Instruments table of the Norwich store via Shops.
3. If Scrape and Blow wanted to buy stock for their proposed Great Yarmouth
shop which had not yet been built, they could not do so—or at least it could
not be represented in the database—until the shop itself had been added to
the database. In other words, insertion of a child attribute is impossible until
its parent exists.
4. Should it ever be necessary to delete a parent node from the database—
imagine Scrape and Blow decide to close their Thetford shop—then deletion
of that parent node means automatic deletion of all its children also. Hence,
if the Thetford shop is closed, all its stock vanishes into thin air.

Hence, as you can see, there are real disadvantages to adopting a hierarchical
DBMS. None the less, such a structure is perfectly adequate for many organizations (and where it isn't, many organizations have had no choice but to retain
it). We do, therefore, need to have a look at exactly how data is accessed from
within a hierarchically structured database. We have so far been looking at the
DBMS from a purely logical or conceptual point of view. Now it is time to look
at its physical implementation.

There are four different means of accessing data. One of the most common
suffers from the uncaptivating label of *preorder traversal*. You tell the database
what data it is that you need to retrieve, alter or delete. (How you do this is
virtually a chapter of its own, and varies from database to database.) The
database, having received your request, proceeds to follow a set path. It starts
at the root, moves onto the first child on the left, then onto its first child, and so
on. Its passage is therefore from top to bottom and from left to right, and this
mode of accession is commonly known as the *hierarchical sequential access*

method, and even more commonly referred to by the inevitable acronym, HSAM. Figure 8.6 shows the technique, with the bold line indicating the accession path.

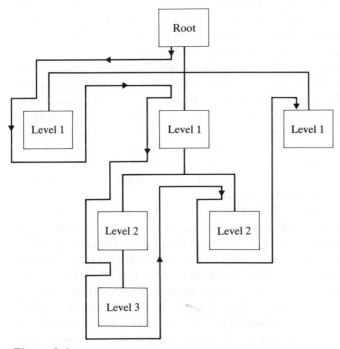

Figure 8.6

Since the database itself has to store rows of data sequentially in order for HSAM to be a workable method of access, it follows that this storage structure is equally suited to tape as to disk. Indeed, since random access is not possible under HSAM, this database structure and its access procedure are best suited to archive material, in other words, data that is kept for historical reasons and is rarely accessed.

It is tempting to say much the same for the second access method, the *hierarchical indexed sequential access method* (HISAM). As you can doubtless infer from its name, random access of a sort is possible here. Hence if we take Scrape and Blow's vestigial database as we have so far developed it, a request to retrieve data about Stowmarket's church choir would be dealt with by starting at the root, moving immediately to Postal business, and then going to the leaf node Choirs. Thereafter, accession would be sequential processing until the row for Stowmarket church choir was reached. Clearly accession would be a quicker operation under HISAM than under HSAM, but true random accession is still not possible, and if the application concerned is a dynamic one and data alterations are consequently frequent, the structure of the database itself will require constant reorganization. As always too, accession will be affected by the underlying operating system upon which the database is resting.

The third method, known as the *hierarchical direct access method* (HDAM), does provide real random access. This is done through a mixture of hashing and pointers, the latter being a data word which contains the location of an address in main memory. Indeed, HDAM is, in most circumstances, the fastest of the accession methods available for a hierarchical database.

The final technique, with its equally forgettable title and acronym, the *hierarchical indexed direct access method* (HIDAM), seems to merge the methods of HDAM and HISAM in that the database itself is organized as an HDAM database, while the index to the database is of the HISAM type. It too is viable for on-line, fast-response systems. I have, however, not found that discussion of this goes down very well at the average cocktail party. As you casually enquire, 'Do you think the HISAM index and the HDAM database are fully congruent in HIDAM?', everyone at the party seems to remember that they have an urgent appointment elsewhere.

You may, while ploughing through this brief list of access methods, have considered a further desirable aspect. All four of the access methods so far mentioned have depended for their successful usage upon the primary key of the data row concerned. What happens though if the infallible Hetty does have a lapse of memory? She knows that she needs to write to Elsbeth Quadrump, but she can't remember which organization employs Elsbeth as its secretary. What salvation can a hierarchical system offer her? If HASM is employed, there is no solution, but, since the other three techniques do employ indexing or hashing, it becomes possible to construct secondary indexes. Indeed, if you know beforehand that secondary indexing is going to be viable, it does give you a little more flexibility in the designing of the logical database itself. Under normal circumstances, the logical database in a hierarchical context very closely resembles the physical database. Indeed, it is imperative that the root node in both is identical. Secondary indexing gives the opportunity for a much greater divergence between the two, though, of course, secondary indexing does slow down processing and increase costs.

Conceptually, a hierarchical database is extremely simple to understand. In practice, though, there is an enormous amount of complexity involved. How does the DBMS know what the nature of the data is? How does the DBMS know how this data is stored? How do you actually tell the DBMS to retrieve some data? How are pointers, indexes and hashing techniques actually implemented? To none of these questions have I provided any answers. Nor shall I do so in full. For instance, the types of commands that you give a hierarchical database are likely to be the commands of a data manipulation language that is a proprietary one, that is, one associated specifically with the hierarchical database that you have bought. I have already indicated that we will have a brief look at one of these in Chapter 11, but an extended look would not be sensible. Furthermore, that data manipulation language is likely to be embedded in the programming language used by the company that bought the DBMS: Pascal, COBOL, PL/1 or whatever. Hence, to communicate with a hierarchical database is in itself a complex task. A very abbreviated glimpse into this world is given in Chapter 12. In part that stems from my own more limited objectives: this book is intended as a genuine introduction. But equally important in the decision to treat hierarchical databases so sketchily was a question of priorities. We must recognize the importance of hierarchical databases in the story of IT, but, compared to network databases, they are a clumsy tool, and compared to relational databases, they are cumbersome beyond endurance. I note, for instance, that the 384 pages of *Practical Database Techniques* (Deen (ed.), 1990) provides only four pages on hierarchical databases. In other words, the hierarchical database is out of date. I have tried to suggest other sources that you can consult if you really do need to learn practically about hierarchical databases (IMS, in particular), and Chapter 12 ends with an extensive bibliography on hierarchical databases. I do not think that it would be of any service to delve into detail here, particularly since IMS, the major operational hierarchical database, is very, very complicated indeed, partly, of course, as a result of trying to remedy inherent hierarchic deficiencies. None the less, out of date though hierarchic technology may be, it can still be the best option for a company that is genuinely organized in a hierarchical fashion. Such a decision does, however, require genuine thought and analysis. As long ago as 1984, the Institute of Administrative Management and the Department of Trade and Industry published *The Barriers and the Opportunities of Information Technology—A Management Perspective*. It estimated that about one billion pounds had been wasted in that year alone by companies investing unwisely in IT 'solutions'. Computerization is not the short-cut to instant success. Unwise and ill-considered computerization can, however, be the short-cut to ruin. None the less, as the management consultants who did the research for the 1984 management perspective showed, an intelligent use of IT can very clearly give a major competitive edge. Intelligence in the IT world does not necessarily mean plumbing for the latest technology. In certain circumstances, a hierarchical database could be the ideal solution. Such circumstances are, perhaps, going to be relatively rare today, but the hierarchical option is still worth bearing in mind. Hence the look at further elements of it in Chaper 12.

Reference

Bowers, D. S. *From Data to Database*, Van Nostrand, 1988.
Date, C. J. *Introduction to Database Systems*, 4th edn, Addison-Wesley, 1986.
Deen, S. (ed.) *Practical Database Techniques*, Pitman, 1990.
Gillenson, M. L. *Database Step-by-Step*, 2nd ed., John Wiley, 1990.
Perkinson, R. C. *The Key to Data Base Design*, QED, 1984.
Pratt, P. J. and Adamski, J. J. *Database Systems: Management and Design*, Body and Fraser, 1987.

9
The network database model

You will recall that a major limitation of the hierarchical database model is that it does not allow the representation of many-to-many relationships. Yet life is full of them. Many organizations employ many accountants; one organization might employ several accountants; an accountant might serve several organizations. Many cricket teams employ coaches; one coach might work for several teams; one team might employ several coaches. A database system does need the ability to show such relationships. It is this deficiency that the network database model does much to correct though it still bears a strong resemblance to its hierarchical forebear.

It is unfortunate too that the network database model brings with it yet more of the vocabulary hassles that IT seems unable or unwilling to circumvent. These we will encounter shortly, but it seems sensible to begin with the word *network*. What does this word mean in the database context? By and large, it means exactly what it means in everyday life. You and I have a network of friends, some of whom know each other. Most countries have a network of roads, some of which are not closed because of roadworks. Most companies have a network of departments, some of which help to raise profits. Indeed, since a database is intended to be a static representation of reality, it is only reasonable that a database itself should be organized as a network. Yet, in a clear and obvious sense, a hierarchical tree is also a network. It is, after all, a series of entities linked together. The linkage may be only a one-way linkage, but it is a linkage for all that. How then can we distinguish between a hierarchical tree and a network?

The examples of networks given in the preceding paragraph provide a clue, and a road network provides a convenient analogy. The road map of Fig. 9.1 will illustrate the matter for us. As you can see, each of the towns (represented by a blob) is connected to one or more other towns by a road. If you were, for instance, at the most eastern town and wanted to reach the most northern town, there would be a dozen or so possible routes, though only two of them would be

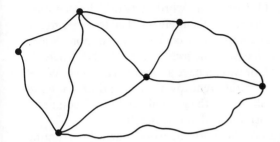

Figure 9.1

sensible ones. The major and obvious difference between that road network and a hierarchical tree is that each point (a town) is linked to other points by more than one path. For a node in a hierarchical tree, this is not the case. Each node is able to move upwards in the tree by only one path. While it is true that any one node may have several children, those children can only access their parent by one path and the parent itself can only access its parent by one path.

Even so, the distinction made above is not entirely accurate. It implies that no member of a network can be connected to only one other member of that network. Yet this is not true. Let us forget roads now and just envisage Fig. 9.2 as a representation of a database model. It is a network, yet most points within it are only connected to one other point.

There is one element in Fig. 9.2 which, by definition, means that it cannot possibly be a hierarchical tree. If you look at point 5, you will see that it has two parents, points 1 and 2. This is impossible within a tree. Hence, by default, Fig. 9.2 has to be seen as a network.

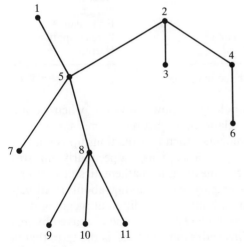

Figure 9.2

It is tiresome that, within the IT world, the word 'network' has another, entirely different meaning. Computers can be themselves linked together so that communication between the various computers becomes easy and rapid. Such a linkage is called a network. We can have a *local area network* (LAN), where the linked computers are all on one site, or we can have a *wide area network* (WAN) where the linked computers may be in different towns or even different countries. The study of such networks falls under the general heading of 'communications', and has no necessary connection with databases at all.

While these two differing usages of the word 'network' might be irritating, the next piece of jargon is positively annoying. We know that data associated with any one entity is stored in a row (often called a record or a tuple) and that each row is composed of fields or data items or elements or attribute values or instances (Fig. 9.3).

A row or record or tuple

00001	A. Flew	*An Introduction to Western Philosophy*	Thames & Hudson

Four attribute values, data items, elements or fields

Figure 9.3

We know too that each collection of rows devoted to an embracing entity is called a table, though many writers refer to it as a record type. Hence a catalogue of books stored on a database within a library is likely to be stored as a series of tables (Fig. 9.4).

00001	A. Flew	*An Introduction to Western Philosophy*	Thames & Hudson
00002	L. Watson	*Supernature*	Hodder
00003	H. Johnson	*Wine*	Nelson
00004	H. Melville	*Moby Dick*	Everyman
00005	R. Blake	*The Conservative Party*	Eyre & Spottis
00006	D. Self	*Creative and Critical*	Harrap

Figure 9.4   A section from a table or record type

So much should be familiar terminology by now. However, when we are confronted with a one-to-many relationship between one table—say, Courses—and another table—say, Students—then that relationship is known, in network database model terminology, as a *set*. This is a peculiarly unfortunate term. The word 'set' has a precise meaning in mathematics, a meaning which it is sometimes necessary to employ when talking about relational databases. To employ the same term with an entirely different meaning does seem to invite linguistic confusion. Elizabeth Oxborrow is so dismayed by this that she (and others) call it a 'coset' instead. However, 'set' is the term that is most commonly used, and so we had better learn how to use it correctly.

A set can be represented by a *data structure diagram*. Such a diagram is normally called a Bachman diagram, after the name of the man who first investigated and developed the network database model concept. It shows, at the top, a table and then, below, a table that is a member or child of the top table (Fig. 9.5). Strictly speaking, of course, the arrow leading from Courses to Students should be a double-headed arrow, since each course has many students, but the norm is none the less only to show a single-headed arrow.

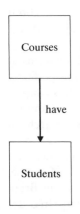

Figure 9.5

To continue speaking strictly, the word 'set' is only a shortened way of speaking of a set type or a set occurrence. Figure 9.5 shows a set type; Fig. 9.6 shows a set type and a set occurrence side by side.

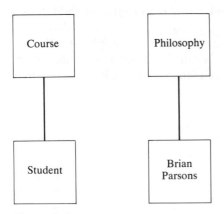

Figure 9.6

The same ruling applies to the other terms that we have been using. For instance, shown is a row, record type or attribute headings:

Book no.	Author	Title	Publisher

This, however, is a row or record occurrence:

002581	J. Austen	*Pride and Prejudice*	OUP

Equally, we can talk about an attribute type or an attribute occurrence, a table type or a table occurrence. Most of the time, of course, we just talk about tables, sets, rows, fields, etc., because the context of our remarks tend to make it obvious as to whether we are referring to a type or an occurrence.

However, now that we have learnt what a set is in network database terms, it has become clear that, while sets represent one-to-many relationships perfectly well, they do not cope with many-to-many relationships at all. Yet this chapter began with my saying that it was the network's ability to represent many-to-many relationships that made it so much more flexible than the hierarchical database model. How, then, is this accomplished?

If we revert to the Courses–Students set, we saw as the set occurrence that one course, Philosophy, taught one Student, Brian Parsons. In fact, of course, the Philosophy course has many more students than Brian Parsons, but Brian also takes other courses. Hence we have a many-to-many relationship. In order to represent this, we have to indulge in a little fudging. In Fig. 9.5, Courses was the owner or parent entity, Students was the member or child entity. This, of course, represented reality: *one* course had *many* students. However, to display a many-to-many relationship, we have to keep Courses as a parent or owner entity but also turn Students into an owner entity. This can only be done by attaching them to an entity that links them both together. Diagrammatically, we want a situation like Fig. 9.7. This Link entity is a member or child of two sets. Hence it will show, as the member of the Course entity, the students who follow a particular course. If the course happens to be Philosophy, it will show Brian Parsons as a member of that course. It will also show, as a member of the Student entity, the courses followed by each student. Hence it will reveal that

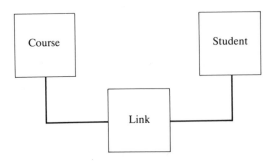

Figure 9.7

Brian Parsons is a member of three courses, Philosophy, Politics and Economics. Thus, by creating two sets which are linked in this fashion, we have created our needed many-to-many relationship. The Link table will have three rows devoted to Brian Parsons, linking that student to three different courses.

Needless to say, there are still vocabulary divergences of which it is well to be aware. Elmasri and Navathe tend to call a set occurrence a set instance, though they use both terms, while Bowers uses only set instance. Gillenson prefers to refer to a link as a 'juncture', though, to his credit, he does say that the many-to-many relationship can be known as a link, juncture, intersection or connection.

It is as well to be aware of how this ability to represent a many-to-many relationship saves us from a redundancy problem which the hierarchical model is unable to avoid. When you have a many-to-many relationship, as we have with Course and Student, which of these tables do you, in a hierarchical database, make the parent and which the child? If you decide to make the Course the parent node, then, because a child cannot exist without its parent, we are going to have a repetition of the course for every student who takes it (Fig. 9.8).

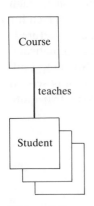

Figure 9.8

If, however, we have Student as the parent node, then we have to repeat that parent for every course that the student takes. Since a student can be involved in many courses, this too can lead to massive duplication. Obviously the designer of the database model has to make a decision, and will choose as the parent node the entity which will have fewer repetitions than its partner, but very often in the many-to-many context, it is an impossible decision to make. The ability to link two tables through creating a link table which is a member of two sets is consequently a major facility of the network model.

Notice, however, that a table can be a member of two sets without fulfilling this link or junction function. Bowers provides a useful example of this overlapping of set types. One set comprises Course and Lecture, the usual

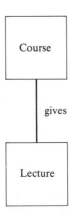

Figure 9.9

one-to-many (or possibly one-to-one) relationship (Fig. 9.9). At the same time there is a table, Lecturer, which is the parent or owner table for Lecture. Consequently, Lecture has two parents, but in both cases the sets are of a one-to-many type, not a many-to-many type employing a link, since each course has many lectures, but any one individual lecture is only being given for one specific course, and although a lecturer gives many lectures, each lecture is only given by one specific lecturer. However, to represent this diagrammatically (Fig. 9.10) does mean that it looks exactly like the Course, Student, Link example that we illustrated in Fig. 9.7. Indeed, were we to show the link sets on Fig. 9.11, it would not be immediately apparent that there were two quite different types of connection being shown.

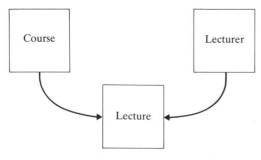

Figure 9.10

I have never subscribed to the view that a picture or diagram is worth a thousand words. Graphic illustrations can clearly be enormously useful, but they are not a substitute for clear and unambiguous language. Following this edict, we need to find a more revealing name for our link table. Perhaps Studies would be appropriate. There is a tendency for textbook writers to use Courses

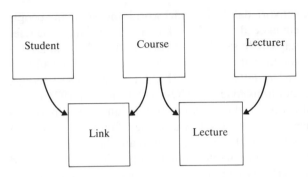

Figure 9.11

and Students as illustrative items, simply, of course, because most textbook writers are professionally engaged with students and courses almost every day. Pratt and Adamski call their link table Student_course_link. Bowers calls his Registration. Clearly it matters little. All that does matter is that one perceives the mode of representing a many-to-many relationship within a network database model.

It will be useful also at this point to introduce a commonly used form of shorthand. It is obvious that there are only three possible types of relationship, and we have met them all:

One-to-one
One-to-many
Many-to-many

Frequently, however, these relationships are presented in an abbreviated form:

1 : 1   One-to-one
1 : M   One-to-many
M : N   Many-to-many

From now on, these shorthand forms will be used.

It is also useful to provide some historical background for the emergence of the network database model, not just because of its intrinsic interest but also because it introduces yet more in-house jargon that it is handy to be aware of. Certainly you need to know about a voluntary organization called the Conference on Data Systems Languages (always referred to as CODASYL). This body was responsible for the development of the programming language COBOL, and, when it had completed that task, it turned its attention to the problem of the standardization of database management systems. A group within CODASYL called the Data Base Task Group (DBTG) was entrusted with the task of developing such a standard. Its proposals, first published in 1969, attracted a great deal of criticism, and as a result, a revised report was produced in 1971. The recommendations of this report have since become the yardstick for vocabulary within the network database model world. Indeed, many people refer to a CODASYL system instead of a network model. Or again, some refer to a DBTG model. Hence it is safe to say that network, CODASYL and DBTG are complete synonyms, though that can give rise to the absurdity of calling a non-CODASYL system, like Hewlett-Packard's IMAGE, a CODASYL model.

Naturally, the recommendations made by CODASYL in their 1971 report have since received modifications and extensions, but the underlying basis has remained unaltered. Hence, if you get to know any one CODASYL system, it does not take too much time or effort to acclimatize to another.

I have been concerned within this chapter to make the existence of sets and relationships between sets perfectly comprehensible. This has been done at a purely conceptual level; I have not been concerned with the physical implementation of that conceptual structure, nor with refining the conceptual model into a logical one suited to the particular DBMS that will be handling it. One more word, therefore, you need to learn. It is a word devised by CODASYL to refer to the logical structure of a database. The word is *schema*. When you develop an overall logical view of a network database, you would call it the schema. Below the schema there is a subschema which represents an individual user view of the database.

Each schema has four components:

1. *The schema entry* This gives the name of the schema, and can cite the author of the schema, its date of completion, and append any introductory remarks which are felt useful.

   SCHEMA NAME IS SCRAPE AND BLOW LTD
   Schema compiled by Xanadu Analysts.   Completed January 1991.

2. *The area (or realm) entry* This identifies the area of the database within which tables of data are stored. Hence it will first of all be stated

   AREA NAME IS AREA__DISTRIBUTION

   and the details of records which subsequently appear will be appended to the appropriate area as follows:

   RECORD NAME IS COURSES
   LOCATION MODE IS CALC
   USING COURSE__NUMBER
   WITHIN AREA__DISTRIBUTION

3. *The record entry* This declares records or tables that exist in the schema. It does so under two subentries:
   (a) Record subentries give the name of each table, how it can be accessed, and whereabouts it may reside.
   (b) Data subentries list the attributes of each column within the table.
   A record subentry we saw above; a data subentry would immediately follow, as is shown below:

RECORD NAME IS COURSES
LOCATION MODE IS CALC
USING COURSE__NUMBER
WITHIN AREA__DISTRIBUTION

02 COURSE__NUMBER   PIC 9(3)
02 NAME   PIC X(20)
02 DEPARTMENT   PIC X(20)

4. *The set entry* This declares the associations among the various types of record. As we know, a table can have more than one parent. It is the set entry part of the schema that reveals this. In most cases, of course, it simply reveals the owner–member relationship within a set. We could devise a set for Simeon Grumblethitch which would cope well with the problem of showing a number of different performances of the same work:

SET NAME IS SYMPHONIES
OWNER IS WORK
MEMBER IS PERFORMANCE

Figure 9.12 gives a diagrammatic representation together with a typical data row alongside each table. Note, though, that each performance has to be given a unique performance number as its primary key. It would not be acceptable to use the record or tape number because you would then have the same primary key for more than one specific row.

As you can doubtless envisage, Simeon and his quaint organization could have several parallel sets of this nature, one for symphonies as Fig. 9.12, one for concertos, one for chamber works, one for operas and so on.

Set: Symphonies

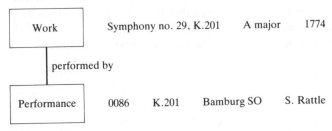

Figure 9.12

Let us now, therefore, make some evaluative comments. It is obvious that the major advantage of the network database model over the hierarchical lies in its ability to cope with M : N relationships. Indeed, a network data model can cope with any type of data relationship. The fact that the network data model is backed by the CODASYL DBTG is also an advantage since it provides a useful consultative and backup organization. In performance terms, a network system is just as good as a hierarchical one, and better than a relational one. A well-constructed network system can cope with most of the desired database functions. It can prevent a deadly embrace, share data, carry out effective recovery procedures, take useful security steps and also provide some integrity support. Perhaps most important of all is the fact that CODASYL database model DBMSs have been available since the late 1960s, and hence provide a wealth of concrete examples that can be followed. No one, therefore, can afford to dismiss the network model without careful consideration. There is, though, one overwhelming adverse factor. The major disadvantage of the network model is its complexity. This merits some explanation.

When we first of all think about acquiring a database, we have a conceptual model of that database. We know what entities will exist within it and what the relationships are between those entities. From this conceptual model, we select the DBMS that seems most appropriate for representing that model. However, the conceptual model has been devised without any thought of the restrictions that an actual DBMS will impose. Hence we now change the conceptual model into what is called a *logical* model, a model that can actually be implemented by the selected DBMS. In devising the links between Courses and Students we have been constructing a logical database model. We have only been concerned to do so at an elementary level, but it has been clear that a full logical model, even for small concerns like Scrape and Blow or Simeon Grumblethitch and MASS, would be a complicated object. This can be taxing. Application programs written for a network system have to provide for some complex navigation from set to set, subschema to subschema. More seriously, though, is the lack of data independence that this complex structure entails. If we change the logical structure of the database, changes are then required to the application programs. This defect, of course, is one that it shares with the hierarchical data model. Indeed, total data independence is the most difficult of the DBMS desired functions to achieve. It is an element that the relational database more fully approaches, and it does so with a great deal more simplicity than either the hierarchical or network models. Thus it is to the relational model that we next turn.

Reference

Bowers, D. S. *From Data to Database*, Van Nostrand, 1988.

10
The relational database model

The relational approach is one with which we are already at least partially familiar. The basis of the relational DBMS rests in the creation of tables of data, and we have seen extracts from many tables so far and have been engaged in ensuring that the data within those tables was in at least third normal form. Let us then just summarize our understanding of the nature of a table (or relation):

1. The values in every field within the table are single values, not repeating or multiple ones. Thus the following row showing the name of an English king, the dates of his accession and death and the number of years of his reign is a perfectly acceptable row because every field is single-valued:

Edward III	1327	1377	51

The following row is, however, defective. It shows the authors of a book, the book's title, publisher and date of publication. However, since two people collaborated in writing this book, it means that the field given over to the author is not a single-valued field. It is instead a multiple value.

Peterson, J. L. & Silberschatz, A.	Operating System Concepts	Addison-Wesley	1983

To eliminate a multiple value, we need to construct rows in which one, and only one, of the multiple values appears in each row. In the example above, for instance, two rows would be necessary in order to eliminate the multiple value:

Peterson, J. L.	Operating System Concepts	Addison-Wesley	1983
Silberschatz, A.	Operating System Concepts	Addison-Wesley	1983

Alternatively, in order to avoid the duplication of title, publisher and date of publication, we could split the table into two separate ones, creating a link value if necessary by giving each book a unique book number:

Authors		Books
Peterson, J. L	934	934 Operating System Concepts Addison-Wesley 1983
Silberschatz, A.	934	

Much the same procedure can be adopted for repeating values. Imagine that you constructed a table showing computer shops in the town of Turingham, and that you wanted to show the name of the shop, its address, and the different makes of computer equipment that it stocked. Your table would look something like Table 10.1.

Table 10.1   Computer retailers in Turingham

Name of retailer	Address	Stock range
Sponge, E. W.	Byte Passage, TU2 7RY	Amstrad, H-P, IBM, Tandon
IT for You	Buffer Road, TU3 5BN	Apple, Commodore, IBM, Olivetti

As you can see, the final field has repeating groups within it. This cannot be accepted within a relational table, and so we employ either of the two techniques available in order to ensure that the Stock range column has only single-valued attributes within it. A single-valued attribute is often called *atomic*, since it cannot be broken down into anything simpler.

2. Each column in a table is given a distinct name which will indicate the nature of the values or attributes within that column. Hence, if we encounter a table with the following column headings, we would know instantly the nature of the attributes placed in that column:

Employee number	Name	Address	Telephone number

Of course, when we came to specify the table for the physical representation of the database, we would need to indicate whether or not the attributes were fixed or variable in length and what type of data (character, floating-point number, etc.) was going to fill that particular field. Self-evidently, having given a column an attribute name like Employee, number or Address, every value in that column must be consistent with the attribute name. A table like Table 10.2 would cause some difficulties. One does, however, feel that it would take a much higher than average degree of idiocy to construct such a table.

Table 10.2

Employee number	Name	Address	Telephone number
0000241	13 Windsor Road	Michael W. Hutchinson	0391–453911
91–872654	0000615	36 Malvern Road	Steve Flood
The Croft	Mary Cunningham	0000723	87–863
0000137	91–833211	41 Uppingham Drive	S. D. Forbes

3. Within a relational database model, it does not matter in what order the rows or columns are placed. What matters is the accuracy of the data. Provided that is observed, it is immaterial as to the ordering of that data. After all, swapping round the order of rows and/or columns will not affect the information content of the table one iota.

4. Each row (or tuple) in a table is unique. This again is self-evident. Imagine that you were filling in these attribute columns:

Employee number	Name	Address	Telephone number

If the data were to appear as it is shown in Table 10.3, then one complete row would be totally redundant.

Table 10.3

Employee number	Name	Address	Telephone number
0000120	Brenda Hastings	9 Scullthorpe Road	87–4720
0000121	David Weidmann	15 Towers Close	87–2994
0000120	Brenda Hastings	9 Scullthorpe Road	87–4720
0000122	Richard Wybourne	44 Slade Avenue	87–3361

It is clear, though, that duplication of one or more attributes is perfectly acceptable. Imagine, for instance, that the defective Table 10.3 were to appear instead as Table 10.4.

Table 10.4

Employee number	Name	Address	Telephone number
0000120	Brenda Hastings	9 Scullthorpe Road	87–4720
0000121	David Weidmann	15 Towers Close	87–2994
0000123	Michael Hastings	9 Scullthorpe Road	87–4720
0000122	Richard Wybourne	44 Slade Avenue	87–3361

In this table, we do have a duplication of both address and telephone number, but this is not redundant because they refer to a different employee who has, as it happens, a unique name but, more importantly, has a unique employee number. As you doubtless deduced, Brenda and Michael Hastings are a married couple who happen to work for the same organization and who therefore appear in the same Employee table. Such a duplication does not produce identical rows since two attributes of those rows remain unique. Furthermore, if the address and telephone numbers were not shown for both Brenda and Michael Hastings, we would have no knowledge as to their respective addresses and telephone numbers. The fact that they are married does not necessarily imply that they share the same address. Hence the duplication here is far from redundant.

We are also well aware of the importance of the primary key for each row within a table and with the concept of functional dependence that such keys entail. In the Employee table at which we have just glanced, it is the Employee number which is the primary key. It is, of course, possible to think of Name as being the primary key. It is, of course, possible to think of Name as being the primary key instead. Where there is an alternative possibility for the primary key, the alternative is often referred to as a *candidate key*. In fact, of course, Name would not be a proper candidate key in such an Employee table simply because it would be possible for two or more employees to have the same name, while it would not be possible for them to have the same Employee number.

A relational database, then, is constructed simply of tables. In that respect, it may be identical to a hierarchical or a network DBMS. The difference between the three lies in the mode of accession. We have seen that within a hierarchical database we can only travel up and down, from parent to child and from child back to parent, though complicated systems of pointers are possible. Within a network database, our travel is less confined. The use of pointers enables some horizontal passage from set to set, as well as the vertical passage fron owner to member. Most significant, of course, is the fact that an entity in a network structure can have more than one parent. In a relational database, however, we can move from any table to any other table, or indeed from any attribute to any other attribute. The relational database model consequently has two significant advantages:

1. Since it is composed entirely of tables, and such tables are the only thing that the user needs to know about, the relational approach has a greater simplicity than the hierarchical or the network, where the user needs to be aware of the structure of the database itself.
2. The greater range and flexibility of the accession procedures (of which the user need never be aware) gives the relational method a greater power in explicitly representing relationships.

Since we have already looked at many of the issues concerned with the construction of valid tables, we will be able in this chapter to look at some of the more advanced concepts. I have already indicated that the construction of well-normalized tables is an advantage for whatever type of DBMS we are ultimately going to employ. Even in some of the more advanced concepts at which we are now going to look, an awareness of such concepts is helpful whatever the ultimate implementation.

10.1   Nulls

I have already commented in passing about the problem of null values. There are two possible reasons for a field to contain a null value.

- There may be a valid entry for the field concerned, but the designer of the table just doesn't happen to know it as the moment. For instance, Barry Pickersgill appears in the Employee table, but his telephone number is ex-directory and you have consequently been unable to include it in the database. It will be inserted when you have had the opportunity to consult Barry in person.
- There may be no valid entry possible at all. Ruth Scargill is an employee and consequently appears in the Employee table. She is not, however, on the phone; consequently, no phone number can possibly be included in her row of data.

As it happens, the examples of null values given above would cause no serious problems, but there are cases where a null value would be extremely damaging, for example:

- It would be absurd and logically impossible to have a null value in the primary key field. Since it is the primary key which functionally determines all the other attributes of the row, we would have the ludicrous state of everything being dependent upon nothing.
- Should the range of attributes contained in the column of a table be involved in some mathematical calculation, the presence of a null value would probably distort the final result. It is, after all, not uncommon to use data within a table to produce an average result. A null value here would invalidate the result.
- Often we need to join elements of one table to elements of another table. Such a merging becomes impossible when one of the common joining attributes is left as a null value.

It would consequently seem that to allow null values in any of the above three instances would negate the purpose of the table or tables concerned. The inevitable conclusion is that null values should therefore not be allowed to exist. Date (1986) does indeed favour this stance. None the less, as Date himself implies, we cannot simply banish null values by a simple edict. It would be not unlike disposing of the advancing tiger by putting your head in a paper bag. Yet it not easy to resolve this problem. We can legislate to some extent by instructing the DBMS to give different default values to the differing types of null so that we do at least know that the null entry represents either ignorance or that no entry is ever possible. It is, however, very difficult to implement such distinctions, and I have to conclude by saying that the problem of null values is one for which an entirely satisfactory solution has not yet been found.

10.2   Data independence

A brief look at this aspect has already been taken. We are already aware that the ability to change the database without such changes requiring any alteration in the application programs accessing that database is a major advantage. We have also seen that such data independence is not achievable in hierarchical or network database models. How well can relational databases achieve this desired end?

Let us begin by making sure that we understand the different aspects of data.

10.2.1   APPLICATION PROGRAMS

These programs are the software that accomplish a specific task for the user. You may have a payroll program. Obviously this program accesses the database in order to retrieve data about the employees of the company who require paying.

10.2.2   INTERNAL SCHEMA

From time to time, you might need to know how the database is physically structured and what indexing systems there are for accessing that data. Obviously, for instance, if the payroll application program is going to perform its function at all, it is going to have to know about the internal schema of the database. It will need to know the whereabouts of the needed data, where it is stored. It will also need to know the access paths to that data.

10.2.3   CONCEPTUAL SCHEMA

It is, of course, the conceptual view that dictates the internal structure. The internal view can only be constructed in accordance with the conceptual vision of the database and its application programs. Thus the conceptual schema is the overall description of the database, a kind of global view. It is not in any way concerned with the details of physical storage structure that the internal schema depicts.

10.2.4   EXTERNAL SCHEMA

This is what the user actually sees. The external view is consequently derived from the combination of the conceptual view and the internal representation, and is presented in accordance with the demands of the application program and/or the specific user. Hence two users might be accessing the same data but could be given entirely different external views of that data.

As is obvious, these four aspects or views of data are closely linked one with another. If you need to add a new member to the payroll, you are adding another element to the internal schema. This does not alter in any way the conceptual schema, but it will alter the external schema in that you, the user, will want to see on the screen data about another employee. Obviously, though, in just adding another row to the database, you will not want to have to make amendments to anything else. That example, however, is an extremely simple one. What happens if it is decided that all employees who possess a company car are going to have alterations made to their income tax assessment and to their National Insurance contributions? Once again, with a DBMS that fulfils the function of data independence, no changes will need to be made other than to the conceptual schema, or, more accurately, no changes will have to be made by you, the user. We need a DBMS that, once a change is made to the conceptual schema, automatically links that change to all the other relevant aspects of the database matrix. This entire process of linking one change in one aspect to all other necessary aspects is called *binding*. There are two kinds of binding:

1. Compilation-time binding which creates all the necessary linkages as the application program itself is being loaded;
2. Execution-time binding which creates the necessary linkages as and when those linkages become necessary during the execution of the program.

These mappings between the various schemas are complex. Clearly, if any alteration is made to the conceptual schema, consequent alterations or mappings are going to have to be made to the other schemas. The DBMS thus needs the ability to do this. Normally any alteration to the conceptual schema will first be linked to the internal schema (IS) and the result stored in a directory that specifically links the conceptual schema (CS) to the internal one (Fig. 10.1).

We now have what is called a CS/IS binding. It is clear, though, that such a binding operation also has to be performed between the conceptual schema and the external schema (ES). This ES/CS binding is then stored in an ES/CS directory. The application program then needs to be compiled against the new external schema, and then, finally, the new application program/external schema linkage needs to be mapped to the CS/IS directory.

Obviously all this takes time and consumes a considerable degree of computing resources. You also have to decide whether to use compilation-time binding or execution-time binding. If you are likely to use a program many times, then

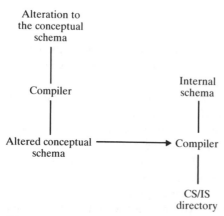

Figure 10.1

compilation-time binding will be the more efficient, but every time any changes are made to that program, the whole binding operation has to be redone. Execution-time binding produces a slower response because the binding has to be completed during the course of the operation or transaction.

It is easy to see, then, that it has been a question of economy in the monetary sense that has prevented data independence becoming the database norm. Most relational systems like DB2 and INGRES do allow a fairly high degree of data independence, and there seems little reason to doubt that this facility will increase.

10.3   Joins and views

We are well aware that the relational database consists of tables and only of tables. This gives the data a stability that is quite independent of the access paths required to access that data. This is particularly useful when specific access paths might only be short-lived. An ad hoc report, for instance, might want a particular combination of entities and relationships that is never required again. The fact that the necessary data is in self-contained tables means that the necessary data can be extracted from those tables without in any way disturbing their structure and content.

In hierarchical and network databases, tables are indissolubly linked to one another, by parent–child in hierarchical, by sets in network. This imposes certain access limitations upon both these database systems, limitations that can, in part, be overcome but which entail a greater degree of processing overhead and a greater awareness by the user of the structure of the database in question. None the less, even in a relational system, it frequently is the case that data from one or more tables is required for a particular transaction. Where it is a frequent necessity to process data from different tables, there are two solutions available in a relational system. You can either join two or more tables together, and in so doing construct an entirely new table, or you can create a view.

A *join* operation is relatively straightforward. Basically the operation is as simple as creating a table in the first place. Exactly how you do create a table in any sort of DBMS depends upon the facilities that you have in terms of data defining languages and data manipulating languages, and these are the topics of Part Four. It does seem useful, however, before we move onto database languages, to clarify the conceptual issues involved. Indeed, Date (1987) goes so far as to say that: 'it is the availability of the join operation, almost more than anything else, that distinguishes relational from nonrelational systems'.

If Table *A* exists, but is normally used in combination with Table *B*, it might be a great deal easier to join the two tables together into a new construct that we will call Table *C*. One aspect, however, is imperative. Table *A* and Table *B* must have one attribute in common for such a join to be made. Let us consider Tables 10.5 and 10.6.

Table 10.5

Student number	Student name	Course number
128473	Siegfried B. Fisher	23

Table 10.6

Course number	Course name
23	Logic

As you can see, Course number is the linking attribute here. Indeed, Course number in this instance is what is called a *foreign key*. A foreign key is an attribute that appears in one table—in this case, Table 10.5—but is the primary key for another table.

Now there are possibly very good reasons for having Table 10.5 and Table 10.6 as two distinct tables. They are both doubtless used in many applications with no reference to each other at all. None the less, it is not surprising to learn that some applications do use both these tables in combination. We therefore create a Join table, our Table *C*. Such a table would explicitly link the student with the course which he or she was following (Table 10.7).

Table 10.7

Student number	Student name	Course number	Course name
128473	Siegfried B. Fisher	23	Logic

Clearly, in terms of processing speed, when we do want to combine the data from the Student table with data from the Course table, it will be quicker and more convenient to use the newly created Join table.

There are, however, times when it is better to create a view rather than a join.

A view is a table that does not exist. Defined like that, a view does not sound of much use. It is, though, very handy, because although it does not exist, it gives the user every impression of really existing. If you create a table in a relational database, that table physically exists as a series of magnetized and unmagnetized spots upon a disk. When you create a join, since a join is a real table, that too exists as a series of 0s and 1s upon the disk. A view, however, is created when you ask the database to combine attributes from one or more tables without physically creating a new table to do so. The nature of that view—what attributes from which tables are required—will be stored in a directory, and every time you indicate that you wish to access that view, the DBMS will create it for you. The user, though, can remain blissfully unaware of all this. The view will, like all the tables, have been given a name. Hence, when the user wishes to access a view, he or she just calls it up by its name in the same way that he or she would call up a table by its name.

If then a view is exactly like a table, why create views instead of tables? In fact, views can have real advantages. If you need to restructure the database in any significant way, this might mean that the user has to define the retrieval of data in a new and different way. Hence data independence will be lost. If, however, the user has created a view, the odds are that the view will still be able to retrieve the necessary data despite its restructuring. The way in which the view retrieves the data will doubtless be different, but there is no need for the user even to be aware of this. Hence usage of views helps to provide a greater degree of data independence.

It could well be that existing tables contain data that not all employees of the organization should be allowed to see. The Employee table, for instance, might contain details of the salary of each employee. Doris, in the ordering department, needs quite often to access the Employee table. It is felt, however, that it would be ill-advised to allow Doris to see that Mervyn Slater, the director of sales, earns £35,000 a year, while Doris herself only earns £8,000. Hence we create a view for Doris that gives her the data from the Employee table that she needs, but withholds other data.

Although data in an organization is a corporate resource, people will want to see different aspects of that data presented in different combinations. The simplest solution is to create a view that gives each user precisely the range and format that he or she requires.

Hence, through using the join and view facilities that most relational databases provide, the user can be granted a flexibility and a convenience that is of considerable value.

10.4   Storage and indexing

Pratt and Adamski (1987) begin a section of their fifth chapter with the unvarnished words: 'Within relational model systems, the main mechanism for increasing the efficiency with which data is retrieved from the database is the use of *indexes*.' Clearly this is true, and, because of its truth, some knowledge of indexing systems is vital if we are to understand the relational data model. Nor can we confine ourselves to indexes. Obviously the kind of storage structure used will, to some extent, dictate the type of indexing system that is applicable. Hence indexing is not just a conceptual matter; it involves some knowledge of the physical conditions under which the DBMS will be operating.

The tape storage of data has been virtually ignored in this book. Nowadays it is seldom used for anything other than backup purposes. We have consequently assumed that all data storage will be on disk. It was also mentioned earlier (though only in passing) that a database might very well be stored upon a disk pack. We need to take a closer look at this now because its presence can affect the indexing technique employed.

A disk pack is a number of disks placed on top of each other with sufficient space between them for a read–write head to be inserted. A read–write head can read data from the disk or write new data onto the disk. Diagrammatically, the disk pack looks like Fig. 10.2. Each disk (or platter, as they are usually called) is coated with a metallic oxide film which stores magnetically encoded information. The platter itself is divided into several hundred concentric rings. Each of those rings is divided into a number of sectors. A greatly simplified impression is given in Fig. 10.3.

Since all the read–write heads move in unison, this means that if the topmost read–write head is accessing track 54, sector 3 of the topmost platter, then every other read–write head is also accessing track 54, sector 3 of their respective

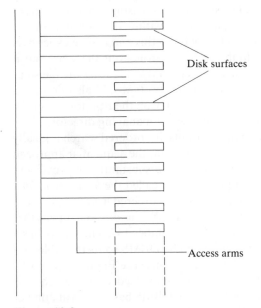

Figure 10.2

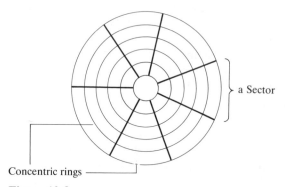

Figure 10.3

platters. Consequently, related information, instead of being stored all on one disk, is frequently stored on the same track and sector of a number of different disks. Hence the read–write heads can simultaneously access all the related information in one operation. Clearly where this is the case, it will influence any indexing system employed.

As we already know, the simplest structure for data is a sequential one where item just follows item, a storage technique sometimes referred to as the *heap* method. As a result, a sequential search looks at every item in turn until it reaches the specific item for which it is looking. Such a process is clearly not very efficient, and there are a number of ways of speeding it up without actually indexing. For instance, the data could be stored in decreasing order of expected popularity so that most searches were successful within the first half of the maximum possible search. Even so, it is tricky to do this and can be expensive. The popularity of data items will doubtless vary throughout the year, and it would be a far from insignificant burden to keep on restructuring the file so as to keep it in genuine decreasing order of popularity. It would also doubtless lead to betting circles within the office placing money on their tip for top of the pops this week, an activity that might not amuse the managing director.

Neither a straight sequential search nor a popularity-ordered search is ideally effective. Indeed, if we want effective finding of data, the sequential approach has to be abandoned. An alternative which shows a substantial improvement on the sequential procedure is a technique generally called the *binary searching* technique. Imagine for the moment that you have an ordered list of pupils from Dothegirls Hall. The order is by means of Pupil number, and it so happens that you want to examine the data pertaining to Pupil number 137. The school has a total roll of 390. In the binary search technique, the DBMS splits the table into half and goes immediately to the middle point, in this case Pupil number 195. Clearly, if by some stroke of luck 195 is the actual data needed, the search ends at once. However, we want Pupil number 137. The DBMS has arrived at number 195. It realizes that the number it needs is less than the number upon which it is currently resting, so it performs another binary search, but this time with 0 to 195 as its range. The midpoint for this range is number 97. Having arrived at 97, the DBMS realizes that the number it needs is higher than the number upon which it is currently resting. Consequently it does another binary search, this time between 97 and 195. The midpoint of that range is 144. Having arrived at 144, the DBMS realizes that the number it requires is now lower than the number it has. So we have another binary split, this time between 97 and 144. This brings us to number 122. All the time our possible range is narrowing. Now it is only between 122 and 144. The midpoint here is number 133, thus reducing the range to 133–144. And so the binary searching continues until the correct record is found or the size of the remaining list is zero.

Figure 10.4 illustrates how many accessions are necessary before the correct row is located. As you can see, the entire operation takes nine steps. This is a great deal fewer than is required by a straight sequential search. Even so, a binary search is much more expensive in terms of processing power than is a sequential one. Note too that binary searching can only be accomplished where you have an ordered primary key. In the case of Dothegirls Hall, the primary key did run from 0 to 390, so it was easy to conduct a binary search. In many cases, because of expense or lack of order, a binary search is not viable.

Problem: to find pupil number 137 from a total number of 390 pupils.

Possible range	Midnumber
0–390	195
0–195	97
97–195	144
97–144	122
122–144	133
133–144	138
133–138	135
135–138	136
136–138	137

Figure 10.4

The first two methods for locating data at which we have looked have been concerned with unindexed sequential files. Sequential files offer an inexpensive means of storing and processing quantities of data on tape or disk. They are, therefore, ideal for batch processing programs that will read and/or write a high proportion of the rows in a file. As we have seen, though, an unindexed sequential file does not lend itself to rapid access. The answer, quite unsurprisingly, is therefore to index the file in question. The rows in an indexed sequential file exist just as they do in an unindexed file. The only difference is that, in addition to the raw file itself, there also exists an index, a sort of 'road map' to the rows. Indeed, the index is a file or table of its own and is handled by the DBMS as an example of system software. Let me give an example of how an indexed sequential file would work. To do so we will return to Simeon Grumblethitch's table of Mozart symphonies. If you recall, this was an extremely simple table. The example that was given was for Symphony Number 34 (Table 10.8).

Table 10.8

Symphony no.	K-number	Key
No. 34	338	C major

Conveniently, the data on the disk is laid out in numerical order. Hence the first row is no. 1, 16, E flat, the second row is no. 4, 19, D major, the third row is no. 5, 22, B flat and so on up to no. 41, 551, C major. (Don't worry about the fact that I appear to have missed out symphonies 2 and 3. They do not seem to have survived, and even Simeon can only store records of extant symphonies.)

As you will also recall, data on a disk is stored in tracks that are themselves split into sectors or blocks. Let us assume that each block can hold the data for three rows' worth of the table, in other words, for three symphonies. Hence you construct your index so that each block is given a separate address. The first block is given the address of 01 and the final block is given the address of 14. Your mathematical prowess is doubtless sufficient for you to work out that 14 blocks, each storing data for 3 symphonies, allows records to be stored for 42 symphonies, which is ample space for Simeon's purposes.

Table 10.9   Index

Symphony no.	Address no.
01	00001
04	00001
05	00001
06	00002
07	00002
08	00002
09	00003

Clearly the primary key of the Symphony table is the symphony no. That key is mapped alongside the Index table as shown in Table 10.9. Hence, if you want to access symphony number 11, the DBMS will take you instantly to block 3 and the read/write head will look at symphony number 9, discard it, look at symphony number 10, discard that too, and then come to symphony number 11 which it will output onto the screen. You have consequently achieved almost direct access. At the maximum, the read–write head will only ever have to look at three symphonies before outputting the one needed.

One consequence of an indexed sequential file may well have occurred to you. They cannot be stored on tape. Only a direct-access storage device—normally a disk—can cope with indexed sequential tables. Furthermore, although an indexed sequential file does have major advantages, problems can be created concerning updates and deletions. If you delete a row of data, you either leave a space where the old row existed (thus wasting space) or you have to rearrange the entire table and its associated index table. The same necessity will hold if some tiresome scholar comes along and 'proves' that K.45b was not written by Mozart at all. Indeed, this entire example that I have been giving has been greatly oversimplified. What, for instance, do you do with K.111 which was originally an overture but which has been joined with K.120 to create a symphony confusingly numbered K.111a but not given a symphony number at all? Resolving such problems could play havoc with your original storage and the consequent indexing. Indexed sequential is an improvement, but it can give difficulties in maintenance. As a result, we turn either to hashing which we have already glanced at, or to a completely random access indexing system like B-trees.

I do not want to repeat or extend what was said about hashing in Chapter 7. There is a great deal more that could be added. Samson (1990) gives a good account. It is necessary though to give some indication as to what on earth B-trees are, particularly since many relational databases give you the option of indexing by means of the B-tree method.

A *B-tree* index is organized exactly like the hierarchical data model. In other words, it is a tree (Fig. 10.5). The root node contains the range of all the data within that particular database. Imagine for the moment that this tiny database only has three hundred rows of data within it. Consequently node *A*, the root node, will be organized somewhat like Fig. 10.6. Should you want to locate row number 239, the DBMS will go to the rightmost field of node *A* which will

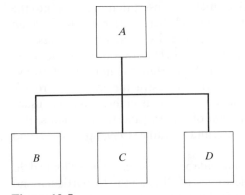

Figure 10.5

Figure 10.6

immediately direct the DBMS to the child node *D*. That node only has two children (Fig. 10.7). This time the DBMS will access the left-placed asterisk which will direct it to node *I*. This node contains pointers to rows between 200 and 250. And so the process continues until you reach a leaf node which contains the address of the specific row that you want, in this case, row 239.

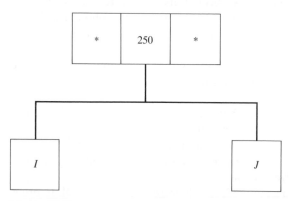

Figure 10.7

While the structure of B-trees is easy to understand, some of their advantages have not, as yet, become apparent. For instance, when a B-tree index is first created, it is done so that the various nodes of the tree are left with space available in them. Consequently, when you make an addition to the database, there will normally be space available to insert that new row into the index system. When a particular node is full and there is no room for such an insertion, then the B-tree automatically reorganizes itself, creating, if necessary, new nodes and even new levels of nodes. If you delete rows of data, the index will again adjust itself to the new situation. As a result, the index itself always remains a balanced index because of this dynamic restructuring. It can provide rapid access, efficient insertion and deletion, and a reasonably economic usage of disk space. For a much fuller treatment of B-trees, and their variants, B+ trees and B* trees, I would suggest Elmasri and Navathe (1989, pp. 114–32) and Chapter 6 of Smith and Barnes (1987).

The aspects of relevance to a relational database at which we have looked do not by any means exhaust the viable topics of discussion. In particular, no mention has been made of the range of additional tools that often come fully integrated with a relational DBMS: report generators, graphic interfaces, screen managers and application generators. As, however, has already been indicated, it is difficult to split any aspect of IT up into separate components. Yet, when discussing databases, it is impossible to ignore the fact that the data in databases has to be inserted, retrieved, deleted or amended by the user giving some command to the database itself. We have gained an overall impression of three of the major data models in this part. It is impossible, however, really to apprehend those data models until you have learnt how to talk to them. Database literacy is the topic of Part Four.

References

Date, C. J. *Introduction to Database Systems*, Vol. II, Addison-Wesley, 1986.
Date, C. J. *A Guide to INGRES*, Addison-Wesley, 1987.
Elmasri, R. and Navathe, S. *Fundamentals of Database Systems*, Benjamin Cummings, 1989.
Pratt, P. J. and Adamski, J. J. *Database Systems: Management and Design*, Boyd & Fraser, 1987.
Samson, W. B. *Practical Database Techniques*, Pitman, 1990.
Smith, P. and Barnes, M. *Files and Databases*, Addison-Wesley, 1987.

Questions on Part Three

1. Why is rollback an important facility for a DBMS?
2. What is hashing?
3. Why is locking a useful technique?
4. What is a deadly embrace?
5. How do familial relationships differ in the hierarchical and network data models?
6. In a network data model, why is it often necessary to create a link or juncture?
7. Explain the significance of each row of data in a relational database possessing a primary key.
8. What is meant by data independence?
9. Show the difference between compilation-time binding and execution-time binding.
10. Distinguish between a join and a view.

Answers

1. Rollback: the ability to move back to the state that existed before the beginning of a particular transaction. It is important because it helps to ensure the database remains in a consistent state.
2. Hashing is a process whereby an attribute value within a row of data (normally the primary key) is converted to a numeric value which is then further used to generate an address. The row of data concerned is then stored at that address (or retrieved from that address).
3. Locking, whereby access to data is temporarily prevented, is a useful technique since it enables a transaction to be completed without the data involved in that transaction being accessed (and possibly changed) by anyone else. Locking consequently helps to preserve the integrity of the database.

4. A deadly embrace is a situation that arises when program *A* wants an item currently held by program *B*. Program *B* cannot release that data until it has itself received another item of data. Unfortunately, the item of data that program *B* is waiting for is currently held by program *A*. Hence we have the situation that program *A* cannot complete a transaction until it obtains data held by program *B*, while program *B* cannot complete a transaction until it obtains data held by program *A*. The two transactions are thus in a deadly embrace, neither of them able to progress any further.

5. A hierarchical data model only allows a child to have one parent; a network data model allows a child to have two or more parents.

6. It is often necessary to create a link in order to represent a many-to-many relationship.

7. The primary key is significant because it functionally determines all the other elements within the row and thus helps to ensure the uniqueness of that particular row.

8. Data independence means that changes to data within a database are handled by the DBMS itself and not by the user. Thus, if some data were to be deleted, the DBMS would make the necessary alterations to the external schema and the internal schema.

9. Compilation-time binding is the linking of changes to the conceptual schema with the necessary changes to the other schema at the time that the relevant application program is loaded. Execution-time binding is the same sort of linking only this time the linkages are only created as they become relevant during the execution of the application program itself.

10. A join is a table created by merging data from two or more existing tables. A view is exactly the same sort of product as a join except that a view is created each time it is called while a join exists as a physical component in storage.

PART FOUR

Speaking with many tongues

11
An introduction to the tongues

A DBMS might be a wonderful creation, but it will not manage your database for you all by itself. If you order DB4, Oracle, INGRES or some other superb (and expensive) DBMS, you cannot load the DBMS onto your disk and merrily say, 'Right, Charlie, it's all yours now; look after the database while I play golf?' The DBMS needs to be told what to do. You will have to issue commands. And those commands need to be precise and in a particular language that the DBMS understands. This chapter is about the sort of language to which a DBMS can respond.

As you will have gathered, IT is jargon-ridden and often somewhat idiosyncratic in its linguistic practices (or, at least, I somewhat neurotically take this to be the case). It seems, consequently, useful just to begin by looking at the entire gamut of languages that you can encounter in IT. Then, having established the range and the purpose of these alien tongues, you can focus on the types that are directly relevant to database management. I shall, therefore, simply provide in this chapter a dictionary of tongues, though the order in which I present them is intended to be a logical and historically slanted order.

11.1 Machine code

As its name would suggest, this is the language that the computer itself understands. It is, therefore, a series of pulses of electricity. We human beings always represent those pulses with the symbols 0 and 1. Should we wish to talk to a computer in its own language, we would sit at the keyboard and type loving notes like this:

100110010011100101010011110100100001011100101011110001

Once upon a time, back in the dark ages (i.e. the 1950s), using machine code or machine language was the *only* way of communicating with a computer. As you might imagine, it is very, very easy to make a mistake when you are entering machine code in at the keyboard. If you make a mistake, the program will not work. You therefore have to find your mistake and correct it. Doing so can take hours and/or send you insane in the process.

11.2   Assembly language

Because machine code is so different to use, computer scientists tried to devise short-cuts that would remove some of the agony of communicating with the computer. The result was assembly language. Instead of using a series of 0s and 1s, a series of symbolic names was substituted for the numbers. Hence L could stand for the instruction to load, ADD speaks for itself, DC could represent define constant, and so on. Software inside the computer was programmed to translate these symbolic instructions into the electrical pulses necessary. Assembly language is still fairly stark. To write computer instructions like these is not the most Wordsworthian of activities:

```
L       1,I
DC      F'2'
mov     i,r
ADD     (HL)
```

It is, none the less, much, much easier than programming in machine code.

11.3   Third-generation languages

Although assembly language was a great improvement upon machine language, it was still not easy to use, and each different make of machine used its own brand of assembly language. Thus you could not learn assembly language for an IBM machine and then go and use the same language on an ICL machine. Computer scientists consequently tried to produce languages that were easier to learn and use, and which could be employed on a variety of different machines. The results of these efforts have tended to be called third-generation languages, implying, of course, that machine code and assembly language were first generation and second generation respectively.

There are vast numbers of third-generation languages. Some of the best known are Ada, BASIC, C, FORTRAN, and Pascal. Every one of these languages is different from each of the others, yet they all have certain things in common that indicate that they are all third-generation languages and not machine code or assembly language. Just look at a short section in each language:

Ada

```
DRAW__AXES ( X__ORIGIN =) 500, Y__ORIGIN =) 500,
   X__SPACING =) 10, Y__SPACING =) 10, FULL__GRID =) FALSE,
   X__SCALE =) 1.0, Y__SCALE =) 0.5,
```

BASIC

```
10 OPEN "I", #2, "TRANS"
20 OPEN "I", #2, "ACCOUNTS"
30 OPEN "I", #3, "TEMP"
40 IF EOF (1) THEN T.NO$ = "9999"
```

C

```
#include ⟨stdio.h⟩
# MAXSIZ 50
# NAMSIZ 50
struct bill__count
```

FORTRAN

```
DIMENSION INDATA(10000), RESULT(8000)
EQUIVALENCE (INDATA(1), RESULT(1))
```

Pascal

```
program timestables (output);
var tablenumber, multiplier:integer;
begin
```

None of these extracts will be at all meaningful. Indeed, they are so tiny as to remain meaningless to those who actually understand the languages in question. None the less, all five of them do illustrate how far removed third-generation languages are from machine or assembler code. The latter are called low-level languages, while third-generation languages are referred to as being high level. You might not understand the tiny extracts shown, but you can easily imagine that instruction in the semantics of those languages would lead to programming output that would be a great deal more rapid than could possibly be achieved in first- or second-generation languages. MacLennan (1983, Chapter 1) gives an extract from a program written in the mid-1950s for the IBM 650 computer:

```
1107   46   1112   1061
1061   30   0003   1019
1019   20   1023   1026
1026   60   8003   1033
1033   30   0003   1041
1041   20   1045   1048
```

As you can see, it would be tedious and time consuming to enter into the computer. It was to relieve the tedium and reduce the time that third-generation languages were developed.

We are entirely justified in asking why so many third-generation languages exist. I have cited five above, yet COBOL, which I missed out, is perhaps the most commonly used language of them all. ALGOL-60, LISP, PL/1, and

Smalltalk all have their supporters, and there are dozens of others. Why the plethora? Chantler (1981) comes to a somewhat cynical conclusion:

> Since one of the stated aims of the programmer is to communicate his ideas to others, including machines, it may be wondered why there is not just a single Universal Programming Language. It is obvious that the availability of such a language would vastly simplify the problems of systems implementation, machine replacement, software exchange and so on. And yet, after 30 years of commercial data processing we are still a long way from this ideal. There are many reasons for this: inertia, isolationism, vested commercial interest, inability to accept other people's ideas, etc.

Yet there are substantive reasons as well for the plethora of programming languages. There is a huge variety of things that we need to do with a computer. Processing business letters is a very different task from computing the path of a spacecraft. Monitoring a process of chemical analysis is very different from running a mail-order business. Hence different third-generation languages have tended to be developed in response to different computing necessities. Schofield (1985) concentrates on BASIC, but devotes his sixteenth chapter to alternatives to BASIC. He points out that FORTRAN was devised in order to aid mathematical processing, specifically in astronomy. COBOL came into existence in 1959 with a completely different aim. As Schofield explains: 'COBOL was designed not for calculation but for data processing—the handling of data files.' Indeed the COBOL name is derived from its full title: common business-oriented language. FORTH, a language we have not mentioned before, was also designed for astronomy in order to cope with elements that FORTRAN was unable to handle. In a similar way, Modula-2 developed as an improvement on Pascal. Ada was devised as a general-purpose language for the United States Defense Department. C was devised to write systems software. LISP was developed for work in artificial intelligence, as indeed was PROLOG. PILOT and LOGO were both invented for educational purposes. There is also, as you know, a vast array of hardware constantly being developed and produced. Some languages arose as a way of maximizing the new hardware. Chantler is doubtless correct in his pessimistic conclusion that there will never be a universal, all-purpose programming language, but his cynicism is not an entirely fair attitude. I note that, towards the end of his book, Crystal (1987) provides a table of the world's spoken languages. There are nearly 1000 of them and he admits that most of those with fewer than 10 000 speakers have been omitted. At least computer science has not devised anything like as many artificial languages as the real world has provided us with real ones. And yet there is a possible similarity between the real and the artificial. In linguistic theory, the Sapir–Whorf hypothesis states that the structure of language defines the boundaries of thought. Although this is not proven, there seems little doubt that certain languages can facilitate certain types of thought and impede others. Surely the same is likely to be the case within IT. Indeed, much of the bias against BASIC that is to be found in academic circles is because computer scientists believe that the limitations of BASIC prevent certain aspects of reality being modelled at all. Hence work on databases leads us into the realm of linguistic philosophy! But then, as Flew (1971) asks: 'What other sorts of philosophy are there?'

This section on third-generation languages has been discursive and of apparently slight relevance to databases. I do not, however, believe that to be true. In the first volume of his *Introduction to Database Systems*, Date has a chapter on semantic modelling. Previously in this book I have always quoted from the 4th edition (1986) of Date's work. It is noticeable, however, that the 5th edition (1990) has a considerably expanded version of that chapter. Within it, Date (1990) makes the following comment:

> *Note*: Semantic modeling is also known by a variety of other names (especially when the activity is being carried out in the context of database design for some specific enterprise or application—see later). Other terms that are frequently heard include *data* modeling, *entity/relationship* modeling, and *entity* modeling.

We have already seen that this operation of semantic modelling is highly relevant to the database enterprise. So, within that enterprise, are third-generation languages. Much of the work with a database is carried out within the embrace of a particular third-generation database. Furthermore, much of the discussion of database that this section has contained is highly apposite when we come to look at the types of language that have been specifically devised for database interrogation. Finally, we cannot understand fourth-generation languages without knowing a little about their immediate predecessors, and it is to fourth-generation languages that we must next move.

11.4 Fourth-generation languages

Although third-generation languages were devised (in considerable numbers as we have seen) to facilitate the construction of computer programs, they all suffered from a shared defect. Watt (1987) expresses it as follows:

> All high level languages that are commonly used in business applications are procedure orientated. They lay down a sequence of events which instruct the computer in the task of processing a series of activities sequentially, one after the other, to solve a problem. In this sense, languages are oriented towards the computer's needs rather than the business problem the human wishes to solve.

As Watt goes on to point out: 'The next step in the evolutionary chain was the database management facility.' We know that within that facility, data independence is an important aspiration, and we have seen that it is the relational model that most closely achieves such data independence. It does so in part by a strict emphasis upon the normalization of data within the database. Hence, as the database systems came into existence, the need was often felt to devise a language in combination with the database, a language that was more user friendly than existing third-generation ones and that could be modified with greater ease than COBOL and all its sisters. In other words, a language was needed which could allow the manager of a business to produce applications for his own purposes and change existing applications to suit changing circumstances.

The situation would hence appear to be one of relatively straightforward evolutionary development. First came machine code, then assembler code, then third-generation languages, and finally database systems with an associated fourth-generation language, a language that enabled the user to enter data into the system quickly, devise rapid reports, derive graphs and charts from existing data, contain a data dictionary, and allow immediate access to any and all data fields. Such is, indeed, the ideal, an ideal which the best DBMS contexts come close to fulfilling. Inevitably, however, there has been, and is, a great deal of imprecision and hype associated with the entire area. There are 'database management systems' which exist that fall so far short of the functional imperatives listed in Chapter 7 that they do not deserve to be called database management systems at all. This is particularly true of products purporting to call themselves relational databases. Nor can we rest content with the thought that, when we buy a database, we will automatically gain an entity that will have its own inbuilt fourth-generation language that will cope with all our database management needs. Hence we do need to look at the types of language that have been developed specifically for database management.

11.5 Database languages

Chapter 13 of Martin (1976) is concerned with the different types of database language. Horrifyingly, Martin lists 11 of them:

1. The physical data description language.
2. The schema (logical database) description language.
3. The subschema (programmer's data view) description language.
4. Application programming language.
5. The data manipulation language used by the application programs.
6. The data dictionary.
7. Inquiry facilities.
8. Off-line database report generator facilities.
9. An on-line database interrogation, search and manipulation language.
10. Application program dialogue facilities.
11. Security control facilities.

Forbidding though this list might well appear, it is useful to reproduce it since it provides a good breakdown of the kinds of activity which we need to be aware of within the database field. Nor is the situation quite as dire as the Martin list might suggest. After all, Martin's book was published in 1976, and there has been some considerable consolidation of the situation since then. Sundgren (1985) looks at database management systems and their associated languages. He subsumes them all under the general label of *database language*, and indicates that there are only two basic functions that such a language needs to perform:

1. To define and describe the information in the database.
2. To manipulate that information by adding to it, retrieving it, deleting it or updating it.

Traditionally known respectively as a data description language (DDL) and a data manipulation language (DML), both these functions are often combined in a so-called *query language*. Now there are a considerable number of such query languages. Scheuermann (1982) has, among its contents, five different essays, each one devoted to a different query language. Yang (1986) looks at four relational query languages. Martin (1981) looks at three, though one of them, Query-By-Example, is included among Yang's quartet. Even so, those three books do describe 10 different query languages, and there are many more. However, for our purposes, the situation can be greatly simplified. One query language, structured query language (SQL), has attained an overwhelming preponderance so far as all relational databases are concerned. The hierarchical market is so dominated by IBM's Information Management System (IMS) that we are reasonably justified in confining our attention to data language 1 (DL/1) which is used on the IBM system. Similarly, the CODASYL model is such a standard in the network database field that we can look at the data definition language (DDL) and data manipulation language (DML) as defined within that model. Hence, from the welter of options that would seem to present themselves, we can, without any real distortion, look at just three predominant languages, one for each database model. It is to these that the remaining chapters of this part are devoted. Furthermore, although there are many languages, the purpose that they fulfil is identical in all cases. The DDL defines each element within the data structure for the benefit of the DBMS, and also defines the operations that can be performed against each data element. The DML is a set of commands within the DBMS through which the application program specifies the data that it requires to be retrieved, changed and/or stored. The first of these, the DDL, can be divided into the schema and the subschema. The data to be manipulated by the DBMS is defined in the schema. The subschema describes the application program view of that data, granting the authority to view and update such data as the program uses, preventing the access to out-of-bounds data, and limiting the functions a program can perform against a database. The DML, on the other hand, validates the user's authority to perform a requested operation by examining the subschema definition. Assuming that the request is accepted as a valid one, the DML then forwards that request for data to the DBMS. How the DBMS copes with such requests depends, of course, upon the nature of the data model that it is managing.

However, whatever data model we are concerned with, we do need to be aware of the data dictionary. That provides the final topic for this chapter.

11.6 The data dictionary

As you know, one of the major advantages of a database is that it can be shared by a number of different people simultaneously. For such sharing to be a viable operation, there has to be a means of ensuring that the data they are sharing is correct, nonredundant, and uniform. It would be unhelpful if one user learnt that stock number TB837 was a lathe and for another user to discover that stock number TB837 signified a vice. It would be wasteful if employee names were stored in nine different places. It would be chaotic if the sales department was also known as the marketing department. Hence, to secure such accuracy, nonredundancy and uniformity of description and format, a data dictionary is compiled. In computer jargon, a data dictionary is known as *meta-data*, i.e. data about data.

As we have seen, one of the early steps in designing a database is to collect information about the enterprise with which you are concerned, be it Simeon Grumblethitch's Mozartian organization, Scrape and Blow's music retailing business, the Yorkshire Cricket Club, or a multinational chemical industry. That information will include the usage of various data items, the relationships between those data items or entities, and the meaning of those data items. As we also know, a database can be apprehended at various levels: conceptual, logical, internal and external. Distinctions between those levels, and the connections between them, all have to be noted. It is the data dictionary that serves as the tool for controlling and managing the information about the data in the design, implementation, operation and expansion of the database. Compiling a data dictionary is consequently not a trivial task.

To begin with, data has to be defined. A data dictionary should contain an understandable definition and description of every piece of data. This in itself is far from easy. Different departments within an organization doubtless use identical data from time to time, but there are almost inevitably going to be vocabulary differences among such users or even conceptual differences. One department has a field for the customer's address, and stores in that field the customer's business address. Another department also has a field for customer's address, but stores within it the customer's home address. One department always refers to customers as clients. Should a customer (or client) be stored as J. F. Knowles, John F. Knowles, John Felix Knowles, Knowles, J. F., or KNOWLES, J. F.? Atre (1980), points to 'balance' as a typically ambiguous word. Do you mean opening balance, closing balance, book balance or available balance? It is the data dictionary that would legislate on all such terminological uncertainties.

Secondly, the data dictionary can serve as an overall view of a business's data. In so doing, it can act as a management resource. All too often, the management of a business do not have an adequate corporate view. Indeed, such a view is impossible unless there is a central repository of data to which management can refer.

Of course, to compile a manual data dictionary would be inordinately time consuming and the finished product would still be subject to inconsistent entries. Fortunately, most DBMSs include among their facilities an inbuilt dictionary facility. Even so, it is tedious to compile such a dictionary, but it is a tedium that must be endured. Yourdon (1989) concludes his chapter on data dictionaries with the terse fact that: 'without a formal dictionary that defines the meaning of all the terms, there can be no hope of precision'. Hence, in the information contained in the remaining chapters of this part, remember always that it needs to be linked to the compilation of a data dictionary. Without so doing, chaos can reign. Let me then conclude this chapter by itemizing the basic parts of a data dictionary:

1. Each data item, data element, attribute, or field (to give most of the synonyms) must be described. Indeed, where there are synonyms for a data item, they too must be listed. By so doing, everyone in the company can be aware of the correct terminology used and the proper meaning of that terminology.
2. Where items are logically related to each other, a group data name should be supplied so that the interdependence of the data items is clear. Each member of the group must also be explicitly defined.
3. Often in data processing, data items are produced as the consequence of a formula or calculation. Such elements should be identified together with the items that led to their existence.
4. The data dictionary should distinguish between and relate together the four views of a database: the conceptual model, the logical model, the external model and the internal model.

Of course, there can be more to a data dictionary than these modest functions would indicate. Date (1990) links it firmly with the whole area of semantic modelling. But that is another story which Date must be left to expound for himself.

References

Atre, S. *Data Base: Structured Techniques for Design, Performance and Management*, John Wiley, 1980.

Chantler, A. *Programming Techniques and Practice*, NCC, 1981.

Crystal, D. *Cambridge Encyclopaedia of Language*, Cambridge University Press, 1987.

Date, C. J. *Introduction to Database Systems*, 4th edn, Addison-Wesley, 1986.

Date, C. J. *Introduction to Database Systems*, 5th edn, Addison-Wesley, 1990.

Flew, A. *Introduction to Western Philosophy*, Thames & Hudson, 1971.

MacLennan, B. *Principles of Programming Languages*, Holt, Rinehart & Winston, 1983.

Martin, J. *An End-Users Guide to Data Base*, Prentice-Hall, 1981.

Martin, J. *Principles of Data-base Management*, Prentice-Hall, 1976.

Scheuermann, P. (ed.) *Improving Database Usability and Responsiveness*, Academic Press, 1982.

Schofield, J. *The Guardian Guide to Microcomputing*, Blackwell, 1985.

Sundgren, B. *Data Bases and Data Models*, Chartwell-Bratt, 1985.

Watt, J. *Applied Fourth Generation Languages*, Sigma, 1987.

Yang, C.-C. *Relational Databases*, Prentice-Hall, 1986.

Yourdon, E. *Modern Structured Analysis*, Prentice-Hall, 1989.

12
The IMS and DL/1

As has been mentioned, IBM's Information Management System (IMS) uses a language called data language/1 (DL/1), a language that combines both the data definition role and the data manipulation role. Since IMS is the major hierarchical system, this chapter will be concerned with showing how DL/1 is used as a query language. If your company does not have a hierarchical system or if your university or polytechnic course only gives very cursory attention to the hierarchical model, then you will naturally be tempted to ignore this chapter completely, particularly since we have already glanced at hierarchical databases in Chapter 8. Naturally, no author likes to think that his bejewelled words and masterly presentation are going to be passed over with no regard. I have, however, gutted too many books myself not to be aware that your reading of a book is determined your own personal priorities: the report that you have to prepare by the end of next week, the essay that is due in tomorrow, the fact that the pubs open in 40 minutes' time and so on. I do, none the less, suggest that there will be purpose in your reading this chapter. It will build on the data given in Chapter 8 about the hierarchical model, and in so doing, will extend your understanding of that model. It will enlarge upon the four methods of accessing data that were outlined in that chapter, thus providing you with a fuller technical understanding as to how a computer operates, whatever the data model with which it is dealing. Most importantly of all, perhaps, it will increase your understanding of the network and relational models. Analogies are always dangerous, but no one would come to an understanding of the theory of relativity without first knowing a considerable amount about the Newtonian universe; no one can fully appreciate the music of Wagner without knowing the music of Beethoven; no one can appreciate the concept of chaos in the scientific sense without being aware of the Laplacian dream of deterministic predictability; Picasso and the cubist movement are better apprehended if you know the paintings of Cézanne, and so on. Furthermore, Tremblay and Sorenson

(1984) point out that the concept of hierarchically structuring a problem is a fundamental one in problem solving:

> It is this form of organization or structuring which permits us to understand a system at different levels and allows us to make changes at one level without having to completely understand more detailed descriptions at higher levels. Also important in this hierarchical structuring process is the desirability of being able to understand a module at a certain level independently of all remaining modules at that same level.

Hence having a proper understanding of the hierarchical model is vital for a proper comprehension of the logical framework of IT.

Clearly we cannot illustrate DL/1 in action without having a database. Indeed, part of DL/1's function will be to define that database. In Chapter 8, Scrape and Blow's retailing business was used, so it will be simplest to return to that and see, in outline, how their database would be defined. This is done in IMS by means of the *database description* (DBD). The process of defining a DBD is called a *DBD generation*, except, of course, that computerspeak reigns and consequently DBD generation is normally abbreviated to the unattractive acronym DBDGEN. For every physical database, there has to be a DBDGEN and the first line of our database description has to begin with a name for the entire database:

```
1. DBA   NAME=SCRAPBLO
```

I have observed the convention imposed by many DBMSs, including IMS, that names cannot exceed eight letters.

Having given the database a name, we next move on to defining the tables within that database, though DL/1 refers to them as segments. As you may recall, the root segment suggested for Scrape and Blow's business was Head-quarters. The second row of our data definition would consequently read as follows:

```
2. SEGM   NAME=HEADQUAR, PARENT=0, BYTES=63
```

As you can see, it gives a name for the table, indicates that it has no parent (and is consequently the root node), and gives the number of bytes that the table (or segment) takes up. Of course, the number of bytes that a table comprises is simply the sum of the bytes consumed by the various fields within the row. Hence the DBD will next cite those fields. What are they going to be? The name and address of the company is obvious, as is their telephone number. Hence we provide a field for each of them. This is defined by giving the name of the field, stating how many bytes are needed for storing that field, and finally specifying where, on the disk, that field is located. Since this is the first segment of the database, its first field starts at the beginning, byte number 1. The next field starts at byte number 20 because the first field took up 19 bytes. As you can see, the fields are listed in the following fashion:

```
3. FIELD  NAME=(CONAME, SEQ), BYTES=19, START=1
4. FIELD  NAME=ADDRESS, BYTES=33, START=20
5. FIELD  NAME=TELNO, BYTES=11, START=54
```

The first of the fields has its name enclosed in brackets and is followed by the code SEQ to indicate that this field is to be stored in a set sequence and is, as it were, the primary key of the row concerned. In fact, of course, there is only *one* headquarters, so no sequencing will be possible, but you take the point. In this way, we have defined the data that would appear in the root node of the Scrape and Blow database. That particular segment would appear on the screen of the VDU as:

Scrape and Blow Ltd
19 Norwich Street
DEREHAM
NR19 5PQ

And if that is all Franklin Scrape and Tiberius Blow wanted in their first segment, we would move on to defining the next segment. Note, however, that we have to follow a specific path in our definition of data. You must define the data in its preorder traversal path. If you remember, the Scrape and Blow hierarchy began like Fig. 12.1. Hence the next segment that we define is the one devoted to Shops:

```
6. SEGM  NAME=SHOPS, PARENT=HEADQUAR, BYTES=83
```

Once again, the fields needed in the Shops segment are fairly obvious, and were listed in Chapter 8. Our field definitions consequently appear as follows:

```
 7. FIELD  NAME=(SHOPNO, SEQ), BYTES=2, START=1
 8. FIELD  NAME=ADDRESS, BYTES=50, START=3
 9. FIELD  NAME=TELNO, BYTES=11, START=54
10. FIELD  NAME=MANAGER, BYTES=20, START=66
```

We next move to the first child of the Shops segment (Staff), then the next child (Payroll), and so on. Having defined all the children of the Shops segment,

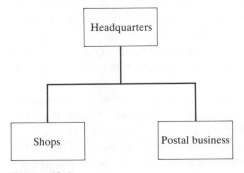

Figure 12.1

the definition moves to defining the segment Postal business, and then on to the children of that segment. The process is fairly straightforward. Here, then, is the physical database of the first four segments for Scrape and Blow:

```
 1. DBA     NAME=SCRAPBLO

 2. SEGM    NAME=HEADQUAR, PARENT=0, BYTES=63
 3. FIELD   NAME=(CONAME, SEQ), BYTES=19, START=1
 4. FIELD   NAME=ADDRESS, BYTES=33, START=20
 5. FIELD   NAME=TELNO, BYTES=11, START=54

 6. SEGM    NAME=SHOPS, PARENT=HEADQUAR, BYTES=83
 7. FIELD   NAME=(SHOPNO, SEQ), BYTES=2, START=1
 8. FIELD   NAME=ADDRESS, BYTES=50, START=3
 9. FIELD   NAME=TELNO, BYTES=11, START=54
10. FIELD   NAME=MANAGER, BYTES=20, START=66

11. SEGM    NAME=STAFF, PARENT=SHOPS, BYTES=96
12. FIELD   NAME=NAME, BYTES=25, START=1
13. FIELD   NAME=ADDRESS, BYTES=50, START=26
14. FIELD   NAME=TELNO, BYTES=11, START=77
15. FIELD   NAME=POSITION, BYTES=10, START=89

16. SEGM    NAME=PAYROLL, PARENT=SHOPS, BYTES=105
17. FIELD   NAME=NAME, BYTES=25, START=1
18. FIELD   NAME=SALARY, BYTES=7, START=26
19. FIELD   NAME=(NINO, SEQ), BYTES=9, START=34
20. FIELD   NAME=TAXRATE, BYTES=3, START=44
```

Of course, if you have examined this DBD with attention, you will have noticed one or two deficiencies. If you haven't, go through it again before reading the next paragraph.

Apart from the fact that it seems to omit a number of essential entities and relationships—Accounts has already been mentioned as a startling absentee—the lack of any named primary key for Staff and the consequent loss of any ordered storage seems very careless. And it is. By this time, however, you should be able to correct this omission with no difficulty. Obviously you cannot use Name as a primary key because of the possibility that more than one member of staff within a shop could have the same name. You would need, therefore, to add a further field to the row, giving each member of staff a unique staff number.

When you have defined all the segments in the ways indicated above, you have completed your definition of the physical database. Within the hierarchical system, however, you now have to go on to define what is called the logical database. This, as you know, is the individual user's view of the database, or section of the database. There can be, as you might readily imagine, a large number of permitted and needed constructs here. Headquarters, for instance, might want to examine the stock of each of their stores in order to assess the respective holdings and the rate of stock movement. The shop in Watton might want to discover whether the local school has ordered anything from Headquarters in recent months. It might be necessary to increase the salary of all managers of the Scrape and Blow shops by 8 per cent. For each one of such actions, you have to define what is called a *program specification block*, an entity that is inevitably referred to as a PSB. The result of the process is called a *PSB generation*, or, equally inevitably, a PSBGEN. Each PSB comprises one or more *program communication blocks* (PCBs).

The process for such definitions is, not unnaturally, very similar to the definition process in a database description. We begin with a first line that indicates that we are constructing a PCB, that the block is of a database type, and then names the database with which we are concerned. Hence the first line would look something like this:

```
1. PCB   TYPE=DB, DBNAME=SCRAPBLO
```

The next lines are likely to name the segments of the database through which we need to traverse. Such segments are referred to as *sensitive segments*, and each line consequently begins with the acronym SENSEG. The segment that we need to travel through is then named, and its parent. By using the PROCOPT parameter, we next indicate what processing option we wish to employ. There are four:

- G for get or retrieval only,
- I for insert,
- R for replace,
- and D for delete.

Imagine then that we wanted to examine the suppliers of the Ipswich store. We define a route through Shops and Suppliers. You will note that, in line 4 of the PCB below, there occurs the acronym SENFLD, standing for *sensitive field*. You may never use SENFLD, but if you do, it has the effect of limiting your access to that specific field. Line 2 of the PCB has indicated that we want to retrieve the Shops segment. However, we only want the Shops segment as an avenue to the Supplier segment. We don't want to bother with reading the address of each shop or finding out who the manager is. Hence, in line 3, we limit our accession of the Shops segment to the primary key only, the Shop number.

```
1. PCB      TYPE=DB, DBNAME=SCRAPBLO
2. SENSEG   NAME=SHOPS, PARENT=HEADQUAR, PROCOPT=G
3. SENFLD   NAME=SHOP_NO, START=1
4. SENSEG   NAME=SUPPLIER, PARENT=SHOPS, PROCOPT=G
```

Assuming that we know the Shop number of each specific store, we can locate the Shop number for Ipswich, and from there proceed to the segment giving us the suppliers of that shop.

Each PSB will comprise a number of PCBs and will close with a **PSBGEN** statement in which the programming language used is named and the PSB itself is given a name. It might be like this:

```
38. PSBGEN  LANG=COBOL, PSBNAME=SONATA
```

And once the DBDs and PCBs have been defined, the database itself can be loaded in, and application programs can be written to manipulate that database.

The precise details of how the DBDs and PCBs interact with the application programs will clearly be slightly different depending upon what language is used in those application programs. If your company uses Pascal or COBOL or whatever, it will not be difficult for you to discover the linkage code that will allow that program to access the DBD and PSBs that you have just defined. As Pratt and Adamski comment: 'What is critical is the process of creating DBDs and PSBs in preparation for manipulating the databases.'

As you can see, the data definition process in IMS can be a prolonged one. I have only given an outline of this process. It does not take a great deal of imagination to realize that, for a full database with a corresponding variety of operations, the process of pure definition within a hierarchical database is an extensive procedure. However, having defined our DBD and PCB, we can begin to manipulate it. The operation is conducted within the framework of the host language used by the particular database concerned. Hence our first line in the data manipulation aspect of DL/1 is going to use the CALL interface. All this means is that you type in the word CALL and then give the host–DL/1 connection. Hence, if your host language is PL/1, the first line begins:

```
CALL PL1TDL1
```

which simply means 'call PL/1 to DL/1'. Thereafter, you manipulate the data required by a series of DL/1 commands. These commands are positively transparent. Indeed, having by this time encountered quite a wide range of computerspeak jargon, DL/1 commands almost affront you by their simplicity. If you want to retrieve a row of data, the key word is GET. It could hardly be more direct! Of course, you can modify GET in various ways:

GET UNIQUE	Retrieve a segment that corresponds to the instructions following the command.
GET NEXT	Retrieve the next segment that follows in the preorder traversal route.
GET NEXT	Retrieve rows within the family of the parent table.
WITHIN PARENT	While GET NEXT will carry on until the end of the database, GET NEXT WITHIN PARENT will stop searching at the rightmost immediate descendant of the parent.

Hence, the three examples above, when applied to the Scrape and Blow database, could read as follows:

```
GET UNIQUE SHOP
GET NEXT SHOP
GET NEXT STAFF WITHIN SHOP
```

Other commands with DL/1 are equally obvious. DELETE, INSERT and REPLACE hardly need any explication. One or two things, however, are worth remembering. DELETE will perform a physical deletion not only of the current record, but also of its descendants. If you do not want this to happen, you can effectively (in a logical sense) perform a deletion by using the REPLACE command instead. If you replace a record with another one, but ensure that the new record has no data within it, then you have effectively deleted the old record while still maintaining all its links to descendants. Note also that, with INSERT you will need to select the parent of the new insertion first of all by means of a GET command, and with REPLACE you will need to set the current record initially with a GET and HOLD command. HOLD is an important command which does need explaining. It simply prevents anyone else from accessing the row or table upon which you are currently working. When you have completed your modification, the holding operation will be automatically released.

By using these commands, you can perform all the necessary database operations. Furthermore, in order to save time and to ensure that, to the outsider, database management remains totally incomprehensible, you can employ abbreviations of the above commands:

```
GET UNIQUE                        GU
GET NEXT                          GN
GET NEXT WITHIN PARENT            GNP
GET HOLD UNIQUE                   GHU
GET HOLD NEXT                     GHN
GET HOLD NEXT WITHIN PARENT       GHNP
DELETE                            DLET
REPLACE                           REPL
INSERT                            ISRT
```

Of course, the actual way in which these commands are performed will depend upon the storage structure of your database. There are two major types, *hierarchic sequential* (HS) and *hierarchic direct* (HD). Each is supported by two access methods, both of which we encountered in Chapter 8:

Hierarchic sequential	HSAM
	HISAM
Hierarchic direct	HDAM
	HIDAM

It is useful to have another brief look at these access methods now that we know just a little about DL/1. In other words, we can refresh our memories about HSAM and the rest within a slightly fuller context than we possessed in our first meeting.

The first, hierarchic sequential access method (HSAM), is very limited indeed and barely deserves being mentioned within a database context. You can only INSERT when the database is being constructed. If you really do need to insert a new item after the database has been constructed, then you have to rewrite the entire database. As for the other operations, only GU, GN and GNP are possible. DLET and REPL calls are not permitted. Nor is this the only restriction. HSAM databases store data in fixed-length rows. In other words, every row of data within an HSAM database is of exactly the same length. Unfortunately, of course, Scrape and Blow failed to establish their shops with this restriction in mind. You can see the sort of disparity that can exist:

Scrape and Blow,	Scrape and Blow,
The Pavilion,	14 High Street,
Cornerbatch Avenue,	DISS,
BURY ST EDMUNDS,	Norfolk.
Suffolk.	

The managers of their shops range from John Hull to Samantha Broadhurston. The musical societies that Scrape and Blow serve range from Ely Bach Club to The Walton-on-the-Naze Operatic and Choral Work Society. Hence, in constructing a database, we have to determine the most efficient storage size for the rows of data within that database. With the best will in the world, however, we are going to have a considerable amount of wasted space. Hence, two adjacent rows of data in the table given over to schools in the Scrape and Blow database could appear as follows, with the wasted space being signified by a series of 0s:

```
SC   DB   West Bergholt Primary School   00000
SC   DB   Holt High School   000000000000000000
```

The codes SC and DB are the segment code and the delete code. The segment code identifies the segment type so that IMS can recognize it. The delete code is entirely irrelevant since deletion is not allowed in HSAM; it is only included so as to make all segments within an IMS context identical. It is, after all, conceivable that HSAM will be the access mode for one database within a company, and that HIDAM (which does allow deletions) is used for another database within the same company. Hence this two-byte prefix to each segment is employed for purposes of compatibility.

HSAM is only used (unless there is no alternative) for data that is kept for historic reasons and is rarely accessed. Its sequential processing makes it too slow for everyday use, its fixed-length segments make it uneconomic, and its inability to accept insertions without recreating the database make it inflexible.

The hierarchical indexed sequential access method (HISAM) is much more acceptable. It does allow both insertion and deletion. It follows from this that not all the database can possibly be stored in strict sequential order. It will, of course, be constructed in strict sequential order, but deletions and additions will alter this. Consequently, by using pointers, HISAM can store segments in an overflow area separate from the primary data set. It not unnaturally follows that a large number of insertions and/or deletions will degrade the performance of the database. Hence, although HISAM is a much more acceptable access method than HSAM, it is still not very convenient for a dynamic database.

The hierarchical direct access method (HDAM) provides fast and direct access to all segments and allows the usage of all DL/1 functions. So too does the hierarchical indexed direct access method (HIDAM). Vasta (1989) shows how each of these access methods operates in IMS, and I do not feel that it is necessary here to go into the sort of detail that Vasta allows himself. Elmasri and Navathe also explain the access methods fairly fully in their twenty-third chapter. What does seem to me to be important is that we understand how the access process can itself be a limiting determinant. HSAM, as we can clearly see, places considerable restrictions upon the user. None the less, even in the more flexible procedures, data independence is not achieved. If, for instance, you need to use many GET NEXT (GN) calls, HIDAM presents you with segments in ascending root key sequence, while HDAM presents them in the sequence in which they are stored. As a result, if you change your access method, you will also probably need to make changes to the application program itself, one of the handicaps that a database system is supposed to obviate. Even more basically, every time that a hierarchy is processed, IMS requires that the first command be a GET UNIQUE (GU), a command that has to start at the root. It is not normally possible within a hierarchical system for an individual segment to be accessed without a hierarchical path being followed for that accession. Nor is the system of having to CALL the programming language without dangers.

IMS does enable you to escape from some of its inbuilt limitations by allowing the construction of secondary indexes. If a key field is not known or if there is a necessity to access data in more than one sequence, it is possible to construct an index to as many other fields as you feel is necessary. While this facility is welcome, there are consequent handicaps. New indexes greatly increase the usage of pointers, and each secondary index also entails additional overhead because it has to be updated every time the source field is added, changed or deleted. The use of secondary indexes can enable the user to escape from some of the restrictions imposed by the hierarchical structure of the database, but such escapes come with an attached cost.

Even with the sketchy glance at DL/1 and at the access procedures that Chapter 8 and this chapter have given, you can now appreciate how IMS is organized. Obviously, you, the user, will be concerned with the application program that you are running: a payroll, a stock inventory, a customer invoice system, or whatever. Your application program will approach the program specification blocks, and will access the one that is specific to itself. If you recall, we illustrated earlier that each application needed to have an individual program specification block (PSB). From the PSB, the relevant program communication block (PCB) is retrieved. That accesses the database definitions, and then, using the appropriate or available access method, the database itself is accessed. Hence we have an internal organization like Fig. 12.2.

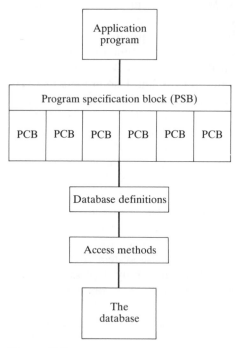

Figure 12.2

I have made little effort to conceal the patent fact that hierarchical databases are clumsy objects. None the less, they are a political and economic fact. IMS in particular is still widely used, though I wonder if it would be quite so prevalent were it not still supported by IBM. DL/1, for which only the briefest of outlines has been provided here, is complicated and difficult to use. Even a small company like Scrape and Blow, who are organized in a conveniently hierarchical fashion, could experience considerable difficulties when one of their postal business contacts also traded frequently with one of their stores. The hierarchical system, when I was writing this sentence, was 23 years old. This, in IT terms, makes it an old-age pensioner. Like many old people, a hierarchical database is still valuable and useful, but, like some old people, it does need considerable care and a great deal of nursing.

Further reading and References

While hierarchical databases are shortly doomed to go onto the scrap heap of history, it is still perfectly possible that you personally, for examination or employment reasons, need to know much more about the hierarchical system than I have provided in Chapters 8 and 12 of this book. I want, therefore, to end this chapter by giving some annotated references to other books. Should you need (or want) to explore the hierarchical database model more fully, then it will be helpful, I hope, to be given some guidance as to useful sources. As always, of course, the list that follows must not be taken as exhaustive. The sources are given in authorial alphabetical order.

S. Atre, *Data Base: Structured Techniques for Design, Performance and Management*, John Wiley 1980, Chapters 4, 6, 8 and 9, pp. 95–109, 163–80, 218–37, 269–73.
   Although Atre's book is quite an old one, there are few better ones for giving a clear breakdown of the essential factors.
D. S. Bowers, *From Data to Database*, Van Nostrand, 1988, Chapter 4, pp. 82–6.
   As you can see, this is an extremely brief treatment. It is a clear and intelligent survey, perhaps ideal for revision purposes.
Malcolm Bull, *Students' Guide to Databases*, Heinemann Newnes 1990, Chapter 8, pp. 156–71.
   This chapter consists largely of diagrams which take up at least half the total space given over to hierarchical databases. Further space is given over to Activities (for which no solutions are suggested). As a result, very little information is imparted.
C. J. Date, *An Introduction to Database Systems*, Vol. I, Addison-Wesley 5th ed. 1990, Appendix B, pp. 753–89.
   This is an appendix specifically on IMS. In the 4th ed. of 1986 it appeared as Chapter 22, pp. 503–40. As always with Date, it is clear and intelligent. It also has the advantage of some excellent questions to which the answers are given.
Ramez Elmasri and Shamkant B. Navathe, *Fundamentals of Database Systems*, Benjamin/Cummings 1989, Chapters 10 and 23, pp. 253–79, 661–704.
   Unlike almost all the other books in this list, Elmasri and Navathe not only look specifically at IMS (in Chapter 23) but also (in Chapter 10) devise their own specimen DDL and DML. They provide a clear and quite full coverage.
R. A. Frost, *Introduction to Knowledge Base Systems*, Collins 1986, Chapter 3, pp. 86–90.
   Hierarchical databases are far from being Frost's centre of interest in this book, but his brief remarks are more thought-provoking than the lengthy chapters of others.

Mark L. Gillenson, *Database Step-by-Step*, John Wiley 2nd edn. 1990, Chapter 10, pp. 188–230.

This strikes me as an excellent chapter. It is particularly good on relationships between segments.

W. H. Inmon and Thomas J. Bird, *The Dynamics of Data Base*, Prentice-Hall 1986, Chapter 11.

Gives a coverage of IMS in this chapter, though I did not find Inmon and Bird very inspiring, particularly for a book which claims to be directed at the uninformed.

Dan Kapp and Joseph F. Leben, *IMS Programming Techniques: A Guide to Using DL/1*, Van Nostrand Reinhold 1978.

If you need a full coverage of DL/1, then this book provides it.

Elizabeth Oxborrow, *Databases and Database Systems*, Chartwell-Bratt 1989, Chapters 3 and 5, pp. 77–81, 161–3.

So brief in its coverage as to add little, and virtually no mention of data definition and manipulation.

Richard C. Perkinson, *Data Analysis: The Key to Data Base Design*, QED 1984, Chapter 10, pp. 169–80.

This has the virtue of being written by an enthusiast for IMS, though I do not find it a masterpiece of clarity.

Philip J. Pratt and Joseph J. Adamski, *Database Systems: Management and Design*, Boyd & Fraser 1987, Chapter 10, pp. 427–64.

Pratt and Adamski are not always as crystal clear as I would have liked, but they do, on the whole, an excellent job.

Naphtali Rishe, *Database Design Fundamentals*, Prentice-Hall 1988, Chapter 6, pp. 255–72.

Full of diagrams but written in telegraphese computerspeak.

Peter D. Smith and G. Michael Barnes, *Files and Databases*, Addison-Wesley 1987, Chapter 11, pp. 281–90.

This coverage is so brief as to add nothing of any real significance to the material contained in Chapters 8 and 12 of this book.

David Stamper and Wilson Price, *Database Design & Management: An Applied Approach*, McGraw-Hill 1990, Chapter 14, pp. 324–31.

A very generalized treatment which, given its brevity, does not add anything of significance.

Tremblay, J.-P. and Sorenson, P. P. G. *Introduction to Data Structures with Applications*, 2nd edn, McGraw-Hill, 1984.

Joseph A. Vasta, *Understanding Database Management Systems*, Wadsworth 2nd ed. 1989, Chapters 4 and 14, pp. 83–112 and 449–72.

A sensible fourth chapter on IMS, clearly expressed, and a full discussion of physical storage in the fourteenth chapter.

Gottfried Vossen, *Data Models, Database Languages and Database Management Systems*, Addison-Wesley 1990, Chapters 6 and 16, pp. 79–86, 301–6.

Vossen admits that, since the hierarchical system is of decreasing importance today, his treatment is very basic. It is even more basic than the one I provide.

Such, then, are a selection of further sources. As you can see, many of them take the attitude that I adopt: namely, that the hierarchical method is so clumsy as to no longer be a viable technique. The world, however, does not necessarily respond to the edicts of computer scientists. As long as companies still find the hierarchical database worth retaining, it will continue to be used no matter how many IT specialists consign it to the lumber room. Hence its appearance in this book; if you need an introduction to the database world, then the hierarchical system must be mentioned. After all, you may need to work with one.

13
Definition and manipulation in the CODASYL context

The hierarchical system was rather like Topsy. If you recall, in Beecher Stowe's novel, *Uncle Tom's Cabin*, there was a little slave girl who asserted that she had neither father nor mother, and, being asked who made her, replied: 'I 'spect I grow'd.' So it was with hierarchical databases. There was no firm theoretical foundation, just applied common sense. There was no attempt at standardization. As a result, each hierarchical database that did develop was anchored to the specific CPU for which it was designed, to the programming language with which it was linked, and to the application programs for which it had been developed. This natural process of just growing does carry with it horrendous problems of conversion whenever some change in the context becomes imperative. Hence, when the Conference on Data System Languages (CODASYL) was established in 1959 to formalize and standardize the programming language COBOL, it carried over this passion for ensuring uniformity when, in 1967, the Data Base Task Group (DBTG) was established. From this, in 1971, there sprang the Data Description Language Committee (DDLC) which was given responsibility for developing a data definition language for the database as an overall entity, defining the sets within the database and the logical relationship between the records (or tables) within a set. At the same time the Programming Language Committee was given responsibility for developing a data definition language for the sets and records as they would be viewed by a user. Thus the role of the DDLC was to establish what is called the *schema* of the database; the role of the Programming Language Committee was to define what is called the *subschema*. In addition, the Programming Language Committee was entrusted with the task of compiling a data manipulation language. It is the purpose of this chapter to outline the nature of these languages.

Before doing so, it is as well to remind ourselves that, although the CODASYL network model was a much more deliberate intellectual creation than the hierarchical model, there are none the less considerable similarities between them. The basic unit of data tends to be called a 'field' in the hierarchical model and a 'data item' in the network, but in both cases it is a single-valued object of interest like name, address and telephone number. Data items (or fields) are linked together in rows of data, called a 'segment' in IMS and a 'record' by CODASYL. The collection of such rows of data devoted to a single entity I have always tended to refer to as a table, but segment and record seem to be applied to the collection of rows as well as to individual rows in IMS and CODASYL usage. Hence this is a segment or record:

| Medoc | Calon Segur | St Estephe | 1979 |

As you can see, it is a row of data showing a wine district (Medoc), a specific wine (Calon Segur), the town of origin (St Estephe) and the year of the wine. A collection of such rows into a complete table is also referred to as a segment in IMS and a record in CODASYL. Regardless of the model, such constructs of tables are fundamental in database design. It is the combination of such tables that constitutes the database. It is irritating that terminological divergences handicap an understanding of databases.

However, let us now have a look as to how data is defined and managed in the CODASYL network model.

13.1   The schema

Let us return to Simeon Grumblethitch and the Mozart Appreciation Sabian Society. The primary reason for so doing is because it provides me with an excuse to listen to Mozart. (I always claim to my wife and children that I have to listen to so much because of the book that I am writing. Fortunately, none of them has yet woken up to the fact that writing this book does not demand that I listen to anybody's music at all.) However, the demands of MASS do provide us with a useful way of illustrating definition and manipulation within a network structure.

The schema definition performs a function similar to a DBD in IMS. The schema name for the MASS database is self-evident:

```
SCHEMA NAME IS MOZART
```

Having given the database a name, we next need to define all the tables (records) within that database. There should be no major surprises here. We are, after all, just defining data in the customary way, and it would, of course, be advisable to observe the rules of normalization. Imagine, then, that Simeon needed a record devoted to Mozart's piano concertos. It seems reasonable to assume that it would be defined as follows:

```
RECORD NAME IS PIANO_CONCERTOS
  K_NUMBER       TYPE IS    CHARACTER 4
  KEY            TYPE IS    CHARACTER 12
  YEAR           TYPE IS    INTEGER
```

So much seems self-evident. The K_NUMBER acts as the primary key to each row, since each piano concerto has one, and only one, K-number, and four characters will be sufficient to store any and all of the K-numbers, even when one encounters oddities like 213a. Twelve characters should be ample for the keys; we are not going to encounter anything longer than B flat minor. Finally, the year of composition will be an integer like 1784. It is all very straightforward.

Of course, because there are a number of network systems, we are going to encounter differences of vocabulary and format. The record above might be defined as follows:

```
RECORD NAME IS PIANO_CONCERTOS
  01 K_NUMBER     PIC X(4)
  01 KEY          PIC X(12)
  01 YEAR         PIC 9999
```

We might also wish to impose some constraints upon the data. For instance, since a K-number is unique, we might want to ensure that uniqueness:

```
RECORD NAME IS PIANO_CONCERTOS
  DUPLICATES NOT ALLOWED FOR K_NUMBER
  K_NUMBER       TYPE IS    CHARACTER 4
  KEY            TYPE IS    CHARACTER 12
  YEAR           TYPE IS    INTEGER
```

In addition, we need to indicate how data is going to be inserted into the database. There are three methods:

- DIRECT
- CALC
- VIA

The first, DIRECT, will just find a vacant space for the data and then give it a database key. The second, CALC, will employ a hashing method, and you can, of course, stipulate that all hash codes have to be unique. The third mode, VIA, allows member records of a set to be located near their owner or near other member records having the same owner. Thus our record definition for piano concertos could appear like this:

```
RECORD NAME IS PIANO_CONCERTOS
  LOCATION MODE IS CALC USING K_NUMBER
  DUPLICATES NOT ALLOWED FOR K_NUMBER
```

```
K_NUMBER      TYPE IS    CHARACTER 4
KEY           TYPE IS    CHARACTER 12
YEAR          TYPE IS    INTEGER
```

There is also the likelihood that one will encounter the mystic entry **AREA NAME IS ...**, but such commands are entirely implementation dependent, whereas the commands and definitions so far provided are valid for virtually all network implementations.

Of course, defining one record is not a strikingly productive achievement. As you know, the basic construct in a network database is the set, so we need to know how to define a set. Since a set comprises two records, we had better construct our second record. Since we have a record for the piano concertos, it seems sensible to have a record which lists performances of those concertos. This time you could construct the record yourself. The first line will be?

[Fill in the missing line]

Then will follow the location mode and any constraints that you care to impose. Finally there will come the list of attributes. This will doubtless entail a duplication of K_NUMBER so as to identify the work in question. Then you will need the name of the soloist, the orchestra and the conductor. Thus the record will be defined, and I am sure that you do not need the formal definition which I now provide:

```
RECORD NAME IS PIANO_CONCERTO PERFORMANCES
 LOCATION MODE IS VIA PIANO_CONCERTO-PIANO_CONCERTO
PERFORMANCES SET
   K_NUMBER      TYPE IS    CHARACTER 4
   SOLOIST       TYPE IS    CHARACTER 25
   ORCHESTRA     TYPE IS    CHARACTER 35
   CONDUCTOR     TYPE IS    CHARACTER 25
```

The only possible surprise in the above is the location mode where I decided to store the record adjacent to the other record, **PIANO_CONCERTOS**, with which **PIANO_CONCERTO PERFORMANCES** makes a set. Note too that duplicates have not been disallowed. There will, for instance, be many performances of K.491. There may even be two different performances of K.491 with the same soloist, orchestra and conductor. Hence, to outlaw duplicates would have prevented the record from giving a full catalogue of the performances available.

As you have seen, we cannot use the location mode VIA without specifying the set to which the record concerned belongs. How, then, do we define a set? The process is again very straightforward. First of all we name the set concerned:

```
SET NAME IS PIANO_CONCERTO-PIANO_CONCERTO
PERFORMANCES
```

then select the owner record for that set. Since it is the piano concerto that forms the centre of this set, it is logical to make it the owner of the set:

OWNER IS PIANO_CONCERTO

It therefore follows that the record **PERFORMANCES** is the member of the set, and we should state this also:

MEMBER IS PIANO_CONCERTO PERFORMANCES

We also need to specify how the two records will be connected in a valid way. Since both records have an attribute in common—K_NUMBER—we can state this:

SET SELECTION IS BY K_NUMBER IN PIANO_CONCERTO = K
NUMBER IN PIANO_CONCERTO PERFORMANCES

Equally, we are likely to need to use the **ORDER** command which specifies the way in which insertions into the database are going to be placed. There are five options:

FIRST The record (or row) concerned is placed at the beginning of the already existing list of records.

LAST The record concerned is put at the end of existing records.

SORTED Records are stored in the order determined by the value of one of the fields within the record.

NEXT Records are placed immediately after the most recently accessed member of the set.

PRIOR Records are positioned immediately before the most recently accessed member of the table.

Clearly, in our current database, it seems most sensible to store the records in an ascending order of K_number. Hence we would need to issue these instructions:

ORDER IS SORTED BY DEFINED KEYS
ASCENDING KEY IS K_NUMBER

Hence, at the end, our **SET NAME** data definition is likely to look like this:

SET NAME IS PIANO_CONCERTO-PIANO_CONCERTO PER-
FORMANCES
 OWNER IS PIANO_CONCERTO
  ORDER IS SORTED BY DEFINED KEYS
 MEMBER IS PIANO_CONCERTO PERFORMANCES
  ASCENDING KEY IS K_NUMBER
SET SELECTION IS BY K_NUMBER IN PIANO_CONCERTO = K_
NUMBER IN PIANO_CONCERTO PERFORMANCES

And, in a similar fashion, we define all our other sets. Having done so, the schema has been defined. There are a number of eventualities that have been omitted in this brief account, but the general nature of the operation has been indicated. We must, therefore, proceed to the subschema.

13.2   The subschema

At any one time, each user of a database almost invariably only wants to use a tiny fraction of the whole. In addition, of course, a specific user may have restrictions as to what particular elements within the database he or she is allowed to access. Consequently, any one occasion of a user accessing the database is likely to involve or concern only a subset of that database.

It follows also that a subschema data definition language is dependent upon the programming language used in the application program. As a result, a subschema designed to be used with COBOL may differ in form from a subschema designed to be used with FORTRAN.

Each subschema can be divided into three elements:

1. The *title*, by which the subschema is given a name and linked with the schema with which it is associated, for example:

   SS SUBSCHEMA_CONDUCTOR WITHIN SCHEMA MOZART

2. The *mapping*, in which any names in the subschema that are different from the names defined in the schema are indicated, for example:

   AD = = K_NUMBER   BECOMES OPUS_NO

3. The *structure*, which itself contains three sections:

   (a) The *realm*, which indicates the area of concern with which this subschema is involved;
   (b) The *record*, in which the records (and fields) to be included in the subschema are listed;
   (c) The *set*, in which the sets to be included in the subschema are also listed.

As has been indicated, the fact that each subschema is linked to the programming language of the application program concerned means that there is not a great deal of point in giving extensive examples of subschema entries, simply because those entries vary so much, depending upon the host language. It is, however, important to see how the creation of subschemas (and there can be a lot of them) does help to provide additional logical independence between the application programs and the schema. We have seen that all a subschema really does is to twist or map the schema into a logical description more suited to the application program in question. Since each subschema normally only accesses a subset of the schema, applications can consequently address the database without having to know the entire schema.

13.3   The data manipulation language

Each application program has a *user work area* that acts as an interface between the application program and the DBMS. What this means is very straightforward. The application program that you are currently running will need, we assume, to update the database in some respect. Hence the application program places the data necessary for this update into the user work area. The application program then asks the DBMS to make the necessary change in the database. Having received this request, the DBMS to make the necessary change in the database. Having received this request, the DBMS places the data needed and any necessary status information into the *user works area*. Only then can the program process these records or modify them in any way. Having done so, the data can then be returned to the database. Hence the user request area is, as it were, a concourse where the data manipulation language (DML) and the DBMS can meet and transact their business. Our primary concern in this section is the DML itself.

By definition, a DML needs to be easy to understand. Hence the DML devised by the DBTG contains common and relatively unambiguous words like READY, FIND, GET, FINISH and so on. Clearly no attempt is going to be made here to teach the DBTG DML, but I do want to give enough information in order to act as a useful background if you do need to manage or use a network database.

The DML is just a tool by means of which you, the user, can navigate your way round the database. Only two things are really essential:

1. You need to know where you are going.
2. You need to know where you are now.

In DL/1, certain commands mark your current position within the database; in the DBTG network version, currency indicators, as they are called, perform the same function. Taking this as read, let us look at the DML itself.

Elmasri and Navathe (1989) divide DML commands into three types: retrieval, navigation and updating. Staniszkis (1990) splits the functions of the CODASYL DML into four types: administration, selection, mapping and update. McFadden and Hoffer (1991) look at data retrieval and what they call data maintenance and control. Again, the verbal differences do not matter a great deal. The commands categorized as administrative by Staniszkis— INVOKE, PRIVACY, OPEN, CLOSE, FREE, KEEP—are not going to be ones accessed by the average user, so we will confine ourselves, as most do, to the more common and updating commands.

Fairly obviously, in order to see any data or to modify it in any way, you have, first of all, to retrieve it. The command for so doing is simplicity itself:

GET

It does remind me of throwing a stick for the dog to retrieve—'Get, Rover'—

but it is a great deal quicker to type GET than it would be to enter the request, 'Excuse me, database, but could you possibly retrieve for me ...?

Obviously, the DBMS cannot get anything unless it already knows where it is. Hence the GET command is normally preceded by the FIND command. There are two common variants of the FIND command:

1. FIND ANY will locate the first row or record of the database that you specify after the command.
2. FIND NEXT will find the next row or record that satisfies the criteria that you set.

Let us have a look at some instances of this.

We will assume that Simeon Grumblethitch wishes to refresh his mind as to the cast list of Mozart's first opera, *Apollo et Hyacinthus*. He recalls that the operas have been stored in ascending order of Köchel number. Hence, if he wishes to look at the first one, he can use the ANY parameter. Simeon consequently types the following:

```
FIND ANY WITHIN OPERA
```

This command will accordingly find the first row within the Opera record. It will, however, do nothing else. It will not tell that it has found the required row and it will certainly not display it on the screen. For that to happen, you use the GET command:

```
GET OPERA
```

Hence, a FIND followed by a GET performs the same sort of function as a GET UNIQUE or a GET NEXT.

Strictly speaking, of course, no commands at all will work until you have indicated that you wish to enter the database. This is done by the command READY, and it is necessary to indicate what sort of operation, retrieval or update, you wish to perform upon that database. Hence, if Simeon just wants to look at the first record in his Opera table, the commands that he will issue will be as follows:

```
READY: USAGE MODE IS RETRIEVAL
FIND ANY WITHIN OPERA
GET OPERA
```

As a consequence, the first row of the Opera record will be placed in the user work area (UWA).

Of course, there are many more options than those mentioned so far. Commonly, in most implementations, you will be able to use the following FIND commands:

```
FIND NEXT  ... WITHIN ...
FIND FIRST ... WITHIN ...
```

```
FIND PRIOR ... WITHIN ...
FIND LAST ... WITHIN ...
FIND OWNER WITHIN ...
```

Followed by the appropriate GET command, you can consequently retrieve the item or items that you wish to see.

Naturally you are unlikely to confine yourself merely to retrieving data. You will, of course, need to modify this data. The operation is simple enough. You FIND the necessary row of data, move it into the UWA by means of the GET command, indicate the kind of alteration that you wish to make, and then issue the MODIFY command. We will imagine that you wish to give all your employees a salary rise of 10 per cent. The sequence will look something like this:

```
FIND ANY EMPLOYEE;
 GET EMPLOYEE;
 EMPLOYEE. SALARY := (EMPLOYEE.SALARY *1.1);
 MODIFY EMPLOYEE:
 FIND NEXT EMPLOYEE
```

Other useful key words or command words are cited in the following short list:

STORE Creates a new record or row.
ERASE Deletes a record.
CONNECT Places a data item within a name set.
DISCONNECT Removes a data item from a set but still keeps it within the
  database.
RECONNECT Moves a row from one set to another.

Hence, with the retrieval commands FIND and GET, and the update commands listed above, you can perform most of the database management that you are going to need.

Even so, the query language commands within the DBTG system often turn out to be quite lengthy. I have glided over such concepts as current record and currency indicators, but they do matter when dealing with the CODASYL DML. As in a hierarchical query language, a network query language is relatively low level in that it searches for and retrieves a single record (or row) at a time. Furthermore, you need to use a customary programming language like COBOL or Pascal, and to embed the DML commands within that language. Nor does the CODASYL system have the uniformity at which it originally aimed. While most commercial network systems do follow the standards of the 1971 report, there have been supplementary reports since then: 1973, 1978 and 1981. Some current network systems therefore incorporate some of the recommendations subsequent to 1971. Hence, despite its undoubted speed, the network system can be encountered in a confusing diversity. Nor can its speed of operation always be taken for granted. Both the hierarchical and network systems are structured with inbuilt associations. Thus, in a network set, there is an inbuilt association between the owner and members within that set, just as there is an inbuilt association between parents and children within a hierarchical database. Processing can be extremely rapid when it entails such an inbuilt association, but accesses based on relationships that have not been designed into the structure can be extremely slow. Nor is it easy to modify the structure of the database itself by, for instance, adding an entirely new record (or table). Network systems are more flexible than hierarchical ones, but they and their query languages cannot match the ease of manipulation provided by the relational database.

This glance at the DDL and DML of the CODASYL system has been extremely cursory. I shall not provide page references for further reading, however, because the references provided at the end of Chapter 12 should enable you to consult any of those books cited with little effort, since material on the network model in those books is normally adjacent to material on the hierarchical model. If you need to consult a book devoted entirely to the CODASYL approach, then Olle (1978) can be recommended. Furthermore, while the network model is still extensively used, it too is becoming of largely historical interest. We have already seen that, structurally, the relational database is a great deal simpler and more flexible than its hierarchical and network peers. In terms of query language interaction, it is also greatly to be preferred, as we shall see in the next chapter.

References

Elmasri, R. and Navathe, S. *Fundamentals of Database Systems*, Benjamin Cummings, 1989.

Deen, S. M. (ed.) *Practical Database Techiques*, Pitman, 1990.

McFadden, F. R. and Hoffer, J. A. *Database Management*, 3rd edn, Benjamin Cummings, 1991.

Olle, T. W. *The CODASYL Approach to Data Base Management*, John Wiley, 1978.

14
SQL, query languages and relational databases

I have attempted to keep the chapters of this book on the brief side. It is easier to absorb something if the element concerned does not weary one with undue prolixity. None the less, this chapter is considerably longer than any of its predecessors. With IMS and CODASYL I was only concerned to give a taste of the data definition and data manipulation languages concerned. If this book is to make any real pretence at being an effective introduction to the database world, then it must cover the hierarchical and network data models and their respective languages. None the less, the relational data model is, for most purposes, superior to its two rivals, and the major relational language, SQL, consequently merits a fuller coverage that DL/1 or NDL (the network database language). Even so, I am not attempting to give a full coverage of SQL, but SQL is a vital tool, and I also want in this chapter to tie together the entire topic of database languages, hence its length. I have, however, subdivided it into four broad sections, so each section can be regarded as a minichapter of its own. The first section, 'SQL in context', tries to place SQL within the broad range of query languages and, more specifically, tries to evaluate its effectiveness as a relational tool. The second section looks at the language itself and provides an outline of its definition and manipulation functions. I must also admit that this chapter owes a good deal to my section on SQL in my INGRES book (Rothwell, 1992). Obviously the book on INGRES does touch on many of the aspects more fully covered in this book, but only in this chapter is the borrowing overt.

14.1 SQL in context

14.1.1 THE NATURE OF QUERY LANGUAGES

It should be evident that the nature and scope of the functions that we can perform on data is conditioned directly by two factors:

1. The nature of the database itself.
2. The nature of the query language used.

Let us, therefore, before turning specifically to the most widespread query language of them all, SQL, consolidate our understanding of query languages in general.

An interface A query language is a connection between the DBMS and the user. The object of the exercise is to make life easier for the user. Quite often this is done by making the query language itself virtually invisible to the user. Instead of having to type in queries and commands, the user is presented with a menu comprising a series of options. By moving the cursor to the required option, the user achieves his or her object without having to use any language at all, though what in fact has happened is that the menu selection has generated a query language statement without the user being aware of it. There are occasions also where the so-called function keys will perform exactly the same sort of service. If you want to save a document, for instance, all that you have to do is to press one of these function keys, and the command will be obeyed. The function keys themselves are normally placed as the top row of the keyboard or as a separate range of keys on the right-hand side of the keyboard.

It was pointed out in Chapter 11 that query languages were nonprocedural. If you recall, this means that the user only has to state *what* is required, but does not, at the same time, have to tell the computer *how* to accomplish the request. Burstein (1986) even exclaims that:

> The beauty of databases really comes into play here, because the user need not have the slightest idea of the storage medium being used for the data item, how the data item's fields are defined, the hashing technique used, the relation of the data item to other data items, and so on.

Hence, in IMS, it is much easier to state GET NEXT SHOP than it is to tell the computer which track of which disk contains the data for the next shop.

When you are seated at the keyboard gazing reverently up at the screen, it is easy to imagine that the query language is in charge. After all, you type a command like

FIND CUSTOMER VIA CUSTNAME USING CUSTOMER-NAME

and, more or less, you gain the information required. The query language appears omnipotent. Do not be misled. The query language is just an interface. It tells the DBMS what it is that you want doing, and it is the DBMS that then goes away and does it. The query language itself has no idea how to find a customer's name (or anything else). Nor is the query language a programming language in the way that Modula-2 or Pascal are; they are more procedurally oriented than a query language. You can, of course, have a query language linked in a kind of partnership with a programming language, but the two objects are different and distinct.

Furthermore, because query languages are designed to make life easy for the user, their vocabulary is much nearer to standard English than any third-generation language. It has even been claimed that SQL, the major subject of this chapter, has a flow like ordinary English. That depends, I suppose, upon the quality of your everyday English, I admit that I rarely write or speak like this:

```
EXEC SQL
  DECLARE CAPTAINS CURSOR FOR
  SELECT  PLAYERNO, NAME
  FROM    PLAYERS
  WHERE   PLAYERNO IN
          (SELECT  PLAYERNO
           FROM    TEAMS);
```

I doubt if you do either. None the less, the common usage in query languages or words like RETRIEVE, DROP, INSERT and UPDATE does make them much more approachable (and easier to learn) than most third-generation languages, let alone assembler or machine code.

The final interface function that demands a mention is the speed with which a query language operates. If Hetty Freezer wants to know how many bassoons are in stock at Harwich, she is not going to be best pleased if she has to wait most of the afternoon for the answer to appear upon the screen. Fortunately, all query languages operate interactively. The commands you give or the questions you ask can normally be dealt with in a matter of seconds.

The dual query role   You are already well aware that a query language performs two basic functions:

1. It defines data.
2. It manipulates data.

In the first function, it helps to create the data structures that the relational system requires. Thus, if you wish to create a database, you begin with a command like CREATEDB. If you wish to alter an item within the database, you use a word like AMEND. Thus a query language like SQL plays a vital role in the creation of the database itself, the tables within that database, and the index of indexes associated with the database. Secondly, of course, a query language allows us to SELECT data or to UPDATE it or to DELETE it. Indeed, it is within data manipulation that you will most frequently encounter SQL. After all, you only define the data once; thereafter, for the entire life of the database, you will be manipulating it.

Sayles (1989) suggests that query languages also perform a data control function. He argues that when you force an order number to comprise eight digits or when you prevent an employee in Plymouth from accessing data relevant only to the Birmingham branch, you are in fact performing a data control function. Most people would, I think, take this as just another example of data manipulation, but the issue is not worth a semantic quibble.

The level of query languages It is obvious that a query language is a high-level language. It is nonprocedural, in that you just issue the command:

```
SELECT    town
FROM      addresses
WHERE     town='Norwich'
```

without worrying about how that command is going to be obeyed. It is high level too in that its vocabulary is so accessible.

As Gardarin and Valduriez (1989) point out: 'All nonprocedural languages have four basic operations.' They are as follows:

1. To retrieve rows of data or attributes from rows of data.
2. To insert new data into a table.
3. To destroy existing data within a database.
4. To change or modify existing data within a database.

Yet, although QUEL and QBE (two effective query languages) can perform all these functions perfectly adequately, it is SQL which has attained a dominant position among query languages. It would be as well, then, to look now at its origin and nature.

14.1.2 THE EMERGENCE OF SQL

IBM was one of the earliest organization to realize that the relational model held the seeds of the future. Hence they initiated a major research effort into a relational DBMS in 1975, an effort which led, in 1979, to the emergence of System R, a complete prototype for a relational DBMS. Linked with System R was a unified language for relational database management. This structured query language was eventually to be known by the unavoidable acronym SQL.

In fact, SQL was a development of an earlier version called SEQUEL, and many people still refer to SQL by its earlier name. While this seems to me merely to confirm that computer scientists have a passion for terminological confusion, it need not delay us here. None the less, the emergence of SQL from SEQUEL (1974), SQUARE (1975) and SEQUEL2 (1976) gives some indication of its checkered emergence, and although the label SQL was fully accepted by 1980, this was by no means the end of the story. It became clear that SQL should be formalized, that a standard version should be codified so as to estblish a uniformity in its usage. The International Organization for Standardization (ISO) did this in 1986, but, in the same year, work began on a successor to SQL, called, unimaginatively but unambiguously, SQL2. So far as I know, this has not yet been standardized, though its being so was anticipated for the early 1990s. Indeed, Gorman (1991) firmly states that: 'the SQL2 project will be technically complete during the first half of 1991, and become an ANSI standard by late 1992, . . .'. We will see.

Meanwhile, while IBM was developing their System R, the University of California was producing INGRES, another relational database. The language that they developed for this database was known as QUEL. Date (1987) clearly regards QUEL as a better language than SQL. Why then did SQL triumph, so much so that INGRES, while it still supports QUEL, has also embraced SQL so that either language can be employed in defining and manipulating the database?

It has to be admitted that the fact that SQL has become the standard language for all relational databases owes a great deal to IBM. Emerson, Darnovsky and Bowman (1989) begin their first chapter with the words: 'In the beginning was IBM, and IBM created SQL.' At the time (1975–79), the dominance of IBM was greater than it is today (and it is still massively significant). Hence, anything that IBM developed was bound to become a de facto standard. In addition, although SQL has its defects, it is, at least in part, a relational language. Pascal (1989) states that: 'It is the relational nature of SQL that has propelled it as the language of choice for connectivity.' It is also a portable language; it can be used, with little change, in a variety of differing contexts. Finally, and most important from the user's point of view, it is a very accessible language. It is easy to learn and easy to understand. Regrettably, although it has been standardized since 1986, there are still many different implementations of SQL. Date (1987) noted that there were more than 50 systems supporting SQL, but each had its own individual variations. Hence SQL, standard though it may be, has not managed to avoid the multiplication of versions any better than the CODASYL query language did.

14.1.3 THE RELATIONAL QUALITIES OF SQL

Codd originally laid down 12 criteria by means of which we could judge how relational or otherwise a database really was. By returning to Codd's criteria, we can estimate how fully SQL lives up to its claim to be a relational query language. Let me just outline these original 12 criteria, commenting upon SQL's observance or nonobservance of the criterion where this is relevant:

1. In a relational database, the data must be organized as values in tables, each table being composed or rows and columns.
2. The values contained within such tables must be retrievable by means of specifying the relevant table name, the primary key value and the column name. In fact, SQL does not always insist on this criterion being observed with sufficient rigour.
3. Codd argued that null values should be supported in exactly the same way as normal values, though SQL does not always observe this rule very consistently.

4. As you know, a proper database consists not only of the data to be managed but also of a data dictionary (or system table or system catalogue). This data dictionary is meta-data, i.e. data about data. In a relational system, the system tables should be handled in exactly the same way as the user tables are. Hence, for the base tables created by the user and the system tables created by the DBMS, there should be a uniform mode of access. As it happens, most implementations of SQL seem to support this rule fully, though the ANSI standard for SQL seems to ignore this factor completely. Nor does van der Lans (1989) raise the issue.

5. Codd confirmed that a full relational system should have a sublanguage which could cope with six functions:

   (a) Data definition.
   (b) Data manipulation.
   (c) View definition.
   (d) Integrity constraints.
   (e) Means of checking the authorization of users.
   (f) Means of aiding in recovery procedures.

   SQL can deal with all six of these.

6. If it is logically possible to update a data item, then the database should permit such an update, though the DBMS needs to have the ability to validate (or deny) any proposed update.

7. A relation within a database should be capable of being inserted, updated or deleted as a single command.

8. The physical location of data upon the disk should be completely irrelevant to the user. Logical operations upon that data should remain unaffected, despite physical changes in the location of that data. This ruling does seem to be generally observed.

9. Changes within the tables of data should not affect the running of application programs.

10. Constraints designed to ensure the integrity (or consistency) of the database should not affect application programs in any way.

11. A query language should work within a distributed database just as effectively as it works within a centralized database. There is, perhaps, still too little documentation for any firm conclusions to be drawn under this heading. As Chapter 18 on distributed databases indicates, this is still an area where standards are emerging rather than established.

12. No alteration to the database should be possible if that alteration violates the overall rules imposed by the relational language being used.

These, then, are the 12 rules laid down by Codd. SQL certainly does not adhere to them all. There seems to be general agreement that SQL observes five of the Codd rules completely and another three in part. This is a better adherence to the Codd criteria than most other products can offer, and it would seem plausible to believe that SQL2 will extend that adherence. Certainly, however, the acceptance of SQL by IBM, the portability and user accessibility of SQL, and its adherence to most of the relational criteria have given it a query language dominance that seems unlikely to weaken. Hence it is to the language itself that we must next move.

14.2 The language itself

14.2.1 DATA DEFINITION

Before you can begin to create a database or anything else under SQL, you will have to 'log on', or, in other words, identify yourself to the computer system as an authorized user. Normally this is done by you entering at the keyboard your user name, ROTHWELL for example. You will then be asked for a password, and you will, of course, enter the password which you earlier informed the computer that you would be using. Of course, you cannot log on to the system unless the database administrator has earlier accepted you as a valid user and has informed the computer system of your name and status. You may approach a computer terminal with the clearest of minds, impressive relation database scholarship, and an expert knowledge of SQL. None of these admirable attributes will be of the remotest relevance to the computer. All that concerns it is that you are allowed to enter the system at all. If you are not, then having read and understood this book so far is quite irrelevant.

However, I shall assume that no such problems confront you. You are seated at your terminal and are anxious to create your database so that you can begin manipulating it. As we have already discovered, there is no universal SQL implementation, and there can be variations between systems. Indeed, there is no ANSI command for creating a database and various implementations create their own 'solution'. Some like dBASE IV SQL and Informix, have taken the most obvious course. If you want to create a database within such contexts, you issue the command CREATE DATABASE and follow it with the proposed database name:

```
CREATE DATABASE icecream
```

INGRES is almost as obvious, merely opting for an abbreviated version of the above:

```
CREATDB icecream
```

The ANSI standard does not seem to recognize the existence of databases at all. Instead it has the command CREATE SCHEMA, which can be a way of combining several tables under one umbrella, i.e., a database

```
CREATE SCHEMA icecream
```

Van der Lans (1989) states that an entire database can contain many schemata, though he provides no further elucidation of this.

Oracle does not seem to recognize the existence of databases either, though it too allows sundry tables to shelter under the umbrella of what it calls a 'cluster':

```
CREATE CLUSTER icecream
```

However, what all systems seem to agree upon is that a relational system is bound to comprise tables. Hence all implementations contain the command CREATE TABLE. Indeed, as you know, tables are the basic building blocks of the relational universe. Hence we do need to make sure that we grasp fairly fully this most essential of data definition usages.

We will imagine that we have created a database entitled 'icecream'. You are the owner of this business which consists of a number of vans that tour the town of Market Prune (population 946 719). Each van is allocated an area of the town which it dutifully covers during a week. Hence our first table is devoted to data concerning the drivers of these vans, the salespeople of our icecream:

```
CREATE TABLE salespeople
```

Having told the DBMS that we are about to create a table, we now need to specify each column within that table, indicating in each case what type of data will be entered into that column. We will need, for instance, a primary key for our Salespeople table. Employee number seems a sensible choice:

```
empno   char(5) not null unique,
```

Thus we name the column, state that it will comprise five characters, that it is not possible to enter a null value, and specify that each value in this column must be unique. In so doing, we ensure that no duplicate rows are ever included, and since we are going to use empno as the primary key, that no row is ever created without an employee number being included in that row. Indeed, the integrity rules NOT NULL and UNIQUE are tested directly after the execution of each relevant SQL statement, and any violation of those commands will ensure that the statement is rejected by SQL.

Unfortunately, although the empno row definition at which we have just looked corresponds to the ANSI standard, actual implementations of SQL are less rigorous. It is not normally possible to use the UNIQUE parameter when defining a table. Ironically, it is possible to use that command when defining an index. Hence, if you want to ensure that a field within a row is unique, and that no duplicates are ever allowed, you have to cite the UNIQUE command when creating the index to the table. Clearly doing so will have the same effect as using the command during the creation of the table itself, and it seems a curious and circumlocutionary way of having to go about it. It is to be hoped that SQL2 will remove this quaint illogicality.

Obviously, having given our salesperson a unique employee number, we need now to list his or her name:

```
surname     char(20),
firstname   char(15),
```

Such an entry is virtually self-evident. Nor, of course, does it matter a great deal if your icecream business has two Fred Smiths or two Mary Jones, since they will respectively have different employee numbers.

Each of your salespeople is allocated an icecream van, and each van has its own specific area to cover. Hence we also need a field indicating for which area this particular salesperson is responsible:

```
area    integer not null unique,
```

Since you decided to give each area of the town a number, it seems simplest to give this field an integer data type. However, since no salesperson can be without an area to cover, it seems sensible to make it a not null field, and, since no sales person can cover more than one area, it seems equally sensible to render this field a unique one.

Finally, as you know only too well, salespeople come and go. It will be useful, therefore, for the table to contain a field indicating the date upon which the salesperson joined your company:

```
datejoined   date,
```

As you can see, this enables us to use a third data type. Most implementations have a default format for the representation of that date. Informix shows the date as 14–10–92. Oracle represents it as 14–OCT–92. The British version of dBASE SQL had 14/10/92. INGRES has a variety of formats, including all three of the types already shown. In addition, most relational databases, apart from having date as an individual data type of its own, like char and integer, also have special date functions for determining the interval between two dates, or for adding and/or subtracting a given amount of time to and/or from a date.

We have, then, created our first table in our relational database. The complete entry would be set out as follows:

```
CREATE TABLE salespeople
 (empno   char(5) not null unique,
  surname      char(20),
  firstname    char(15),
  area     integer not null unique,
  datejoined   date);
```

Differing implementations may have slightly differing ways of indicating the data types. A character string can be signified, as it is above, by the abbreviation 'char', though char might signify a fixed-length field. If you wanted more flexibility, you may need to use 'vchar', standing for variable-character field. Again, both of those could be further abbreviated to 'c' and 'vc'. Equally 'integer' can be abbreviated to 'int' or 'i', and some implementations have ways of specifying the range of integer with which you are concerned:

integer1 represents − 128 to + 128
integer2 represents − 32 768 to + 32 767
integer4 represents − 2 147 483 648 to + 2 147 483 746

There are also a variety of other data types used within SQL. Most of them are numeric ones like SMALLINT, FLOAT, REAL and DOUBLE PRECISION, though there is also a Money data type, which in most implementations, does allow the representation of various currencies.

Obviously, in defining a real database, we would be concerned to define many tables, possibly also some views, and, certainly, indexes to those tables and views. The procedure is normally reasonably straightforward. Let us imagine that we wanted to create a view to show us how many, if any, of our salesforce had been working for us since 1988. The view would be defined as follows:

```
CREATE VIEW LONGSERV
SELECT *
FROM EMPLOYEE
WHERE datejoined=1988
```

The line SELECT * indicates that we want all the data from the table, subject, of course, to the condition expressed in the WHERE line.

Creating an index is not something that standard SQL explicitly allows, nor, apparently, are there any plans to include it in SQL2. None the less, most databases do make such a provision, and its format is normally fairly common-sensical. You set up an index with the most obvious of commands:

```
CREATE INDEX
```

Clearly you need to give this index a name, a name that will relate to the column of the table which you wish to index. Thus, if you wanted to construct an index for our salespeople table, the most obvious column upon which to create that index would be surname, particularly since you would be able to remember the names of your icecream salespeople but might not remember their employee numbers. Creating an index on name would consequently speed up access to the employee number and all the other salesforce data. All that you have to do is to give the index itself a name, specify the table concerned, and then, in brackets, the column of that table which is to be indexed:

```
CREATE INDEX name ON salespeople (surname)
```

Of course, there is no reason why you should not create an index on more than one column value. Thus you could, in one command, create indexes on two or more columns of the salespeople table:

```
CREATE INDEX namearea ON salespeople (surname, area)
```

You could, indeed, create indexes for every column in every table in the entire database, but to do so would be absurd. Every time that you create an index, you are taking up space and consuming more time. Hence it only makes sense to create indexes for attributes or values that are commonly accessed. Indeed, since our imagined icecream database is so small, it does not make a great deal of sense to create any indexes at all. When the system searches an unindexed column, it does so by looking at each row, one by one. Since our icecream database has few tables, each of which will only have about nine rows, creating indexes would be foolish. When, however, a table has hundreds of thousands of rows, an index becomes indispensable, and it is consequently vital that you are aware of the facility of creating them.

In glancing at the creation of databases, tables (and views) and indexes, we have virtually completed the data definition functions with which we need to be concerned. One other command certainly needs to be mentioned. While we often need to create tables and the database within which those tables rest, we also from time to time need to destroy such tables, or, indeed, an entire database. The operation is simplicity itself. To destroy a database, we use the word DROP followed by DATABASE and the name of the database concerned:

DROP DATEBASE icecream

It is the same for destroying a table:

DROP TABLE salespeople

To destroy an index, we just follow the command with the name of the table and the name of the index itself:

DROP INDEX salespeople, namearea

Thus, with three short and simple commands, you can obliterate months (even years) of painstaking work. Fortunately, most systems do try to prevent your indulging in random destruction. Some systems will only allow the database administrator to destroy data. Others will, when you issue the command DROP, flash up a concerned query:

Are you sure that you want to drop this table?

Yet, whatever safeguards the system employs, mistaken destruction still takes place. There may, even so, still be ways of salvation available, but I can only recommend with the utmost force that you never put the system to the test. *Never use the DROP command* until you have consulted with the database administrator, the managing director, the entire computing staff, had three cups of tea and taken a five mile reflective walk. Even then, do ensure that you have a copy on tape of the database and/or tables that you are about to destroy.

There is another command that is fractionally less destructive than the DROP command. This is the DELETE command which enables you to remove all the data from a table of a database but still preserve the structure of that table or database. However, since an entirely empty table or database is not a great deal of use, you should employ exactly the same safeguards in using DELETE as you would when using DROP.

Having created your database and its component tables, and having learnt how to destroy those artefacts, you have virtually completed the data definition facilities necessary. It is, of course, occasionally necessary to alter a table (or database) that you have already created. You might, for instance, wish to add another column to a table or destroy a particular column. Again, very oddly, standard SQL provides no means of so doing, but most implementations of a DBMS do by providing the ALTER command. Its implementation is fairly obvious. You just use the keyword ALTER followed by the entity that you wish to alter: DATABASE, TABLE or VIEW. You then give the name of the database or table concerned. Hence, if you wanted to alter our salespeople table, the command would read as follows:

ALTER TABLE salespeople

Naturally you need to indicate what sort of alteration is going to be made. There are only two possibilities: ADD or DROP. After the action word, you cite the relevant column name, and, if adding a new column, the data type of that column. Hence, if you wanted to remove the column 'datejoined' from the table, you would issue this command:

ALTER TABLE salespeople DROP datejoined

If you wanted to add a new column called 'd_o_b' date (standing for date of birth), you would issue this command:

ALTER TABLE salespeople ADD d_o_b date

Obviously, you cannot add a new column to a table by giving the new column a name that has already been used for an existing column within that table. Nor can you remove a column from a table if it is the only column that exists within that table. Apart from such restrictions, the ALTER command is, as we have seen, very easy to handle. There are, of course, various differences in differing implementations, but they are easy enough to learn as you encounter the systems concerned.

With CREATE, DROP and ALTER, we have completed the data definition commands of SQL, though the last is not strictly part of SQL at all. Clearly, data definition is an integral and vital aspect of database communication; without having created a database in the first place, there would be nothing to handle. None the less, most of your time and energies are employed in manipulating the databases that you have created, and it is to this aspect of SQL that we must next turn.

14.2.2　DATA MANIPULATION UNDER SQL

While there are only two or three commands that we need be concerned with in data definition. SQL has at least 12 manipulating commands. To cover them all would be absurd here. All that will be attempted is a partial glance at some of the more frequently used commands. There are a number of excellent books that do cover SQL in full, none the less, the outline that is provided here will serve for most people under most circumstances, and, more importantly, will guide you in using not only SQL but any other query languages as well.

Obviously, once you have created a database, you are going to want to retrieve elements from that database. You may just want to check an entry. You may need to alter an item. You may even need to delete something. Not infrequently, you will want to compare something from one table with something else from another. Whatever the operation may be, the most common command word that you will required will be SELECT. If you know, in SQL, how to use SELECT, then the bulk of your learning has been completed. Hence it is at this vital instruction that we first look.

SELECT   Van der Lans (1988) devotes 111 pages to the SELECT operation alone. Furthermore, I entirely agree with Emerson et al. (1989) when they begin their fourth chapter with the following words:

> In many ways, the SELECT statement is the real heart of SQL. It lets you find and view your data in a variety of ways. You use it to answer questions based on your data—how many, where, what kind of, even what if. Once you become comfortable with its sometimes dauntingly complex syntax, you'll be amazed at what the SELECT statement can do.

Just so. Yet even so, there is an element of oversimplification here. The SELECT command is entirely useless by itself. A moment's reflection will indicate to you that any SELECT command in SQL demands two parameters. Obviously there has to be the basic SELECT instruction itself:

```
SELECT ...
```

The keyword is then followed by the attribute or attributes that you wish to select:

```
SELECT name, salary
```

or

```
SELECT Supplier_no, Tel_no
```

Self-evidently, though, such a command is entirely useless by itself. A DBMS cannot be told to select anything without also being told from which source it needs to obtain the data. Consequently, the SELECT command *always* needs to be followed by the FROM instruction. Hence the two commands just given would be effective if they actually read as follows:

```
SELECT name, salary        SELECT Supplier_no, Tel_no
FROM [name of table];      FROM [Name of table];
```

The DBMS will only select attributes if it is also told from which table those attributes are to be garnered. Hence it is the SELECT and FROM construct that is our basic framework.

Still within this basic framework, we can insist on one or two further conditions being obeyed. If, for instance, we wanted to know what operas

Simeon Grumblethitch had on record or tape, but were not interested in knowing what different recordings he had of the same opera, we would issue the command:

```
SELECT DISTINCT opera
```

As a result, we would learn that he did have a recording of *The Magic Flute*, but we would not learn that he had three different recordings of the same opera. The DISTINCT command excludes all repetitions.

Conversely, we might occasionally need to insist that SQL really did give us every instance of an attribute even if that entailed considerable repetition. In fact, by default, SQL will give us all the mentions of a named attribute unless it is countermanded by DISTINCT. If you want to make absolutely sure of this, you merely need to issue the instruction:

```
SELECT ALL
```

followed, of course, by the appropriate FROM command.

And that is all there is to it. However, we can build on the SELECT ... FROM construct a range of further conditions, and it is at these that I wish to look now.

While the SELECT and FROM clauses are essential, most users find the WHERE condition so useful that they come to think if it as virtually essential as well. After all, SELECT and FROM will give you the totality of the rows and domains specified, but nine times out of ten you want to limit those rows and domains by some further condition. If you are living in Leeds, and want to go out for an Indian meal, you do not just frame the required 'SELECT Indian FROM restaurant'; you are much more likely to say 'SELECT Indian FROM restaurant WHERE restaurant is within five miles of my house.' Fortunately, the WHERE clause in SQL will perform this sort of operation with no difficulty:

```
SELECT Manager, address
FROM Shops
WHERE shop_no='7';
```

And, not surprisingly, you can extend this WHERE clause:

```
SELECT Manager, address
FROM Shops
WHERE shop_no='7' AND '11';
```

Indeed, you can use the AND conjunction so that you select from two or more different domains:

```
SELECT Name, salary
FROM Payroll
WHERE shop_no='7' AND salary <'10,000';
```

Equally, in place of AND, you can use the condition OR. Imagine that you wanted the details of the Scrape and Blow stores in Chelmsford and Holt. The SQL instruction issued would be as follows:

```
SELECT *
FROM Shops
WHERE address='*Chelmsford'
OR    address='*Holt';
```

You will, I trust, have recalled that the use of the symbol * indicates that you want all the data available, so that when you indicate that you want to SELECT *, you want to select all the columns from the table concerned. Equally, the * symbol represents the missing parts of the address in the two final lines of the instruction.

Just imagine, though, that you wanted to issue the command that SQL should give you the name and position from the Staff table of every employee except the manager. You might, of course, do it like this:

```
SELECT Name, position
FROM Staff
WHERE position='assistant'
OR    position='driver'
OR    position='cleaner'
OR    position='janitor'
OR    position='sales_dir'
OR    position=...
```

You would rapidly become tired of issuing such commands, because of their length, and would then, after your labours, be unamused to discover that you received no information from your query. You cannot pile up multiple ANDs or multiple ORs. They merely have the effect of cancelling each other out. But you could, of course, do the whole thing much more concisely and obtain the information for which you sought:

```
SELECT Name, position
FROM Staff
WHERE position!='manager';
```

As you will have deduced, the exclamation mark performs a negative role, indicating that you want all the staff listed *except* the manager. In fact, there ought to be two ways of selecting the names and roles of all the Scrape and Blow employees except managers. You can do it the way given in the example above or you can do it by using the symbol < >. It might be worth checking that your terminal accepts both formats of the not-equal-to qualifier.

The WHERE clause can also be linked with the condition word LIKE. Again an example should illustrate the nature of the query:

```
SELECT Manager
FROM Shops
WHERE Manager LIKE 'B%';
```

In fact, the above query is simply asking which Scrape and Blow managers have a surname beginning with the letter 'B'. The % sign stands for an unspecified number of characters, just as the * sign does. It follows, therefore, that one can use the % sign in a variety of ways. One could, for instance, ask for managers ending in the letter 'm':

```
SELECT Manager
FROM Shops
WHERE Manager LIKE '%m';
```

There are a number of these condition words that can be used with **WHERE**. I shall not attempt to survey them all, but one or two other examples may be helpful. You can, for instance use BETWEEN as follows:

```
SELECT description
FROM stock
WHERE reorder level BETWEEN 5 AND 20;
```

In a somewhat similar fashion you can use the IN operator. Let us imagine that you wanted to know which salespeople in our icecream database had been taken on in 1985, 1986 and 1987. Your query would be expressed like this:

```
SELECT *
FROM salespeople
WHERE hiredate IN (*85,*86,*87);
```

There are other such operators—words like ANY, ALL, NULL and EXISTS—but I am sure that you have now seen the basic fashion in which queries are expressed in SQL.

In a relational database it is a matter of complete insignificance as to what order the rows of a table are placed in. You, however, in having data presented to you, may well wish to impose a specific order for the presentation of that data. This can be done by means of the GROUP BY instruction.

We will assume that you want the entire list of employees of Scrape and Blow, but that you want them grouped by the specific store in which they work. The command to effect this result would be as follows:

```
SELECT *
FROM staff
GROUP BY store_no;
```

The UNION ... SELECT combination is also very useful since it enables you to perform more than one query within a single statement. As always, an example will illustrate this perfectly well. Imagine then that you enter the statement below:

```
SELECT name, position FROM staff
 WHERE store_no >3
 UNION
SELECT name, position FROM staff
 WHERE position='assistant';
```

As you will have worked out, the above command will give you the names and roles of all assistants in shops numbered higher than 3. I can't imagine anyone wishing to collect such data, but the technique is, I hope, clear. Do note, however, that the column name or names which follow the SELECT command must be identical. You cannot SELECT shop_no FROM shops and then, using UNION, go on to SELECT supp_no FROM suppliers.

We have seen that, in SQL, it is possible (indeed essential) to use both logical and arithmetic operators. For instance, when dealing with more than one condition in a WHERE clause, we use the logical operators AND, OR and NOT. We have used the first two already, and the last, NOT, is fairly self-evident. Let me, however, just summarize their logical function:

AND joins two or more conditions but only gives a result when all of the conditions are valid.

OR also connects two or more conditions but returns a positive result provided any one of the conditions is valid.

NOT (normally represented by the != sign) disallows the expression which follows it. Hence, if you wanted to select all the schools from the schools table except those where the headmaster's name began with the letter L, your query would look like this:

```
WHERE headmaster !='L%'
```

or like this:

```
_ NOT headmaster='L*'
```

Both expressions should work, though you may find that your system only allows the * operator (or the !). It is, of course, difficult to imagine ever wanting to execute such an absurd exclusion.

The *arithmetic operators* $(+,-,/,*)$ we have also encountered—doubtless at primary school. However, it is worth pointing out that SQL allows the arithmetic operators to be used on any numeric column. If you do so use one, the result required will be presented to you on the screen, but the data in the database itself will naturally remain unaltered. Possibly too, if your system provides date functions, then arithmetic operations can be performed on date columns also. Some systems also contain a *modulo* operation. All this means is that it will give any remainder left as the result of an arithmetic operation. Thus, if you wish to divide 10 by 4, the modulo will be 2 because 4 goes into ten twice leaving 2 left over. The modulo function is performed by using the % sign.

What I am primarily concerned to point out is that operations within SQL, like operations in programming or general computer work, take a kind of pecking order. Thus, if you ask, within a single expression, the addition and multiplication functions to be performed, then the multiplication will be performed before the addition is carried out. Take the following expression:

$4 + 4*2$

The answer given will be 12 because 4 and 2 are first multiplied, and 4 is then added to the result. If you want the addition to be carried out first, you must surround the 4 + 4 with brackets, because brackets have the highest precedence of all. Consequently, if you do enter $(4 + 4)*2$ you will be presented with the result 16 instead of 12.

From this it follows that it is important, if you want to get accurate results, to know the order of precedence in which SQL carries out its operations. The hierarchy is as follows:

1. Brackets
2. Multiplication and/or division
3. Subtraction and/or addition
4. Not
5. And
6. Or

As you can see, the logical operators come below the arithmetic ones. It is clearly important to be aware of this hierarchy when carrying out complex SELECT queries.

And so we end our survey of SELECT. If, as I mentioned at the beginning, van der Lans can devote 111 pages to the SELECT command alone, there is clearly a great deal more that you could learn. Even so, I do feel that we have now covered the basic essentials of this powerful command.

Other commands   The SELECT command is the primary command in dealing with the extraction of information from the database, and we have looked at various permutations of that command. It would, however, be absurd to ignore completely other commands which are concerned, not with retrieval, but with modifying the database itself. There are three vital commands here:

* DELETE – Removing items from the database;
* INSERT – Adding items to the database;
* UPDATE – Changing items in the database.

I shall make no attempt to cover these commands fully, but, even with a brief examination of them, you will be able to use SQL in a meaningful fashion.

DELETE – You can, in SQL, only delete entire rows of data; it is not possible simply to remove a single attribute value from a row. You can also only delete from one table (or set) at a time; if you want to remove several rows from a number of different tables, you must issue a separate command for each table (or relation). The command itself, however, is very straightforward. Let us imagine that we have a table devoted to students at the University of Exeter, a table with the unsurprising names of Students. One of those students, so overcome by the pressure of work expected of him, decides to leave the university. Hence that student needs to be deleted from the student table. I have little doubt that you could issue the command without any guidance from me. It would be, of course:

```
DELETE FROM student
WHERE student_id='1427'
```

You will note that the relevant row has been identified by citing the unique primary code for that row. There could be problems if we attempted the deletion on the name of the student:

```
DELETE FROM student
WHERE name='Smith'
```

The result of that command could mean the disappearance of half a dozen earnest and hardworking undergraduates. Be careful too that you do not press the Enter key after typing DELETE FROM student. You could find then that the university has no students left at all. You would, however, still have a table left, although it would be an empty one. It was mentioned earlier that, if you want to destroy a table completely, you need to use the command DROP.

INSERT – This is an equally straightforward command. Imagine that the university allowed the late arrival of a new student. His or her name would then need to be added to the student table:

```
INSERT INTO Student
VALUES (1635, 'Humberstone', 'Nigel Jeffries', 061173)
```

This command would insert the student identity number, surname, forenames and date of birth into the relevant table. You must, however, state the values of your row in the correct order, i.e. the order in which they are currently arranged in the table concerned.

UPDATE – This is a little more complicated. It is very easy to update a particular value throughout an entire table. The Market Drayton Printing Association wish to increase the salaries of all their printers by 10 per cent. The relevant table is called Printers:

```
UPDATE printers
 SET salary=salary*1.1;
```

Should you, however, only wish to change a value in one row of a table then you need to use a WHERE command also:

```
UPDATE printers
 SET salary=salary*1.1
 WHERE name=Caxton;
```

This will leave the salaries of all the printers in the Market Drayton Printing Association totally unchanged except that of Fred Caxton whose salary increase came as a consequence of his allowing his name to be used in an advertising campaign.

Clearly much more could be written about these commands, none the less, the items of SQL at which we have looked should have given you an overall understanding of data creation and manipulation within that particular query language. There are, of course, many more query languages—ALPHA, DEDUCE, FWL, QUEL, TAMALAN and so on—but the principles are common to them all and SQL is certainly the most widespread of such languages.

A query language is an integral component of a database system. It is so crucial to the overall effectiveness of such a system that it is worth gaining a clearer idea of how these languages actually work. Hence the next section.

14.3 The technical mechanics

It will already have become obvious that I am not a passionately practical person. To mend a bicycle puncture normally takes me about an hour and a half. Even changing a plug takes about 20 minutes. Consequently this book has contained very little about voltages, read–write heads or shadow paging. It has, instead, concentrated on an intellectual understanding, with little concern as to how the conceptual operations discussed are actually translated into practice. However, query languages in general and SQL in particular are an important topic, and it seemed to me to be appropriate to include in this quite long chapter on SQL a brief explanation as to how precisely, in practical terms, a computer does implement the requests of a query language.

I shall use SQL as my example of a query language, but the comments which follow will be apposite for any query language whatsoever. Clearly, too, the processing involved will be done by the DBMS , though again the pattern will be virtually identical for whatever DBMS is employed.

Let us begin with the assumption that you have a database packed with data about the Miss World competition. One of the tables in that database is called Winners, and lists the people who have, over the years, been graced with the title of Miss World. (I ought to add that I know absolutely nothing about the Miss World competition, and that all the data which I shall cite is entirely fictitious.)

The attributes for this Winners table are as follows:

Winner_number; Name; Age; Nationality; Win_year

I think that the attributes are reasonably self-evident. Each winner has been allocated a unique four-digit number. Her name and age then follow. The country of her origin is the penultimate attribute value, and the year in which she won the context concludes the row. As a consequence, the first four rows of this entirely mythical table look like this:

0001	Rosine Engel	22	Spanish	1921
0002	Ena Flugel	19	Brazilian	1922
0003	Michelle Amani	21	Tunisian	1923
0004	Sara Plutch	20	Hungarian	1924

Now, for reasons best known to yourself, you want to obtain the name and age of all Miss World winners whose nationality happened to be French. The query itself is very straightforward:

```
SELECT Name, Age
FROM Winners
WHERE Nationality='French';
```

How, then, does the computer cope with this when you type in your query at the keyboard?

The SQL statement processor does three things whenever it is presented with a query. The operations involved are known as *parsing*, *planning* and *executing*. As you type your query, it passes through the SQL *user interface*, which is simply a screen format controller. It immediately sends the query on to the SQL *statement processor*, and it is here that the statement is parsed. In other words, the statement processor analyses your query. It checks that the syntax of your query is correct. It identifies any key words, table names and/or column names with which it is presented. It detects any conditions that apply. Most of this it does this by referring to the schema tables. Hence, in the example given above, the SQL *control system* identifies that a retrieval operation is required; the keyword SELECT indicates this. It identifies that the column fields for Name and Age are needed for outputting. The FROM instruction tells it that those columns will be located in the Winners table. Finally, the necessary condition is given by the WHERE statement, which further indicates that the field for Nationality will need to be examined. The statement processor also confirms that the query in question is syntactically correct.

The query is next the subject of a planning process. In other words, the statement processor works out a method for answering your query. In the query that we are considering at the moment, little planning is necessary. The keyword SELECT has already been recognized. So has the table Winners, and the column headings Name, Age and Nationality. Thus the processor plans to move through the Winners table looking for the nationality 'French'. Whenever that nationality is encountered, the processor plans to output the Name and Age of the row concerned. The statement processor is helped in its tasks by the filters which provide printout processing steps.

The final stage, execution, is simplicity itself. The processor passes the requisite data back to the SQL user interface which arranges the necessary screen format and then propels it to the screen where you can read it.

The whole transaction seems so obvious that you can be forgiven for wondering why it has been given a separate subsection all to itself. In fact, of course, the Miss World query at which we have just looked was the simplest possible query with which a database could be faced. If we now look at a slightly more complicated one, you will see that the three-part operation— Parse, Plan, Execute—is quite important to our understanding of how SQL or any other query language is implemented.

We shall move this time to a realm rather more humdrum than that concerned with Miss World, though it is a much more important realm. We are confronted again with a college database. You want to know the titles of courses given by Dr Richard Saunders where Dr Saunders is not only the lecturer for those courses but is also the personal tutor for those students. There are three relevant tables. The first is called Course and comprises the following attributes:

Course_code;   Title;   Site;   Day;   Time

The first column contains the unique primary key, a four-digit number. The second column gives the title of the course with that number. The third column states where the lectures or tutorials for that course are actually held, while the fourth and fifth columns give the day on which that course is held and the time of that day. Hence the first four rows of our table might look like this:

5137	Pragmatism in the Third World	Walter Knox Hall	Tues	10–11
2864	The American Novel	Leavis Room	Wed	14–15
1993	The Rise of Meritocracy	Houghton Room	Mon	11–12
6338	Systems Analysis	Babbage Lab.	Fri	14–16

The second table is called Tutors. All students at the university are given a personal tutor. Every effort is make to ensure that a student's personal tutor also has some academic connection with the courses that the student is following. The Tutors table has four attributes:

Tutor_code;   Course_code;   Day;   time

Each tutor group is given a unique five-digit code, a code that is identical to the staff number allocated to the member of staff who happens to be the tutor for that particular group. The second field cites the course which all the students in that particular tutor group happen to be following. The final two fields contain the day and time of tutor group meetings. Thus you would see entries like this in the Tutor table:

10014   2864   Thur   09–10

As you can see, one field, Course_code, can also be located in the Course table.

The final table with which we need to be concerned is the staff table. As its name suggests, this is a listing of all the members of staff employed by the college. There are four attributes:

Staff_no;   Name;   Department;   Title

These attributes are fairly self-evident. The primary key is a unique five-digit number, one for each member of staff, and, when a member of staff is also a personal tutor, the tutor number given is identical to his staff number. Name and Department hardly need any explication. The final field, Title, simply cites any position that the person concerned holds: lecturer, senior lecturer, professor, etc.

By this time you may well have forgotten exactly what our query is. You want to know the titles of courses given by Dr Richard Saunders where Dr Saunders is not only the lecturer for those courses but is also the personal tutor for the students following those courses. The three relevant tables from the database contain the following attributes.

Course_code;   Title;   Site;   Day;   Time
Tutor_code;   Course_code;   Day;   Time
Staff_no;   Name;   Department;   Title

And this is where knowing something about the technical mechanics of coping with an SQL query becomes relevant, because, as you may have already realized, there is more than one way of arriving at an answer to our query.

The first method takes the tables in the order in which they are presented here. Hence it takes Course and Tutors and combines together the data that it needs. We know that it needs the title of the courses because titles are to appear in the final output. It also needs Course_code because that is the common attribute between the Course table and Tutors table. It also needs Staff_no because that will eventually be a link between the table formed from the joining of Course and Tutors and the Staff table. Hence the SQL statement processor works out that it needs to extract from the Course table just the Course_code and the title, and to join that data with the Staff_no and Course_code from the Tutors table. As a result, the first row of the Course table is extracted from the disk storage and placed in a buffer. (If you remember, a buffer is an area for temporary data storage.) Let us imagine that the first row extracted is this one:

2237   The Anglo-Saxons   Tawney Hall   Thur   10–11

The statement processor will next ask for the first row from the Tutors table. It too will be placed in a buffer;

10007   1732   Wed   12–13

The two Course_codes will now be compared. Since they are not the same, the first row from the Tutors table will be discarded, and the second row brought:

10018   1106   Thur   15–16

Since the Course_codes here do not match either, the second row will also be discarded. And so the operation will continue until a match is found:

10014   2237   Mon   11–12

Once such a match of the Course_codes has been achieved, the two rows will be merged and placed in an internal table, the filters being the operative agency in this process:

2237   The Anglo-Saxons   Tawney Hall   Thur   10–11   10014   Mon   11–12

And so the operation will continue, as each row of the Course table is compared with each row of the Tutors table in order to achieve a linking of their respective course_codes. The resulting new table will rest in the special area reserved for internal tables.

Having produced a new table, the statement processor will next want to link the new table with the staff table. This time the matching code is Staff_no. The first row of our new joined table is placed in a buffer, and the first row of the Staff table is extracted for comparison. If the Staff_no matches the Tutor_code row of the internal table, then that row will also be stored in another internal table. Eventually, after a great deal of processing, there will be two linked tables which can then be joined so that they show the Course_code, the Title of the course, the Staff_no and Name of the lecturer giving that course.

Finally, from the internal tables that have been produced, the SQL control system will need to extract from them the instance where the staff number of Dr Richard Saunders is identical to a tutor code. This is a simple operation of retrieval, and, at the end of it, the necessary data will be output to the screen:

Richard Saunders   The Nineteenth-century Novel

No lecturer can be the tutor of more than one group; hence only one connection will be located. The steps that have been taken to arrive at the answer are illustrated in Fig. 14.1. These steps, as we have seen, entailed a great deal of processing. It is not, however, the only method available. Let us see if we can devise a more economical procedure.

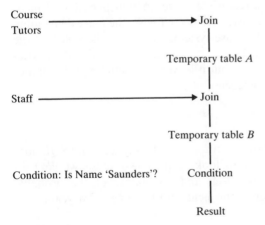

Figure 14.1

We know that our result is bound to include the name of Dr Richard Saunders. Consequently the SQL statement processor could decide to look first at the Staff table and extract from it the name Richard Saunders together with his staff number. This would not be a difficult or complex operation. With that information placed in an internal table, the statement processor could then go through the Tutors table looking for the only occasion upon which the staff number it has already retrieved matched the tutor code. That instance would also then be placed in the internal table area. Finally, the processor would look at the Course table, trying to find an instance where the course code matched the course code that had already been extracted from the Tutors table. Again there could only be one specific instance where this was the case. Hence, if the statement processor adopted this method, there would be a great deal less processing involved.

Finally, there is a third method which would be even more rapid. If the Staff table had an index on the name attribute, Richard Saunders could be extracted from that table almost instantly. Then, if there were an index on the Tutor_code for the Tutor table, that correspondence could be performed instantly. Finally, if there were an index on Course_code, the title of the relevant course could also be located at once. The existence of indexes would speed up the operation markedly, but, as always, there are no free lunches. The existence of those indexes would take considerable areas of disk space and consume considerable resources. For any context, the DBA needs to work out whether the convenience and speed provided by indexing justifies the expense and increased load that the system in consequence suffers.

From this glance at the pure mechanics of executing an SQL query, it is clearly a far from trivial business. The whole operation is, of course, concerned with query optimization, and there is an excellent chapter on this topic in the first volume of Date (1990).

Query languages, as we have already seen, are an indispensable element within the database context, but, the easier they are to use, the more demanding they are for the resources of the database system. Yet this is the way that the database world is moving and will need to move. SQL is already a vital component of most computer systems, but it is worth concluding this chapter by having a look at some of its deficiencies.

14.4   The limitations of SQL

SQL may be the de facto standard now, but we have already seen that SQL does have a number of clear imperfections. By looking at some of these, we can gain a better awareness of the language itself and an inkling of the probable advances that are going to be made in this field within the next few years.

14.4.1   JOIN

We already know that the join facility is one of the most valuable features of the relational data model. Data from two or more tables can be combined, thus greatly easing our handling of the material contained within the database.

Despite what I have just implied, there is in fact no join command in SQL at all. Instead, SQL, with a coy diffidence, only allows you to join tables (or sections of tables) by you gently implying that you would like to see such a join. You do so by means of the WHERE clause. Hence your request structure is going to be as follows:

```
SELECT ...
FROM table1, table2, ...
WHERE table1, column1=table2, column4
```

I hope that the above is very straightforward. First of all, you state what it is that you need to select. Just imagine that we wanted to link products supplied to stores with the address of the supplier that had delivered those products. The first line of your instruction will simply specify all the column names of the desired data in the order in which you wanted them to be displayed. Thus your SELECT command could read as follows:

```
SELECT supp_no, supp_name, supp_address, product
```

Notice, however, that although there is no need for you actually to have the supplier number, it has to be specified because it is the only field that links the appropriate tables.

Having specified the columns that you actually want to see, you next indicate from which tables those columns are going to be retrieved, merely separating the tables concerned with a comma. Hence our FROM line would read as follows:

```
FROM supplier, products
```

And now you specify the join needed in the WHERE clause by making the one common field in both the above fields explicit:

```
WHERE supplier supp_no=products supp_no;
```

Thus, as you can see, the preconditions for creating a join in SQL are that the FROM clause must contain the name of more than one table and that the WHERE clause provides a valid connective element between those tables. In the example provided above, the connective element was complete equality in that the names of the respective columns were identical as well as the contents of those columns being identical. In fact, provided the contents are identical, the columns could have different names. Nor, provided a match is specified between two tables, do you have to display the matching column at all. Hence we could have achieved the join that we have just looked at without the suppliers number being displayed. Our instruction would then read as follows:

```
SELECT supp_name, supp_address, product
FROM supplier, products
WHERE supplier supp_no=products supp_no;
```

Obviously too, there are very different kinds of joins that can be accomplished. I have illustrated the most common type where there is a join on specified columns. You can equally achieve a join where the condition of equality upon which I have so far been insisting does not exist. In such a case, instead of using the equals sign, you substitute it for $>$, $<$ or $<>$, depending upon which condition you want to be fulfilled. There are, of course, other sophistications on offer, but enough has been done to indicate the nature of the join condition within SQL. I have put it under the heading 'The limitations of SQL' because it seems to be a limitation when you cannot specify directly the nature of the operation that you want.

14.4.2 SUBQUERIES

We are all acquainted with the situation of a question resting upon the response to an earlier question. Such nested queries are the staple fare of discussions:

Obviously we don't know if the President of the USA will decide to invade Tasmania, but, if he does, what will be the ecological effects upon Tasmanian marsupials, especially if the American invasion destroys the King William and Huon pines on the mountain slopes.

Such a query is absurd, but we all construct queries of this nature (though not, perhaps, on such topics), and it is clearly important for any self-respecting query language to be able to do the same. It is not, in fact, a difficult process, though the SQL expressions containing subqueries do look both ugly and complicated (hence its inclusion in this section). None the less, subqueries can save considerable effort. Let me illustrate.

Let us imagine that you wanted to find out how many products sold by IBM cost exactly the same as a DuraWand bar code reader (another absurd query). You clearly have two operations to perform:

1. Find out the price of a DuraWand.
2. Find out all the products that cost the same as the DuraWand.

Obviously you could answer the query by making two separate queries. (I am assuming, for the sake of argument that we do have the relevant data to hand.) The first SQL instruction would look like this:

```
SELECT purchase, price
FROM purchases
WHERE purchase='DuraWand';
```

Then, having gained the first necessary piece of information, you could incorporate it into your second SQL instruction:

```
SELECT purchase
FROM purchases
WHERE price='495';
```

If, however, you can express the whole thing as one query, it will save time, not because you have less typing to do but because you will not have the break between the first operation and the second. All you need to do is just to merge our previous two queries into one:

```
SELECT purchase, price
FROM purchases
WHERE price=
  (SELECT price
   FROM purchases
   WHERE purchase='DuraWand');
```

Of course, again just for convenience, we have so arranged the universe that we only have one type of DuraWand at one set price, but it should not be too difficult to see how subqueries could be so nested as to incorporate a whole range of possibilities.

The example given had a subquery that needed to address the same table as the primary query. It is, of course, perfectly possible to have subqueries that address tables other than the ones cited in the first query. Thus, for instance, you might want to find out how many products bought by a company cost the same amount as a manager's annual salary. The resulting instruction would look something like this:

```
SELECT purchase
FROM purchases
WHERE purchase=
  (SELECT salary
   FROM emp_store
   WHERE role='Manager');
```

And the basic structure of subqueries should now be clear. Of course, a great deal more can be accomplished by using a whole variety of keywords or keyword phrases. The purpose of these is self-evident:

```
IN   NOT IN   HAVING   GROUP BY   ANY   ALL   EXISTS
```

We can also have subqueries that repeat themselves, continuing to ask exactly the same question on an entire sequence of data delivered to it by the primary query. So the use of subqueries can be a valuable aid.

Even though we have once again only skimmed the surface, it is clear that subqueries can only operate in an ordered universe. The theoretical background upon which SQL (and relational DBMSs) is based has to be logically stable enough to cope with multiple subqueries as well as all the other complex commands (and careless errors) to which it will be subjected. Hence looking at a query language is an appropriate time to take a closer look at the entire rationale of relational development.

14.5   Logical foundations

If you think about the entire operation of communication with a DBMS with which this part of the book is concerned, you will realize that it is a remarkably complex operation. For it to be done effectively, a great deal (of which you and I are normally unaware) has to be taken for granted. To start with, the database or databases upon which we are operating have to have been sensibly constructed. Data within it will be normalized data. The process of entity–relationship modelling, a topic to which whole books have been devoted, will have been rigorously carried out. Having constructed the database, we move on to operating upon the data contained therein. As we have seen in this chapter, such operations are carried out by means by a query language (even that query language may be encapsulated in on-screen prompts). So far as the user is concerned, the query language (or screen instruction) is all that matters, and so it should be in a nonprocedural language. None the less, while a non procedural language like SQL is a major boon for ease of operation, it does entail gigantic acts of faith. You, the user, just have to trust that the query language is behaving in a proper and correct manner. In other words, you and your intelligence have opted out of the entire operation. Yet what the query language has to do is to submit the queries that you have made to a *query optimizer* which then analyses your query. It breaks your query down into its component parts, possibly rearranges them so that they will be dealt with in the most efficient manner, and then searches for the most useful indexes to aid it in the solving of the query. Should it not succeed in finding any such indexes, it is then forced to resort to checking the database line by line in order to provide you with the data you need. You will, or course, get your data eventually, but it may be several days or weeks later, depending upon the size of the database.

Such a scenario is rare, of course. Almost invariably, the query optimizer is able to perform its task with admirable efficiency. With how much efficiency depends upon the structure of the database it is searching, upon the effectiveness of the query optomizer itself, and, of course, upon the operating system which forms the entire context within which the procedure is being conducted. And as far as all this is concerned, you personally have about as much influence as an American bison or an antipodean wombat. In other words, you are irrelevant.

This total irrelevance while operating a relational database has never caused me to lose any sleep. I have found the humble operation of framing the SQL queries in the first place quite sufficient to keep my mind engaged and my soul content. None the less, there seem to have been scores of writers who have been seized with some passionate desire to disturb my tranquillity. They have insisted that I cannot possibly understand any relational database or any query language without being instructed in some arcane topics such as relational algebra and relational calculus. Thus the Hursches entitle their tenth chapter 'The relational algebra and SQL'. In the first paragraph, they inform me that

SQL owes much to relational algebra, and in the second paragraph, they begin their explanation:

> Given a finite set of attributes $U = (A_1, A_2, \ldots, A_U)$ with domains dom(A_1), a relation scheme is a subset of U. A relational database scheme D over U is a collection of relations schemes, $(R_1, R_2, \ldots, R_d)$, such that the union of the R_1 is U. Given a relation scheme R, a tuple, t, over R is a single-valued mapping from the members of R to the domains of the members of R such that . . .

And so it continues. It may be that such impenetrable prose is child's play to someone trained in mathematics. Unfortunately, my own training in mathematics comprised learning the two-times table and not much else. Given the avidity with which universities and polytechnics are now offering conversion courses in IT to graduates of whatever discipline, it is highly likely that hundreds of others will also view the Hursch prose as gobbledegook. Yet, if you make more than a superficial acquaintanceship with relational databases, you are bound to come across a great deal of this esoteric jargon. Smith and Barnes (1987) feel it necessary to explain that there are three levels of DML commands, relational calculus, relational algebra and tuple-by-tuple processing, and conduct their explanation with only marginally greater clarity than is found in the Hursch book. Even Bowers (1988) devotes 18 pages to relational algebra and calculus, and, although less impenetrable, his explanations still do not thrill the spirit or animate the heart. Yet I lay stress on this simply because it seems to me to be so unnecessary. I am prepared to believe (trusting soul that I am), that relational algebra and calculus are necessary tools for the designer of relational databases and relationally orientated query languages, but few people in business and few undergraduates are ever going to be concerned with such acts of creation. Certainly the readers of this book are unlikely to aspire to such heights. Hence, my argument is, simple users of a DBMS or a query language have absolutely no need whatsoever to concern themselves with such theoretical underpinnings. I note, for instance, that Atre (1980) makes no reference to such matters at all. I note with even more pleasure, that Laurie (1985) explicitly states that relational calculus, 'is another example (so common in the high-tech world) of a solution looking for a problem'. Indeed, he relates the appearance of sections on relational calculus in textbooks to an antiquated historicism. Laurie argues that relational calculus had perhaps some relevance when computer systems were tape driven. Now that they are all disk machines, the complications of tape management have become redundant. Unfortunately, the writers of computer textbooks have failed to notice this. It is, Laurie claims: 'as if the captain of the first steamship insisted on tacking to windward as if he were still under sail because it had taken him a lot of time and trouble to learn the art and he was not going to abandon it now just because it was obsolete'. Hence, all the mathematical jargon which I quoted above, merely confuses, in Laurie's words again: 'the real issue with masses of difficult and spurious theory'. He sums up by stating that: 'It is excellent for setting examination questions, useless to help real computer users.' Yet I devote some relative length to this issue because I recall only too well the personal alarm and despondency that I felt when I first encountered these issues, an alarm and despondency that I have witnessed with sundry undergraduates also. There is, however, no need for such paranoia. When you meet sections on relational algebra and calculus in texts that you are using, just treat such sections as you would a textbook on alchemy.

None the less, we do need to be concerned about the logical validity of the database management system that we are using and the query language that we employ for its interrogation. You will recall that one of the most crucial tenets in the construction of relational tables is that each row within a table must be a unique row. This does not mean that individual values within an attribute column are all different from each other. Indeed, many of them can be identical. Take the example of the perennially useful John Smith. Let us imagine that there are two John Smiths who work in the same department, have the same salary, are members of the same pension scheme, and belong to the same social club. None the less, their respective rows are unique because each row has, as its primary key, the relevant national insurance number (or social security number) for the John Smith concerned. And this is all that matters. That primary key renders each row unique. No other row in the entire database is identical to it.

Since the uniqueness of each table row is a vital element of a relational system, we do therefore need a relational database and/or a query language that will enforce the uniqueness of those rows or, failing compulsion, will report on any duplicate rows that do occur. It therefore comes as a considerable regret to discover that no such animal exists. SQL will do what you tell it to do, but it possesses no syntax for designating primary keys, and, as you are aware, it is almost invariably the primary key that enforces the uniqueness of the rows concerned.

This is a serious deficiency, and SQL has been severely criticized for this omission. Fortunately, however, it can be circumvented. First of all, since it is the primary key that normally guarantees the uniqueness of each individual row, you can instruct SQL to ensure that the primary key is never allowed to be a null value. By so doing, you help to ensure the uniqueness of each row. Secondly, you can create a unique index for each table. This does not prevent you from entering a duplicate row into your database, but it does ensure that any duplication is picked up by the index which will refuse to allow you to perform an INSERT or UPDATE command in such circumstances. Ironically, the ANSI standard allows each user to specify any column or columns as being unique (though you would also have to link it with a not null command). Clearly this would be the most sensible procedure. If you specify a column upon creation as UNIQUE, you thereby ensure that no duplicate entries can possibly be made. Alas, most actual implementations only enforce the uniqueness criterion with respect to indices. I hope—and expect?—that suppliers will eventually get round to implementing uniqueness in the creation of data tables, but at the moment this is certainly an instance of where the ANSI standard is better than the reality. Were you to be in the position of buying an SQL for your company's relational database, this is one item that you should certainly check beforehand in the documentation provided for your proposed SQL purchase. It is, after all, lunacy that UNIQUENESS, obviously a property of the table concerned, is only enforced in the subsequent index.

To conclude: not everything is perfect in the SQL garden, and it would be too much to expect SQL2 (or even the proposed SQL3) to resolve all the complex issues with which a query language has to cope. We can, however, be fairly confident that SQL is going to remain the major relational query language, and as such it is imperative that anyone within the database world has at least a basic understanding of that language. It is this understanding which this chapter has sought to give.

References

Atre, S. *Data Base: Structured Techniques for Design, Performance and Management*, John Wiley, 1980.

Bowers, D. S. *From Data to Database*, Van Nostrand, 1988.

Burstein, J. S. *Computers and Information Systems*, Holt, Reinhart & Winston, 1986.

Date, C. J. *Introduction to Database Systems*, Vol. II, Addison-Wesley, 1985.

Date, C. J. *A Guide to the SQL Standard*, Addison-Wesley, 1987.

Date, C. J. *A Guide to INGRES*, Addison-Wesley, 1987.

Emerson, S. L., Darnovsky, M. and Bowman, J. *The Practical SQL Handbook*, Addison-Wesley, 1989.

Gardarin, G. and Valduriez, P. *Analysis and Comparison of Relational Database Systems*, Addison-Wesley, 1989.

Gorman, M. *Database Management Systems*, Butterworth Heinemann/ Computer Weekly, 1991.

Rothwell, D. M. *Ingres and Relational Databases*, McGraw-Hill, 1992.

Sayles, J. *SQL Spoken Here*, QED, 1989.

Smith, P. and Barnes, M. *Files and Databases*, Addison-Wesley, 1987.

van der Lans, R. F. *The SQL Standard*, Prentice-Hall, 1989.

Questions on Part Four

1. What are the advantages of indexes for data processing?
2. What are the disadvantages of indexes?
3. Why is it unfortunate that SQL permits the presence of duplicate rows?
4. If someone said that the major difference between the hierarchical data structure and the network data structure concerned the question of parent-hood, what would you take their remark as meaning?
5. Imagine you had a table in a database given over to Shirts. The attributes within that table are as follows:

   collar_size; colour; material; price.

   You wish to change the data so that all shirts which are listed as being coloured green are instead amended to the colour blue. How would you make this change by using SQL?
6. What do you understand by the operation of parsing within a query language system?
7. Under what circumstances would you be likely to use the DISTINCT command?
8. Why is it often useful to create views?
9. You have a table Teams which lists the bowls teams for a county (or state). You also have a table Scorers which lists the scorers that each team possesses. The attributes within each table as as follows:

   team_no   team_name   address   tel_no
   scorer_no   surname   forenames   team_no

   How would you express an SQL query which found the scorers for the team known as the Litcham Lightning?
10. You have a table Characters which lists the characters who appear in the novels of Charles Dickens. The fields or attributes of that table are

    name; novel; sex; d_o_p;

the final field being given to the date of publication of the novel in question. You wish to make an addition to this table because you have just become aware that Benjamin Allen from *The Pickwick Papers* (1837) has been omitted. How would you make the insertion using SQL?

Answers

1. The advantages of indexes are that they speed up the direct access of an indexed field, since otherwise a sequential search would be required.
2. Indexes carry the disadvantages of consuming a considerable amount of space and furthermore in slowing down all UPDATE operations.
3. The presence of duplicate rows, apart from the fact that they serve no viable purpose, also ensures that query optimization can be handicapped.
4. The hierarchical data model only allows one parent per child, whereas the network data model allows a child to have two or more parents.
5. UPDATE Shirts
   SET COLOUR='Blue'
   WHERE COLOUR='Green';
6. Parsing is the process of the query optimizer checking to determine whether or not the query presented is syntactically correct.
7. You would use the DISTINCT command when you wanted to exclude any repetitions of an attribute or entity.
8. Views can be useful in that they can create tables which have been tailored for a specific purpose or person. Thus you can create a view which links data from a number of different tables but which will only be needed for that particular operation and hence does not demand the creation of a formal join table. Equally you can create a view which omits data that the personnel using that view are not supposed to see.
9. SELECT surname, forenames
   FROM SCORERS
   WHERE team_no IN
    (SELECT team_no
     FROM TEAMS
     WHERE team_name='Litcham_Lightning';
10. INSERT INTO CHARACTERS
    VALUES (Benjamin Allen, The Pickwick Papers,
            m,1837);

PART FIVE

Looking after a database

15
The database administrator

Ann Rossitor was an able student. Having read English at Sheffield University and gained an outstanding First, she then went on to Gumthorpe College of Higher Education to do a diploma in computer management. Ann was never entirely sure as to what prompted this switch. She had, after all, been urged to do a Ph.D., and there could have been little doubt that a safe and satisfying academic career was hers for the asking. None the less, after three years of Chaucer to Yeats, Shakespeare to Shaw, Ann felt like a break from the rarefied world of imagistic control, narrative modes, allegorical techniques and linguistic structures. She also had a sneaking suspicion that the world of Eng. Lit. was merely a sophisticated form of hedonism. She enjoyed the controlled savagery of Pope's *Dunciad* and the semantic richness of James Joyce, but it did all seem at several removes from the things that really mattered in the world.

While at Sheffield one of Ann's friends had been reading information technology. It was easy for Ann to see that IT was the career opportunity of the 1990s, and she was fascinated by the insights into communication that the precision (and stupidity) of the computer provided. Hence her removal to the more literal milieu of Gumthorpe.

It cannot be said that Ann's immersion into bits and bytes had been entirely delightful. Most of the work demanded a memory but not much else. Any fool, she felt, could master HIPO charting in a spare 10 minutes. The advantages and disadvantages of batch processing were virtually self-evident. Normalization had a certain disciplined charm, but made little demand upon imagination or insight. And most of her teachers at Gumthorpe had the mechanical approach of a word processor and the visionary flair of an ALU. None the less, Ann felt, the tedious experience had been worth it. It had given her a job.

In 1990, the Conservative government, decided to open yet another new university. Signalled as the start of a 'new era of higher education for all', the University of Eastwood was due to open in September 1991. Naturally, being a new university, they wanted some type of gimmick. Since Eastwood was the birth place of D. H. Lawrence, it was not unnatural that the pioneers of this new university should decide to make it a resource centre for the writings of its native poet and novelist. Accordingly there appeared in the *Times Educational Supplement* for 4 January 1991 the following advertisement:

DATA MANAGER: D. H. LAWRENCE STUDY CENTRE. The University of Eastwood, due to open in September 1991, is establishing a resource centre for the study of D. H. Lawrence. We wish to appoint an English graduate with computing and administrative skills to organize the facilities of this centre and to liaise with users and outside bodies so that those facilities can be most effectively used.

Ann liked D. H. Lawrence. She had read all of his novels and much of his poetry. Such a post would enable her to combine her computing skills (such as they were) and her literary awareness. Above all, for Ann was young, idealistic and naive, it would enable her, she thought, to make a significant contribution to international scholarship. Under her expert control, the D. H. Lawrence Study Centre would become the Mecca for all Lawrentians. Consequently Ann applied for the post and was duly appointed. Even in the computerized world of 1991, there were not many English graduates with first-class degrees who knew anything about relational databases, fourth-generation languages and network structures. The University of Eastwood regarded Ann Rossitor as manna from heaven. Ann too was delighted. To be in charge of the data resources of a newly founded academic centre was more than she had ever hoped for.

Ann had been appointed in January. The post did not begin until September and, indeed, Ann's course at Gumthorpe did not finish until July. It was not surprising that much of Ann's work at Gumthorpe between January and July was directed more towards Eastwood than the tedious assignments that her diploma course still demanded. Fortunately there was a considerable degree of correspondence between the two, and Ann could feel with a certain amount of justification that the work she was doing in preparation for her Eastwood post would also help in the Gumthorpe exams that awaited her in July. It is of interest to take a brief survey of the tasks that Ann set herself. Having once read that genius was 99 per cent perspiration and only 1 per cent inspiration, Ann had never stinted on the pure graft upon which all real understanding ulti-mately depends. Hence, having been appointed data manager for the D. H. Lawrence Study Centre, Ann set to work to codify her knowledge and under-standing of the data world.

The first thing that Ann decided to do was to draw up her own dossier of database terminology. Often in her early months at Gumthorpe she had been confused by terminology. Computer science was supposedly precise and un-ambiguous. Ann had often found the plethora of definitions that IT lavished upon her both imprecise and ambiguous. She therefore decided to compile her own set of definitions. Armed with a card index—Ann did not possess her own computer—Ann began establishing a set of coherent and meaningful terms.

Category   a label which describes any set of objects which share common attributes; e.g. Department, Book, Borrower.

Database model   a representation of the realities of the world in such a way as to be comprehensible to a computer. There are four common types of database model: binary, hierarchical, network, relational.

Object   any concrete or abstract item in the real world.

Value   the state taken by a specific instance of a category. Thus an entry in the Borrower file could have the value 'P. G. Smith'.

And so it went on, each word placed in alphabetical order in the card index box. It was Ann's tiny database. It was also, despite the ulterior motive which animated Ann's procedure, an excellent way of codifying and revising her computer management course at Gumthorpe. The July exams came. Ann found it second nature to write a suitable set of primary and foreign key constraints for a mythical database. It was easy to draw an entity–relationship diagram for an education database. She even managed to write a perceptive essay on the issue of an SQL database being permitted to contain duplicate values. The result was inevitable. Ann gained the diploma with a distinction. There followed an enjoyable month and a half with her family in Church Stretton, and then, on 16 September, Ann reported for duty at the University of Eastwood.

Ann was not an arrogant person, but she did know that she had a good mind. She felt confident that she could cope with the demands of her new role. During her sunny stay in the south Shropshire hills she had reread a great deal of Lawrence and tried to absorb as much as she could of *Database Design Fundamentals* (Rishe, 1988) a book that lacked the emotive and rhapsodic prose of Lawrence but which was excellent in the methodical rigour with which it defined its terms. Indeed, it played a major part in the construction of Ann's own card index of definitions. There were the inevitable butterflies in her stomach when Ann reported to Dr Tom Matthews on Monday morning, but they soon disappeared.

'Morning, Ann,' Tom boomed as she entered the room, 'Welcome to chaos.'

The D. H. Lawrence Centre had been allocated a small suite of rooms on the first floor of the newly built arts block. Dr Matthews escorted Ann to her domain. There was a library devoted to Lawrence's works and books and articles about him. There was a study room comprising eight long tables, each of which possessed a solitary computer terminal. And there was Ann's study comprising a desk with a Tandon computer resting in dominant grandeur upon it, a wall of bookshelves antiseptically empty, a filing cabinet, a telephone and a wastepaper bin.

'This, Ann, is your citadel,' Tom somewhat dismissively announced. 'From here you will engineer the most dynamic research centre in the academic world.'

Ann grinned.

'And precisely how am I expected to do that?' she enquired mildly.

'That, my dear, is your problem,' was the comforting reply. 'Personally I think that Lawrence is the most overrated writer of the century, and I trust that I shall live another 30 years or so without reading another word of his neurotic meanderings. However, there are scores of others who take a different view. Your *raison d'être* is to cater for these benighted souls. You have a capitation allowance of £3,000 per annum to buy books, subscribe to journals, procure copies of unreadable theses, and so on. You also have first call on my secretary every Tuesday and Thursday morning to cope with correspondence. If you do encounter any problems with which you cannot cope, just let me know. I won't be able to cope with them either, but I might be able to put you in touch with someone who can. And incidently, you aren't expected to sit in solitary isolation in your office all day and every day. The senior common room bar will, I am assured, be open every day from 11.00 a.m. to 3.00 p.m. so, if you want to talk to me or just drown your sorrows in drink, pop along to the SCR.'

'Thank you,' Ann replied, feeling, all of a sudden, slightly intimidated.

Tom Matthews gave her a conspiratorial smile and left. Ann sat down in front of the terminal and switched it on. The screen lit up showing ID? in its top left-hand corner. Fortunately Ann had been informed of her computer user number and obediently typed it in. She also knew that Eastwood had a multiuser INGRES database management system. She accordingly logged into that. 'Well,' she thought, 'if this research centre is to be of any use, I'd better start creating its database.'

Not surprisingly, Ann had already given some thought to the database that she would need. She therefore began to create her first table, one devoted to a simple list of all Lawrence's writings from *The White Peacock* in 1911 to the first professionally edited edition of his plays published in 1965. This was an easy task and Ann was halfway through it when the phone rang.

'Hello. D. H. Lawrence Study Centre, Ann Rossitor here. Can I help?'

'Hello. Dick Rogers here from the English department. I'm taking some tutorials on Lawrence's short stories this term. Is there any chance of your providing a chronological list of his stories so that I can give one to each of my students.'

'Of course, I'm fairly sure that I can let you have one by tomorrow. Where would you like me to put it?'

'Oh splendid. Just put it in my pigeonhole in the SCR would you please. Thanks very much.'

Only when Dick Rogers had replaced his receiver did Ann realize that it was not quite as simple as she had at first thought. She knew that *The Prussian Officer and Other Stories* had first appeared in 1914, to be followed by *England, My England* in 1922, but presumably Dick Rogers wanted the publication date of each individual story. Still, this was no real problem. Indeed, since she was going to look them up for Dick Rogers, she could include them in the table that she was already compiling. Ann trotted off into her adjacent library, found the bibliography compiled by Warren Roberts, and returned to her INGRES table.

The phone rang.

'Hello. D. H. Lawrence Study Centre. Ann Rossitor here.'

'Oh, do excuse me. My name's Miriam Nunnerley. I teach at Brinsley Comprehensive. I want to do something about D. H. Lawrence this term with my GCSE fourth form. I wondered if it would be possible to bring them for an afternoon to your Study Centre.'

'Well, er . . . yes,' Ann hesitantly replied. 'But I'm not sure that there would be very much of interest for your pupils.'

'Oh, I don't want to deluge them with material,' Miriam Nunnerley replied. 'I just wondered if it would be possible to show them the books by and about Lawrence that you have, and I was hoping that you or someone could give a short talk to them about the kind of work you do. The point is, you see, they are not a bad class, but they have no idea what academic study really means. I thought that if they could just see for themselves what real people do in connection with a writer who lived and worked in their own area, it would broaden their horizons.'

Ann was all in favour of broadening people's horizons.

'Well, yes,' she said. 'I'm sure we could put on something that would be of interest for them. When did you have in mind?'

'Oh, marvellous,' the harassed teacher exclaimed. 'Would next Tuesday afternoon be all right, a week tomorrow?'

'Certainly,' Ann replied. 'I don't honestly think that I can fill more than 45 minutes. Would 2.15 till 3.00 be all right?'

'Wonderful,' came the relieved response. 'See you then. And thank you.'

Ann replaced the receiver and noted Brinsley Comprehensive's visit in her diary. She was just about to resume work on her first table, when there was a short knock at the door and in walked a university porter.

'Here's your post, miss.'

'Oh, thank you,' Ann replied, and received one package and three letters in her hand.

The package turned out to be some slides of Nottingham in the early years of the century, the Nottingham that Lawrence knew. Ann immediately thought that she could perhaps use them for Brinsley Comprehensive. There was a letter from the chief librarian of Nottingham sending his good wishes to the Centre and hoping that they would be able to cooperate to each other's advantage. There was a letter from the Houghton Library, Harvard University offering photocopies of their collection of Lawrence's letters, and the final letter was from a Simon Platt in Exeter wanting to know if the Study Centre had any tapes of Lawrence reading his own poetry. Ann made a note in her diary to reply to those letters when she had the use of a secretary tomorrow afternoon.

For the next hour, Ann worked in peace and completed her first table, Works, DHL, in the D. H. Lawrence database. What next, she wondered. In answer, the phone rang again.

'Hello. D. H. Lawrence Study Centre. Ann Rossitor speaking.'

'Morning, Professor James Barford here, history department. I take it that you are in charge of this new jewel in the academic crown.'

'Yes,' Ann tersely replied, irritated by the pompous and overbearing tone of Professor Barford.

'Good. I'm running some seminars on the socio-economic matrix of Britain in the industrial decline. Early twentieth-century Nottinghamshire provides a good case study. I'd like some references from Lawrence that would illustrate the theme. Just shove them in my pigeonhole, but no later than Friday, please. Bye.'

Ann sat and quivered with rage. She never responded well to domineering presumption. She turned to her computer, accessed the word processor and began typing.

Dear Professor Barford,

With respect to your demand for material on the socio-economic matrix of early twentieth-century Nottingham, I fear that it can only be your complete ignorance of information technology that occasioned such a request. The purpose of the D. H. Lawrence Study Centre is to provide the facilities for individuals to do their research on the writings of Lawrence. It is not the intention (or capability) of the Centre to do the research itself.

Yours sincerely,

A. H. Rossitor.

Ann read through the letter she had so rapidly typed, smiled to herself and, with a degree of regret, reached for the Delete key. At that moment, the door of her office opened and Tom Matthews entered.

'Come on, Ann,' he said. 'You must have earned yourself a cup of coffee at least by now. Come and join me in one.'

Ann turned, smiled, and asked the first question that popped into her head.

'Do you know Professor Barford?'

'Good Lord, who doesn't?' Tom replied. 'James claims that he's a modern historian, but most people think that he's a reincarnation of Attila the Hun. Why? Has he been giving you some hassle?'

'He phoned me this morning and demanded that I prepare this week some resources for him that would need all D. H. Lawrence's novels and short stories being on disk and an expert system to manipulate them. He hung up before I could even explain that it was beyond our resources and outside our remit. I've just written him a letter,' Ann added, 'but I don't think that it would be a good idea to send him the note as it stands.'

'Is this it?' Tom asked, approaching the screen.

'Yes,' Ann answered.

Tom read Ann's undiplomatic note and grinned.

'That would certainly have James demanding your expulsion,' Tom stated. 'Frankly, I think that it would be good for him to receive it, but it might not be the wisest move from your point of view. James Barford and I were colleagues at University College, London before we came here. Actually I quite like him, but he is an irascible and vindictive so-and-so at times. A more tactful response would be better, I feel. Come and have a coffee. Then you'll have cooled down enough to write a more measured reply.'

'OK,' Ann replied. 'Perhaps that would be a good idea.'

Together Ann and Tom Matthews walked across to the senior common room, with Ann reflecting upon the first two hours or so of her new job.

'Well, how's it been?' Tom asked. 'Apart from James Barford, have you felt reasonably at home?'

'It's the usual difference between theory and practice,' Ann replied. 'When I left home on Saturday to come to my digs in Nottingham, I felt excited and, frankly, reasonably confident. I know about Lawrence; indeed, I did a course paper on him at Sheffield. I've just had 12 months of systems analysis, relational databases and so on. Foolishly I felt that the job of running a resource centre, creating the databases to equip that centre, and dealing with user queries was right up my street. After only a couple of hours, I'm a great deal less sure.'

'Why?' Tom asked. 'You are God there. You do things at your own pace and in your own order. Nobody expects miracles overnight.'

'Maybe,' Ann replied, 'but I'm already feeling overwhelmed. Quite apart from the irritation of Professor Barford, I've already agreed to provide Dick Rogers with a chronological list of Lawrence's short stories and to give a party of schoolchildren a gripping introduction to the Centre next week, and I shall have to do some preparation for that. I already have three letters to reply to, as well as other letters that I want to write to institutes in Great Britain and the USA about the Centre. And that is in less than two hours. My major work of creating a relational database to aid all scholars of Lawrence was hardly begun. I'm beginning to fear it never will get done.'

By this time they had reached the SCR. Tom got them both a cup of coffee and they sat on some chairs near the south-facing window.

'Look, Ann,' Tom began, 'I know nothing about database administration, or whatever it is that you term your mystic art, but we are all going to feel overwhelmed for the next couple of weeks or so. Don't let it get you down. The D. H. Lawrence Study Centre only opened this morning. Everyone will be amazed if you have managed to make it even remotely useful by next September. Neither I nor the professor of English are going to be breathing down your neck, so relax.'

Ann smiled.

'Thank you Dr Matthews,' she said.

'Good Lord, woman, my name's Tom. Now, if you want to be really useful, I've got lumbered with a course on Scott Fitzgerald. You couldn't produce some lecture notes on him in your spare time, could you?'

The preceding narrative was only concerned with presenting a picture of some of the pressures on and functions of the database administrator. This second part of the chapter merely tries to formalize and categorize those functions.

You will have gathered that the DBMS is an important and complex entity. While it is designed to facilitate the operations of the business or organization that owns it, it needs considerable care and attention lavishing upon it in its own right. If an enterprise depends upon data (and most enterprises do), then the repository and guardian of that data, the database and its DBMS, need the sort of coddling that you would give to an aged relative who might be persuaded to leave you a fortune. The person or persons delegated to perform this caring function are generally known as the database administration staff. In a small company or academic department, this may comprise only one person, as was the case in the Ann Rossitor situation; in a large company, it is likely to be a significant department of its own. Whatever the staffing situation, it is a vital role. McFadden and Hoffer (1991) are merely expressing a truism when they write: 'Actual experience with computer databases has established a fundamental principle: The data administration function is *essential* to the success of managing the data resource.' It is unfortunate that managing directors often come to recognize this truth only as a consequence of some preceding database catastrophe. They then go on to establish the database administration that should have been set up even before they bought a computer.

One obvious element about the computer world in general and the database field in particular is that there is rarely much chance of just idling along. No sooner is one system installed than some other seminal breakthrough arrives. 'They also serve who only stand and wait' was written by Milton in a sonnet on his blindness; it is, alas, not a maxim appropriate for a database administrator (DBA). An essential aspect of his or her role is to plan for the future. Since that future will involve the implementation of new systems, the modification of existing systems, and the administration of the entire operation, the DBA cannot afford to stand and wait. What then, in outline, does the DBA do? What will Ann Rossitor's role really be when she has become established in her domain?

I shall divide the functions of the DBA into two categories:

1. Data control
2. Overall administration

The first of these can be split into five subsections, all relatively humdrum, but important and constituting the bulk of the DBA's work. To call them humdrum is not to suggest that they are either insignificant or simple. They are not. The second category reflects personnel aspects of the DBA's work as well as technical awareness. I might add, however, just one word of warning. There is even less standardization of nomenclature in the DBA world than there is in the more technical aspects of computer science. Hence the terms I use may well not correspond to the vocabulary that you encounter in any other books. None the less, despite the different terms, the functions will be identical.

15.1 Data control

Since data lies at the core of a database system and does so because data is the central entity of any business, it follows that the prime function of the DBA is to safeguard and protect that data. Clearly, much of that safeguarding and protection is built into the functions of the DBMS itself, but not even the most sophisticated DBMS can cater for or predict all the eventualities that are likely to confront a company or organization and its database. Hence, in the following five functions, the DBA has to monitor and perhaps modify the DBMS.

15.1.1 DATA SECURITY

Most people within a company are going to have access to data. Often that data will be shared or accessed by many different people. It is clearly important to ensure that sensitive data is only allowed to be accessed by the relevant and authorized personnel. It is important that no data at all is obtainable to an outsider. Hence the DBA has to assess the level of risk for varying aspects of the data, and the viable means of securing that data. Total security is not difficult to achieve. You just install the database in a concrete building with no doors or windows into that building. You further ensure that there are no electrical contacts leading into or out of that building. The database will then be perfectly safe. The only handicap will be that no one at all can use it. Total security is consequently an impossibility. A database is designed to be used. The moment it becomes available for use, it becomes insecure. There are, though, various ways of reducing that insecurity.

All authorized users can each be given a different password. Access to the database can only be accomplished by using the relevant password. All individuals allowed into the database building can be subjected to some form of biological identification: retina scan, palm print, voice verification. Certain sections of the database itself can only be accessed by the input of a further code. The data itself can be encrypted, and then only decrypted by inserting an encryption key. Certain protective devices can be employed in SQL itself. Use of the GRANT command (and its converse REVOKE) ensures that data is only accessed by the authorized personnel.

Hence there are a number of techniques which the DBA can employ to ensure that the data remains secure. It will be the DBA who has the ultimate responsibility for arranging the security measures to be taken. Nor, of course, will this be something that needs doing once and can then be forgotten about. New applications will be introduced. Crucial data will, with the passage of time, merely become of historical interest. Priorities within the company will change. Hence concern with the security of data will be a continuous preoccupation. This is a function that Ann Rossitor did not even begin to consider, but it is one that she will have to face even in the academic cloister in which she finds herself.

15.1.2 TUNING

The only thing that most users of a database system are ever concerned about is the speed of response. A managing director wanting to know what the last order to Bombay comprised tends to become fractious if he has to wait two hours for the answer. Indeed, some managing directors tend to become fractious if they wait more than two seconds. Hence the DBA needs to tune the database so that it gives the fastest possible response. Needless to say, of course, to do so requires knowledge, judgement and a measure of luck. In a large database, it is just not possible to satisfy every request for data in 0.0001 second, particularly when those requests may entail the simultaneous yoking together of data from three or four entirely different tables. Consequently, what the DBA needs to do is to determine what types of query are the most frequent in the organization to which he (or she) belongs. The design of the database and its applications can then be modified in order to facilitate those types. Yet again, of course, the frequency of types of request are going to vary as time passes. The DBA needs to modify the database structure so as to cater for changing needs. The database is also going to grow. As it does, acceptable access times cease to be so. The DBA has to monitor performance statistics constantly so as to take corrective action when and where it is needed. As Ann Rossitor builds her database tables, this is an aspect that she will need to keep in mind.

15.1.3 STANDARDS

Although each user of a database system tends to regard him or herself as the most significant user, all users do share the same data items. They may view such items in differing contexts, but the items themselves—department, customer, purchase, etc.—remain identical. It is important that the DBA establishes uniform standards for the naming of such entities. Equally, standards must be imposed for a whole variety of common functions: testing procedures; the changing of control procedures; the measurement of performance standards; the maintenance of the data dictionary; system documentation; and so on. Without the maintenance of such standards, there is no real data control at all.

15.1.4 DATA INTEGRITY

Standards imply data integrity, yet the preservation of integrity within a database is sufficiently crucial to warrant a mention of its own. As you know, the DBMS does a great deal to preserve the integrity of a database, but it cannot cope with all hardware errors or, for that matter, wayward eventualities during a batch operation. Hence it has to be the responsibility of the DBA to cater for such circumstances. That means that the DBA needs to lay out contingency plans to cope with all conceivable threats to the integrity of the database.

15.1.5 QUALITY MAINTENANCE

The purpose of standards, of safeguarding your data integrity, of imposing security checks and of tuning your system is to maintain a high quality level of performance. Yet it is not just the system itself where qualilty control is important; each individual program that the system uses must also maintain a high quality level. Hence the BDA can act as a sentinel, ensuring that no applications are taken on that contravene the standards that have been established.

15.2 Overall administration

15.2.1 PLANNING

Much of the work of a DBA has to be of an ad hoc nature. No one can predict the demands and imperatives that are going to arise. None the less, a DBA who does not plan is going to preside over a company or establishment whose inefficiency becomes a topic of universal chit-chat. The scope of the necessary planning can be subdivided into three broad areas:

1. The DBA needs to plan for the implementation of the database system if joining a company that is just about to invest in one. More commonly the DBA needs to plan for the implementation of new systems, since all companies and organizations grow out of their existing system or need to add parallel ones. Ann Rossitor is likely to find, in the not too distant future, that she wants to expand her growing database into a more versatile knowledge system, using, perhaps, an object-oriented network. There will be a little more about such an entity in Chapter 19.
2. The DBA needs to modify the current working database system. Eventually the degree of necessary modification becomes so overwhelming and so uneconomic in terms of time and money that a new system has to be installed, but this is an evil day (evil in terms of monetary burden) that a DBA can postpone for a long time if the existing system is modified with judgement and skill.
3. The best planning in the world does not have much point if there is not an administrative structure to support that planning. The DBA needs to have an administrative machinery to support the implementation of a database system and to support and reflect the modifications to that system.

Hence planning is the cerebral cement of database administration.

15.2.2 DATABASE DESIGN

A DBA does not normally design a database, but it is a foolish company that does not have the DBA intimately involved in design discussions. As you will already have gathered, the ideal situation is when the DBA is appointed before a database system has even been chosen, before a DBMS has been selected. The DBA can then make their rightful contribution to the logical context that the database system will inhabit. Rarely does this happen, and the DBA is normally appointed to look after a system that has already been chosen, bought and set up. Even so, database design is an iterative process. Hence the DBA will often be required to amend an existing schema, to monitor the capture and location of new data, and to alter existing definitions. Ann Rossitor has been placed in a strange midway position. The DBMS and the terminals had been chosen for her, but she was free to construct her own database.

15.2.3 COORDINATION

One of the vital criteria that impinges directly upon the tuning of a database system lies in the degree of coordination that is possible in such a system. Everybody who has access to a computer system as an essential element of their work suffers from precisely the same delusion: each of them regards their own function within the company system as crucial. The person in charge of order entry argues that if orders are not input promptly and correctly, the company will rapidly have no orders at all. The person in charge of accounts payable argues that if accounts are not dealt with promptly and correctly, there soon won't be any accounts to deal with. The *raison d'être* of the DBA for such people is to ensure that *their* vital role is given the priority it deserves. Hence the DBA, confronted with 10, 20 or however many vital functions, has to ensure that each of those receives the service that they want. Clearly this is a question of database design. The DBA has to review the needs of all the users and choose the design pattern which most fully satisfies those users. Equally clearly, no one design is going to provide the optimum performance for all the personnel involved. The DBA can only use judgement and tact and have a thick skin.

Such, then, is the role of the DBA. I could, perfectly validly, have extended this role and talked about the training functions of the DBA, or the specific task of managing the data dictionary. I could have talked about how vital it is for the DBA to keep up to date with current technology. None the less, all of those were implied, both in the formal itemization that we have just concluded and in the imaginative glimpse of Ann Rossitor's day at work. It is not possible or helpful to grade database aspects into a league table; is a good DBA more important than fully normalized data? does the data model adopted virtually determine the range and scope of database administration? Such questions of priority are not helpful. What is, however, vital is that we learn that the database administrative function is a very important one indeed. A good DBA can be the competitive edge between one company and another. Nor is this surprising. A good DBA needs intelligence, tact, industry and knowledge. It is not a frequent combination.

References

McFadden, F. R. and Hoffer, J. A. *Database Management*, 3rd edn, Benjamin Cummings, 1991.
Rishe, N. *Database Design Fundamentals*, Prentice-Hall, 1988.

16
Protecting the database

The title of this chapter is a fraction ambiguous since there are a number of ways in which we may wish to protect a database:

1. To ensure that only authorized personnel are permitted to use the database in question;
2. To ensure that those authorized persons do not damage the database in any significant respect;
3. To ensure that the database in question retains both semantic integrity and transaction integrity.

All of the above and their associated issues have already been touched upon. None the less, protecting our data resource is so vital an issue that it seemed necessary to devote an entire chapter to the matter. It fits too into this part because protecting the database is very much one of the functions of the DBA. I was amused when preparing for the writing of this chapter to encounter a comment in *Where Next for Computer Security?* (NCC, 1974): 'Although few DBAs are "in post" yet, it is suggested that the DBAs of the future will carry substantial responsibility for security of the systems for which they are responsible, ... '. Indeed they do. Hence this chapter.

Even so, there will be a great deal omitted from this chapter. For instance, legal and moral issues clearly impinge upon the whole question of security. Such issues will, however, be ignored. All that I am concerned to do in this chapter is to expand upon the paragraph devoted to security in the preceding chapter. None the less, brief though that paragraph was, it did imply a frighteningly large number of eventualities. So far as security alone is concerned, clearly there are three broad divisions:

1. The unauthorized access of data from outside;
2. The spite or vengeance of someone inside the company concerned;
3. Accidental damage or deletion.

The frightening implications of the first of these was highlighted in the film *Wargames* where a teenager gained access to a military computer system and almost caused a nuclear war as a consequence. Less dire but very expensive is the deliberate infection of systems with viruses. An example of this in November 1988 caused the failure of over 6000 workstations. A few years earlier, as an example of internal malice, a sacked employee deliberately erased thousands of records before he left. And the final category, accidental events, must be too numerous to count. It is, therefore, a vital role of the DBA to establish the most strict security and integrity procedures. As I pointed out in the previous chapter, total security is impossible, but much can be done to safeguard the data of an organization.

Related to security, though none the less a very distinct aspect, there is the question of ensuring that the database maintains an internal integrity. Without such an integrity, the database loses much of its point. It is vital that the data within a database should not be changed by system errors, but to ensure this, the DBA will need to run system checks that will themselves infringe the very levels of security that would, elsewhere, be operative. Hence the question of integrity not only is important for the status of the data itself, but also has repercussions on the whole topic of security. None the less, connected though they are, it will be useful to consider the two aspects of protecting a database, security and integrity, as independent elements. Only when we have seen their individual needs can we fully apprehend their interrelatedness.

16.1 Security

As far as security itself is concerned, there are three broad avenues that can be explored:

1. We can make it physically difficult to gain access to the data processing department.
2. Even if someone gains access to a terminal, it can still be ensured that the data itself is diffficult to access by unauthorized people.
3. Finally, even if the data itself is breached, it can none the less be rendered useless to unauthorized personnel.

Let us, therefore, glance at each one of these approaches.

16.1.1 PHYSICAL SECURITY

As I pointed out in the last chapter, it is easy to secure the complete physical security of the database and its management system. To do so, however, does mean that no one can use it. Indeed, given the proliferation of computers and terminals these days, the whole question of physical security has become increasingly difficult. With terminals in every office and with the widespread sharing of data, pure physical protection certainly cannot by itself be a sufficient safeguard. Indeed, since access to a database is now commonly possible by means of the telephone system, in certain circumstances, physical safeguards are not even a relevant option. Even so, simple physical security cannot be dismissed out of hand. It can still play a significant role. I do not imagine that I will cover every safeguard that can be used, but the following techniques are ones that certainly still have a part to play in the vital work of database security:

- Each terminal within an organization should have a lock. As a result, only those with the relevant key can use the terminal at all.
- While most departments—perhaps all—have terminals, those which are used in the computer science or data processing department itself, and hence are accustomed to dealing with more sensitive material, should, in the ideal world, be physically placed as a unit in a location where other members of the company have no need to visit. If the data processing department is placed on the ground floor next to reception and adjacent to accounts, then it is easy for a large number of people to have physical access to that department. If, however, the data processing department is physically separate from all other departments, then a much tighter rein can be maintained upon physical access to that department. Directors with a fanciful or historical frame of mind might care to invest in a moat.
- Even if the computer department is a separate and distinct entity, it is still a good idea for all members of that department (and any others where computer usage is possible) to be forced to provide some personal form of identification before being allowed into the department. There is a range of these available; from biological ones like fingerprints, voiceprints, and retina scans, to simple physical ones like access codes or badge readers. Which type is adopted depends to a large degree on the significance of the data that is being protected.

Clearly the above strategies are not mutually exclusive; you could employ a combination of them. Equally clearly, the more techniques that you do employ, the more difficult you make it for a potential invader. It will be a rare being who is able to enter the remote data processing department, type in an access number, and then unlock a terminal. Should such a thing happen, the invader will be further discouraged to discover that access to the data itself is also difficult. It is to this aspect that we next turn.

16.1.2   DATA SECURITY

Having gained access to a terminal, it is not difficult to ensure that the data obtainable from that terminal is made difficult to access by unauthorized personnel.

1. *Password* All staff should have a password. Only by their typing in that password will access to the database become possible. Each company should

ensure that passwords are changed regularly so that any security slips only have a short duration. Nor should passwords be made obvious. The usage of an employee's initials or date of birth as a password should never be acceptable. Nor, when passwords are changed, should the new password have any obvious connection with the old password.

2. *User view* This is a facility that is available with most DBMs. Any particular user of the database within a company is only likely to want to see certain sections of that database. As a result, that user can have a particular configuration compiled for his or her particular use. Let us assume that one employee only deals with exports to the Far East, and therefore only needs access to the tables dealing with shipments to the Far East, to accounts dealing with Far Eastern companies, and to the names and addresses of Far Eastern companies with which the organization deals. Consequently a view can be set up that gives the employee all the data required and only that data. As a result, the employee can access no other data; nor can any one else access the employee's data. Thus, by providing user views, an extra degree of security is built into the workings of the company.

3. *Hardware access* If users are provided with user views, a further level of protection can also be implemented by restricting specific operations to specific terminals. Hence, if our employee devoted to Far Eastern shipments can only carry out that function at a specific terminal, then a hardware restriction is added to the software restriction, making the interloper's task even more difficult.

4. *Logging off* In order to have access to the database or any section of that database, each user has to log on to the database in question, using a password and possibly using a specific terminal. If it is made a company rule that *everybody* logs off from their terminal every time they leave it un-attended, then once again the security risk is diminished. It is not unusual for employees to have their coffee break with colleagues or even to go out for lunch while still leaving their terminal switched on. During their absence, anyone can then have access to the data available on that terminal. Clearly any employee who is detected leaving his or her terminal unattended but still switched on would have to be dismissed. If data is vital, so is its protection, and a few dismissals, *pour encourager les autres*, should be perfectly effective.

None the less, even the best physical security and data access prevention can be circumvented. Hence we have to make the data useless even if it is accessed. This brings us to our final technique.

16.1.3 DATA ENCRYPTION

If someone evades the physical safeguards and the data access safeguards, life can still be rendered difficult for him or her. An authorized user will be presented with plain or clear text, that is, data presented in a plainly or clearly intelligible form. However, it can be ensured that all data in a database is automatically encrypted, with the consequence that any unauthorized user who does manage to access that data will merely be presented with an entirely meaningless text. Hence the intruder will need to decrypt the text before it becomes of any use whatsoever. A standard algorithm for encrypting text can make this more than a little difficult since employing a hit-or-miss method of deciphering it can take over 50 years to accomplish. Hence our interloper would require an almost infinite number of lunch breaks to make sense of the data accessed. Indeed, you can gain a good impression of the advances made in data encryption by comparing Van Tassel (1972) with van Tilborg (1988).

These then are the basic procedures to provide data security. It is a huge topic and discussion in depth would not be appropriate here. Even so, it is useful to look at just one practical implementation. We have looked briefly at SQL, but structured query language also provides security capabilities. Given our basic awareness of SQL and of the fact that it is the predominant query language, it will be useful to see how it can be used for protecting data.

16.1.4 PROTECTION WITH SQL

Access to data, or, indeed, to the SQL system itself, is controlled by the use of the word **GRANT**. Hence the DBA will grant facilities to a particular user:

```
GRANT TO Petra
```

'Grant what?' you may enquire. There are, in fact, three different levels of access. Thus you could have:

```
GRANT CONNECT TO Petra
```

This would enable Petra to select, update, insert and delete data from other user's tables. She would not, however, be able to create her own tables or drop anyone else's.

Secondly, you could have the level:

```
GRANT RESOURCE TO Petra
```

This would enable Petra to do everything that CONNECT had allowed, and to create and drop her own tables.

The final level, called the DBA level, allows its possessor to carry out any operation whatsoever on all and every table. Hence, were the DBA to issue this command to the database:

```
GRANT DBA TO Petra
```

the DBA would be granting Petra exactly the same rights as the DBA possessed. Such an action would, we hope, be very rare.

Of course, this GRANT command needs to be linked to a password. Hence you could have:

```
GRANT CONNECT TO Petra
  IDENTIFIED BY diesel
```

or

```
GRANT RESOURCE TO Herbert
  IDENTIFIED BY scrannel
```

or

```
GRANT DBA TO Ariel
  IDENTIFIED BY matex
```

And if you need to remove the rights for using such commands, then you employ the new command **REVOKE**. Hence, to remove Petra from the system entirely, you would issue this command:

```
REVOKE CONNECT FROM Petra
```

It should be clear that the same format of command will be used for the removal of any of the other authorizations.

Of course, the GRANT and REVOKE commands are most frequently used with reference to specific tables within the database and, indeed, to specific elements within those tables. Hence, if you had a table entitled Products and wished to give Susan the right to insert and update elements within that table, you would issue the following command:

```
grant insert, update
on products
to susan
```

When you subsequently discovered that it was not a good idea to allow Susan to update such a table because it led to problems within the department, you could then remove the permission so to do as follows:

```
revoke update
on products
from susan
```

Note, of course, that in most implementations, the use of upper-case or lower-case letters is immaterial; either will do.

You can not only grant a permission to a user but also give that user the right of passing on that particular permission to others. Hence, if you wanted to give Brian the right to select from the table Parts and also wished to let him have the right to allow others the same right, you would issue the following command:

```
grant select
on parts
to brian
with grant option
```

The examples above are concerned with granting rights to entire tables, but you may wish only to grant such rights to particular columns within such a table. In that case the command would be along the following lines:

```
grant update
on parts (price)
to leslie
```

which would only allow Leslie to change the prices of parts listed in the table but not alter the part_number, part_description or whatever.

I hope, therefore, that it is clear that within SQL you can tailor access to the database and rights within that database so that each employee only has access to the data to which he or she is entitled. You can, of course, extend this monitoring process by creating views for particular employees, views that give the employee concerned access to the data which they need but that exclude access to other data to which they are not entitled. In this way, an employee can be granted access to an entire table with the exclusion of certain columns within that table, or can be shown all the available columns but only for a limited subset of the table concerned, or even a subset of another view.

It is consequently not difficult to see that SQL itself provides very useful facilities for safeguarding the security of the database. It also plays a useful part on questions of integrity, and it is to this that we must next turn.

16.2   Integrity

You will, perhaps, recall that, in Chapter 7, integrity was presented as one of the functions of the DBMS. My comments then were as follows:

> Perhaps a synonym for integrity would be consistency. Imagine that an organization decided to have as a primary key for its Employee table an Employee number. New employees were entered into the database by the manager of the department that employed the employee. The manager of the advertising department prefixed all employee numbers with the letters AD. The manager of the sales department prefixed all his employee numbers with a 0 followed by a decimal point. And so it went on. As a result, there was no uniformity whatsoever. A DBMS should be able to prevent such idiosyncracies by imposing what are called *integrity restraints*. These can be of a very varied nature. The DBMS may prevent you deleting a customer's record if that customer still owes money. A DBMS should be able to prevent a salesperson being awarded a commission of 45 per cent. The DBMS must be able to ensure that all the employee numbers are of an identical type. Hence integrity constraints both prevent certain types of invalid updates from being entered and dictate that a certain type of processing must (or must not) be implemented.
>
> Obviously, integrity constraints could be imposed by the users of the

database, but this would be highly undesirable. Inconsistency might result. Users might forget. The result in both cases would be a lack of integrity in the database. It is clearly a great deal better for this aspect to be a DBMS responsibility.

This seems to imply that the DBMS enforces integrity constraints through an operation of inherent wisdom, and, of course, there are factors which the DBMS does enforce as an integral part of its business. Such constraints depend upon the type of DBMS with which we are dealing. The hierarchical DBMS imposes different constraints from the network model, and that, in turn, has different constraints from the relational model. It is, thus, impossible to create a table in a hierarchical database (other than a root table) that does not have an owner. The DBMS prevents such a creation. The DBMS for a network model imposes some structural constraints on 1 : N relationships. None the less, in all three database models, and almost exclusively so in the relational model, a DBMS only enforces implicit constraints if those constraints have been expressed in the data definition language. It is the process of database design that creates the implicit constraints. The most obvious example is the matter of data type. If you have specified that the data attribute 'quantity' belongs to the data type integer, then you ensure that no one can enter 'five' or '67.83' into that column. The DDL compiler stores the constraints in the DBMS catalogue, and they will thereafter be automatically enforced. Clearly, however, it often becomes necessary to impose specific constraints upon particular transactions or upon particular employees. Explicit constraints of this nature are the responsibility of the DBA, and I want to look at the range of options available.

Note, first of all, that we can be concerned with two different types of integrity: *data integrity* and *referential integrity*.

Data integrity is relatively straightforward. The object of the exercise is to ensure that only valid data is entered and that data entries are consistent across all tables of the database. This is normally done by means of the data type specifications at which we have already glanced. Hence, if you wanted to ensure that no employee was paid more than £65,000 p.a., you would insert a maximum constraint in your data definition. You might also want to insert a minimum constraint so as to ensure that no one was mistakenly paid less than £7,000 p.a. Clearly such a constraint is very imprecise; the managing director, who ought to be earning £47,000, is unlikely to be appeased when, having only received £27,000, is informed that at least you had ensured that he could not get less than £7,000. Even so, this type of constraint can be useful in safeguarding against gross errors. You can also use the UNIQUE and NOT NULL quali-fications upon relevant columns within the tables.

Referential integrity is concerned with the relationship between values in the tables of a database. You might, for instance, have a Parts table which listed products and the suppliers of those products. You would also have another table, the Suppliers table, which gave the necessary data about the suppliers

Table 16.1 Parts

Part_no	Part_name	Supplier_no
135	wozer	11
218	matchy	27
119	clude	03

Table 16.2 Supplier

Supplier_no	Supplier_name	Address
11	Grubits	Harlene
27	Scrath	Burllum
03	Zenths	Cardon

with whom your company dealt. Extracts from both are shown in Tables 16.1 and 16.2. Abbreviated though these tables are, it is not difficult to envisage a conceivable integrity problem. In the Parts table, the final attribute, Supplier_no, is a foreign key, since it is the primary key of the Supplier table. It is not difficult to see that chaos could result if a part were listed to a nonexistent supplier. It ought, therefore, to be possible to implement a referential integrity constraint so that a value in a foreign key column matches the same value in a primary key column of another table. In theory, there are two possible ways of ensuring that this does happen:

1. A specific integrity constraint should be included in the data definition of each relevant application program.
2. The DBMS should have the ability to enforce this type of constraint.

The first of these conceivable solutions is not desirable. It is easy to forget to include the necessary referential constraints. Even if there were no forgetfulness by the database staff, it would still be possible to install constraints that conflicted with one another. It is easy to see that real consistency would only be possible when the DBMS was in charge. Unfortunately, by no means all DBMSs enforce referential integrity, and even those that do often operate in a somewhat partial or clumsy fashion. INGRES, for instance, modifies each user request before execution in such a way as to ensure that it cannot possibly violate any constraints. While such security is welcome, it does look very much like a case of putting the cart before the horse, and clearly necessitates considerable superfluous processing. A number of writers suggest the use of the keyword ASSERT in SQL. By using what is in effect a declarative statement—e.g. ASSERT role_constraint ON employee—you can easily implement the safeguards that you need, such as ensuring that the employee enjoying the role of sales manager earns £18,000 p.a. and has a company car. Unfortunately, although ASSERT is mentioned confidently by Elmasri and Navathe, Pratt and Adamski, Gardarin and Valduriez and others, it is not a command included in the ISO standard for SQL and, indeed, makes no appearance whatsoever in van der Lans' (1989) book devoted to that standard. I have to conclude that integrity constraints are an area of database management that still need both definition and standardization. Given the significance of integrity control—Vossen (1990) describes it as being of 'central importance to various aspects of database processing', though, ironically, he devotes remarkably little to the issue—and given too the fact that I mentioned a moment ago that explicit integrity constraints are going, perforce, to be the responsibility of the DBA, I would like to clarify the nature of this task. Blethyn and Parker (1990) discuss integrity rules in Chapters 6 and 7 under three different headings:

1. Transition integrity rules
2. Domain integrity rules
3. Table integrity rules

It will be convenient to adopt their classification for what follows in this chapter, particularly since it will enable us to consolidate some of the understanding that we have already achieved on the area of database design.

16.2.1 TRANSITION INTEGRITY

It may not be immediately clear as to what is meant by a transition integrity rule. Fortunately it is a relatively straightforward concept. Entities within a database undergo transitions from one state to another. In other words, they experience changes. A customer buys a product. As a result, the customer's account experiences a transition from being in credit to being in the red. The product table is decreased by one item. The sales table is increased by one item. Hence, as you can see, the simple action of one customer buying one item necessitates changes to at least three tables of data, and possibly more. It is important that these changes remain consistent. They will only do so if there are rules incorporated into the database structure or if the procedure set out embraces the relevant interactions. That last sentence was somewhat gnomic, so let me expand.

If you incorporate rules into your database, those rules must be concerned to ensure that the integrity of that database remains unimpaired. Hence, if you are trying to insert a new order into the Order table, you must establish, as rules, a number of other constraints. A valid order will affect the Product table. Hence, while the specific order that is being currently processed is in operation, the Product table must be locked until the relevant alteration contingent upon that Order has been performed. Not until the Order has been processed and the relevant Product been subtracted from the Product table can both tables become free for other processing. Equally, the implementation of an Order will have an obvious impact upon the Customer account table. Not until that table has been made consistent with the Order table and the Product table can any of the three tables become unlocked. Hence, in the very design of the database, rules have to be incorporated so as to ensure that integrity is maintained. Such rules will entail the simultaneous locking of all the relevant tables until the entire transaction has been completed.

It is, however, difficult to ensure that all conceivable eventualities are catered for in the design of the database. Hence, from time to time, the DBA will need to check that a procedure for a particular transaction will not in any way infringe the integrity of the database. The object of the exercise is identical, but whereas rules are an integral part of the database structure, the procedural approach defines the necessary steps in a sequential fashion. Clearly this will entail frequent use of the IF ... THEN ... ELSE construct:

```
IF the Order is acceptable
 THEN increase Order_number by 1
  ELSE output 'Order not valid';
```

In reality, it is rarely possible to include rules for all the complex processing possibilities, and most transactions entail a mixture of rules and sequential procedural instructions. It is ultimately the function of the DBA to create the environment where this integrity preservation is always observed. It can be said with some confidence that such a role for the DBA is impossible. In a large establishment with dozens of highly qualified people using the database daily, it is not viable for the DBA and staff to monitor all processing so as to ensure that integrity is maintained. Of course, for the vast majority of the time, integrity will continue to exist; most operations are not going to degrade the database in any way. Until, however, we have reached the state where integrity can be handled much more fully by the DBMS itself, it is not realistic to claim that this is an issue which is fully resolved.

16.2.2 DOMAIN INTEGRITY

A domain is a set of values. Hence each column within a table constitutes a domain. A consequence of this we have already encountered: any foreign key must be of the same domain as the primary key to which it points. Indeed, should any value or attribute appear in more than one table, regardless of its status, then the domain definition should always be the same. Ensuring that this is the case is not too difficult. When the database is established, the DBA needs to set out the domain definitions and, consequently, the permissible values for any attribute contained within that domain. Consider, for instance, an Employee table with the following columns or domains:

Employee_no;   Name;   Address;   Phone_no;   Joining_date;   Role;   Salary

We can legislate that the primary key, Employee_no, is an integer between 0 and 5000 (or whatever is a reasonable maximum for the company concerned). We can make the Name field a character string of fixed or variable length. We can decide on whether to make the Phone_no an integer or a character field; it would have to be a character field if you wanted to separate the code number from the individual number. We can legislate as to the precise format of date we wanted: 1.1.91, 1st Jan 1991, 1/1/91 or Jan 1, 1991. We can impose a character limit on Role so that no one is credited as being 'supervisory lavatorial executive' when the lengthiest role allowed is only of 10 characters. Linkages could be created between Role and Salary so that the managing director could not be credited with £7,000 p.a. and a cleaner with £43,000. Clearly all such definitions would be contained in the data dictionary, and it could be made mandatory that no new domains were created without the DBA's permission, so that consistency was retained by the DBA.

Of course, none of this data definition will prevent incorrect data being entered. If the employee's name is J. F. Smythe, the database won't object if you enter J. F. Smith, though it will object if you try to enter J. F. Smi3th. If J. F. Smythe joined the company on 4 September 1991, the database won't know or care if you enter 4 October 1991, though it will know and care if you enter 32 September 1991. There is no total safeguard against human error.

There is also the question of the range of data definition available. The more precisely you can specify the type of data each field requires, the more firmly you can safeguard against erroneous entries. Unfortunately, many DBMSs only allow a relatively limited range of data types, thereby preventing the safeguarding precision that certain DBAs might desire. In addition, SQL also only supports a relatively small selection of data types. Finally, while most DBMSs use SQL, the data types of those DBMSs do not always correspond to SQL nomenclature. Hence, just to illustrate this issue, Table 16.3 lists the approved standard SQL data types and the data types permitted in two successful relational databases, INGRES and Oracle.

Such data types are significant when working with a database because they ensure that, when you add or change data, the new data must be of the type specified for that column when the table was created. Thus integrity is preserved. Unfortunately, there is such a divergence between particular implementations of data types that it is easy to become confused. As you can see from the listing of Table 16.3, SQL does not support the data type DATE, yet every implementation of SQL upon which I have worked did, in fact, offer DATE as a data type. As most DBMSs and their associated query languages accept NULL values, so it is always advisable to specify NOT NULL alongside each data entry.

Table 16.3 Data types

SQL	INGRES	Oracle
CHARACTER (or CHAR)	C (or CHAR, VCHAR, VARCHAR)	CHAR (or VARCHAR)
NUMERIC	INTEGER1	LONG (or LONGVARCHAR)
DECIMAL (or DEC)	INTEGER2	NUMBER
INTEGER (or INT)	FLOAT4	NUMBER(n)
SMALLINT	FLOAT8	NUMBER(n,m)
FLOAT	DATE	RAW(n) (or LONGRAW)
REAL	MONEY	DECIMAL, INTEGER and
DOUBLE PRECISION		SMALLINT are the same as NUMBER.

16.2.3 TABLE INTEGRITY

Transition integrity rules deal with the changes that are allowed in database values. Domain integrity rules specify what values are allowed to exist in a database. Table integrity rules are concerned with the question of referential integrity at which we have already glanced. We can, therefore, just itemize the rules that ought to be included in a relational database. You will recall that referential integrity is concerned with the validity of references to one item in a table that also appears in another table or tables. We need, therefore, rules for insertion and deletion.

1. *Insertion rule* A row or field that refers to another row or field in another table should not be inserted unless the other row or field which it matches already exists. The purpose of this rule is virtually self-evident. It is absurd to have a supplier listed in the Product table who does not exist in the Supplier table.
2. *Deletion rule* It follows, therefore, that you should not be able to delete a row or field if that row or field is referred to by a parallel row or field in a different table. You basically have two alternatives:
   (a) The delete request can be disallowed completely.
   (b) The delete request can be accepted, but all parallel rows or fields in other tables should automatically be deleted at the same time.

To conclude: it is clear that both security and integrity are issues of considerable importance in database management and that they need to be given due weight by any DBA. Security is relatively straightforward. It can never be foolproof, but the available security techniques are well known and their implementation will depend upon the significance of the data to be protected and the amount of money available for such protection. Integrity, though, is a thornier issue. Given the chaos that a degraded database can create, it is shameful that most books deal with integrity in a somewhat off-hand fashion and even more shameful that we are not yet at the stage of having DBMSs which can cope adequately with integrity issues. McFadden and Hoffer (1991) are hopeful: 'Unfortunately, not all DBMS products today enforce referential integrity; newer releases of some DBMS products do, however, and this feature will probably become standard for most products in the future.'

Let us hope that they are right.

References

Blethyn, S. G. and Parker, C. Y. *Designing Information Systems*, Butterworth-Heinemann, 1990.
Van Tassel, D. *Computer Security Management*, Prentice-Hall, 1972.
van Tilborg, H. C. A. *An Introduction to Cryptology*, Kluwer, 1988.

17
The data dictionary

The preceding two chapters have, I hope, shown that the role of the database administrator is a vital one. I have already indicated that, in a small company, all the DBA functions might devolve onto one person, while in a large company, it might merit a department of its own. Whatever the situation may be, it is an unhappy one. The accounts department is aided by spreadsheets, database reports, archive material and sundry accountants. The marketing department can call upon database files, report formats, graphical facilities and scores of salespeople. The research department has the ability to store, recall and manipulate data from as many database files as it needs to access. The managing director can obtain an instant snapshot of any aspect of the business merely by pressing a few buttons on a keyboard. They all rely upon and depend on the data processing department to ensure that the resources of the database are configured for their convenience and that the database concerned is permanently accurate and up to date. As we have seen, this is the *raison d'être* of the DBA. The DBA's department, however, has no such aids. Needed by everybody, blamed by everybody, the DBA has to construct tools to help everybody else, but has no such tools personally, or at least if they exist, they are tools constructed by the DBA.

There is, however, one invaluable tool which can help to relieve the parlous lot of the DBA. As Deen (1985) points out: 'The key to effective use of the data in a database is its proper documentation, without which a user is bound to get lost.' This documentation is customarily called the data dictionary, and I devoted a short section on it towards the end of Chapter 11. It is, however, so crucial an element, and can be so indispensable in the work of the DBA and in the overall protection of the database itself that it needs a fuller examination.

Given the significance of the data dictionary, its partial coverage by respected writers in the world of IT is confusing. Gardarin and Valduriez (1989) give the topic 10 lines out of 435 pages. Rishe (1988) only provides one page out of 421. Laurie (1985) does not mention them at all, and neither do Smith and Barnes

(1987). Frost (1986) only manages 14 lines out of 653 pages. Matthews (1991) provides six lines, Abdellatif *et al.* (1990) rise to a page and a half, Korth and Silberschatz (1991) also only manage a page and a half out of 678. Even Date (1990), normally so thorough and precise, only devotes a four and a half page chapter to the data dictionary out of 835 pages of text in volume 1, and no expansion at all in volume 2. Yet Date does, by implication, suggest some explanation for the partial treatment of data dictionaries. The chapter that he devotes to the topic is entitled 'The system catalog' and is devoted, not to data dictionaries in general, but to the specific implementation in DB2. Earlier on in his book, he refers to the data dictionary and provides the following footnote:

> Once again we are touching on an area in which there is much terminological confusion. Some people would refer to what we are calling the dictionary as a *directory* or a *catalog*—with the implication that directories and catalogs are somehow inferior to a true dictionary—and would reserve the term 'dictionary' to refer to a specific (important) kind of application development tool .... Other terms that are sometimes used to refer to this latter kind of object are 'data repository' and 'data encyclopedia.'

Nor is it necessarily a simple question of terminological confusion. McFadden and Hoffer (1991) state that: 'Information repositories are replacing data dictionaries in many organisations'. Unfortunately, the distinction that McFadden and Hoffer make between a data dictionary, which they term a simple data element documentation tool, and an information repository, which they see as being used to manage the total information processing environment, is not an entirely satisfactory one since the very aspects of a repository upon which they comment are often cited by other writers as being functions of the data dictionary. We have already seen that databases are a relatively recent entity in the world of computer science. As the database world has developed, so has the related one of data dictionaries, and the two have progressed together, though not necessarily in tandem. We have seen that there are three basic types of database model: hierarchical, network and relational. As we shall see shortly, there are also three basic types of data dictionary. But, as we shall see in Chapter 19 of this book, there are now emerging types of database that do not fit into any of the three models at which we have looked. In the same way, data dictionaries have developed so that current examples are much more versatile than earlier ones in that they are capable of not only aiding users and applications but also playing a part within computer-aided software engineering (CASE). McFadden and Hoffer place considerable emphasis upon this, and it almost seems as if it is this facility which distinguishes a repository from a dictionary. Clearly then it is a question of terminology, but not a straightforward one. Latin and Italian are two different and distinct languages, but the latter developed from the former. When did Latin cease to be Latin and become Italian? The analogy seems a fair one, and it is this fluid situation which helps to explain at least some of the terminological chaos with which computer science seems to be constantly beset.

I cannot resolve the terminological and/or conceptual imprecision, but I can do my best to evade it. The rest of this chapter is divided into sections, each one of which will try clearly and unambiguously to define an aspect of data dictionaries. By so doing, the section will convey a precision and preciseness that is not an entirely fair reflection of the IT world. In other words, I shall attempt to express the core of the matter, but will ignore the penumbra. This seems to me to be useful in exactly the same sort of way as the rule 'i before e except after c' is useful. As we all know, there are a number of exceptions—'neighbour', for example—but the rule helps us in the majority of cases. So it is with data dictionaries. A data dictionary is a central storehouse of data about an organization's entire data handling. That handling is inevitably complex and not necessarily entirely coherent. Computer science is a rigorous and exact study; information technology is an intuitive and idiosyncratic art. If databases are the core of IT or computer science, as I believe them to be, it is no wonder that they exemplify the conceptual breadth (or ambiguity) of the subject of which they form a central part.

17.1   Types of data dictionary

There are three different types of database dictionary system. On this point. Oxborrow (1989) and Pratt and Adamski (1987) agree, though they use different nomenclature to describe those types.

1. An *independent* data dictionary (i.e. a *free-standing* or *standalone* one) is a dictionary that describes the database or databases concerned but is not connected or tied in any way to that database or those databases. It follows, therefore, that every time an entity or object is added to the database, a parallel entry (or entries) need to be made to the data dictionary. This is not a very satisfactory situation. It is almost inevitable that discrepancies will exist between the database and the dictionary.
2. An *integrated* or *interfaced* or *dependent* dictionary overcomes this problem because it is stored and managed by the DBMS and can consequently relate more closely to the data within the database itself. The degree of interaction between the dictionary and the database which it is describing varies, but there is normally a basic integration between data and meta-data.
3. An *embedded* or *active* dictionary is really a totally and fully integrated dictionary. Indeed, it is a constituent member of the DBMS itself. As a consequence, other database elements like query languages and programs can be incapacitated if the correct information is not already held by the dictionary. It is this type of dictionary that comes close to what McFadden and Hoffer seem to mean when they talk about a repository.

It is not difficult to see that these three types represent three progressive developments within the data dictionary field, and that the embedded dictionary is by far the most effective of the three.

17.2 Entities and the dictionary

As you know, whatever type of data dictionary an establishment might possess,
the fundamental purpose of that dictionary is to store information about the
data within the database. The database, of course, is going to be packed with
data about objects or entities. There will be a file or table about employees,
providing the essential data about the workforce of the company concerned.
Table 17.1 is an abbreviated version. It is the purpose of the data dictionary to
describe Table 17.1 and to establish its parameters. Hence each element within

Table 17.1

Emp_no	Surname	Forenames	Address
0001	Robinson	Peter Nigel	12 Slade St, Frindham
0002	Percy	Stephen Ian	49 Hastings Ave, Bull
0003	Wardall	Matthew Brian	3 The Grove, Chotlem

the table will be described in the data dictionary. As you can see, the first
column of the table is devoted to an employee number. The data dictionary is
likely to itemize it in the following fashion:

Name	Length Max	Min	Type	Where used	Allowable values	Sequence field
Emp_no	4	4	Numeric	Employees	9999	Yes

The data dictionary first identifies the data item concerned by naming it.
Although not shown in the example above, the data dictionary must also cite
any synonyms or aliases for the name; Staff_no might be an example. It then
sets out the length of that data item. In this case, the employee number is forced
to be four characters long, thus taking up four bytes of space. The data type for
Emp_no is, obviously enough, numeric, and, since it is a maximum (and
minimum) of four digits long, its maximum allowable value is 9999. The final
entry—sequence field—is concerned to establish whether or not the attribute is
an identifying attribute. Since Emp_no is the primary key of the row in
question, it clearly is an identifying attribute.

As well as the column entries shown, the data dictionary may also add a brief
description of the attribute:

Name	Length Max	Min	Type	Where used	Allowable values	Sequence field
Emp_no	4	4	Numeric	Employees	9999	Yes

Description: a number which uniquely describes each employee

Nor must this be taken as representing any specific data dictionary, I have simply taken the sample illustration provided by Vasta (1989) and adapted it slightly. Certainly the column headings chosen by Vasta will vary from time to time in differing data dictionaries. you might, for instance, have a format like the following:

Domain	Data type	Data width	Picture	Values	Key
Emp_no	Numeric	4	'9999'	0000 to 9999	Mandatory

You might also be using a dictionary that allows more information to be given. It might, for instance, give the number of occurrences of this particular field. It might indicate who is allowed to access and change the data item concerned. If there is more than one database for the company concerned, the data dictionary should show which other databases also show this field. There might also be some indication of the frequency of usage of this field. Bull (1990) gives an illustration of quite a comprehensive entry for a single field on a product information file. It is, I think, perfectly comprehensible without further explication:

DATA-ITEM: QUANTITY
TYPE: ATTRIBUTE
DESIGNED: 10 APRIL 1990
LAST UPDATED: 10 APRIL 1990
LOCATION: LM34/V/9
FILE: PRODUCT, MASTER
ATTRIBUTE: 3
PASSWORD: ABS445
UPDATE AUTHORITY: HEINE
DESCRIPTION:
This field indicates the current stockholding of the item which is physically present in the warehouse.
It does not include any incoming stock which has been ordered but not yet received.
It does not include any outgoing stock which has been ordered by clients but not yet issued.

FORMAT:
  NUMERIC
  INTEGER
  MAXIMUM VALUE: 9999999999
  LEADING ZEROS: NONE
  DISPLAYED: RIGHT JUSTIFIED
SYNONYMS:
  QTY
  QUANTITY-IN-STOCK
  HOLDING
  STOCKHOLDING
THE DATA IS USED BY THE FOLLOWING PROGRAMS:
  CREATED: MB1001
  READ: MB1003
                                 MB1004
                                 MB1034
                                 VALN0001
  DELETED: MB1003
                                 MB1002

The data dictionary will, of course, contain a row for each attribute of the entity concerned. After the employee number came the employee's surname:

Name	Length		Type	Where used	Allowable values	Sequence field
---	Max	Min	---	---	---	---
Surname	18	2	Character	Employees		

And so it goes on until you have covered every attribute in the Employees table, and then, of course, you would move on to the next table, and so on until every entity in the entire database had been described in the dictionary. In this respect, the data dictionary is not unlike the English dictionary that we all use in order to discover what 'effusive' means or how to spell 'parallel'. The next section, however, shows a facility of the data dictionary that is not shared by language dictionaries.

17.3   Relationships and the dictionary

As Gillenson (1990) points out; 'The relationship between virtually any pair of data dictionary entities can have value to some part of the data processing organization.' Not unnaturally, data dictionaries vary in the scope with which they fulfil this function, some being more limited than others. It is important therefore to have a proper understanding of exactly what we mean by the term 'relationship'. It has been used often enough already in this book, but it will help to codify our understanding if Michael Gorman's definition (Gorman, 1991) is kept in mind:

A relationship is the manifestation of a business rule between two or more data record instances from the same or different data record types. As an example, a company might require that all employees be assigned to a project, or that an employee be assigned to a department, or (in the case of a university) that all teachers must belong to a college and teach at least one course. Such business rules, manifest in a database as relationships, can be either arbitary or computed. A relationship is arbitrary when the set of rules that binds records together is not reflected in the set of values stored in one or more data record elements contained in the data record instances. A relationship is computed when the set of rules is manifest as commonly shared data record element values.

We already are aware of the fact that some attributes within a database are going to appear in more than one file or table. Indeed, the issue of foreign keys, where an attribute that is the primary key of one table appears as a nonprimary key in another, has already been mentioned. Clearly, though, no matter how rigorous our attempts to escape redundancy may be, some fields are going to appear more than once within a database. The employee number in the Employes table at which we have just been looking might well reappear in the Department table or the Project table or the Pension table or the Social club table or, indeed, in them all. Fortunately, it is not difficult to itemize the types of relationship which can be represented within a database.

17.3.1 ONE TO ONE

This is a relatively rare relationship. It signifies the situation when one element from one table has a relationship only with one element from another table. The company of Daniels Decorative Tables (better known as DDT) has a number of stores scattered round the country. Each store has a managing director. It so happens that the Daniels database has two tables, one devoted to its managing directors, the other devoted to its separate stores. The managing directors table has a field devoted to the store number of the shop which that particular employee manages. Not surprisingly, Store_no is the primary key of the Store table and thus acts as a link between the store table and the Managing directors table. It is, however, a matter of company policy that one person can only be the managing director of one store, and that one store can only have one managing director. There is, therefore, a simple one-to-one relationship between row one in Table 17.2, and row three in Table 17.3.

The fact that there is this simple one-to-one relationship should entail a certain amount of housekeeping by the DBMS. If you wanted to enter F. S. Berkerly as the managing director of store number S13, the DBMS should prevent you so doing, because W. B. Quilp is already the managing director of that store. If, however, the DBMS does not support such one-to-one relationships, then a programmer has to construct a specific appliction which will perform the necessary checking. Note too that the fact that Store_no appears in two

Table 17.2   Managing directors

Emp_no	Surname	Initials	Home_address	Store_no
128	Quilp	W.B.	111 Cadge Lane, Burden.	S13
032	Pecksniff	M.T.	37 Smarm Close, Yarnd	S02
064	Magwitch	B.I.S.	2a The Mounds, Statis	S04
005	Gargery	G.	19 Smith Row, Burden	S12

Table 17.3   Store

Store_no	Store_town	Store_address	Tel_no
S01	Plund	11–15 Quint Way	281–99437
S09	Hersham	9–13 Dowager Road	472–82391
S13	Burden	1–5 Ronald Street	893–11742
S05	Newmare	105–7 Whippet Road	922–56293

tables is a matter of some importance, because if you update a field in one table, it is vital that the identical field be updated in all the other fields in which it may appear. Nor is this all. The field itself may not be changed, but some policy decision relating to that field may be implemented which requires some change to one or more of the tables in which that particular attribute appears. Under such circumstances, it is extremely useful if the data dictionary can inform you as to the respective files in which the attribute in question makes an appearance.

17.3.2   ONE TO MANY

These are much more common relationships than one-to-one instances. Often known as owner–member relationships, it is not difficult to think of common examples:

department–staff
company–employees
author–works

17.3.3   MANY TO MANY

This too is a common relationship type, and we have already seen some of the difficulties that we can encounter in representing many-to-many relationships within a database model. One or two examples will clarify the situation:

• *Lecturer–student* There are obviously many lecturers and many students, but the relationship is best envisaged as:

    one lecturer   one student
    teaches   is taught by
    many students   many lecturers

- *Cricketers–matches* There are obviously many cricketers and many matches, but the relationship is best envisaged as:

one cricketer	one match
plays in	is played in by
many matches	many cricketers

Decomposing the relationship into two one-to-many relationships is frequently the only viable way of representing many-to-many relationships at all within the confines of a database.

17.3.4 RECURSION

A recursive relation is when something refers to itself. This might sound an odd arrangement at first, but recursive relations are not uncommon. The county of Wessex has a database devoted to its chess organization. One table or relation is devoted to teams operating within the county. By and large, each town or large village has an entry within the Teams table, and indeed, the town or village name is made the primary key for the table itself. Thus there is a row given over to Yeovil and another to Dorchester and another for Launceston and so on. It is, of course, often the case that a town has more than one chess team. Where this is the case, the various teams are looped or nested within the table, and we have a recursive situation. Not all network DBMSs can directly simulate the recursive relationship, and clearly the insistence within the relational model upon each table being devoted to single-valued entries excludes recursion from direct representation within a relational database. Date (1990) links recursion to the emergence of more logic-based database systems, and I can only refer you to his Chapter 24 (and its excellent biography) should you wish to explore this area.

17.3.5 OWNER–MULTIPLE-MEMBER

This is hardly a self-explanatory heading, but the concept is not difficult. In essence it is the same as a one-to-one relationship, except that one of the entities within the relationship has more than one type within itself. An example will help to clarify matters.

If you have a Department, then that department is likely to possess Employees. Such is a simple one-to-one relationship, provided that each employee can only work for one department. However, the Employees table might itself be split into varying options: full_time_employees, part_time_employees, retired_employees. This would be an example of the owner–multiple-member relationship.

There are other relationship-types, but the five listed above are the ones that you are most likely to encounter.

17.4   Functions of data dictionary systems

Providing information about entities (and their attributes) and relationships
clearly fulfils important functions, but it is useful if we can itemize the functions
of a data dictionary system more formally. In so doing we can gain a fuller
understanding of the database world.

1. In the most straightforward sense, a data dictionary is, as has been implied
   already, just like a dictionary from which you check spellings or definitions.
   It performs much the same sort of function as the Glossary at the end of this
   book in that it defines the entities encountered in the database context.
2. A data dictionary, as well as defining the entities within the system, can also
   exercise control over data entry and maintenance so that; no entity is ever
   defined twice (possibly in slightly differing ways); all synonyms for each
   entity are listed; entities are cross-referenced within the dictionary; and all
   the operations under entry and maintenance are under the control of data
   administration.
3. The data dictionary should have the means of checking the access authorization of a user and debarring such access from any potential user who
   cannot submit the correct authorization.
4. The data dictionary system should be able to provide a variety of reports to
   database users, both standard reports and user-defined ones. In this way, the
   data dictionary is an indispensable element in the administration of the
   organization, being able to provide report formats for accounts, sales, costs,
   etc.
5. As we have already seen, a very important feature of the data dictionary is its
   ability to show relationships: relationships between attributes and the tables
   to which they belong; relationships between tables (often shown by a
   common attribute); and the relationship between a table (or record) and the
   logical schema of the entire database. Such connections create in many
   cases the *raison d'être* of the database itself, and it is clearly vital that
   those linkages should be maintained during all update and/or deletion
   operations.
6. Access to data is a prime requirement in database handling, and the data
   dictionary can play an important part in such access by providing pointers
   to further relevant meta-data or to the actual stored data itself.
7. The data dictionary needs to have some means of responding to commands
   in the host language or languages of the database system concerned. Indeed
   there needs to be quite a full interface between programming (and query)
   languages and the dictionary itself so that the building of databases structure
   or access to the data dictionary itself is made as reciprocal a process as
   possible.

I could continue. The functions of the data dictionary can be relatively confined
within a small and primitive system; they can be extensive and embracing within

a larger concern. Braithwaite (1990) produces Fig. 17.1 to show the central role of the data dictionary in the entire system development life cycle (SDLC). He spends a couple of pages explaining the ramifications of the diagram—I have never believed that a picture is worth a thousand words; it often needs the thousand words to explain the picture—but it should be relatively self-explanatory to readers of this book. The data dictionary rests at the core of the SDLC. The meta-data about the various phases of the SDLC surround this core. Then, outside the system itself, lie its various interfaces. Such a diagram indicates the crucial role of the data dictionary, and makes the failure of some writers to mention it at all very difficult to understand.

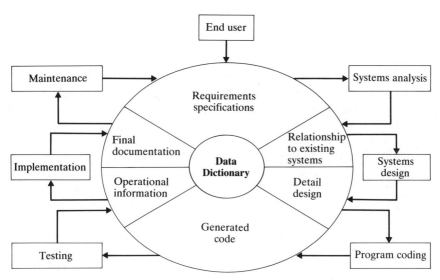

Figure 17.1

Do not, of course, forget that the basic function of the data dictionary is to communicate, not with you, the user, but with the database itself. The data dictionary is a significant aid in facilitating access to data, in preserving relationship integrity and in preserving security. You can use a database for months and not even be aware that it has a database dictionary, yet that dictionary will have been aiding your operations in countless ways. One of those ways, the preservation of integrity, is, as we saw in Chapters 15 and 16, a question of the utmost concern. Hence it is worth while returning briefly to this issue, particularly since it enables us to make a further distinction within the database area itself.

17.5 The integrity of relations

As you may recall, the usual term for referring to the defined set of rules and actions that apply to relationships is 'referential integrity'. When we mention referential integrity, we are talking about the types of relationships that need to be maintained, and the actions necessary to ensure such observance. The rules of referential integrity only involve relationships where there is an owner–member construct (normally one-to-one or one-to-many), and the actions of relevance are those of insertion or deletion. Thus referential integrity is concerned to ensure that nothing is deleted when such a deletion would have repercussions upon other data items. Equally, referential integrity is concerned to ensure that all additions to the database are congruent with existing data items. In addition, referential integrity is affected by the nature of the DBMS itself, in particular as to whether the DBMS uses static or dynamic facilities. It is this which requires some explication.

When relationships within a database tend to be stable, then it follows that the tables of that database and the rows within those tables tend also to be well defined and stable. A context where relationships are in a constant state of flux tends to be a situation where data is also often transient and variable. Clearly such disparate states have considerable implications for referential integrity. A static context with formally defined relationship clauses is clearly a very different entity from the point of view of integrity maintenance than is a dynamic context with no formally defined relationship clauses. Gorman (1991) argues that the static or dynamic nature of a database is more important than its data model, and you can see what he means. In a database with static relationships, those relationships can be implemented through traditional pointers all under the control of a single schema within a well-engineered and controlled database. A dynamic context, however, can pose more serious integrity problems because the relationships, and the data items expressing those relationships, tend to be under user control. Hence, when a data field is updated, any repercussions on other data fields either have to be handled by the user (with the consequent risks of omission) or by a complicated system of locks to be handled by the DBMS itself. Let us glance at each in turn.

So far as insertion is concerned, within both the static and dynamic environments, a new row of data is only allowed to be inserted if there is an appropriate table or set in which such a row (or data item) can be relevantly inserted. The advantage of the static context is that such insertions can be more quickly performed because the structure and location of the relevant files is clearly indicated. A dynamic context tends to entail the use of secondary keys and probable consequent search of a list of primary keys. With regard to delations, the data model concerned is also of considerable importance because it is only the hierarchical and network models that explicitly declare relationships. Hence, in such instances, a *cascade* effect of a deletion can be experienced in which not only the data item (or record) in one location is deleted but all other matching instances also. This cascade effect can equally affect both static and dynamic contexts. The interactions of data model, static or dynamic contexts and the nature of the data dictionary itself clearly constitutes a complex matrix, and it is not surprising that most writers (myself included) fail to explore the issues in any depth. In one sense, this is inevitable. There are so many available options that it would be self-defeating to explore them all. Each reader would only be interested in the combination relevant to their situation, and any exploration in depth would consume pages greater in number than this entire book. Yet it is this matrix which has profound repercussions upon the question of referential integrity. It would consequently have been dishonest not to have made you aware of the issue, even though real guidance is beyond the scope of this introductory book. You may, however, want (or need) to explore the issue more fully. Hence I attempt, in the next, concluding section, to make some useful suggestions for such an exploration.

17.6 Additional information

I have already commented that many books give little space for the important topic of the data dictionary, and I have suggested some reasons for this unfortunate lacuna. There are already well over 100 differing types of data dictionary in operation. There is also the seemingly inevitable terminological problem. As computing technology has advanced, and high-level languages and CASE tools have become more common, writers have tended to move away from talking about the relatively simply concept of a data dictionary to the more complex concept of a data repository which is itself a component within an information repository dictionary system (IRDS). McFadden and Hoffer (1991) do so, as does Gorman (1991). Nor do writers on specific DBMSs necessarily give any attention to the data dictionary that is allied to that DBMS. Abdellatif *et al.* (1990) only give a page and a half and Matthews (1991) gives even less. Both Malamud (1989) and I (Rothwell, 1992), in our respective books on INGRES, do devote a chapter to the topic, and I try to show how the data dictionary in INGRES (and all relational databases) is made up of tables just like the database itself. The following extract tries to indicate the general layout of a relational database dictionary, though I have excluded specific references to the specimen database which I was using in that book.

First of all, we must understand that INGRES stores its data in a particular fashion. In fact there are eight alternative methods in which INGRES can store the data with which it is presented:

Heap   Btree   Cheap   Cbtree   Hash   Isam   Chash   Cisam

None of these storage structure names will be at all meaningful to you at this moment, and there is no reason why this blissful unawareness should not continue. All that matters for our purposes is to know that each of the above

names represents a different way in which data is stored. In some, for
instance, duplicate rows are permitted; in others, not so. In some, the data is
stored sequentially; in others, it has a tree-like structure. Whatever the
method, however, INGRES constructs an index in order to enable it to
access the data accurately and rapidly. None of this, of course, concerns the
user of the database, who can happily remain ignorant of what INGRES is
doing. None the less, it is the creation of these indexes which allows the data
dictionary to be accessed .... Since indexes in INGRES are, like everything
else, tables themselves, you can frame a query asking for the specific data that
you want:

```
RANGE OF A IS ATTRIBUTE

 SELECT (A.ATTRELIO)
WHERE A.ATTNAME='town'
```

The first line of this query—RANGE OF A IS ATTRIBUTE—is only
present in order to save some writing, as is clear when you look at the next
two lines. Their meaning is fairly self-evident. The query is asking INGRES
to select an attribute from all the possible tables whenever that attribute has
the name 'Town'. As a consequence, INGRES will present upon the screen a
table like the following:

attrelid
store

Obviously, in a full database, the attribute name 'town' would appear in a
number of diffrent tables, and each of them would be listed in the data
dictionary response to our query.

Equally, if you cannot remember how many columns the Supplier table
possesses or what those columns are called, just enter the query

```
 SELECT (A.ATTNAME)
WHERE A.ATTRELIDL = 'supplier'
```

The result will be as follows:

attname
supp_no
supp_name
address
tel_no

You can also enquire about the indexes themselves. If, for instance, you want
to know how many indexes have been constructed on the Purchases table,
simply ask

RANGE OF X IS INDEXES

SELECT (N = COUNT (X.IRELIDI WHERE X.IRELIDP = 'Purchases'))

IRELDI is the INGRES name for the name of the index, and IRELIDP stands for the name of the indexed relation.

Other writers give examples from hierarchical or network databases. Elmasri and Navathe (1989) give specimen catalogues for relational and network DBMSs in their seventeenth chapter. Gillenson (1990) gives an extract from a dictionary report describing a DL/1 hierarchy, Date (1990) as I have mentioned, confines himself to DB2, Yourdon (1989) provides no specific data model examples, but does give a quite useful guide to data dictionary notation. On the whole, however, general books on databases do not expand very much on this topic. If you want a more detailed survey, then the proceedings of the British Computer Society for 1983, *Data Dictionary Update* (Baker, 1983) gives a number of specific presentations. A somewhat more up-to-date approach is provided by Narayan (1988). He gives a most useful paragraph summarizing the nature of a data dictionary:

The data dictionary is an automated repository of all definitive information about an organisation's data resources. This includes the key data elements that are used in conducting a business enterprise, generating standard names, mnemonics and sizes, and enforcing the use of these standards in all application programs. The data dictionary provides information about the meaning of data elements, system components, and machine configurations where they are located and used. The definitions in the dictionary are meaningful and useful to personnel who are engaged in the systems development life cycle, maintenance of computer systems, and the operational aspects of computer systems.

This chapter has only attempted to be an introduction to such a range of facilities. Nor have I indulged in any of the cost/benefit considerations that are inescapable. A data dictionary comes as an integral part of some DBMSs, but by no means of them all. The third chapter of Atre (1980) provides a sane and readable assessment of such issues. It must have become evident that I regard a data dictionary as an essential element of the database context, but real organizations performing real functions have none the less often chosen (or been forced) to do without 'essential' elements, and of those elements, the data dictionary has often been a casualty. Frankly, to establish a database without an associated dictionary or repository alongside it seems to me about as sensible as walking across the Sahara without a bottle of water, but the world of IT is not always a rational world.

References

Abdellatif, A., Le Bihan, J. and Limame, M. *Oracle: A User's Guide*, Macmillan, 1990.

Atre, S. *Data Base: Structured Techniques for Design, Performance and Management*, John Wiley, 1980.

Baker, G. J. (ed.) 'Data Dictionary Update' in *Proceedings of British Computer Society*, 1983.

Brathwaite, K. S. *Database Management and Control*, McGraw-Hill, 1990.

Bull, M. *Students' Guide to Databases*, Heinemann Newnes, 1990.

Date, C. J. *Introduction to Database Systems*, 5th edn, Addison-Wesley, 1990.

Deen, S. M. *Principles and Practice of Database Systems*, Macmillan, 1985.

Elmasri, R. and Navathe, S. *Fundamentals of Database Systems*, Benjamin Cummings, 1989.

Frost, R. A. *Introduction to Knowledge Based Systems*, Collins, 1986.

Gardarin, G. and Valduriez, P. *Analysis and Comparison of Relational Database Systems*, Addison Wesley, 1989.

Gillenson, M. L. *Database Step-by-Step*, 2nd edn, John Wiley, 1990.

Gorman, M. M. *Database Management Systems: Understanding and Applying Database Technology*, Computer Weekly/Butterworth Heinemann, 1991.

Korth, H. F. and Silberschatz, A. *Database System Concepts*, 2nd edn, McGraw-Hill, 1991.

Laurie, P. *Databases*, Chapman & Hall, 1986.

Malamud, C. *INGRES: Tools for Building an Information Architecture*, Van Nostrand Reinhold, 1989.

Matthews, P. *Ingres User Guide: Visual Programming Tools*, Prentice-Hall, 1991.

McFadden, F. A. and Hoffer, J. A. *Database Management*, 3rd edn, Benjamin Cummings, 1991.

Narayan, R. *Data Dictionary: Implementation, Use and Maintenance*, Prentice-Hall, 1988.

Oxborrow, E. *Databases and Database Systems*, 2nd edn, Chartwell-Bratt, 1989.

Pratt, P. J. and Adamski, J. J. *Database Systems: Management and Design*, Boyd & Fraser, 1987.

Rishe, N. *Database Design Fundamentals*, Prentice-Hall, 1988.

Rothwell, D. M. *Ingres and Relational Daterbases*, McGraw-Hill, 1992.

Smith, P. and Barnes, M. *Files and Databases: An Introduction*, Addison-Wesley, 1987.

Vasta, J. A. *Understanding Database Management Systems*, 2nd end, Wadsworth, 1989.

Yourdon, E. *Modern Structured Analysis*, Prentice-Hall, 1989.

Questions on Part Five

---

1. What would you understand by the phrase 'login security'?
2. 'Tuning a piano is just like tuning a database.' Would you agree?
3. Why is it useful for the DBA to be involved in database design?
4. Why is transaction integrity difficult to achieve?
5. What do you understand by the phrase 'referential integrity'?
6. What is meta-data?
7. Why do many organizations insist that a computer user changes his or her password every week?
8. What is a recursive relation?
9. What does the acronym SDLC stand for?
10. Can you name two other phrases that are sometimes used as synonyms for the data dictionary?

Answers

1. Login security means that a user, wishing to gain access to a database system, has to provide a valid user's name and/or a password.
2. Tuning a piano means that you ensure that the instrument plays in tune; tuning a database means that you ensure that it answers queries in the fastest and most effective way. There is hardly a lot of similarity between these tuning operations.
3. The DBA is going to look after that database, modify it for changing circumstances, restore it after crashes and protect it during daily usage. It is consequently useful if the DBA can be involved in the design of the database so that he or she can fully understand its structure and possibly ensure that it contains elements that will aid DBA planning and administration.
4. Transaction integrity is difficult to achieve because a complex transaction can affect or impinge upon so many elements within the database that ensuring consistency is maintained can be an equally complex operation.

5. Referential integrity is concerned to ensure that each foreign key in a row of data corresponds exactly to the primary key of the associated table.
6. Meta-data is data about data.
7. In an organization it is easy for passwords to become known to others. Careless talk or observation of someone at the keyboard can result in this. If, consequently, passwords are changed every week, breakdown of security can be minimized.
8. A recursive relation is one where something in an entity refers to something within the same entity.
9. Systems development life cycle.
10. The system catalogue; the data repository.

PART SIX

Current developments and future progress

18
The nature and purpose of distribution

So far in this book we have inhabited a simple world. We have learnt what a database is and how it is managed. We have learnt how to communicate with a database and how to look after it. The database itself, however, has been static and unambiguous. We have assumed that the database is positioned at point A, and that any terminals wishing to access the database will have to be connected, in some way or other, to point A. Such an arrangement is referred to as having a *centralized* database. Indeed, centralization would seem to be an inherent object of database management. After all, we only create a database because we want to give controlled access to data, and in order to control and monitor that access fully, the data needs to rest on a single site.

Such a scenario is simple and straightforward. A little thought will indicate that it is virtually impossible as well, or at least impossible for many, many companies and organizations. Let us take the situation of the Association of Evil Barons. This organization comprises members of the aristocracy from all the countries of the world, members who are concerned to exploit and maltreat the peasantry of their respective countries. In earlier centuries, members of the association could only communicate very infrequently, if at all, by chance meetings in the spas of Europe. The computer age has changed all this. In 1983, after considerable negotiation, it was decided to establish a computer system with its headquarters in Transylvania, a region of Romania, where, you may recall, Count Dracula had earlier established his own activities. In the high-tech world of the late twentieth century, it was decided that certain items of information were vital for all reactionary noblemen. Data was needed on the international stock exchanges of the world. It was necessary to know the extradition policies of all the countries of the world. Government attitudes and actions with respect to issues like liberty, employment and immigration were needed. It rapidly became obvious that a centralized database was not viable. The database was going to be accessed by Islamic rulers, Japanese samurai, South American landlords and Basque terrorists. A daily perusal of exchange rates or the varying legislations on prostitution was going to be impossible when the data was stored in Romania. The costs of transferring data from Romania to Japan or Alaska on a frequent basis would have been prohibitive. Hence commonly accessed portions of the database needed to be replicated at a number of different sites. Equally, of course, certain tables within the database tended to be of relevance only to a small proportion of the association. It was, for instance, only Spanish noblemen who were particularly concerned with Basque nationalism. Consequently, the table concerned with this issue, though available to all, was physically placed in Madrid. Equally, data on the Indian caste system was stored at Delhi, though someone in London or Tokyo could access it if they needed to.

From this mythical example, you can gather the overall nature of a distributed database system. None the less, that passion within the IT world for as much terminological ambiguity as possible, has inevitably afflicted the distributed database realm. Coulouris and Dollimore (1988) in their preface wearily remark that: 'The term "distributed system" has been applied to so wide a range of multicomputer and multiprocessor computer systems of differing designs and goals that its usage has become somewhat devalued.' Ozsu and Valdureiz (1991) even go so far as to claim that: 'The term *distributed processing* (or *distributed computing*) is probably the most abused term in computer science of the last couple of years.' We cannot pursue this here, and since there is such mayhem in computer terminology, I would be reluctant to establish any kind of league table of ambiguity. None the less, there would be wide agreement upon the general nature of a distributed database system. Ceri and Pelagatti (1984) define it as being:

> ... a collection of data which are distributed over different computers of a computer network. Each site of the network has autonomous processing capability and can perform local applications. Each site also participates in the execution of at least one global application, which requires accessing data at several sites using a communications subsystem.

In a book published seven years later (Korth and Silberschatz, 1991), the broad definition remains identical:

> A distributed database system consists of a collection of sites, each of which may participate in the execution of transactions which access data at one site, or several sites. The main difference between centralized and distributed database systems is that, in the former, the data resides in one single location, while in the latter, the data resides in several locations.

Korth and Silberschatz go on to explain the difference between local and global applications which Ceri and Pelagatti had assumed was self-evident.

> Each site is able to process *local transactions*, those transactions that access data only in that single site. In addition, a site may participate in the

execution of *global transactions*, those transactions that access data in several sites.

From these definitions, certain conclusions regarding the purpose and benefits of distributed database management systems become apparent:

1. A DDBMS (distributed database management system) provides users with a greater degree of local autonomy. This can have very significant benefits in terms of user satisfaction.
2. Since a DDBMS entails processing at several sites, the failure of one of those sites does not cripple the entire system.
3. A DDBMS normally has sections of the database replicated at more than one site. This can produce the advantage of better data availability since, if a node is down, the chances are that its data can be found at another site.
4. Since it already possesses a modular structure, it is normally easier to increase processing power or add new sites within a distributed system than is the case in a centralized construct.
5. Data that is frequently accessed at site A tends, in a distributed system, to be stored at site A. Consequently the response time within a DDBMS tends to be faster than in a centralized system.
6. A further consequence of local storage of frequently accessed data is that communication costs can be significantly lower than those in a centralized system.

Hence the very definition of a distributed database management system reveals to us some of its advantages.

Though the overall definition may be straightforward enough, the nature of distributed databases raises a number of apsects that are both different and important. It is the purpose of this chapter to introduce these aspects. Distributed databases are still a relative newcomer to the world of IT, which does help to excuse the terminological confusion already referred to, but they are likely to become increasingly common. Hence no book on databases, not even an introductory one, can afford to ignore them.

Obviously, if the database itself is distributed, there needs to be the means of transporting the data from one site to another. This action is performed by networks, and it is at those that we first look. Networks are a different entity from a database. In a purely intellectual demarcation, they have no place in a book on databases, and I note that Ozsu and Valduriez (1991) in the 562 pages of their book on distributed systems only refer to networks rarely and in passing. None the less, you cannot implement a distributed database without using a network. Omitting a section on networks therefore seems to me to be about as sensible as writing a book about milk without mentioning cows.

There are a number of different ways of structuring a distributed database management system (DDBMS). That structure has a number of implications for the capabilities of the system. Hence it is at this structure or architecture that we next look.

We need to make some evaluation of the DDBMS. Until we can perceive its benefits and its drawbacks, we can make no considered judgement of the advisability of adopting one or the other system, centralized or distributed. Some criteria for this evaluation process are next suggested.

Finally, the drawbacks of distributed systems tend to spring from the very factors which make them different from centralized systems. By looking at these problematic areas, we can gain a valuable insight into some of the more complex aspects of the database world.

18.1   Computer networks

There are, of course, whole books devoted to computer networks. What follows will be a breathless sprint through the basics of the topic.

A *computer network* is an interconnected collection of autonomous computers that are capable of exchanging information among them. Computers on a network are commonly refered to as *nodes*, *hosts* or *sites*. A process running at any site can send a message to a process running at any other site (provided, of course, that the wind is in the right direction and there is enough coffee in the office). I commented in my book on INGRES (Rothwell, 1992) about the Bank of Montreal which operates North America's largest real-time banking computer system. The bank's computer network links 1302 branches throughout Canada by using more than 150 000 miles of telecommunications lines. A teller at any one of the 500 branch terminals may access any customer's account information in less than three seconds. More than three million transactions are processed each day. You can see, therefore, that networks are more than fractionally useful in the database world, and imperative in the distributed context. We need consequently to glance briefly at some data about the actual operation of data communication, and then to look at the types of network that exist for carrying out this communication.

18.1.1   DATA COMMUNICATION CONCEPTS

Equipment in a data communication environment is connected by *channels* or *links* in either digital form or analogue form. Each communication link has a capacity of transmitting so much data within a set time, a capacity normally known as its *bandwidth*. In digital networks, a channel that transmits 9600 bits per second (bps) is said to have a *baud rate* of 9600. There are three ranges of communication links, classified according to their bandwidth:

1. Voice-grade channels—600 to 4800 bps.
2. Subvoice channels—less than 1200 bps.
3. Broadband channels—50 000 or more bps.

Where digital data is transmitted via an analogue channel, it has to be modulated. With a higher bandwidth channel, the data can be *multiplexed*, i.e. more than one item sent along the channel at the same time. Furthermore, a communication line may operate in a simplex, half-duplex or full-duplex mode:

- *Simplex* Data only travels in one direction.
- *Half-duplex* Data can travel in both directions but not simultaneously.
- *Full-duplex* Data can travel in both directions simultaneously.

Obviously a full-duplex arrangement is by far the most convenient and flexible, but it is also the most expensive. Our invented Association of Evil Barons could probably be perfectly adequately served by a simplex connection, and many businesses, where communication is rarely of critical immediacy, cope very well with a half-duplex set-up.

The parameters which characterize data communication are:

- Delay time—how long does the communication take?
- Cost—how expensive will the communication be?
- Reliability—how great is the error rate in communication?

Clearly it is the assessment of these parameters that guide the choice of network, or even whether or not to become distributed at all.

18.1.2 TYPES OF NETWORKS

It will come as no surprise to learn that there are a variety of differing networks. The distinctions between them can be subsumed under three criteria:

- Interconnection structure or topology—star, ring, hierarchical, meshed, irregular
- Geographic distribution—WANs and LANs.
- Mode of transmission—point-to-point or multi-point networks.

These three items will not be very meaningful stated baldly as above, so let us expand them a little.

Topology Interconnection structure or topology simply means the way in which the network is physically arranged. The names given to the various topologies indicate their nature. Thus a *star structure* has a computer at the centre and other computers radiating from that centre (Fig. 18.1). The computer at the centre is the host computer for the satellites surrounding it. An example of a star network could be a number of department stores each linked to head office. Note, however, that the satellite nodes do not communicate with each other except through the host computer at the centre.

A *ring structure* has the component computers arranged in a ring sequence so that data is simply passed round the ring until it arrives at the computer for which it is intended (Fig. 18.2). Travel round the ring is in one direction only.

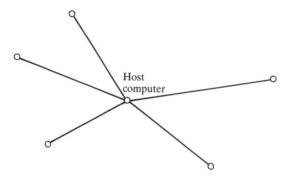

Figure 18.1

With no central computer, all those within the system are equal and communicate with one another. A business with widely scattered warehouses, each of which does most of the processing for its own orders, might choose to use a ring network.

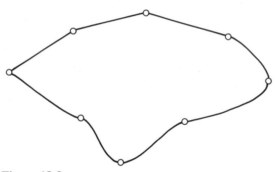

Figure 18.2

A *hierarchical topology* is one we have already met in considering data models. It comprises a host computer to control satellite processors and devices, which in turn may control other satellite processors and devices (Fig. 18.3). This type of structure might be used by a large organization that must retain central control of the information system and yet needs to delegate substantial computing power to individual departments within the organization.

A *meshed network* is one in which the interconnections between the component computers can be varied so that computer *A* can receive data from computer *B* by a variety of routes (Fig. 18.4). There are nomenclature problems here since a meshed network might be called a multiple connected network, a complex network or a distributed network. If there are cross-communication

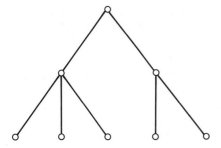

Figure 18.3

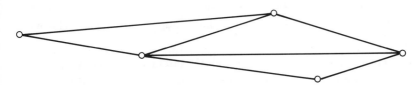

Figure 18.4

links between all the computers, then it might be referred to as a complete network. Figure 18.5 illustrates the situation.

Although any kind of complex network saves time, it does require a much more elaborate communications control, which increases the complexity of the system. A business that relies on interoffice communications for the sharing of resources and up-to-the-minute information about the activities of any branch location might decide to use a complex network.

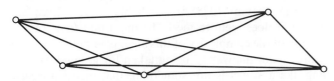

Figure 18.5

Nor do these examples exhaust the possibilities or the vocabulary. There are bus networks, interconnected rings, irregular ones and, doubtless, others. Fortunately, though we do need to know about networks in order to understand the database world, we need not be concerned with becoming experts.

Geographic distribution Geographic distribution—WANs and LANs—is simply a reference to the range of communication offered by the network. A WAN is a *wide area network* which can span an entire country or even the world. A LAN is a *local area network* which is normally confined to one site. A distributed system can be used in either context, and it is quite important to learn about some of the conventions associated with WANs and LANs.

Wide Area Networks   Topologies can be either point-to-point or multipoint, using media like radio, satellite or microwave. Star and irregular are the most common topologies, though you can have hierarchical or meshed.

Obviously, a typical WAN has to connect many disparate types of equipment. So that the transmission media can handle the heterogeneity of equipment, an open systems interconnection architecture has been devised by the International Organization for Standardization (ISO) which lays down seven layers of protocols for such interconnection. A protocol states how the sender and receiver can reach an agreement on exchanging a message, how they can recognize and identify eath other, how many messages they exchange, whether a message requires an answer or not, and similar aspects. The seven layers are:

Physical layer transmits the data through the circuits of the network.

Data link layer ensures error-free transmission between adjacent sites.

Network layer controls how the messages are sent from the source site to the destination site.

Transport layer implements virtual point-to-point channel between the source and the destination.

Session layer establishes and maintains sessions between processes.

Presentation layer deals with the conversion of information between forms of data representation, e.g. ASCII and EBCDIC.

Application layer deals with the development of all user applications.

This bare listing is not very informative, and indeed only the first three layers have been precisely defined in terms of international standards. For a fuller discussion of protocols, Tanenbaum (1988) is a reliable source. Even so, despite this sketchy outline, it does seem to me to be important that readers should gain some impression of the complexity of this area. Computers, despite their brief history, are already on the way to being taken for granted, yet the technology of something like a WAN is not something that merits a casual shrug.

Local Area Networks   Almost invariably this is a communications network privately owned by the organization using it. Using coaxial cables or fibre optics, it may adopt a star, ring or complex configuration. Indeed, local networks have been developed by many major computer manufacturers like Xerox and Wang. In the UK, the Ethernet network from Xerox is probably the best known. It uses a coaxial copper cable to connect various pieces of information equipment. Information travels over the cable in *packets* of data that are sent from one machine to another. Each packet contains the actual message that is being transmitted as well as information identifying the sending and receiving devices. Error control information is included to help ensure correct transmission.

Ethernet uses the *collision concept* or *contention* to decide which piece of office equipment on the network gets to communicate next. When one device is transmitting, all other devices must wait. When the current transmission stops, other devices may attempt transmission. If their transmissions collide (that is, if several devices attempt to transmit at the same time), all devices stop transmission. Eventually, one of the devices begins transmitting again, no collision occurs, and that device is able to complete its transmission while the other devices wait. This collision concept allows Ethernet to operate without *central network control*, thus making it much easier to add new devices to the network after initial installation.

The contention approach to sharing the network may at first seem inefficient. It is, however, fast (transmitting at 10 million bits per second), reliable and economical. The network operates so quickly and the packets are so short that each transmission lasts less than one thousandth of a second, so the number of collisions is small. Because the control is provided by each individual device, the reliability of the network is very high. If an individual device fails, the network keeps functioning. This is called *distributed network control*.

Some sort of comparison between WANs and LANs is interesting. The following points about LANs exemplify some of the differences between the two:

1. Cost of communication is lower than WANs, as indeed we would expect.
2. Higher bandwidth than WANs.
3. Shorter delays than in WANs.
4. Can cope with one large-scale circuit as an interface, rather than the large computer needed for WAN switching.
5. Transmission usually digital rather than WAN analogue.
6. Simpler protocols necessary.
7. LAN is owned by the organization using it.

Mode of Transmission   The mode of transmission has already been glanced at, and there is no real need to expand. It is simply a reference to the actual sending of data, and is concerned with the medium, rate and nature of such transmission: simplex, half-duplex or fully duplex; the bandwidth of the communication channel; the type of that channel—coaxial cable, radio, etc. I merely refer to these aspects again so as to emphasize that they too are an integral part of our concerns when considering the topic of networks. They are an exciting aspect of computer science.

However, although we need a network for most database contexts, and we cannot do without a network in the distributed database environment, they are not themselves databases, and it is to our primary concern that we must now return.

18.2   Distributed DDBMS architecture

The architecture of a system defines its structure. This means that the components of the system are identified, the function of each component is specified, and the interrelationships and interactions among these components are defined. Let us begin by looking at the sort of facilities that we would ideally expect from our perfect distributed database system.

18.2.1   DESIRED DISTRIBUTION QUALITIES

The jargon word that is crucial in discussing the desired qualities of a DDBMS is 'transparency'. As you will, I trust, recall, 'transparency' within the computing context is a synonym for being invisible. In other words, all the complicated technical techniques that are required to do the job remain invisible to the user who can blissfully only concern his or her mind with the conceptual requirements of the job. The transparency problem in a distributed system lies in the fact that, from the user's point of view, a distributed system should look exactly like a nondistributed system. It follows hence that the most obvious element of transparency that is needed is a transparency as to the location of the hardware and software that make up the DDBMS network.

Location Transparency   Needless to say, there can be various levels of location transparency—Coulouris and Dollimore identify three in the second chapter of their book—but the basic aim is obvious: wherever the data may be located, the user must gain the impression that it is all in one place. Imagine, for instance, that the managing director of a chain of clothes shops wanted to know how many white shirts were currently in stock in the chain as a whole. The SQL query is not difficult to formulate:

```
SELECT DISTINCT Stock_no, Stock_name, quantity
FROM Stock
WHERE Stock_name=''Shirt''
AND Colour=''White''
ORDER BY Store_no
```

As you can see, the result will list the white shirts available store by store, but for the user, the whole operation should feel as if the computer is just checking a file next door. Clearly such an operation needs an accurate and up-to-date data dictionary for its successful completion. It is also clear that the desired impression of adjacent and centralized storage can only be achieved with a very effective system of data communications. Location transparency is a different problem for a DDBMS on a single site to a DDBMS where its sites can be separated by hundreds of miles. In the latter case, there is bound to be some delay in processing.

Nor, of course, should location transparency be confined to simple retrievals like the instance above. It should apply to updates and deletions also, and this, of course, raises the question of data independence.

Data Independence   At one level, the logical structure of the data is defined: the schema definition. At the other level, the physical structure of the data is defined: the physical data description. We can therefore talk about two types of data independence:

Logical data independence refers to the immunity of user applications to changes in the logical structure of the database.

Physical data independence deals with hiding the details of the storage structure from user applications.

As we have already seen in previous chapters, it is not easy to achieve high levels of data independence, even in a centralized context, but in distributed databases, the further aspect of distribution transparency is also added. Indeed, data independence is not, in itself, a transparency issue, but it affects most of the transparency elements which follow.

Network Transparency   Ideally the user should not be aware of the network or its structure, so that there should be no difference between database applications that would run on a centralized database and those that would run on a distributed one.

Replication Transparency   It is usually desirable to be able to distribute data in a replicated fashion across the machines on a network, but if the operations of those users are predominantly update oriented, it may not be a good idea to have too many copies of the data. It then becomes too easy for data at one location to be updated, but for the same data at another location to remain unmodified. However, of course, no matter how many or how few examples of replication there may be, the user remains unaware of the issue. If he or she is modifying or just retrieving a collection of data, it is immaterial to that user how many more versions of that data there are in existence. Indeed, as you can doubtless see, replication transparency is implied by location transparency.

It will have been painfully apparent to you that I have merely set out the areas where transparency is necessary, but not indicated the ways in which such transparency can be obtained. It is inevitable that any introductory book upon a subject has no alternative but to leave many issues unexplored. I note that Ozsu and Valduriez (1991) also refer to fragmentation transparency, though, as they themselves point out, this is more a question of query processing than of transparency proper. McFadden and Hoffer (1991) also refer to failure transparency, and concurrency transparency. These, however, are also problems within a centralized database, and discussing them here would not significantly increase our understanding of the issues.

Having then identified the desirable qualities for our DDBMS, what sort of structures can be devised to deliver such qualities? This is still very much an emerging area within information technology, and few really firm answers can be provided.

18.2.2 ANSI/SPARC ARCHITECTURE

Having glanced at some of the desirable facets that we would like within our distributed database, we need to look at how that database could be structured. Two important events in the late 1960s and early 1970s influenced the standardization activities in database management: first, the DBTG of the CODASYL Systems Committee issued two reports, one providing a survey of DDBMSs, and the second describing the features of a network; and second, the publication of Codd's original papers on the relational data model. As a result, ANSI established a study group under the auspices of its Standards Planning and Requirements Committee (SPARC). They drew up three views of data:

1. The internal view which deals with the physical definition and organization of data;
2. The external view which is concerned with how users view the database;
3. The conceptual schema, which is an abstract definition of the database.

The major component that permits mapping between these different data organizational views is the data dictionary/directory, which is a meta-database.

All of this has been referred to earlier, but a brief reminder seemed advisable since it is the ANSI/SPARC architecture which forms the bedrock for the distributed implementation. Clearly, however, the increased complexity of the distributed environment has led to complicated extensions of the ANSI/SPARC architecture. Yet, in its basic structure, it is not difficult to grasp. Clearly, as the embracing core of a DDBMS, you do need a global schema, a schema which will describe every entity and attribute within the database. Since the global schema describes everything, there is nothing within its structure or contents to indicate what sort of database it is intended to serve; the global schema would serve a centralized database just as effectively as a distributed one. The only proviso that we might wish to make is that the global schema will be easier to handle if it is constructed along relational lines.

Assuming that we are operating within a relational context, the global schema will consist of the definition of a number of tables (probably a very large number). Each of these tables can be split into several nonoverlapping portions. Each portion is called a *fragment*. There are perfectly good reasons for such fragmentaton. Imagine, for instance, that we have a table called Employees for that sterling establishment, the International College for Examination Success. That table, in the global schema, looks like Table 18.1. Obviously this is only a tiny section, but it is sufficient to indicate its nature. Now it so happens that, in the International College for Examination Success, each department is housed

Table 18.1

Staff_no	Surname	Forenames	D. of B.	Department
22591	Curtain	Annette	03.05.70	Home econ.
17288	Ford	Cortina Zodiac	16.02.63	Science
12431	Card	Valentine	30.07.45	History
18663	Cart	Orson	14.05.51	Languages
20014	Lamb	Shawn	02.11.53	Geography
10873	Plumber	Bib Brace	12.06.40	Maths

in a separate building and has its own local database. Hence it makes sense to place, within each department, a fragment of the Employee table, the fragment concerned being confined to members of that department alone.

There are different types of fragmentation—horizontal fragmentation and vertical fragmentation being the most common. Ceri and Pelagatti give quite a thorough description of fragmentation in their book on distributed databases, and in so doing illustrate the superiority of the relational data model for effective data handling. However, the example given of fragmentation from the International College for Examination Success (hereafter known as ICES) was an example of horizontal fragmentation in that complete rows from the global schema were combined on the criterion of department to form each specific fragment. We can also produce a vertical fragmentation by splitting the original table on the basis of certain attributes. For instance, if our Employee table also contained the attributes Salary, Tax code, National insurance number and Pension scheme, it might be that the accounts department of ICES wanted to extract those columns, but were not interested in name, date of birth or department. In either or both cases, the details of the fragmented tables are stored in a fragmentation schema which describes the mapping between global relations (or tables) and the fragments themselves (Fig. 18.6).

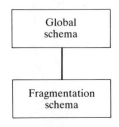

Figure 18.6

In our first example of fragmentation, the data about the employees of ICES was kept within the department to which they belonged. It is obviously important that the database keeps track of where specific data is stored. Hence there is a third schema which defines the site or sites at which a fragment is located (Fig. 18.7).

These three schema are site independent. They describe the entire database, and although the allocation schema describes the location of the various fragments into which that database is split, it is not itself tied logically to any one of those sites. It follows, however, that a distributed database will need site-dependent databases. In our invented college, each department will have its own database with, of course, its own DDBMS to manage that database. There consequently needs to be a schema for each local database which performs the mapping from the allocation schema to that local DDBMS and database (Fig. 18.8).

Clearly, if ICES had a database for each of its departments, there would need to be many more than three sites, but you can gain the general idea from

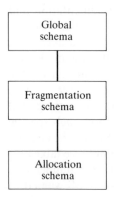

Figure 18.7

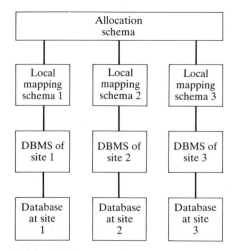

Figure 18.8

Fig. 18.8. Equally clearly, while this instance has given us a general conspectus of the architecture of a distributed database, no actual DDBMS is likely to be exactly like the one just drawn up. It has only been devised in order to give a general conceptual framework. In fact, there can be a DDBMS that does not possess a global schema, or a DDBMS that does not have multiple databases. The whole area does not yet possess very firm procedures.

It is obvious from the above that a DDBMS is going to engender many more difficulties than a centralized database. Let me just give a real-life example. In 1986 I was asked to write a report for a major manufacturing company of trucks and trailers. The company wished to consider the issues surrounding the possible reorganization of their data processing facilities and they were particularly concerned with the question of centralization versus distribution. My report, which considered the parameters of processor costs, storage costs, telecommunications costs, resource sharing, availability, data, skills and company attitudes, was only able to provide very tentative conclusions since the time given for producing the report was brief and no access to managerial thinking was possible. Yet I learnt recently that it was only at the beginning of 1991 that hardware and software for a new database system had been purchased and that, even after the expenditure of so much money in that purchase, it took over seven months before any firm decisions as to its implementation were made. It is relatively easy to write a book describing the database world; it is a great deal more difficult to operate within that world.

What, then, are the major problems that are thrown up by the more complex architecture of a distributed system? It would be unrealistic to look at them all, but the questions of autonomy and meta-data do demand some attention.

Autonomy Since a distributed database contains replications of the same database (or portions of that database), there is an increased difficulty over the question of autonomy. For instance, each database (or portion of the database) will need to be engaged in two types of activity:

1. Local operations which only affect its own section.
2. Global operations which call upon and affect many sections of the database.

Within these two broad types, there will be other associated factors. Some nodes, for instance, may have fewer processing powers than other nodes. Some users will have greater rights than others. Communicating equipment can be of differing types. Consequently, there can be a considerable degree of interaction, all of it posing a potential threat to data autonomy. There appear to be two structural 'solutions':

1. An arrangement whereby the data is *tightly integrated* so that the users, wherever they may be, always gain the impression that they are dealing with the entire database.
2. A *semiautonomous system* in which each DDBMS operates as an independent

entity but with an agreement that all or part of its dependent database can, none the less, be shared by other DDBMSs.

The first 'solution' provides greater safeguards for the consistency of the data, but less individual autonomy for the users. It also entails a massive processing overhead because of all the checking and validation such a system needs to perform. The second 'solution', while greatly increasing user autonomy, poses many greater threats to the consistency of the data. In the real world, decisions on such matters probably depend less on computing efficiency and more on internal politics. Should you need to gain a fuller understanding of distributed databases, the books and articles mentioned in the reference section of this chapter should provide very adequate coverage.

Brief and cursory though our glance at distributed databases has been, it would be unfortunate to end the chapter on the somewhat negtive note of problems within that world. The final section therefore tries to show why a distributed database might well be the most effective solution in a large number of circumstances.

18.3   The benefits and drawbacks

While I just indicated that this final section was going to be a positive one, we must keep a sense of proportion. Rarely are things in life unconditionally plus or minus, and it would be foolish to suggest that a distributed database was invariably better (or worse) than a centralized one. None the less, it is important to see the elements of evaluation on this issue. It is, after all, far from being a simple either/or choice. The question is not simply a centralized versus distributed issue. We could, for instance, have local databases that were not integrated with each other, and did not consequently constitute a distributed database. The three broad options are as follows:

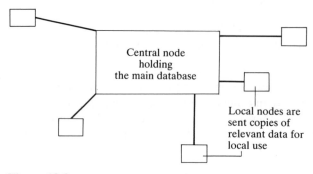

Figure 18.9

1. *A centralized database* In such a context, data transmission tends to take place first thing in the morning and again at the end of the day (Fig. 18.9):

(a) Data is sent from the central database to the local nodes early in the morning so that those local nodes can then get on with the business of the day.

(b) The local nodes send their data back to the central database at the end of the day so that the central database can process all the updates overnight.

2. *A decentralized approach* Local databases are not integrated with each other.

3. *A distributed approach* Separate nodes are each capable of processing data and accessing data whatever its location.

18.3.1 ADVANTAGES OF CENTRALIZATION

1. One DDBMS stored at the centre is cheaper to run than having several nodes each with its own DDBMS.

2. Control is simpler with only a single node to worry about as far as updates are concerned.

3. With all the data being in one place, it is easy to ensure that the data is modelled according to one conceptual basis rather than a variety. Thus all data can be modelled in a relational fashion (or network, or whatever), thus making everything homogeneous and compatible.

18.3.2 ADVANTAGES OF A DDBMS

1. *Local autonomy* Each node is effectively independent and can proceed with its own concerns untrammelled by the constraints of others.

2. *Improved performance* Often a consequence of 1. For instance, if different divisions within a company have very different processing requirements, then they can have hardware particularly suited to them.

3. *Improved reliability/availability* The replication of data means that a crash does not render the entire system inoperable.

4. *Economics* You can tradeoff between telecommunications costs and data communications costs, opting for the most economic configuration. Also it costs less to put together a system of smaller computers than it does to invest in a mainframe.

5. *Expandability* It is easier to accommodate increasing database sizes.

6. *Shareability* It is easier to share data in a distributed system.

18.3.3 DISADVANTAGES OF A DDBMS

1. Lack of experience in using them.

2. Complexity.

3. Cost.

4. Distribution of control creates problems of synchronization and coordination.

5. Security.
6. If you already have a centralized system, it is not easy (or cheap) to convert to a distributed one.
7. Since data is often replicated, the integrity problem is more difficult.

Thus I have, as you can see, attempted to be fair, but, despite the problems, there can be no reasonable doubt that distributed database technology does provide solutions that are greatly superior to those offered by a centralized context. Of course, not every business has need of a distributed database, but where its facilities are relevant, the advantages far outweigh the disadvantages—or at least they do so where the personnel of the business are adequately prepared for its effective implementation. Let me conclude then by recommending an article which, in part at least, addresses this very issue. With admirable clarity, Davis (1989) discusses many of the questions with which this chapter has been concerned and concludes that: 'the microcomputer environment is poised for rapid growth in distributed database technology'. Distributed databases are one pathway to the future, a remark which provides an ideal lead into the next chapter.

References

Ceri, S. and Pelagatti, G. *Distributed Databases: Principles and Systems*, McGraw-Hill, 1984.

Coulouris, G. and Dollimore, J. *Distributed Systems: Concepts and Design*, Addison-Wesley, 1988.

Davis, M. 'Sharing the wealth,' *Byte*, Sept. 1989.

Korth, H. F. and Silberschatz, A. *Database System Concepts*, 2nd edn, McGraw-Hill, 1991.

McFadden, F. R. and Hoffer, J. A. *Database Management*, 3rd edn, Benjamin Cummings, 1991.

Ozsu, M. T. and Valduriez, P. *Principles of Distributed Database Systems*, Prentice-Hall, 1991.

Rothwell, D. M. *Ingres and Relational Databases*, McGraw-Hill, 1992.

Tanenbaum, A. S. *Computer Networks*, Prentice-Hall, 1988.

19
Present and future trends

With possibly wearisome repetition, I have insisted that this book has been aimed at a noncomputerate audience. I have tried to explain the practices and procedures, the attitudes and aims of the database world to those who have not known the difference between a bit and a byte, a field and a file or a program and a procedure.

As you may know, whenever a book is in progress, publishers tend to demand sundry chapters of said book for their assessment. They then farm out these fragments to various docile academics who write a review of the chapters received. On the basis of those reviews, the publisher concerned decides whether or not to offer a contract for the book in question. Should the publisher decide that the reviews are favourable enough to merit continued interest in the book, he or she tends to send those reviews to the author concerned so that the author can amend sections, alter emphases, or, indeed, ignore them completely. I was fortunate in the writing of this book. I was able to see about four different reviews, and I am grateful to the anonymous academics who wrote them even though, alas, they will be able to see little evidence of their comments being implemented in any way. Let me explain.

One reviewer was alarmed at the attention that I paid to the hierarchical and network database models. He (or she) took the view that, since these were outmoded techniques, they should be ignored in an introductory book of this nature. Instead, total attention should be paid to the relational data model. I ignored this suggestion simply because the hierarchical and network data models are still in use on many, many sites. As you are now aware, they both have grave limitations, and the relational model is more appropriate in almost all respects. None the less, if you are working in a company that has a hierarchical or network database, you will want at least a survey of those models. If you are a student at university, you will need the intellectual awareness of those data models even though you may never do any practical work within them. Hence this is what I have attempted to supply.

Another reviewer was alarmed at the relative paucity of my diagrammatic illustrations. This reviewer firmly believed that one picture was worth at least a thousand words. As I have indicated earlier, I have never been entirely convinced by this cliché. The considerable number of diagrams in this book does show that I accept the validity of illustrative techniques, but, for me, the word remains prime. If something is clearly explained in text, then there seems to me to be a better guarantee of a genuine understanding being achieved within the reader's mind. If you too share the attitude of my reviewer, then I am sorry that you have been visually deprived.

So much then for apologias. I wanted to make them at the beginning of this chapter for a particular reason. Because of the way in which I have approached the topic of databases, I now believe that you have a sound understanding of the three major database structures, that you understand the concept of conversing with a database, that you have a realistic comprehension of safeguarding that database and maintaining its consistency, and that you have an adequate awareness of the operations that can be performed within a database context. If you really did begin with no knowledge whatsoever of the database world, this corpus of knowledge and understanding that you now have does not seem to me to be a negligible achievement. It is, of course, almost entirely a theoretical knowledge. The only practical awareness that you can gain comes as a result of working upon an actual database, but it has been the object of this book to provide you with such an awareness that you will find the transition to actuality a relatively easy step to take. Hence my reliance upon the printed word. While you should be able to normalize data, draw a dataflow diagram and construct an E–R diagram, you should, even more importantly, understand what the point is of normalizing data, why a dataflow diagram is useful, and how an E–R diagram helps to clarify the database context. You should, in other words, have a full conceptual knowledge. The physical knowledge will come when you grapple at the keyboard with IMS, DB2, or Oracle.

Furthermore, the conceptual knowledge that you have so far attained is relatively secure knowledge. Despite the irritations of terminological idiosyncracies, there is widespread acceptance of the three database models at which we have looked. The issues of integrity, security and data independence are universally understood. The roles of database administrator and query languages are not dogged by too much ambiguity. In other words, we have been treading relatively firm theoretical and practical ground, confined by the comforting walls of universally accepted principles.

In this chapter we will be leaving these safe havens. We have already seen that information technology, in its brief history, has developed at a frightening pace. Every discipline, as it develops, proceeds with uncertainty, pushing at previous frontiers, dismantling earlier ramparts and exploring new avenues. During this process, lines of demarcation become blurred, new concepts become viable, old ones no longer look so secure. This is the case in every area of human intellectual activity; the only difference between IT and other areas of study has been the speed at which IT has progressed. In 20 years we have seen the hierarchical and network data models progress from inception to obsolescence. They were (and are) perfectly sensible ways of constructing a database. They have, however, been virtually replaced by the relational data model, and it is the relational model which has been assumed as the norm for the bulk of this book. Inevitably, however, that relational model is itself now under attack. New approaches proffer themselves as being more effective database constructs. It would be absurd in an introduction to the database world not to give some guidelines as to current movements within that world.

It is here that we return to the theoretical slant that this book has adopted. It is quite impossible to understand current thinking within database development without having a firm theoretical grasp. It is possible to manage a database without having a very clear theoretical understanding of that database (though never, it seems to me, desirable), but it is quite impossible to understand semantic modeling, object-oriented systems, natural language processing or hypermedia (all objects of current interest) without having a basis of theoretical comprehension. Indeed, since some of the new approaches within the database world specifically and the computer world in general are questioning the entire foundation of data processing, it is only possible to understand their positions if you already know about all three data models—hierarchical, network and relational. So it has always been. You cannot really understand the Einsteinian universe unless you have a firm grasp of the Newtonian one.

However, before plunging into current developments, one obvious question presents itself. We have seen that the nonrelational data models have serious deficiencies. Mittra (1991) itemizes two of them:

1. The nonrelational databases impose a rigid structure on data in the form of owner–member relationships that new users find difficult to understand.
2. To formulate a query in a nonrelational database, users have to navigate through the schema and use a procedural language.

We have seen how the relational model, with the simplicity of its tables, the ease of access which it provides and the way in which it can secure data independence shows a marked improvement over its hierarchical and network forebears. The obvious question then is, 'What is wrong with the relational system?' If the hierarchical and network databases provided an integration which was infinitely superior to the clumsy file system which preceded them, why does the successor to those databases itself need improvement? I know that when I was doing my own M.Sc. in IT, the relational system was presented as the answer to every maiden's prayer. It has been a constant assumption throughout this book that the relational system has major strengths. And so it has. Let us, however, now begin to cast a more critical eye upon it. In so doing we will gain some understanding as to why it is now regarded as seriously inadequate.

19.1 The deficiencies of the relational database

As its name indicates, the relational system is concerned with relations. We have looked at those relations which the relational data model handles with such competence: 1 : 1, 1 : N and N : M. The trouble, however, with the real world is that it constantly presents relations which are a great deal more complex than these three examples. It seems to me to be unfortunate that many moderately high-level books on databases fail to explore the question of relationships in adequate depth. Gorman (1991) is a most honourable exception, and I am indebted to his itemization of all eight possible relationship types. Brathwaite (1990) gives a fuller than usual survey. Hughes (1991) looks at a number of instances which the relational model cannot handle. Ashworth and Goodland (1990) give an interesting discussion and although they do not explore the issue with the completeness of Gorman, they are much more approachable in terms of clarity. Elmasri and Navathe (1989) and McFadden and Hoffer (1991), both books which have often been cited before, also discuss the relationship issue with some rigour, both linking their discussion to the E–R diagram, just as I did in Chapter 3. Yet, although I implied that 1 : 1, 1 : N and N : M relationships were the only ones with which we need to be concerned, let us now, having by this time extended our conceptual understanding considerably, look more fully at the various types of relationship that can exist.

19.1.1 ONE TO MANY

This we have already encountered many times, and it is the most common relationship type (Fig. 19.1). Thus *one* company has *many* employees. *One* company produces *many* products. *One* company has *many* customers. This type hardly needs any further explication.

19.1.2 OWNER–MULTIPLE-MEMBER

This one we have not formally encountered before, though the concept is not a difficult one. It is, indeed, implied in Fig. 19.1 that represents the one-to-many relationship. A company does have many employees, and those employees need to be gathered within a single table so that the company–employee relationship can be adequately and fully expressed. But there are, of course, different types of employee. Some are full-time workers. Others are part-time workers. Others still are retired, but still members of the database because they receive a company pension (or a company Christmas card). So it will be with products. This company makes some products from wood or from metal or from plastic. Within each class—wood, metal or plastic—there are hundreds of product items. So it is with customers. Some pay cash, others have an account. Some are individuals, others are companies. Of course, in the instances given above, all the multiple members belong to the same class of entity: all the employees,

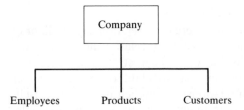

Figure 19.1

whether full-time, part-time or retired, are human beings. All the products, whether metal, wooden or plastic, are manufactured goods. But this congruity need not apply.

A particular product, let us say the INGRES database management system, is represented as a product item within the database. Each product has attached to it a particular salesperson, but attached to that salesperson are the individuals and/or organizations to whom he or she has sold the INGRES DBMS. Hence we would need to represent the situation diagrammatically as Fig. 19.2. Hence the relationship shown involves three different entity types: a product (INGRES), a person (Ann Jones) and three organizations.

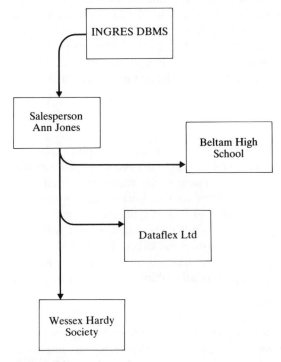

Figure 19.2

19.1.3   SINGULAR–SINGLE-MEMBER

This is the oddest relationship type because there is no relationship at all, or at least not one directly represented. There is no explicit relationship because the singular–single-member type, as its name would suggest, only contains one member. There cannot, therefore, be any parent–child or owner–member representation. Yet there can be such relationships implicit in the entity itself. Take the INGRES DBMS that we had as an entity in our preceding example. That single entity can itself be divided into sundry sections. There are, for instance, the tools and techniques for database handling that are commonly referred to as the front end. Then there is the data manager itself which controls the usage of those tools and techniques. Finally there is the database itself. Hence our single entity, the INGRES DBMS, consists of at least three inter-dependent components which have a close and vital relationship with each other. Gorman (1991) cites Family as a singular, single member. There is no owner because all the members of any particular family are all members of the same entity of which they are merely attribute values.

19.1.4   SINGULAR–MULTIPLE-MEMBER

We can have an entity which is itself composed of members that come from different entities. The members of a family all come from the same entity, Family, and hence have an internal relationship, but the table comprising all the students in Shropshire who passed 'A'-levels in 1992 draws its data from various pupil tables of the various colleges and schools of Shropshire. Hence, while the table compiled of 'A'-level passes is itself a single unit, the data of which it is compiled comes from the pupil tables of The Grove School, Market Drayton, Telford Sixth Form College and so on.

19.1.5   RECURSIVE

While in a singular–single-member relationship there are no explicit relation-ships because there is no owner–member construct, in a recursive relationship there is an explicit owner–member relationship of an entity with itself. For instance, a large company might divide itself into various organization units. While all belonging to the same entity type or record type, those organization units will exist at different levels of responsibility and function and will have relationships with each other. Such relationships are called, by McFadden and Hoffer, unary relationships, though, as Gormon points out, they have also been known as nested relationships, looped relationships and bill-of-materials relationships.

19.1.6   MANY TO MANY

These we have already encountered, and we have seen the strategems employed to represent them within the flat-file nature of a relational database. While it is perfectly possible to decompose a many-to-many relationship into two one-to-many relationships, it is not an ideally elegant solution. A third data type has to be created to act as the member that both owners point to (Fig. 19.3). Thus, as you can see, while there are many students who are taught by many teachers, a many-to-many relationship, that relationship can only be implemented by creating a third entity class Course.

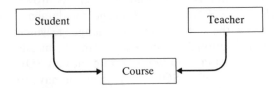

Figure 19.3

19.1.7   ONE TO ONE

We have encountered this type already too, though it is worth pointing out that it is not particularly common. While each employee is only employed within one department, each department tends to employ many employees. Thus the one-to-many situation is much more common than the one to one. None the less, the one owner instance and the one member instance can easily occur (Fig. 19.4). Branden Golf Club has one golf professional, and he is the professional player for that club and only that club. Hence we have a one-to-one relationship.

Figure 19.4

19.1.8   INFERENTIAL RELATIONSHIPS

This type of relationship tends to exist between two different attributes of two different tables. It is not an explicit relationship but is one that is implied. We encounter them often enough in everyday life. Hence, if we know that Meg Soper is employed in the English department, we are likely to infer that she does her teaching in an English room. If component number AS285 fits exactly into container B101, we may well infer that the container was made to package that particular component. As you can see, an inferential relationship links two attribute values from two different tables.

These, then, are the relationship types with which we can be confronted in life. It is clear that none of the data models at which we have looked, hierarchical, network or relational, can represent all these relationships, or at least they cannot do so without some very complex and time-consuming amendments and additions. Thus we have one deficiency of the relational model; it is only capable of representing directly relationships that are relatively simple and which do not have connections with large numbers of other complex and changing entities.

Not surprisingly, query languages that have been developed for use with relational databases, SQL in particular, share the deficiencies of the data model itself. We have seen the power of SQL, but it is a very limited power. As Brown (1991) comments: 'Databases which use SQL as the language for database access are a prime example of systems with a data manipulation language which is relationally complete, but not computationally complete.' By this he means that if you want to manipulate the data that you are inputting into an SQL query or data that is received as the result of an SQL query, then you have to resort to the power of the programming language that you are using because SQL lacks the manipulative range of most adequate programming languages. Consequently you have to embed SQL within the relevant programming language, an operation which increases processing overhead, slows down transactions and can lead to problems. Hughes (1991) points out that it is often convenient to be able to specify the action to be taken if a certain condition becomes true. This can be done by using what are called 'triggers'. Hughes comments that, although a DEFINE TRIGGER statement is provided in SQL, few implementations actually support it. Date (1990) comments a number of times about the imperfections of SQL. Elmasri and Navathe (1989) itemize some of the SQL shortcomings:

1. It does not provide a means of declaring the primary key of a relation.
2. It cannot cope with the problem of referential integrity posed by foreign keys.
3. It does not show the meaningful relationships among tables to the user.
4. It provides no mechanism for specifying strategies for view updates.

Elmasri and Navathe go on to list nine more imperfections, but you get the picture. All these imperfections can be circumvented, in part at least. Khoshafian and Abnous (1990) talk about Intelligent-SQL. Bielawski and Lewand (1991) discuss a number of instances where SQL can be tailored to perform a function for which it is not inherently designed. But you only have to look at the number of new logic-based languages that are currently being developed to realize that SQL is not regarded as the adequate tool for semantically complex and dynamically changing database contexts. Nor, of course, are the claimed deficiencies of SQL entirely argument free. Date, for instance, criticizes SQL because it provides alternative methods of expressing exactly the same query, a situation that Date feels lends itself to confusion and ambiguity. Others, however, as Beynon-Davies (1991) points out, have praised this aspect as pointing to the creative nature by which humans exploit redundancy. None the less, disagreement though there may be, few can doubt that the shortcomings already identified as well as SQL's failure to declare foreign keys, its failure to support the relational algebraic operation of DIVISION, and the cumbersome nature of its dealing with nested subqueries are serious handicaps.

There is, however, a genuine difficulty in what follows next. It is not too difficult to demonstrate the limitations of the relational database, but it is extremely difficult to explain clearly the direction in which advances are currently being made. Partly this difficulty stems from the fact that progress is being made in a number of different areas that are none the less related. We have, therefore, to keep two or three areas of interest in mind simultaneously. I referred at the end of Chapter 11 to semantic modelling. This is an area rich with database implications. The titles of some of the books that I have recently cited would suggest that object-oriented databases are the likely successor to the relational reign. Mention of referential integrity, logic and Intelligent-SQL might lead you to think that databases are beginning to enter the realm of artificial intelligence. And, of course, all this is true. Our problem is how to separate the wood from the trees.

You will, perhaps, recall that as long ago as Chapter 3 I pointed out that systems analysis entailed the consideration of four elements:

1. An organization
2. People
3. Data
4. Technology

There has been a tendency for database experts to concentrate, understandably, upon the third of these elements, data. Today, however, there is a growing realization that, if a database is to be of the utmost value to the organization that designs it, it needs to be a database which encapsulates the developments in technology, the complexity of the organization and the precise requirements of people. In other words, as computer science, still very young, begins to grow up, so it begins to take a broader view of the world which it reflects and upon which it impinges. Hence, if we want to understand the current developments in the database world, we need to re-examine the very foundations of that world. An attempt to do so forms our second section.

19.2   The integrated approach to databases

As you know, a database is an example of software. One of the disparities in the computer world over the last decade or so has been the imbalance between the development of software and the parallel development of hardware upon which to run that software. Computers have become smaller in size but larger in terms of power. The memories of computers have risen from a few thousand bytes to millions or billions of bytes. The cost of hardware has plummeted downwards. The business world has learnt to accept computers and is employing them in an increasing variety of ways. Hence the hardware side of the hardware–software equation has developed exponentially. With this development, of course, there has naturally been an increasing demand for increased software sophistication so that the software can utilize the increased power of the hardware. This, though, has not been easy to produce. The development of hardware and the development of software belong to qualitatively different universes. To develop effective new software, you need to be aware of, and indeed liaise with, managerial objectives. Large-scale software entails the work of many pro- grammers and software developers; they all have to liaise effectively with each other, or at least the work of one has to be congruent with the work of the others. The software being developed has to relate to the possibly heterogenous hardware upon which it will work. The operating system, itself a piece of software, has to provide the facilities that the software application or database model requires. The data processing department of a company might want to yoke different systems and support tools: Jackson structured design, dataflow diagrams, E–R diagrams, etc. The specific organization that is developing the database system might have a whole series of individual constraints. Thus the development of a significant piece of software demands what is often called an *integrated project support environment* (IPSE). Let us, therefore, look at what is implied by this environment.

Let me begin by underlining an element. The key word in IPSE is the first word: integrated. Now, of course, a database represents an integrated view of a company's data. Hence, not surprisingly, a database is at the centre of the IPSE operations. All the current developments looked at in this chapter depend upon a database. I have, more than once, described a database as the core of the IT environment. That has been true for the last 30 years and, so far as I can see, will continue to be true for the next 30. Indeed, in an important sense, that belief provides the motivation for this entire book. The builder managing his small business needs a database. The scholar researching into the Petrarchan sonnet form needs a database. We all of us, in differing ways, need and use databases. As the computer revolution extends itself more and more into the fabric of our lives, more and more of us will find it convenient to keep our database in a computerized form. If then IPSE depends upon a database, what more do we need to know about databases?

The conventional database used in a college or a business, be it hierarchical, network or relational, does tend to display common features. Data is at the centre, but it is established, static data. When you draw up a table of data, you do so in the expectation that it will be constantly accessed for years to come. In your Employee table, for instance, you know that some employees will leave and have to be deleted, and that new employees will join the company and have to be added to the database table. You do not, however, expect such events to occur every hour. Indeed, you know that many employees will continue with the company until they retire and that even those who leave will only do so with relative infrequency. Consequently your database table, although it allows deletions and additions with no difficulty, is going to be relatively static. Nor will the format of the table itself change. The attributes that form its column headings are likely to survive for the entire existence of the table itself.

Yet circumstances in real life do not always follow this stable pattern. The monitoring processes within a drug research establishment are having to deal with constantly changing data and the environment within which that data is administered is also constantly changing. Relational tables of the type to which we have become accustomed would be in such a constant state of flux as to become unmanageable. Furthermore, within the customary database environment, the entity types of which the database is composed tend to be relatively few. There may be 30 or so tables, but there are not 300. The data items contained within those tables are single-valued and constant, yet in many contexts, the data values with which we are dealing could be rapidly changing values or values of which there were numerous versions. Again, within the conventional database, typical transactions are brief: a simple update, a quick retrieval or the rare deletion. Yet, of course, in many contexts, a transaction can involve many entities and entail many hours. Where such is the case, locking the relevant data until the transaction has been completed no longer looks a very viable procedure. To do so would prevent any concurrent access and possibly delay other operations for an insupportable length of time. The database models at which we have looked are viable within relatively static environments. They are a great deal less effective, or, indeed, totally inappropriate, within a dynamic context handling very large numbers of entities and complex relationships between those entities.

You may recall that in Chapter 3, the E–R model was briefly discussed. It is obvious that the existence of entities and the relationships between those entities lies at the core of information handling and therefore is a prime concern of databases. Relatively static though a database may be, its *raison d'être*, in part at least, is to model the connections that exist between the entities (and attributes) that exist within that database. If concern has been manifested about the static nature of the hierarchical, network and relational data models, clearly that concern must also extend to the E–R model which is often a tool employed in designing the database in the first place. Indeed, I pointed out in Chapter 3 that: 'an entity–relationship model is inevitably a somewhat static construct'. Yet the facts remain unalterable: information consists of entities and the relationships between them. The two entities John Milton and *Paradise Lost* are meaningless in isolation. Only when we learn that *Paradise Lost* is a poem which was written by John Milton do those two items of data become information. In other words, they become information when we perceive the relationship between them.

Clearly then, if databases are deficient because they inadequately reflect the rapidly changing world, then it is in part because the E–R diagram used to help design that database has itself been inadequate in the same way. As a result, there have been moves to extend the E–R diagram so as to make it truer to the complexity and transience of reality. In particular, two types of abstraction, *aggregation* and *generalization*, have been added to the E–R model.

Aggregation is a process which allows you to look at an entity and do one of two things to that entity:

1. You can break up the entity in question into smaller component entities, or
2. You can take the entity in question and group it with other related entities that can, together, be regarded as a single entity.

While the first process decomposes an entity into smaller entities and the second process aggregates entities together into a higher level entity, both operations are subsumed under the same label, aggregation.

Generalization, just like aggregation, is a label used to describe two opposite processes:

1. The first process, called specialization, entails breaking down objects within a set into their specific types.
2. The second process, generalization, entails combining objects together into a higher level object.

With aggregation and generalization, information technology has displayed its customary linguistic skill. Not only does each label describe two different activities, but those activities are the converse of each other. Nor is it easy at first glance to see how the two procedures subsumed under aggregation are any different from the two processes included in generalization. But they are different, and it is important to see how.

Aggregation is concerned with components of an object. Either it breaks an object up into its separate components, or it groups components together to make a higher level object. Hence I decompose my fountain pen into a number of separate entities: nib, filling tube, top, barrel. Alternatively, I aggregate my nib, filling tube, etc. into a higher level object known as a fountain pen. Either way, I am dealing with concrete objects.

Generalization is concerned with types or conceptual objects. Hence, if you have the entity 'swimming class', you may chose to break it down into activities: stroke tuition, stroke practice, endurance test, play, speed test, etc. Alternatively you may wish to include all swimming classes into the broader category of physical activity, a heading that will include hockey, athletics, football, tennis, etc.

These operations of aggregation and generalization can be diagrammatically represented. Thus, in an aggregation diagram like the one in Fig. 19.5, if you start at the top and proceed downwards, you are decomposing, while if you start at the bottom and proceed upwards, you are aggregating. And, of course, you could decompose each of the three elements of the CPU even further: main memory into program storage, working storage, input storage and output storage; the ALU into mathematical gates, logic gates and registers; the control

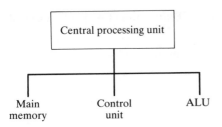

Figure 19.5

unit into sequence control register, memory address register, current instruction register, and so on.

It is exactly the same for generalization, though for a generalization diagram we use a triangle labelled 'is a' to show that the entities below are all types of the entity shown above (Fig. 19.6). And once again, of course, each type of course could be subdivided into further categories.

Having explained what aggregation and generalization are, it is barely necessary to explain their utility. Clearly both operations enable us to capture more precisely the complexity of the reality that we are seeking to describe. Furthermore, they provide a welcome flexibility. We can relate higher object entities where we need an overall conspectus, and lower level components when we need a more detailed approach. Hence such extensions to the E–R model can be of aid in the IPSE. They can increase the degree of integration, more adequately mirror requirements definition and even help in controlling data integrity.

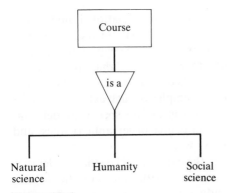

Figure 19.6

We are still, of course, confronted by the limitations of the query language. SQL and languages like it do not have any deductive or inferential capabilities. Indeed, to make a database 'intelligent', we need to incorporate the rule-based structure of an expert system. None the less, extensions to the E–R model can help to make the database more cohesive. Nor, of course, are we limited to E–R diagrams in the development of our database. Brathwaite (1990) lists seven of them:

1. Data-model diagrams, of which E–R diagrams are a subset,
2. Dataflow diagrams,
3. Activity-decomposition diagrams,
4. Activity-dependency diagrams,
5. Activity-process-logic diagrams,
6. Dataflow-content diagrams,
7. State-change diagrams.

It would not be appropriate to expound on all these options here, but the mere listing gives some impression of the variety of tools that is available these days for creating an IPSE. The mention of Brathwaite's book also enables us to encounter yet another acronym. Computer-aided software engineering (CASE) is often taken as being synonymous with IPSE, though it often seems to me that CASE is more tools-centred than IPSE which takes a more conceptual view. Whatever precise meaning is attached to these acronyms, they are both a witness to the efforts over recent years to find a more inclusive approach to the database world and the reality which that world is seeking to encapsulate.

You may also, at this point, have become aware that in this mention of IPSE and CASE, we are really entering again the field of semantic modelling which I stated at the end of Chapter 11 was not an area to which we could devote a full discussion. This remains true, but semantic modelling is the operation which underlies the creation of any fully integrated project support environment or computer-aided software engineering, so we do need to glance again at what exactly we mean by semantic modelling.

As this chapter has already indicated, the traditional relational model does not allow the expression of all the relationships that exist in the real world. Semantic models, of which the E–R diagram is an example, have consequently been developed or extended so as to capture more 'meaning' than the relational model can conveniently embody. We have looked at the forms of abstraction known as aggregation and generalization as examples of such extensions to the E–R context. We have not, however, looked at some of the specific models that have been developed so as to capture a greater degree of semantic richness and hence present a fuller and more integrated view.

The most obvious with which to begin is the extended relational model that has been developed by Codd and Date (both names with which you should now be fully familiar). This model has the advantage of being based upon the relational model itself, which Codd, after all, was the first to develop. It does, however, extend the concept of an entity. Entities in RM/T (the abbreviation normally used for the extended relational model) are split into three classes:

1. Kernel entities
2. Characteristic entities
3. Associative entities

The first type refers to the real-world objects in which we are interested and about which we wish to store data. Thus Student would be a kernel entity in a college database. A characteristic entity is one which helps to describe another entity. Date cites an employee-dependent as being a possible characteristic of an employee. An associative entity represents relationships between entities. Ricardo (1990) cites Enrol as a specimen associative entity showing a relationship between the two entities Student and Class.

There is more to RM/T than this, of course, but you can see how the three entity classes help to extend the capabilities of the basic relational model.

Preceding RM/T, Abrial (1974) introduced the concept of the binary model. Abolishing the distinction between entities and attributes, the Abrial binary model comprises entity sets and binary relationships. Binary relationships between the sets become *facts*. By linking entity sets with other entity sets, a complex mesh of binary relations can be shown (Fig. 19.7).

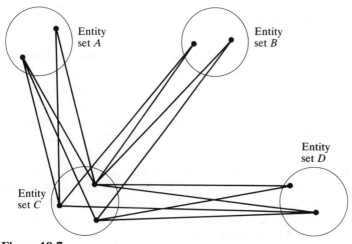

Figure 19.7

Extending the binary model is the construct known as the *semantic binary model*. This drops the name 'entity' completely and instead refers to 'objects', concrete or abstract as the case may be. Objects can be grouped together into categories, though an object can belong to more than one category, thus increasing the semantic richness of the model. Furthermore, while relationships between objects tend to be binary relationships, the semantic binary model can also represent nonbinary relationships, which are relationships between more than two objects.

Other models have also been developed. The semantic database model (SDM) devised by Hammer and McLeod allows multiple perspectives on the same data. The functional model of Kerschberg and Pacheco expresses relationships as functions or mappings between entity sets. In them all, the object is the same: to extend the expressive and associative power of the basic relational model. Chapter 22 of Date (1990) and Chapter 11 of Ricardo (1990) will be useful extensions of the bare outline that I have provided here.

One of the most interesting implementations of such semantic developments has been the emergence of the so-called object-oriented database, and it is to these that we must next turn.

19.3   Object-oriented databases

There have already been a number of books devoted to the object-oriented database. Nor, given the wealth of articles published on the topic in learned journals, can anyone reasonably doubt that object orientation is a matter of intense research and debate. Yet, as I warned at the beginning of this chapter, we are not yet in the realm of generally agreed parameters. In the object-oriented model, the entities of interest are called objects, yet Brown (1991) admits that: 'We cannot give a precise definition of what an object is.' Khoshafian and Abnous (1990) baldly state that: 'Standards are *not* emerging.' Hughes (1991) sounds almost despairing:

> It might be expected that after almost 25 years of development there might be some agreement on the fundamental principles of object-oriented programming languages and systems. On the contrary, the programming language community is still experimenting, while the database and AI [artificial intelligence] communities are faced with considerable difficulties with regard to efficient implementation of a wide range of powerful object-oriented concepts.

Yet, methinks, the writers do protest too much. It may not yet be possible to state that object-orientation will come to replace the relational model as that model has virtually replaced the hierarchical and network constructs, but it is possible to make at least some relatively unambiguous statements about the object-oriented model. Let us, therefore, do so.

19.3.1   WHAT IS AN OBJECT?

The traditional reply to this question is 'everything'. As Stonebraker has reportedly said, 'If I hear the phrase "everything is an object" once more, I think I will scream.' There is, though, no escaping the fact that objects are the crucial concept in object-oriented databases.

At one level, the word 'object' is simply a synonym for the word 'entity'. In other words, an object is an item of interest for the business or organization concerned and about which it wishes to store data. However, while this concept of an object makes it directly synonymous to an entity, object-oriented systems (hereafter shortened to OO-systems) do not just define the identity of an object; they also embrace the operations that can be performed upon that object. Thus an object is defined, not just by its data properties, but also by its functional properties. Hence we are presented with a more integrated picture. We see not just what an object is, but also how it can behave.

Clearly, of course, objects will interact with each other. This is done by the passing of messages from object to object. When an object receives a message, it works out from the message which of its available methods is appropriate for applying in this instance. Note, therefore, that there is a useful degree of 'information hiding' contained here. The human user will doubtless know what method or operation the receiving object should apply after receiving its message, but he (or she) does not have to concern himself (or herself) with the details as to how the required event needs to be implemented. Hence the user only needs to be conceptually aware of the broad context, as shown in Fig. 19.8, where we see an object with eight viable methods receiving a message. The object decodes its message and decides which of its available eight methods or operations needs to be performed in the light of that message. Thus the whole operation is perceived at a fairly high level of abstraction.

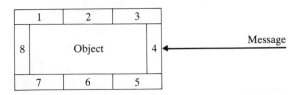

Figure 19.8

In addition, objects can be grouped into classes. This, of course, is comparable to entities being represented in tables. Thus, if you have an object History course, that object will belong to the general class Courses. In fact, the terminology in OO-systems is slightly different. Each individual object, like our History course, is not given a name but has a system-generated *object ID* that is guaranteed never to change. Hence you can change some (or all) of the attributes of an object while still, perforce, retaining its identifier. As a consequence, data independence is strongly implemented. Indeed, in the formation of an OO-database, it is classes that are initially created, because each class has a definition of the attributes available to the objects within that class and the methods of handling each of those objects. A class is consequently a kind of template for the objects which appear within it.

19.3.2 INHERITANCE

The outline in the preceding paragraph of objects and their existence within classes helps to introduce another fundamental aspect of OO-systems. Let us imagine that you create a class of all living animals. This class is given certain attributes and certain methods applicable to handling that class are defined. Clearly, however, it is an enormous class; indeed, we might describe it as a superclass.

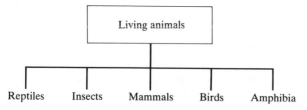

Figure 19.9

From that superclass, certain subclasses can be developed. The ones in this instance are fairly obvious (Fig. 19.9). Each of the five subclasses shown *inherits* the properties and methods of its superclass but can then add further properties and methods to make it a more specialized categorization. And so the process continues. The subclass Mammals can be further subdivided (Fig. 19.10). Each of these subsubclasses can be split in a similar fashion, each of the divisions inheriting the properties and methods of its predecessor.

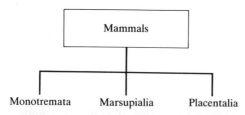

Figure 19.10

While the tiny amount that I have written about OO-systems is clearly inadequate for the formation of any valid evaluation, certain elements are clear. The procedure of inheritance is an elegant and economic way of creating increasingly specialized hierarchies. There is, though, one obvious consequence. Any individual object will have its properties and methods basically defined by its class, but that class might itself have its properties and methods (or most of them, at least), defined by a preceding class. And so the inheritance trail could continue. Just imagine that you wanted to access the class Humans. To discover fully all its properties and viable operations, you would have to regress from class to class in this sort of fashion:

Human
|
Anthropoids
|
Placentalia
|
Mammalia
|
Living animals

Thus the complete knowledge of an object's behaviour is not held in any one place but has to be garnered from a sequential search. None the less, inheritance saves an enormous design effort; a new class can inherit most of its behaviour and representation from a preceding class. Indeed, other aspects of OO-systems like reusability, object identity and user interfaces clearly link OO-systems with the whole concept of artificial intelligence.

19.4 Artificial intelligence

This section will be brief. For a book about databases I have already transgressed the code of academic demarcation by talking about such topics as systems analysis and networks, both specialist areas in their own right. To move into artificial intelligence (AI) as well would be to carry intellectual breadth to the point of lunacy. Yet AI has to be mentioned. If the relational database is too confined because of its lack of semantic flexibility, then what we are looking for is a database that can relate elements within it over a wide spectrum of areas using a broad range of criteria. In other words, we are looking for a database model that will behave intelligently.

It would be useful to begin by defining AI, but that is no easier than it is to define object-oriented databases. Personally I would prefer to define AI as being concerned with the development of computer systems that can do the sorts of things which, if human beings did them, would be regarded as evidence of intelligence. Others, however, wish to extend AI into the science of intelligence in general, with no necessary connection with IT. Certainly too, writings on AI have concerned themselves with the biology of neural networks, the psychology of consciousness, the philosophy of cognition and the nature of logic. Given that a database is an inert collection of magnetized marks, we have clearly moved a long way if we now need to talk about cognition in the database field. Yet the connections are clear. Cussins (1990) writes as follows:

> If cognitive science involves getting a psychological theory out of a computational model, and if a theory of representation is the way to do this, then in order to understand the nature of cognitive-science theorizing we need to understand the relation between computation, representational vehicles, representational content, and psychological explanation. The task is inherently multidisciplinary.

Hence, to become really expert in databases, you need to become the twentieth-century equivalent of Renaissance man.

Clearly we cannot pursue such avenues, but I did want to raise the question of AI because we can already see some manifestations of the linking of database design with AI. As we have seen or implied, there are a number of imperfections within the standard relational database.

1. Secondary storage (or external memory) has to be brought to the main memory before the CPU can examine its contents and process it. It would be

more efficient if the processing could be performed upon initially locating the data, particularly since transmission from secondary to primary storage can only be performed one block or sector at a time.

2. Data is stored by address. These addresses tend to be computed every time the data in question is accessed. This increases overhead and slows down the access. Yet the user of the database neither knows nor cares what the address may be of the relevant data. The user is only interested in the content of the data. Hence it would be logical and convenient if data could be accessed by content rather than by an irrelevant and artificial number.

3. Processing is performed much more quickly than data transfer. Hence the constant toing and froing between secondary and primary storage can easily lead to bottlenecks. The processor can stand idle while it waits for the tardy arrival of data.

4. In a multiuser environment, the fact that only one user can upgrade or amend a data block at a time can cause considerable delays to other users.

Yet solutions to these related database problems have been devised, and in each case the solution has depended upon adding a little more 'intelligence' to the system. Let us look at one or two examples.

The solution to the first problem that was mentioned is obvious enough. If the read–write head that searches secondary memory had enough intelligence to go to the correct address *and* then extract from that address only the precise data that was needed for the question in hand, then a great deal of input/output (I/O) work could be eliminated. At the moment the read–write head transfers an entire block or sector. When the CPU examines that block or sector, most of the data within it has to be sent back to secondary storage. Yet already there are several systems whereby what are called cellular-logic devices are capable of intelligently searching the whole disk in one revolution. The data still has to be brought to the CPU for proper processing, but the overhead cost of locating data by address is eliminated, and the I/O bottlenecks are eased.

A more direct assault on the wasteful practice of creating addresses for data has been made by ensuring that the external storage is so constructed that data can be retrieved by specifying its content rather than its address. Such an approach is called an *associative memory system* and, apart from its logical convenience, also turns out to be quicker than address-based schemes.

Computation in general can be speeded up by employing a system of multiprocessors. Instead of having the CPU handle all processing operations, there are instead a number of processors, each of which is designed to perform one specific function. Thus the data goes to the relevant processor, is dealt with very quickly, and is then passed on to the next relevant processor. Hence, in a complex computer transaction, the operation is split up into a number of subtasks, each dealt with by a separate processor and, indeed, with each subtask possibly being performed concurrently.

All these 'improvements', and others, are discussed in Su (1988), yet I return to an element which has been constantly referred to in these pages. A database itself is an inert object. What we want is for the large collection of data to be handled in such a way that relationships between those items of data can be revealed quickly and economically. In other words, we want the DBMS to behave intelligently. Many products—expert systems, knowledge-based systems, management information systems, etc.—already, in part, do so. Yet there remains a major hurdle. In order to communicate with a database, we have to use a language. Clearly, if a DBMS could use and respond to a natural language, with a natural language's capability for association, generalization, particularization, metaphor and the whole cultural framework that metaphor implies, then we would have taken a gigantic step towards the creation of a genuinely intelligent database. Powers and Turk (1989) approach the issue in their fascinating book. They conclude with these words:

> We have demonstrated that we are now at the point where our centuries of pursuit of knowledge have finally reached the stage where we may be able to reproduce, artificially, just those first distinguishing steps of intelligence that each newborn baby takes.

Breathtakingly exciting though such developments may be, one central fact remains. Data reigns supreme. Without data, there are no relationships. Without relationships, there is no thought. If this book had been titled *The Core of Information Technology* it would not have been hyperbole. Whether stored in the mind, written on paper or packed onto a computer disk, man cannot operate without data. The computer revolution is simply an extension of a process that began when man scratched symbols upon the walls of caves. Perhaps it was Sumerian priests recording deposits in and withdrawals from temple storehouses round about 3000 BC who created the world's first database. INGRES, Oracle, DB4 and the rest are merely ways of carrying on a process that has occupied man for the last 5000 years.

References

Ashworth, C. and Goodland, M. *SSADM: A Practical Approach*, McGraw-Hill, 1990.

Beynon-Davies, P. *Relational Database Systems*, Blackwell, 1991.

Bielawski, L. and Lewand, R. *Intelligent Systems Design: Integrating Expert Systems, Hypermedia, and Database Technologies*, John Wiley, 1991.

Brathwaite, K. S. *Applications Development Using CASE Tools*, Academic Press, 1990.

Brown, A. *Object-Oriented Databases*, McGraw-Hill, 1991.

Cussins, A. in M. Boden (ed.), *The Philosophy of Artificial Intelligence*, Oxford University Press, 1990.

Date, C. J. *Introduction to Database Systems*, Vol. I, 5th edn, Addison-Wesley, 1990.

Elmasri, R. and Navathe, S. *Fundamentals of Database Systems*, Benjamin Cummings, 1989.

Gorman, M. M. *Database Management Systems: Understanding and Applying Database Technology*, Computer Weekly/Butterworth Heinemann, 1991.

Hughes, J. O. *Object-oriented Databases*, Prentice-Hall, 1991.

Khoshafian, S. and Abnous, R. *Object Orientation: Concepts, Languages, Databases, User Interfaces*, John Wiley, 1990.

McFadden, F. A. and Hoffer, J. A. *Database Management*, 3rd edn, Benjamin Cummings, 1991.

Mittra, S. S. *Principles of Relational Database Systems*, Prentice-Hall, 1991.

Powers, D. M. W. and Turk, C. C. R. *Machine Learning of Natural Language*, Sprinter-Verlag, 1989.

Ricardo, C. *Database Systems*, Macmillan, 1990.

Su, S. *Database Computers*, McGraw-Hill, 1990.

PART SEVEN

A concluding case study

20
Case study: the small company

This short chapter is in marked contrast to the rest of the book. I have tried in the preceding pages to give a sound theoretical background to the database world. This brief chapter is my only incursion into reality.

This chapter can, by a stroke of good fortune, present a paradigm case. Most of this book was written in a small Norfolk village. In that village there exists a small company, established in 1906, that makes trailers and mechanical handling equipment. Clearly, in the rural environment of East Anglia, the bulk of its market over the years that the company has existed has been the farming community of Norfolk. None the less, with a refreshing degree of entrepreneurial flair, this small company has developed a substantial market (in combination with another company) worldwide as well as in the whole of Great Britain. Hence, in 1990, one of its directors decided that the company was ripe for an element of computerization. An accounts package was brought to run on a Tandon PC, and, even more significantly, a Hewlett-Packard (H-P) standalone terminal was purchased upon which to run the H-P Mechanical Engineering Series 10 package.

From this brief introduction, one thing is obvious: the company, G. T. Bunning and Sons, has no formal database. It may consequently seem bizarre to devote an entire chapter to a company that does not even possess the entity with which this book has been concerned. Yet this, of course, is the point. G. T. Bunning and Sons make trailers. For many years they have successfully been so doing. As you know, it is customary in the making of trailers to have drawings prepared by a professional draughtsman. Bunning and Sons possess hundreds of these drawings compiled over the years and all stored in a variety of cabinets, though, ironically, the drawings have tended to have been produced after the trailer has been made rather than before. These ex-post facto drawings are their database. Yet it is a database more bulky than effective. No one is entirely sure how to find a particular drawing when one is needed, and anyway, as you will have gathered, the workforce at Bunning's tends not to bother too much about the drawings anyway. For the last eighty-odd years, making a trailer has been a combination of experience, commonsense and intuitive flair. Indeed, even when presented with a drawing, some of the workforce have considerable difficulty in interpreting it. The drawing has been constructed by reference to a set of standards of which they know nothing and employing a range of geometrical and arithmetical conventions of which they are unaware. In other words, G. T. Bunning and Sons has been (and is) a traditional craft firm employing experience rather than science, knowhow rather than precise measurements. Try to understand their position. You may well have constructed an entirely adequate go-cart for your child, but would you be able to understand the drawing shown in Fig. 20.1?

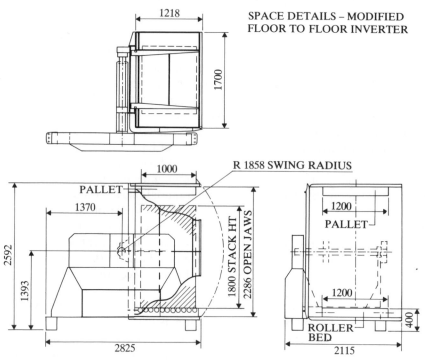

Figure 20.1

Clearly, with the decision to introduce at least a partial computerization, this *laissez-faire* approach has had to change. When a drawing is produced on the computer, its specified materials and measurements are not rough guides; they are precise determinants. Hence, from the introduction of the H-P Mechanical Engineering package, the design engineer appointed to manage that package has had to start building up a database. The drawings are no longer done on the drawing board. Instead they are constructed on the screen and then printed on the adjacent printer. In the first 14 months of the new package, the design engineer has produced over 1000 separate drawings. In other words, the design engineer has been building a database, though building that database has very much been a consequence of his primary objective, producing the drawings to fulfil the next order. It does, however, now mean that if he wants to incorporate a drive shaft or a support column into some trailer that has been ordered, he now just calls up onto his screen the standard drive shaft or support column that has already been placed in the database.

It is interesting to look at the role of this design engineer. He is a qualified draughtsman but has no formal training in computers. He did go on a course for the handling of computer engineering packages and he does have considerable experience with the H-P Mechanical Engineering package, but, other than that, he knows virtually nothing about computer science, database design or systems analysis. Hence, upon his taking up this post some 14 months ago, he has had to cope with the new technology without any of the theoretical understanding that this book has been concerned to provide. How did he go about it?

The design engineer, whom we shall call Peter, partly because it happens to be his name and partly because Peter comprises five letters as opposed to the 14 required for design engineer, decided that he needed to construct a kind of file structure so that relevant objects could be stored under meaningful headings. The H-P package provided a root directory, users/me10, and from this Peter developed a number of subdirectories and subsubdirectories as shown in Fig. 20.2. I do not imagine that the diagram is any more meaningful to you than it is to me. I have no idea what a bowser or a retriever is—breeds of dog seem somewhat unlikely in a trailer manufacturing database—but the technical terminology need not trouble us. The object that Peter was trying to achieve is obvious enough.

If, however, you do look at Fig. 20.2 with a little care, certain inadequacies are likely to become apparent. Peter admits this with a regretful shrug. It was Peter himself who pointed out one of them to me. 'If I was setting up this

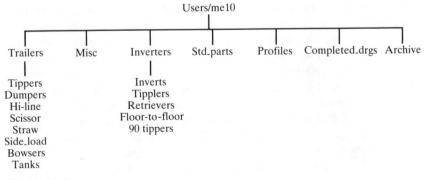

Figure 20.2

file structure today,' he said, 'I'd do something about the std_parts directory.' As you can imagine, it is very useful to have a file devoted to standard parts, but the heading is too general to be of enormous use. The standard parts for an inverter—whatever that might be—are different from the standard parts for a dumper which are in turn different from the standard parts for a tipper. In some cases, of course, a standard part for an inverter could also be a standard part for a tanker, a bowser, a scissor and most other implements. Hence it would have been, as Peter admitted, much more useful to have subdivided the standard parts directory into a series of subdirectories, each devoted to a specific type of part. Surely the same argument could be applied to the completed drawing directory. If, in only 14 months, you have already compiled 1000 completed drawings, it is clearly tiresome to access the entire listing of those plots in order to find the specific one that is required. Strictly speaking, the situation is not as dire as I have painted it. The directory which the H-P package compiles for the completed drawings does have a labelling system which makes it easy to identify each specific drawing, and that directory can be sorted in alphabetical order. Hence it does not take too long to access the specific drawing that Peter requires. But the system is still young and the database of drawings is going to increase greatly. Therefore a more overt classification system would be helpful.

If this seems painfully obvious, do bear in mind the context. Peter's job is to produce drawings for specific orders which the company receives. In other words, he is primarily a draughtsman. He is not also a database administrator. Yet, because of the circumstances, Peter has had to design his own database within a company where there has not been a single computer literate member, himself included. Just look, for instance, at the digitizer tablet (Fig. 20.3) that, together with the normal computer keyboard, constitutes for Peter the user interface of the package that he is running.

Clearly, with actual orders needing to be implemented, Peter has had quite enough to do in becoming fully familiar with the H-P package itself without having to concern himself with the niceties of database structure. Hence, what has happened with the company of G. T. Bunning and Sons is what happens with an enormous number of small companies that decide to pursue the path to computerization. The new system has had to be welded onto old and well-established practices. This welding process has had to be done with inadequate time or training. Yet I said that this was a paradigm case. And so it is. G. T. Bunning and Sons have entered the database world. Already, after only 14 months, the virtues of that database world are evident to the company as a whole. Not long ago, the company received a phone call asking for a plot for a particular type of trailer. By using his database, Peter was able to send the completed drawings for the specified trailer to the company concerned by lunchtime of the same day. A noncomputerized company still operating by means of the drawing board—and hundreds of companies still do—could not have had those drawings delivered to the requesting company inside four days.

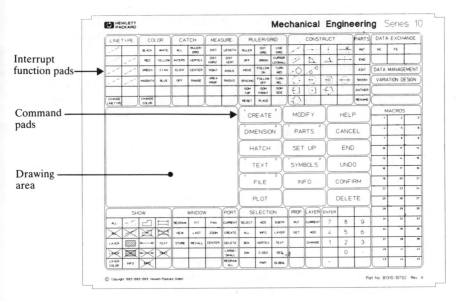

Figure 20.3

G. T. Bunning and Sons were able to do it inside four hours. Such an example illustrates, if illustration is necessary, the power of the computer.

The accounts package adopted by G. T. Bunning and Sons—the Pegasus Senior Range—is also relevant. The company has not purchased the complete range produced by Pegasus Software Ltd, confining themselves to stock control, invoicing, purchase ledger, bought ledger and sales ledger. They may decide to extend into payroll, job costing, and bill of materials at a later date. However, you do not habitually think of databases when you are considering an accounts package, but what is a listing of your stock if it is not a database? So too is a record of your purchases or details of your invoices.

I remember merrily playing with bought ledger, purchase ledger, etc., when doing my M.Sc. course. I too was using a Pegasus package, and it was remarkably straightforward to use. G. T. Bunning and Sons were kind enough to lend me the documentation for their Pegasus components, and, although I still prefer a detective novel, the documentation was admirably clear and well organized.

Obviously, when you buy a package, you are constrained by the rules of that package. It was noticeable that, in order to log in with the Pegagus package, you had to provide an initial password provided by Pegagus, a master password provided by Bunnings themselves, and a personal password to identify the specific person using the system at that point. The H-P engineering module allowed passwords to be used, but did not insist upon it. As a consequence, no password security has been implemented on the me10 at all. Peter, perfectly sensibly, claims that it is unnecessary for a variety of factors, but you still wonder. I would not find it too difficult to delete every drawing that Peter had compiled. I would, however, find it impossible to even enter the Pegasus system at all. That is as it should be.

My major concern with G. T. Bunning and Sons is that they have become meaningfully computerized in an entirely amateur fashion. The Hewlett-Packard terminal and software package cost £30,000, but apart from that expense, G. T. Bunning and Sons have spent nothing on training (Peter had experienced his training course before joining them), only employed one new member of staff (and that as a draughtsman, not as a computer engineer) and still know nothing about normalization, entity–relationship diagrams or data processing. In other words, the database world can be entered by anyone. The database that Peter is currently constructing is not a perfect database. Peter readily admits that. But it is none the less a very useful one. One of my concerns in this book has been to banish the mystique that tends to surround information technology. G. T. Bunning and Sons provide an excellent example. Peter himself knows virtually nothing about computers, yet he is the only person in the company who can operate the H-P Mechanical Engineering Series 10 package. In doing so, he has been forced to construct his own database. If he can do so with little more than common sense to guide him (and with more pressing concerns constantly at hand), then you, having absorbed the information contained in this book, should come to the task infinitely better prepared. Doreen, who operates the accounts package, has received some limited instruction from the Pegasus representative, and has the documentation to refer to (though she very rarely does). Yet Robin Bunning, the director of the company who was largely responsible for the adoption of computerization, states with pride that the two systems, the H-P and the Pegasus, have already amply demonstrated their utility.

Of course, having introduced G. T. Bunning and Sons, I have laid myself open to one obvious and potentially embarrassing question: if G. T. Bunning and Sons can construct a database without knowing anything at all about the subject, is there any real need for all the information that this book contains? Surely G. T. Bunning and Sons have merely demonstrated the entire irrelevance of this book.

It will come as no major surprise if I state my disagreement with the above conclusion. I believe that the information which I have tried to present in this book is *essential* for anyone wishing to enter the database world in an informed and intelligent fashion. I do, therefore, want to have a look at the inadequacies of the G. T. Bunning context. This is not intended as any sort of cheap sneer at my village company. On the contrary, I am full of admiration for what they have achieved, but we do need to put that achievement in a computer context. Staying for the moment with their H-P Mechanical Engineering package, let us look at what they do not achieve with it.

First of all, and in computing terms, most wasteful of all, G. T. Bunning and Sons have no developed CAD/CAM system (computer-aided design and computer-aided manufacture, if you are suffering from acronym surfeit). To be sure, Peter designs the components by means of a computer, but having done so, it would be the most efficient utilization simply to send those designs digitally to the workshop and for the machines then to act upon those digital instructions and, in so doing, to manufacture the components concerned. Thus the company has the CAD but not the CAM. As a result, they are only exploiting half the facilities available. It would, though, be fearsomely expensive to convert to CAM; the existing workshop would have to be totally transformed and a great deal of new equipment purchased. It may well be that G. T. Bunning and Sons will move over to CAM, but they will need to do so relatively slowly and in discrete stages. There is, though, given the necessary finances, no impediment to their so doing. By moving into CAD, they have made it possible to move with relative ease into CAM also. Other extensions of their computer management will be less easy.

Peter's database, adequate enough for current purposes, lacks the potential for advance or significant extension. It is, as we have seen, nothing more than a collection of drawings arranged in a rough hierarchical fashion. Its major deficiency is that it lacks any means of ever relating to any other element. Let us imagine that Bunning in future wanted to relate specific orders to specific drawings which were prepared for fulfilling those orders. There is no means of so doing. Let us imagine that Bunning wanted to relate specific components with the suppliers who had provided the materials for the construction of those components. There is no means of so doing. In other words, the H-P Mechanical Engineering package has been regarded as an entity all on its own with no thought given as to the useful ways in which that designing tool can be integrated into the broader commercial and administrative functions of the company as a whole. Indeed, Peter's database currently exists partly on paper and partly on disk. The drawings themselves are on disk, all 1000 of them, but the itemization of what each drawing comprises is still kept in a book lying on Peter's desk. This, of course, is absurd. If Peter could construct a table of those drawings, with the drawing number as the primary key, then a simple indexing system would be able to relate each drawing number to the relevant drawing. Furthermore, since each drawing entry in the table given over to drawings would indicate the client for whom that drawing was constructed, there would be a simple one-to-many relationship between drawing number and customer or customers who had purchased the trailer represented by that drawing.

You also know that G. T. Bunning and Sons have an accounts package on a separate Tandon PC. There is no interconnection between the Tandon and the H-P terminal. It is consequently impossible to relate bad payers with the artefact which they bought, products with the suppliers who provided the materials for the building of that product, and so on. Nor, although the accounts package exists, is there any computerization of payroll. Yet, as we know, payroll is one of the easiest and most cost-effective elements in the computerization of a company.

Furthermore, while I have indicated that the H-P Mechanical Engineering Series 10 package lies at the core of the G. T. Bunning and Sons computerization, it is only a small section of that H-P package that they have adopted. For instance, H-P provides a data management system linked to their mechanical engineering package. The manual accompanying that data management system has an entire section devoted to system administration. That section explains how to set up a database, how to create tables with primary keys, how to manage the system catalogue (i.e. the data dictionary), and how to back up, archive and restore. In other words, H-P regards proper database management as an integral part of their mechanical engineering package, G. T. Bunning and Sons have chosen not to implement this aspect at all. The decision may have been a forced one; economic constraints may have prevented the purchase of the entire package, and, furthermore, if they had bought the entire entity, they would have needed a database administrator. Peter could not have doubled roles in the way in which he has been doing.

All this, of course, is the way of the world. We, throughout this book, have been pleasantly divorced from the real world. We have been able to plan our database implementation unfettered by reality. G. T. Bunning and Sons have not been so lucky. They have had to cope with finances. They have had to cope with a workforce whose attitude towards computerization verged from the indifferent to the antagonistic. They have had to cope with an economic climate in which it has been much more common for small businesses to enter the bankruptcy courts than to experience expansion. They have had to cope with the limiting factors inherent in all small companies. Yet the danger that they now face is that, having entered the database world, they have done so too partially, too incompletely and too casually to enable significant advances to be made hereafter. G. T. Bunning and Sons have done very well. They illustrate that computers and databases are accessible to all. But they also illustrate that amateurism and information technology are uneasy bedfellows. G. T. Bunning and Sons have made great advances, but in so doing, they may have impeded their own progress in the future. Having now got a database of sorts, they may come to find that they have crippled themselves for entry into the efficient database world. Certainly, if they do eventually decide to extend their computing facilities and to integrate those facilities, they will not be able to do so by adding on to their current system, or at least they will only be able to do so in part. They could implement a CAM system onto their current CAD, but no other meaningful integration seems possible.

As I said at the beginning, G. T. Bunning and Sons are a paradigm case. They show two things:

1. The computer world is not beyond the reach of the noncomputerate.
2. The noncomputerate do need some guidance if they are to make the best decisions.

This book has been aimed at the noncomputerate public. I hope that it has given you the guidance that was needed.

Glossary

Here you will find all the remotely technical words or terms that are used in this book given a brief, self-contained definition. Where necessary, reference will also be given to the pages within the book where the item is more fully explained.

While the selection and formulation of the definitions that follow are clearly my own responsibility, I would like to acknowledge the help that I gained in compiling this glossary from the following:

Sandra Carter, *Computer Terms*, Chambers, 1988.

The *Glossary of Computing Terms* produced by Computing Services of Leicester Polytechnic.

Glossary from Michael M. Gorman, *Database Management Systems*, Butterworth-Heinemann/Computer Weekly, 1991.

Glossary from Carl Malamud, *INGRES: Tools for Building an Information Architecture*, Van Nostrand Reinhold, 1989.

'Appendix B, Glossary of Terms' from Richard C. Perkinson, *Data Analysis: The Key to Data Base Design*, QED Information Sciences Inc., 1982.

Ellen Thro, *The Database Dictionary*, Microtrend Books™, 1990.

Equally importantly, perhaps, has been the guidance provided by Humpty Dumpty:

When I use a word, Humpty Dumpty said, in rather a scornful tone, it means just what I choose it to mean—neither more nor less.

Lewis Carroll, Alice Through the Looking Glass.

A few (very few) of the definitions below are identical to those given in my earlier book on INGRES (Rothwell, 1992).

ABF   An acronym (q.v.) for Application-By-Forms, which is an environment within the relational database INGRES that allows the development of computer applications that are conducted within the framework of INGRES but are none the less entirely personal to the company or individual who has devised it.

absolute value   Used to indicate the magnitude of a number regardless of whether it is a positive or negative number. Thus the absolute value of −793 and +793 are identical.

access   This is normally used as a synonym for 'retrieve'. Hence, if you want to retrieve some data, you may say: 'I want to access this data'.

access method   The way in which the computer system retrieves (or stores) items of data. The method itself will be determined by an algorithm (q.v.) within the operating system software.

access strategy   The way in which a DBMS works out the best method of finding data within the database.

acoustic coupler   A portable modem (q.v.).

acronym   A major trait within computer science is to construct words which are composed of the initial letters of other words. Hence, if you wish to talk about random access memory, you refer to RAM. If you want to mention a personal computer disk operating system, you refer to PC-DOS. The prevalence of such acronyms allows you to construct pages of indigestable prose: e.g. 'The WP gives NLQ and the VDU is WYSIWYG' means 'the word processor gives near letter quality and the video display unit is what-you-see-is-what-you-get'.

Ada   A high-level programming language developed by the US Department of Defense which has since been used in many other contexts. It is a very large and highly structured language.

address   The label given to a specific location within a computer memory. The word can also be used as a verb—'to address memory'—when its meaning is almost the same as 'access'.

aggregation   An operation by which objects can be decomposed into more detailed components or aggregated into more general ones. See Chapter 19.

AI   See artificial intelligence.

algorithm   The recipe from which a computer can solve a particular problem. Hence, if you want the computer to increase the salary of all staff by 7 per cent, you have to input an algorithm for this operation.

alias   Another name for an object or entity. Hence 'attribute' can be an alias for 'value', or 'memory' is an alias for 'storage'.

analogue   A form of measurement or representation which represents changes or a process rather than a series of discrete results. Thus speech is transmitted along a telephone wire by means of an analogue signal.

AND   A logical operator used in computer gates (q.v.). The processor accepts two inputs. Only if input 1 AND input 2 are both positive will a positive output be given.

anomalies   When data within a database shows inconsistencies, the database is said to have anomalies.

ANSI   American National Standards Institution, an organization devoted to the development of standards within the computer industry.

append   A verb meaning to add data: 'He appended the new results to the table'.

application   A specific job or purpose to which the computer is currently devoted: 'It's running the payroll application at the moment'. The word is also used for specific pieces of software like a spreadsheet or a word processor, software which is concerned with accomplishing a specific task.

application generator   A program used to generate other applications. ABF (q.v.) is an application generator.

architecture   The design or layout of the various components of a computer system, i.e. are the terminals linked to each other in some sort of network? how many printers (if any) are linked to the system? Such questions are concerned with the architecture of the system. However, the word 'architecture' is also sometimes used when describing the capabilities of an individual microprocessor. Hence you might hear (or read) about a 16-bit architecture, indicating that the microprocessor handles two bytes of data at a time.

archive   A term normally used to refer to files which are not normally used but are kept (often on tape) either as a backup or as a historical record.

array   An ordered collection of variables of a similar type.

artificial intelligence   A research area within computer science that seeks to devise computers that more completely resemble the characteristics of the human brain.

ASCII   American Standard Code for Information Interchange. This is a character set in which all the letters (upper and lower case), all the numbers, all the punctuation marks and common symbols like £ or $ are represented by a unique series of seven bits plus an extra parity bit for error checking. Always pronounced 'ass-key', it is the most widespread computer character set in existence, though its failure to cope with most foreign languages or with graphics has led to numerous extensions of ASCII.

ASCII file   A collection of related data that is made up only of characters drawn from the original 128 characters of the ASCII standard.

assembler   A program that converts a program written in assembly language into the appropriate machine code.

assembly language   A low-level programming language in which each statement is easily translated into a parallel statement in machine code. Hence an assembly language is bound to be a procedural language. It also runs extremely efficiently, though it is difficult and tedious to write.

asynchronous communication   A method of sending data messages whereby each bit of data follows the preceding bit in an unbroken line. A start bit and a stop bit are used to indicate the beginning and end of each specific communication. Compare it with synchronous communication where bits of data are sent in parallel along separate wires.

atomic   This refers to a single value within a table. All such values should be atomic in that they cannot be broken down into anything simpler. The word is also used to refer to the integral nature of a data transmission. A transmission is atomic in that it only makes sense if the whole of the transmission is completed. Hence, should a transaction be halted before completion, a DBMS needs the facility to revert back to the state that existed before the transaction in question even started.

attribute   In a table comprising rows and columns, the headings at the tops of the columns are known as attributes. Hence if you have a table devoted to books, the columns are likely to be headed: Author, Title, Publisher, Date of Publication. These will be the attributes of the table. Each entry in the table will give specific values to these attributes. However, an instance or value of an attribute is often referred to as an attribute, just as a DBMS is often simply referred to as a database. You may, however, also encounter the word in referring to the facilities of a word processing program, i.e. attributes like underlining, printing in italics, etc., or in describing the facilities of a graphics program.

back end   The portion of a database system that gets data for a user. An application is a front end and it dispatches query language (q.v.) statements to a back-end data server, which in turn returns the relevant rows of data.

backup   The copy of a program or of data which is kept in a safe place just in case the computer crashes while working on that program or with that data and possibly damages or destroys the data concerned. As a verb, the word means 'to copy data or a program so that it can be stored safely in a separate place'.

bad sector   An area of a disk, floppy or hard, that will not reliably record data. These are common faults, normally the product of some manufacturing defect. Fortunately they do not normally result in any major problems since the operating system tends to pass over them. Hence, although the disk in question will lose some of its potential storage space, no reading or writing problems should ensue.

bandwidth   Normally this means the transmission capacity of a communication channel measured in bits per second (bps). In a local area network, the bandwidth is a measurement of the network speed.

bar code   A printed pattern of wide and narrow vertical lines which represent a numerical code. Bar codes are normally used to identify a particular product. By passing the bar code over an optical scanner, the product concerned can be identified and matched with its price. Bar codes are consequently used in supermarkets or for the purposes of inventory control in businesses.

BASIC   An extremely common programming language developed in 1964 to make computer programming easier for people who were not trained computer scientists. It is widely agreed that it is not a very good language since it allows, and even encourages, poor programming techniques.

basic input/output system   Always known by its acronym BIOS, this is a set of programs in read-only memory (ROM) that eases the transfer of data and control instructions from the computer to the disk drive or other peripherals.

batch processing A type of operation in which program instructions are carried out, one after the other, without any user intervention. This is efficient in the usage of computer resources but inconvenient in that, unlike interactive processing, you only discover any errors *after* the entire job has been completed.

baud A measure of the number of times per second that switching can occur in a communications channel. The word is most frequently encountered as the measurement of the speed of a modem.

baud rate A unit for indicating the speed of data transmission. Normally a baud is taken as being the transfer of one bit per second. Hence, when a modem (q.v.) is advertised as transmitting at 300 baud or having a baud rate of 300, it means that the modem will transmit 300 bits per second.

bells and whistles Commonly used to refer to the so-called 'extra' and desirable facilities that a system or product possesses.

benchmark A grading given to a piece of equipment or an application program which purports to signify the standard of performance of that equipment or program. The idea of a benchmark as a measure of effectiveness is a sound idea, but it is not easy to test either equipment or programs in a fully comprehensive fashion. Consequently most computing professionals treat benchmarks with a considerable degree of scepticism.

BCD See binary coded decimal.

binary coded decimal A way of coding long decimal numbers so that they can be processed with precision in a computer that only uses an 8-bit data word.

binary numbers A number system that consists of only the numbers 0 and 1.

binary search A method of finding data by starting in the middle of the relevant file or database and then progressing in the right direction, upwards or downwards, by moving to the middle of the remaining records.

BIOS See basic input/output system.

bit A single unit in a binary numbering system (i.e. a 1 or a 0) is called a bit, an abbreviation of BInary digiT. The so-called word length of a computer indicates how many bits it can cope with simultaneously. Thus a computer with a word length of 32 can process 32 bits at the same time.

block A unit of information that has been processed and can be passed from one computer to another or from a computer to some peripheral of that computer. Normally a block is a number of rows (or records) that are grouped together on a physical device such that all can be read into memory with a single I/O, thus making sequential reading of files more efficient. On some machines, block is synonymous with page.

buffer A memory location in the processor that is allocated to holding information temporarily, often while it is just waiting for some other aspect of the operation concerned to be completed.

bug   An undetected mistake made in the programming of some software of which you only become aware when the software is being used.

bus   A pathway along which signals are sent from one part of the computer to another.

byte   A unit of eight bits.

C   A high-level programming language.

cache memory   A part of the random-access memory (RAM) that is reserved for the storage of frequently accessed data and which deals with such data very rapidly indeed.

CAD   Computer-aided design.

candidate key   An attribute value that functionally determines other values within the row and hence could be chosen as the primary key of the row. It is not uncommon for a row of data to have more than one attribute value that could be selected as the primary key. Such instances are referred to as candidate keys.

cardinality   The number of columns or attributes in a table.

CASE   Computer-aided/assisted software engineering, that is, tools devoted to automating various stages of information systems development.

cell   The rectangle formed by the intersection of a row and column in a spreadsheet. Each cell has an address. Thus A1 means the first cell in the first row, and so on.

central processing unit   Comprising the control unit, the arithmetic/logic unit, and primary storage, the central processing unit (CPU) is the kernel of a computer. Discussed in Sec. 2.3.

character   A letter, digit, punctuation mark or other symbol.

character set   The fixed set of keyboard codes that a particular computer system uses. ASCII (q.v.) is an example of a character set.

chip   An electronic circuit etched onto a tiny wafer of silicon. Devised in the late 1950s, it had become possible by 1990 to place 16 million components on one tiny chip, and then mass produce it.

CHKDSK   A command that leads the computer to check the directory and file allocation table of a disk.

clock speed   The speed at which a computer performs its operations.

clustering   The process of storing logically related records close together on some secondary storage device.

coaxial cable   A cable which is often used to connect terminals in a local area network (q.v.). Although more expensive than ordinary telephone wire, which is one of its alternatives, coaxial cable is able to carry more data.

COBOL   Common business oriented language, a third-generation language widely used in business and commerce.

CODASYL model   An instance of the network database model that was originally defined by the Database Task Force (DBTG) of the Conference of Data System Language (CODASYL) organization. Discussed in Chapters 9 and 13.

column A vertical component of a table. The name at the top of the column is the name of the attribute, and at each place within that column there will appear an attribute value or instance. Their place in tables of a relational database is explained in Chapter 10.

command A signal that the user gives to a computer program in order to initiate (or end) a particular function or operation. Thus the user can give the command DELETE, either by typing the command at the keyboard or by choosing it from a menu, in order to remove a file from the memory or to disable a particular function.

communications program An application program that enables the computer to send or receive data from other computers, usually by means of the telephone system. Discussed in Chapters 7 and 18.

compiler A program that transforms instructions written in a programming language like C or Pascal into instructions that can be executed directly by the computer.

compression The process of removing trailing blanks from alphanumeric fields and leading zeros from numeric fields.

computer-aided design A method of using a computer so as to help design something in architecture or engineering.

computer-assisted instruction A method of employing a computer so as to help someone learn a procedure, a series of instructions, or a set of facts.

computer system The combination of elements like disk drives, printers, monitor and keyboard that, together, make up a complete computer installation. Described in Sec. 2.5.

concatenation The combination of two or more elements into one unit.

conceptual schema This is the overall information model of the enterprise which the database has been set up to serve. The data representing the conceptual schema is stored in the data dictionary.

concurrency The state whereby two or more operations are being processed by the computer at the same time.

consistency A state of the database in which, since there are no partially completed updates, all the data is internally consistent.

contention A situation that occurs when two or more users are attempting to access the same data simultaneously.

control unit The component of the CPU that obtains the program instructions and ensures that they are carried out.

CP/M An operating system for personal computers.

crash The unwanted and unexpected termination of a computer program.

cursor An on-screen blinking character that indicates where the next character will appear when you press a character key.

cylinder In disk drives, the name given to a set of tracks that occupy the same position.

daisywheel printer An impact printer that used to be widely used in offices, but its noise, the difficulty experienced in changing fonts, and the development of inexpensive laser printers has seen its virtual disappearance.

data Factual information stored on tape or disk that can be used in the making of decisions or in mathematical calculation.

data analysis In this book the term is used to signify the identification of the data elements which are needed to support the data processing system of the organization, the placing of these elements into logical groups and the definition of the relationships between the resulting groups. In data analysis the emphasis is on data structure, not data flow.

data communications The name given to the transmission of computer data between computer systems and terminals. The trend today is toward networks (q.v.) of cooperating computers that can share information.

data control language That part of a data model that is concerned with defining data structures.

data definition The process of creating the data definition language.

data dictionary A catalogue of all the hardware and software entities used within a specific system or operation. A data dictionary is an example of meta-data, i.e. data about data. Dealt with briefly in Chapter 7 and more fully in Chapter 17.

data element A distinct unit of data. It could be referred to as a data item or an attribute value.

data flow A named representation of data that is passed between processes. Data flow is often depicted in diagram form.

data independence The facility whereby the users of a database can access the data that they need without having to know anything about where that data is specifically located. In other words, data independence occurs when changes to one database aspect (logical or physical) are taken care of by the DBMS and require no user intervention. Discussed briefly in Chapter 7 and more fully in Chapter 10.

data integrity The accuracy, completeness and internal consistency of the information stored in a database.

data manipulation Used in database management to embrace the four fundamental database operations of retrieval, modification, deletion and insertion.

data model An architecture for data. It is composed of three primary components: data structure, data operators, inherent integrity rules.

data processing The activity of preparing, storing or manipulating information with a computer.

data record In a relational database, often used as a synonym for a row of data.

data redundancy The repetition of the same data in more than one place. A certain amount of data redundancy is inevitable, but it needs to be minimized as much as possible because of the problems with update and integrity that such redundancy produces.

data type The kind of data that a database management program will accept.

Thus a DBMS is likely to accept character, integer, logical and date data types.

database   A collection of ordered and related information about a subject, so arranged as to provide the ability to retrieve, add, delete and combine that information in ways necessary to the user. In a sense, a database can be thought of as an electronic filing cabinet.

database administrator   The person or persons given the responsibility for the definition, organization, protection and efficiency of an organization's databases. Normally abbreviated to DBA, the role is discussed in Chapter 15.

database design   The arrangement of data in a database to facilitate the manipulation of that database. Database design is briefly discussed in Sec. 2.2 and is the underlying concept throughout Chapter 3 and, to some extent, Chapters 4 and 5.

database management program   An application program that provides the tools for the manipulation of a database. Such tools include ways of sorting the data into a required order, outputting such data onto screen or printer, inserting new data, deleting unwanted data and so on.

database management system   Often abbreviated to DBMS, this is a series of programs that not only manage the data within a database but also provide the complete context for the structuring and transmission of such data.

database structure   A definition of the data tables in which information is stored.

database system   A system composed of a database and database management system.

dBASE   A well-known and popular DBMS for personal computers.

DBMS   See database management system.

DCL   See data control language.

deadly embrace   The situation which exists when two or more application programs have locked data needed by each other.

debugging   The process of removing the mistakes from a program.

decryption   The process of translating encrypted data back into normal language.

default value   The value chosen by an application program when the user does not specify one.

degree   The number of rows in a table.

dependency   A state whereby one data item is dependent upon another data item. Hence, if item A appears, it follows that item B, which is dependent on item A, must also appear.

desktop publishing   The procedure whereby a personal computer can be used to produce text and graphics akin to that produced by a professional newspaper or magazine.

determinant   A data item of which all the other attribute values in the row are logical derivatives. For instance, the employee number given to a worker in a company functionally determines his or her name. The part number given to a part will determine its size, name, function and location.

directory   An index to the files or tables stored on a disk. Normally you can see the contents of a disk directory by simply typing DIR at the keyboard.

disk   See 'floppy disk' and/or 'hard disk'.

disk drive   A secondary storage medium such as a floppy disk drive or a hard disk, though the term is normally only applied to floppy disks.

disk pack   A disk pack is a number of hard disks stacked on top of each other and connected by a spindle. Each disk, or platter, usually 14 inches in diameter, is coated with a magnetizable material. As with floppy disks, information is recorded in circles called tracks, but hard disks have greater storage capacity than floppy disks. Consequently they tend to be used in conjunction with mainframe or minicomputers. A disk pack is placed into the disk unit which is connected to the drive mechanism. Once the pack is loaded into the unit the read–write mechanism, located inside the unit, positions itself over the first track of each surface. The mechanism consists of a number of arms at the ends of which there is a read–write head for each surface. All arms are fixed together as one when accessing a surface on the disk pack.

distributed database   A database which is stored, in whole or in part, at more than one site, all the relevant sites being connected by a network of some description. Chapter 18 deals with distributed databases.

documentation   The printed material in the form of instructions, handbooks or reference brochures that is provided with a computer program or computer system in order to aid the user in its operation. Traditionally, such documentation is unreadable and/or inaccurate which is why books like this one keep being written.

domain   The pool of values assigned to a column or an attribute.

DOS   Disk operating system.

dot-matrix printer   An impact printer that forms text and illustrations by pressing the ends of pins against a ribbon. The more pins a printer possesses, the clearer the result.

downloading   The process of receiving and storing data that has been passed on from another distant computer.

driver   A disk file that contains information needed by a program to operate a peripheral such as a monitor or a printer.

DTP   See desktop publishing.

dump   To transfer data from one location to another, normally from internal memory to external memory or from memory to a printer.

e-mail   See electronic mail.

EBCDIC   See extended binary coded decimal interchange code.

electronic mail   A method of sending messages such as letters and memos by means of electronic communications media like the telephone system.

encryption   The process of turning a message into a coded transmission that cannot be understood by anyone who does not possess the key for translating it back into its original form. Encryption is a useful way of safeguarding the privacy of communications. Discussed in Chapter 16.

entity An object of interest to the organization concerned and hence needing representation in the database. It is difficult to be more precise about entities, though an attempt is made in the answer to the first question following Part One. Beynon-Davies (1991) is succinct in describing an entity as: 'Some aspect of the real world which has an independent existence and can be uniquely identified.'

entity–relationship diagram A diagram that illustrates entities and the relationships between entities. Dealt with in the second part of Chapter 3.

entity–relationship model A data model devised by P. P. S. Chen which models data in terms of entities and relationships.

EPROM Erasable programmable read-only memory. Whereas a read-only memory (ROM) chip cannot be altered by the user, an EPROM chip can be erased and then reprogrammed.

E–R diagram See entity–relationship diagram.

error detection Error detection routines should occur during processing. Thus data can be checked to ensure that all the necessary fields are present, and the fields themselves can be checked to ensure that they contain the correct number of characters and that those characters are of the correct type (letters or numeric). In any system there are certain instructions that are illegal because the system is incapable of responding to them. An obvious example is an instruction with a function code to which no meaning has been attached, or an attempt to store a word that has overflowed in the accumulator. In such cases (and others), the condition should be detected by hardware, and control is then transferred to an executive or operating-system routine resident permanently in store, which handles the condition in an appropriate manner. Should an error not be detected during input or processing, its presence only becomes obvious during output (and not always even then). If an error becomes obvious during output, it is clearly too late to remedy it there and then. Virtually the only approach to the problem is to attempt a *trace*, that is to attempt to find whether the program followed the expected sequence, and whether the values of the variables at every stage were reasonable.

Ethernet A method of implementing a local area network (q.v.).

even parity An error-checking technique whereby the final bit in a byte is set to 1 if the number of 1s in the data item adds up to an even number. This final so-called parity bit is set to 0 if the number of 1s in the data item adds up to an odd number.

expert system A computer program designed to help solve problems in a closely and narrowly defined field. Discussed in Sec. 6.2.

extended binary coded decimal interchange code A computer character set coding scheme whereby each one of 256 standard characters is assigned a unique digital representation. While not as common as ASCII (q.v.), it is used on IBM mainframes.

fax   A quasi-acronym of FACSimile, this word refers to the transmission and reception of a printed page via the phone service. A machine scans the relevant page, converts it into a form that can be transmitted by telephone, and then dispatches it. A fax machine at the other end then receives the coded message, translates it back into its original form, which it prints as a replica of the original page.

field   This word can be and is used a little loosely, but it basically refers to the area in which a data value or item is placed. Hence, each column of a table is composed of fields. The value that occupies that field is called an attribute (or, more correctly, an attribute value), but quite often people use field and attribute as synonyms.

field definition   Each field has a series of characteristics. It has a name like 'Part Number', 'address' or 'colour'. It belongs to a particular data type, like integer or character. It may have a maximum width. If it is a numeric field, it may have a specified number of decimal places. Hence a field definition is the list of defining characteristics that each field has been allocated.

field name   The name given to a data field that enables you to identify the contents of that field. Depending on the DBMS concerned, there will be limitations of length placed upon the field name. Thus a field could be called Phone_no or Address, but it is unlikely that it could be called Management_configuration.

file   A collection of related information. Thus all the details necessary for dealing with a payroll is likely to be called the payroll file. Although files are thought of as a unit, they can be stored on a disk as separated fragments. (See the last two paragraphs of Chapter Seven.) A file, then, in terminology that I feel is preferable, is equivalent to a table which is itself composed of rows, each row being made up of atomic data items contained in a field. The two columns below give alternative nomenclatures:

Database	Database
composed of files	composed of tables
made up of records	made up of rows
each of which is composed	each of which is composed
of data elements or fields	of data items or attributes

floppy disk   Made from flexible plastic and reminding most people of small gramophone records, floppy disks are widely used on personal computers. Three sizes of floppy disk are common, 8 inch, 5¼ inch and 3½ inch, though 3 inch is used on the very successful Amstrad PCW8256. Some floppy disks only use a single surface, though the bulk are double-sided these days. Each side has tracks, normally between 40 and 100 tracks per inch. Normally, because their relatively small size means that floppies cannot carry vast stores of information, floppy disks tend to be used with microcomputers. With a floppy disk, used with a microcomputer, the disk is placed into a narrow slot in the front of the disk drive. Once the disk is placed firmly in the slot, it engages a turntable which rotates the disk and also brings a read–write head into contact with the disk. The read–write head is moved to and fro across the disk either to record data onto the disk surface (i.e. 'write') or to 'read' back data which had been previously recorded.

flow chart   A chart which portrays how a particular program works. Standard symbols like rectangles and diamonds are used to signify all the various computer operations or entities like processing, data store, taking a decision, etc.

font   The specific typeface of the letters, symbols and numbers on a key-board.

foreign key   An attribute within a row of attributes that happens to be the primary key of another row in another table.

format   Any method of arranging information for printing or storage.

formatting   The operation of placing a floppy disk in the disk drive and making it ready to accept data.

FORTRAN   A high-level programming language often used in mathematical and scientific work.

forward chaining   In expert systems, a way of drawing inferences by working through the relevant rules in order to determine whether or not more data is needed and, if it is not, how to draw a correct inference from the data available.

functional dependence   The state of one item or items only being identified via the primary key of the row in question.

gateway   A device that can link two dissimilar local area networks together or allow a local area network to communicate to a wide area network.

generalization   An operation whereby objects of different types can be generalized into examples of a more general type, or specialized into more specific types. See Chapter 19.

gigabyte   Approximately one billion bytes or 1000 megabytes.

graphics   The creation, modification and printing of computer-generated diagrams, sketches and pictures.

hacker   A strange being who loves proving that he or she is smarter than any given computer system. Hence the hacker often devotes time to mastering a system so well that sections that are supposed to be inaccessible can be entered, programs can be altered, and generally gives nightmares to the database administrator.

handshaking   A method of controlling the flow of serial communication between two devices so that one device transmits only when the other device is ready.

hard disk   A secondary storage medium that is supplied as an integral part of some computers (unlike a floppy disk).

hardware   The electronic components of a computer system including such items as the monitor, keyboard, printer and CPU.

hashing   A means of access strategy in which the data element's value is used to generate a physical location for that element.

hertz A unit of measurement of electrical vibrations. One hertz (Hz) equals one cycle per second.

heuristic A technique for solving problems that is impossible to define because it depends upon experience, flair and general knowhow. Since children are brought up almost entirely by heuristic methods, it is comforting to know that much progress in computer science has also depended upon such rule-of-thumb techniques.

hexadecimal A numbering system that has 16 different symbols: 0,1,2,3,4,5, 6,7,8,9,A,B,C,D,E,F. Programmers often use this number base of 16 because it translates easily into binary, which is the number base that the computer uses, but is much less cumbersome to use than binary digits.

hierarchical data model A data model organized like a tree. See Chapter 8 for details.

host language The normal programming language—Pascal, C, or whatever—which acts as a host for a data manipulation language like SQL. The host language allows the query language to be embedded within it.

hypermedia The technique of combining a variety of different formats like text, graphics and sound.

index In database management programs, an index contains pointers (q.v.) which indicate the physical location of data contained in the table or file concerned. Consequently the location of such data is greatly speeded up.

inferential relationship A relationship between two data record types in which neither relationship is dependent on the primary key of either.

inkjet printer A nonimpact printer that creates characters by spraying ink from a matrix of tiny jets.

input device A peripheral that facilitates the entry of data into a computer. Common examples include the keyboard, a mouse or a modem.

insertion The action of adding a record to a database.

integrated circuit A semiconductor circuit containing transistors and other electronic components that acts as a processor for a computer or other electronic device such as a hearing aid or washing machine.

integrated program A program that combines two or more software functions. Thus we can have a database, word processor and spreadsheet combined.

integrity A state of database consistency.

interface A device or electronic circuit that acts as a link between two different pieces of hardware. Sometimes also called a port.

interpreter A translator for a high-level language into machine code. Unlike a compiler, an interpreter translates a small section which it then runs before moving on to translate the next small section. Interpreters are therefore less speedy than compilers, but are useful in that they provide the means of spotting errors in a program at more or less the very spot in which they occur.

interrupt A microprocessor instruction that halts processing temporarily until another operation (like input or output) has been completed.

ISO International Organization for Standardization.

iteration   The repetition of a command or series of commands.

job   A unit of work to be performed by the computer, often one that does not require any human intervention (such as printing a file).

join   The operation of joining two or more tables, or sections of tables, together. See Sec. 10.3 and the discussion of SQL's treatment for joins in Chapter 14.

key   A key is a particular type of data item or data element. In fact there are four possible types: primary (q.v.), candidate (q.v.), foreign (q.v.) and secondary: a primary key that is not required to be unique.

keyboard   The most common input device; a typewriter arrangement that allows you to type data into the database or issues commands for the retrieval of data from that database.

kilobyte   1024 bytes of data.

knowledge base   The portion of an expert system that expresses the necessary knowledge by means of a series of rules.

LAN   See local area network.

laser printer   A very rapid and effective method of printing by using laser beams to transfer the image to the page.

leaf node   Any node of a tree that has no descendants. See Chapter 8.

LISP   A high-level programming language often used for the manipulation of text, particularly in artificial intelligence research.

local area network   An arrangement whereby computers within a limited area (normally a single site) are linked together for the sharing of resources and memory.

logic   The science of reasoning.

logical value   In computer terms, a logical value is either *true* or *false*. Such values are sometimes called Boolean values.

logic gate   An arrangement of electronic circuits so that given inputs will produce the logically necessary output. AND, OR and NOR gates are typical examples.

lock   A restriction placed upon some data which prevents that data being accessed by anyone until the current accession has been completed. See Chapter 16.

log on   The operation of gaining access to the data and devices of a computer system. Normally you log on by inputting a password.

low-level language   A programming language which is close to the exact procedures required by the CPU. Machine code and assembly language are both low level.

machine language   Each computer can directly understand only one language —its own machine language. Machine languages are so closely related to the structure of a particular computer that they are said to be *machine dependent*. Programs written in machine language are not portable, that is, they may not be run on other computers with different machine languages. When you write a program in machine language, no translation process is necessary for the machine to use it. The main features of machine language are: each line of machine language refers to one operation represented by a series of 1s and 0s; the first few binary digits give the operation code (or op code) which instructs the computer what operation to perform; following the op code comes one or more operands. Machine-language programs can be applied to any application area. If you have the patience and skill, anything written in a higher level language can be accomplished in machine language; after all, the other languages have to be converted in machine language to work.

mainframe   A large, multiuser computer designed to meet the needs of a large and complex organization.

main memory   An element of the CPU, it is very fast (data is almost instantly accessible from main memory (storage) because of its electronic operation and close proximity to the rest of the CPU) and data *must* be transferred from main memory before processing can take place.

many-to-many relationship   A relationship type in which one entity can be related to many instances of a second entity, while, at the same time, that second entity can be related to many instances of the first entity. Thus a courtroom can be related to many solicitors, while a solicitor can be related to many courtrooms.

map   Generally used as a verb, it refers to the representation of a relationship (normally physical) between two entities. Thus you might want the means of mapping some data onto a bar chart.

meta-data   Data that describes other data.

module   A self-contained component of a program.

natural language   Almost invariably refers to the language that a DBMS uses to communicate to the database. As a consequence, such languages tend to be tied to the DBMS concerned, though SQL (q.v.) is becoming increasingly widespread. The phrase implies that the language concerned is procedure-oriented and such types are sometimes called fourth-generation languages. In vocabulary and syntax they are much closer to normal intercourse than one finds in a third-generation language.

NSL data model   A form of the network data model standardized by ANSI.

network   An arrangement of transmitters and receivers for the purpose of data communication. Thus terminals can be arranged in a star, ring or bus network.

normalization   Data that has been normalized has been arranged in a simple tabular structure in which each item of data is single-valued. There are five viable stages of progressive normalization (see Chapter 5).

null   A state in which a data item is either unknown or impossible. Hence a telephone number may exist but be unknown to you, or it may not exist at all, in which case it is impossible to represent. Nulls of either variety can cause problems within a database because their presence can distort other operations.

object   Apart from the casual way in which we all use the word to signify a physical thing or a conceptual thing, an object is also the basic entity for an object-oriented database. In such a context, an object is a package of information and a description of the ways in which it can be manipulated.

op code Operation code.

operating system The software that controls the resources of the computer and the processes that use those resources. See Chapter 2.

operation code The part of an instruction that specifies the operation to be performed by the instruction.

OR gate An electronic logic gate where the output is false (0) only when all the inputs are 0.

output Computer outputs destined for immediate use by people are produced as *hard copy*, which provides a permanent record of the output, or as *soft copy*, which is output in a temporary form.

Hard copy consists of three broad types:

1. Printed output by means of
   (a) Character-at-a-time impact printers, i.e. serial printers—daisywheel or dot matrix.
   (b) Character-at-a-time nonimpact printers, i.e. inkjet or electrothermal.
   (c) Line-at-a-time impact printers, i.e. chain or drum printers.
   (d) Page-at-a-time nonimpact printers, i.e. laser or electrostatic printers.
2. Computer output microform (COM) such as
   (a) Microfilm—a continuous strip.
   (b) Microfiche—a rectangular piece of film divided into frames, each capable of storing a page of output.
3. Output from graphic plotters such as
   (a) A drum plotter.
   (b) A flatbed plotter.

Soft copy consists of two broad types:

1. Display output, e.g. VDU.
2. Audio output, e.g. answering machines.

Yet, in addition to the above, one of the most exciting technologies of the century lies in robotics, in which output is produced by programmed mechanical means.

overflow The condition that arises when an arithmetical operation produces a result too large for the space provided for that result.

parameter A distinguishing characteristic or identifier of a data item or set of such items.

parity A system whereby the final bit in a group of binary values can be used as a check that the preceding bits are correct.

parse If a query is submitted to the database, that query is automatically parsed in order to establish that it conforms to the syntactical rules of the DBMS.

Pascal   A high-level programming language.

password   A character string that allows its user to have full or limited access to the system and/or the data contained within the system.

PC   See personal computer.

peripheral   Any device that is connected to a computer. Examples are keyboards, printers, etc.

personal computer   A general-purpose single-user microcomputer.

physical database   The physical existence of all the software components go to compose the database: rows of data, indexes, methods of accession, etc.

physical schema   The full definition of all the physical definitions needed to describe the storage of a database. Thus, if a data type is described as numeric, the physical schema will have to specify that it is packed decimal, floating point, or whatever.

pointer   A DBMS-created addressing mechanism which links or relates data record instances of the same or different types.

primary key   The key within a row upon which all the other elements within that row are functionally dependent.

program   A set of instructions by means of which a computer can be instructed to perform a task or series of tasks. The program can be written in a variety of languages from machine code (q.v.) to fourth-generation language.

protocol   Any agreement that governs the procedures used to exchange information between cooperating objects.

query language   Used with a database management system (DBMS), it enables you to retrieve items from the database, and to add elements or delete them from the database. The most widely used query language is SQL (q.v.). Part Four is largely concerned with query languages.

queue   Data waiting to be processed. The processing is normally performed in the order of the queue (FIFO—first in, first out).

QWERTY keyboard   The first six letters of the top letter row of a typewriter are QWERTY. Hence all keyboards which follow this pattern—and most computer input keyboards do—are known as QWERTY keyboards.

RAM and ROM   Each bit in semiconductor memory is represented by a single cell which may be regarded as a microscopic electronic circuit with two distinguishable states used to represent 0 and 1. In ROM each cell state is a permanent fixture set during the manufacturing process. In RAM each cell is a temporary storage unit and its contents disappear as soon as the machine is switched off. In a microcomputer ROM is used for storing data or instructions that the computer needs all the time from the moment it is switched on. RAM is used for holding the data needed during an application program.

random access   Access to data directly without the need to search through the data sequentially.

read   Commonly used as a synonym for retrieve. Thus to read a file means that the file in question is retrieved and displayed upon the screen.

read–write head   An electromagnetic device that is used to read or write data from or to the database.

real time   A real-time computer system is a system which responds immediately to various occurrences. As a consequence, results from a real-time system can arrive so rapidly as to affect the very operation in progress at the time. There is often a need for multiprocessing and a front-end processor in these systems. One example of a real-time computer system can be seen in an airline booking system. Records of seat availability on all its planes will be kept by an airline on a central computer. The computer is linked via terminals to a worldwide system of agents. Each agent can gain access to the flight records and within seconds make a reservation in respect of a particular flight. This reservation is recorded immediately so that the next enquiry for that flight (following even microseconds after the previous reservation) finds that particular seat or seats reserved. Another example can be seen in industrial process control systems such as petrol refining. Again it is the immediate responsiveness of a real-time system that is vital. If a signal from a petrol refinery indicates that the temperature in a mixing vat is rising too quickly, the real-time operating system must in turn respond quickly.

record   Often used as a synonym for row (q.v.).

recovery   The process of restoring normality after a crash.

recursive relationship   A relationship whereby an entity can have a relationship with itself. An example can be seen in a table devoted to Programs in which a particular program could be divided into subprograms and even subsubprograms.

redundancy   The state whereby some data within a database is unnecessarily duplicated.

register   A storage location in the CPU which stores addresses, instructions and data during processing.

relation   An alternative term for table (q.v.).

relational database   A system whereby separate tables of data can be easily linked together. See Chapter 14.

response time   The time taken by a computer to reply to a command.

retrieval   The process of obtaining stored data from a database.

return   The key on a computer keyboard (sometimes labelled Enter) which is pressed when you want to enter data into the CPU.

ring   A network structure whereby each node is linked to another in a ringlike fashion so that data for node C will visit nodes A and B until it arrives at C when the data is picked up.

ROM   See RAM and ROM.

root   The unique note in a hierarchical database that has no parent.

row   A group of related fields which together make up a complete set of information about an entity.

run   Normally used with reference to the execution of a program. Hence you run the payroll or the report generator or whatever.

schema   Used to describe a database organization. Defined in terms of syntax and semantics, there are commonly conceptual (or logical) schemas, physical schemas, external schemas and internal schemas.

scroll   To move text up and down a screen so that the user can view the whole document or whatever portion is of relevance at that time.

search   The process of examining data until the specific item or items are located.

secondary storage   Computers process massive amounts of information at incredibly fast speeds. At any given time, only a small part of that information must be immediately accessible. That information is kept in main storage or main memory. The other data, generally thousands of times more than can be placed in main storage, is kept in external storage devices known as secondary storage or auxiliary storage or backing storage or external storage. Speed and cost are key concerns in computer science. Secondary storage is cheap and slow.

segment   In IMS, a group of fields treated as a unit, i.e. a row. It is also used to refer to a division of a large computer program.

select   Apart from its normal usage, SELECT is also a major function of a query language.

semantics   The meaning to be attributed to a syntactical form in a language.

sequential search   The access of data according to the order in which that data is stored.

serial   One thing after another. Thus the word can refer to the transfer of data down a wire, one bit after another.

set   In a network database, a named logical relationship between tables of data.

silicon   The substance most commonly used to make computer chips.

simplex   A connection between two terminals or computers whereby data can only travel in one direction as opposed to semi-duplex or full duplex transmission where data can travel in both directions.

software   A generic term which describes the programs that control the operation of the hardware (system software) or that perform some specific function for the user (application software).

software life cycle   The complete lifetime of a software system from its conception to its death. See Chapter 3.

sort   The arrangement of data into a meaningful order.

source code   The instructions given to a computer by the user are normally written in a high-level language. These instructions are called the source code. The computer then translates them into machine language instructions, i.e. the object code.

spreadsheet   An application program normally used for financial management. See Sec. 6.1.2.

SQL   The most widespread of query languages. See Chapter 14.

star network   A simple network topology whereby all the nodes within the network are connected to a central node.

storage capacity   Quite simply, how much data a computer will hold. It is sometimes referred to as the size of the computer. This has nothing to do with its physical size; it simply means how big a memory the computer in question possesses. The storage capacity of a computer is measured in K. Thus you can see microcomputers advertised as being 48K or 64K or 128K and so on. The K (see explanation in Sec. 2.5) of a computer consequently tells you how many bytes the computer in question can hold. Since K is short for kilobyte, each K represents 1024 bytes (2 to the power of 10). Hence a 32K machine will have 32 × 1024 bytes, which comes to 32 768 bytes.

storage structure   The physical organization of a database.

system   A word that has, in normal usage, such a penumbra of meanings that its adoption by computer science has altered little. Broadly speaking, a system is a set of components which interact as a whole.

systems analysis   The procedure of investigating an existing organization and its procedures with a view to designing an improved method of working. See Chapter 3.

tab   Short for 'tabulation' which means the laying out of data in the position on the page that you want it.

table   A collection of related data arranged in columns and rows in such a way that each row represents a unique collection of values about a specific entity. Thus, if you have a table given over to countries of the world, the columns could be headed as follows: Country name, Area in sq miles, Population (1990), Main language. Each column is known as an attribute. Thus this table has four attributes.

telecommunications   The transmission and reception of electronic data between two terminals. See Chapter 18.

teleconferencing   A way by which physically separated users can communicate with each other by computer links or television.

terminal   A keyboard and screen linked to a computer. A terminal can be intelligent, which means that it has the capability of storing and manipulating data, or it can be dumb, i.e. lacking this facility.

toggle   To switch backwards and forwards between two different processes.

track   The path on a disk upon which data can be stored.

transaction   The job or series of jobs needed to be completed in order to accomplish a complete and coherent operation. Thus giving employees a 9 per cent pay rise will entail the retrieval and emendation of many rows of data, but the whole is one transaction.

transparent   Something is transparent if it carries out its function without the user needing to be concerned about how it performs that function.

trigger   A means by which one operation can act as a trigger for the doing of an associated operation.

trim   Text on a form not associated with a field.

truth table   A tabular description of the inputs and outputs of a gate.

tuple   Another name for a row within a table.

UNIX   An operating system.

user   A person who uses a computer system for applications.

user friendly   Software that is easy to use.

value   A characteristic of an attribute. Thus, if you have the attribute Colour in a table, the entry 'blue' will be a value of that attribute.

variable   An item of data whose value can change.

VDU   See visual display unit.

verify   To check that data has been input into a computer accurately.

view   A table that does not physically exist in memory but which is created each time it is called.

visual display unit   The screen on which the output of computer can be viewed.

VMS   An operating system normally used on VAX computers.

volatile store   Computer storage which loses its contents when the power is switched off.

WAN   Wide area network, a network which links widely separated sites.

wildcard   A symbol, usually ∗, which represents a group of characters. Thus you might input the instruction f∗ which indicates that you want the computer to retrieve (or copy or delete) all files that begin with the letter 'f'. A question mark can be used as a wildcard for a single character.

word   A set of binary digits that the computer treats as a single unit. Thus a computer might have a word length of a byte or 16 bits (two bytes) or 32 bits.

word processing   The process of storing, editing and manipulating text.

Bibliography

This bibliography, confined almost entirely to books and articles referred to in the text, is divided into the following sections:

1. Introductory texts on computer science.
2. The general field of information systems.
3. General textbooks on databases.
4. Query languages and SQL.
5. Types of DBMS.
6. Distributed databases.
7. Systems analysis.
8. Operating systems.
9. Current trends in database development.
10. Articles.

While many of the books listed have comments appended to them, those comments are clearly a personal reaction with which you are very free to disagree. The absence of comment implies neither approval nor disapproval.

Introductory texts on computer science

Naturally there are scores of these. The few that I referred to or occasionally used are listed below. They are rarely commented upon because it does seem genuinely difficult to make a textbook very exciting, and most of these were competent but uninspiring.

Ron Anderson, *Computer Studies: A First Year Course*, Blackwell, 1990.

D. E. Avison, *Mastering Business Microcomputing*, 2nd edn, Macmillan, 1990.

Peter Bishop, *Computing Science*, Nelson, 1982.

William S. Davis, *Concepts*, 3rd edn, Addison-Wesley, 1991.
  Brief, clear and intelligent, this is an excellent introduction to computer science for the beginner.

C. S. French, *Computer Science*, 3rd edn, DP Publications, 1989.
A very workmanlike A-level textbook.
Noel Kalicharan, *Computer Studies for GCSE*, CUP, 1988.
D. C. Palmer and D. B. Morris, *Computing Science*, Arnold, 1980.
Robert A. Stern and Nancy Stern, *An Introduction to Computers and Information Processing*, 2nd edn, John Wiley, 1982.
G. G. L. Wright, *Mastering Computers*, 2nd edn, Macmillan, 1984.

The general field of information systems

C. Ashworth and M. Goodland, *SSADM: A Practical Approach*, McGraw-Hill, 1990.
A good introduction to structured systems analysis and design method.
Robert Behling, *Computers and Information Processing*, Kent Publishing Company, 1986.
A most approachable book.
J. Bingham, *Mastering Data Processing*, Macmillan, 1983.
An elementary text.
Stan G. Blethyn and Carys Y. Parker, *Designing Information Systems*, Butterworth-Heinemann, 1990.
Jerome S. Burstein, *Computers and Information Systems*, Holt, Rinehart & Winston, 1986.
Beautifully produced and most readable.
R. A. Frost, *Introduction to Knowledge Base Systems*, Collins, 1986.
Large and technical, but clear and intelligent.
James O. Hicks, *Information Systems in Business: An Introduction*, West Publishing Company, 1986.
Despite its title, this could virtually have been placed in the preceding section.
Kenneth A. Kozar, *Humanized Information Systems Analysis and Design*, McGraw-Hill, 1989.
Henry C. Lucas, *The Analysis, Design, and Implementation of Information Systems*, 3rd edn, McGraw-Hill, 1985.
Sound and sensible.
James A. Senn, *Analysis and Design of Information Systems*, 2nd edn, McGraw-Hill, 1989.
Donald A. Waterman, *A Guide to Expert Systems*, Addison-Wesley, 1986.
Interesting and readable.

General textbooks on databases

S. Atre, *Data Base: Structured Techniques for Design, Performance, and Management*, John Wiley, 1980.
Clear and sensible, though a little out-of-date now.

D. S. Bowers, *From Data to Database*, Van Nostrand, 1988.
Bowers states that his book: 'is intended for second or final year students of computing science or related disciplines'. I enjoyed Bowers' book, but much of it would have been incomprehensible had I not already possessed a degree in information technology.

Kenmore S. Brathwaite, *Database Management and Control*, McGraw-Hill, 1990.

Malcolm Bull, *Students' Guide to Databases*, Heinemann Newnes, 1990.
Despite its title, this is not a beginner's guide. Bull admits in the preface that: 'we are assuming a certain preliminary knowledge of the general concepts of data processing and information technology and of the elementary features of the hardware and software which is used.'

C. J. Date, *Introduction to Database Systems*, 5th edn, Addison-Wesley Vol. I 1990, Vol. II 1985.
I do not think that may people would quarrel with my belief that this is the most outstanding work of them all on database systems.

S. Misbah Deen, *Principles and Practice of Database Systems*, Macmillan, 1985.
Aimed at the undergraduate audience, Deen's book is less wide-ranging than mine but much more technical. Thus there is very little indeed on security, systems analysis or query languages, but much more than I provide on data and file structure, pointers and indexes.

S. Misbah Deen (ed.), *Practical Database Techniques*, Pitman,   1990.
A collection of 12 essays of varying quality and clarity, though the best are very good.

Ramez Elmasri and Shamkant Navathe, *Fundamentals of Databases Systems*, Benjamin/Cummings Publishing Company, 1989.
The authors announce that they 'assume that readers are familiar with elementary programming and data structuring concepts'. It is very clear but forbidding for the initiate.

Gordon C. Everest, *Database Management*, McGraw-Hill, 1986.
I have little but praise for this work. It is clearly and intelligently written, and the bulk of its material could be comprehended by a beginner to the subject. Even so, Everest's book is not ideal from the point of view adopted here. As Everest states in his preface: 'This text is aimed at professionals in business and government organisations, and students of business administration and computers preparing to develop or use information systems in organisations.' Certainly such an aim is shared by this book also, but there is a considerable difference in approach between this book and Everest's. The slant in this book is towards the database system itself; Everest much more regards the database system as a tool for effective business management and considers matters through this perspective.

Lars Frank, *Database Theory and Practice*, Addison-Wesley, 1988.
Frank points out that this book is 'primarily designed for computer science

courses in higher education and for refresher courses for data processing staff'.

R. A. Frost (ed.), *Database Management Systems*, Granada, 1984.

Mark L. Gillenson, *Database Step-by-Step*, 2nd edn, John Wiley, 1990.
Gillenson assumes that the reader 'understands elementary computer principles and elementary concepts of computer programming'.

Robert C. Goldstein, *Database Technology and Management*, John Wiley, 1985.
While an excellent book in many ways, I did not find Goldstein's treatment of the network and relational data base management systems ideally clear, and the book as a whole is directed towards business management with databases as a necessary aid rather than being a book focussed on databases in their own right.

Michael M. Gorman, *Database Management Systems: Understanding and Applying Database Technology*, Computer Weekly/Butterworth-Heinemann, 1991.

Jan L. Harrington, *Making Database Management Work*, Dryden Press, 1989.
Very elementary.

D. R. Howe, *Data Analysis for Data Base Design*, 2nd edn, Arnold, 1989.
Excellent but not easy.

W. H. Inmon and Thomas J. Bird, Jr., *The Dynamics of Data Base*, Prentice Hall, 1986.
The authors do state that they assume no previous knowledge, but they do not always rigorously sustain that claim, and, although I found the book very interesting in parts, it was only in parts. Certainly I could not recommend it for a computer novice.

J. A. Jones, *Databases in Theory and Practice*, Chapman & Hall, 1986.

Peter Laurie, *Databases*, Chapman & Hall, 1985.
A book about which I was extremely complimentary in an earlier book of mine, and I have certainly not come to take a dimmer view of Mr Laurie's work. None the less, in only 139 pages, not even Mr Laurie can give anything like a detailed understanding of such a vast topic, though it remains a superb introduction.

Daniel Martin, *Advanced Database Techniques* MIT Press, 1986.

James Martin, *Principles of Data-Base Management* (1976), *An End-Users Guide to Data Base* (1981), and *Managing the Data-Base Environment* (1983), all published by Prentice Hall.
Between them, the Martin books constitute a lot of pages, and a lot of expense in buying three books, particularly since Martin is prone to include material from one book into others as well. Secondly, superbly readable though Martin's books are, they are not always as precise or as up to date as they ideally ought to be. They convey enthusiasm and excitement extremely well, but they do not always provide the hard, factual information to support that excitement and enthusiasm. Finally, and this may be merely a personal prejudice, I sometimes find the hectoring, self-righteous tone of James

Martin more than a little wearing. Superb propagandist though he undoubtedly is, it does become wearisome to be constantly told that only the Martin path is the way to true righteousness. A certain amount of intellectual humility would be welcome.

McFadden and Hoffer, *Database Management*, 3rd edn, Benjamin/Cummings, 1991.
An excellent book of over 700 pages, more technically oriented than this one.

Elizabeth Oxborrow, *Databases and Database Systems*, 2nd edn, Chartwell-Bratt, 1989.
Useful, though less approachable than the author seems to have intended.

Richard C. Perkinson, *The Key to Data Base Design*, QED, 1984.

Philip J. Pratt and Joseph J. Adamski, *Database Systems: Management and Design*, Boyd & Fraser, 1987.
An excellent textbook.

Catherine Ricardo, *Database Design*, Macmillan, 1990.
An excellent book requiring very little previous knowledge for its comprehension, though its author points out that a knowledge of data structures would be a helpful prerequisite for reading it.

Peter Scheuermann (ed.), *Improving Database Usability and Responsiveness*, Academic Press, 1982.

Peter Smith and Michael Barnes, *Files and Databases: An Introduction*, Addison-Wesley, 1987.
In their preface, Smith and Barnes announce that they 'assume a certain amount of knowledge on the part of readers and expect familiarity with basic data structures such as records, lists and trees'. Indeed the book opens with this paragraph:

Our major objective in this book is to present concepts about file and database processing. In doing so we will cover two broad areas. The first is the application of data structure techniques to secondary memory. The second is the evaluation of alternate solutions to the problem of mapping user views of data onto physical storage. We will examine this problem both in the file environment (the file addressing problem) and the database environment (database models). We will discuss at length a variety of techniques used to store and retrieve information maintained in secondary memory.

This is a perfectly clear and sound paragraph if you already know about the distinction between files and databases, understand what is meant by data structure techniques and mapping user views, and have no problem with phrases like secondary memory and physical storage. If, however, all of that is a form of alien jargon, then the Smith and Barnes book is not for you.

David Stamper and Wilson Price, *Database Design and Management*, McGraw-Hill, 1990.
Clear and sensible.

Bo Sundgren, *Data Bases and Data Models*, Chartwell-Bratt, 1985.
Slim but interesting and intelligent.

Joseph A. Vasta, *Understanding Database Management Systems*, 2nd edn, Wadsworth, 1989.

An extremely useful and intelligent book.

Gottfried Vossen, *Data Models, Database Languages and Database Management Systems*, Addison-Wesley, 1990.

Vossen makes it plain that the book is 'an introductory text on database management' and that 'Part I is particularly meant for readers without prior knowledge in the area'. Yet, on only the fourth page of the first chapter, we encounter the following two paragraphs:

> The *third generation*, which roughly coincides with the 1970s, but actually started in the late 1960s, is characterized by the introduction of a distinction between *logical* and *physical* information, which occurred parallel to an increasing need to *manage* large collections of data (as opposed to pure processing mentioned earlier). During that time, *data models* were used for the first time to describe physical structures from a logical point of view; however, the then emerging approaches such as the hierarchical or the network model have to be classified as 'implementation-oriented'.
>
> Starting from, this distinction between the (logical) meaning of data, that is, the syntax and the semantics of its description, and its current (physical) value, systems were developed which could *integrate* all the data of a given application into one collection (which was hence forth termed a *database*), and which provided individual users of this collection with a particular 'view' to it only.

Mr Vossen seems to believe that placing words in italics dispenses with any necessity of explaining what they mean. It is not an approach that the beginner in the subject will find very illuminating.

Gio Wiederhold, *Database Design*, McGraw-Hill, 1977.

A pioneer book.

Query languages and SQL

Sandra L. Emerson, Marcy Darnovsky and Judith Bowman, *The Practical SQL Handbook*, Addison-Wesley, 1989.

Robert S. Epstein, *Query Processing Techniques for Distributed, Relational Data Base Systems*, UMI Research Press, 1982.

Carolyn J. Hursch and Jack L. Hursch, *SQL: The Structured Query Language*, TAB, 1988.

Dan Kapp and Joseph F. Leben, *IMS Programming Techniques: A Guide to Using DL/1*, Van Nostrand Reinhold, 1978.

Rick F. van der Lans, *Introduction to SQL*, Addison-Wesley, 1988.

A full, encyclopedic treatment, tending to share some of the tedium of the average encyclopedia.

Rick F. van der Lans, *The SQL Standard*, Prentice Hall, 1989.

Elizabeth Lynch, *Understanding SQL*, Macmillan, 1990.

This book is most clearly and interestingly written.

Soren Vang, *SQL and Relational Databases*, Microtrend, 1991.

John Watt, *Applied Fourth Generation Languages*, Sigma Press, 1987.

Types of DBMS

This heading is perhaps a little ambiguous, but I could not think of an alternative. By it I mean books that discuss the various data models to which databases adhere and books which deal with specific implementations of a particularly data model.

A. Abdellatif, J. Le Bihan and M. Limame, *Oracle: A User's Guide*, Macmillan, 1990.

Paul Beynon-Davies, *Relational Database Systems*, Blackwell, 1991.

C. J. Date, *A Guide to INGRES*, Addison-Wesley, 1987.

Candace E. Fleming and Barbara von Halle, *Handbook of Relational Database Design*, Addison-Wesley, 1989.

Georges Gardarin and Patrick Valduriez, *Relational Databases and Knowledge Bases*, Addison-Wesley, 1989.

Georges Gardarin and Patrick Valduriez, *Analysis and Comparison of Relational Database Systems*, Addison-Wesley, 1989.

Glenn A. Jackson, *Relational Database Design with Microcomputer Applications*, Prentice Hall, 1988.

Carl Malamud, *INGRES: Tools for Building an Information Architecture*, Van Nostrand Reinhold, 1989.

Peter Matthews, *Ingres User Guide: Visual Programming Tools*, Prentice Hall, 1991.

Sitansu S. Mittra, *Principles of Relational Database Systems*, Prentice Hall, 1991.

T. William Olle, *The CODASYL Approach to Data Base Management*, John Wiley, 1978.

James T. Parry and Robert F. McJunkins, *A User's Guide to dBaseII*, Reston Publishing Company, 1984.

Dan Remenyi and James Dalby, *dBase II & III*, Longman, 1985.

David Rothwell, *INGRES and Relational Databases*, McGraw-Hill, 1992.

Chao-Chih Yang, *Relational Databases*, Prentice Hall, 1986.

Distributed databases

Stefano Ceri and Giuseppe Pelagatti, *Distributed Databases: Principles and Systems*, McGraw-Hill, 1984.

George F. Coulouris and Jean Dollimore, *Distributed Systems: Concepts and Design*, Addison-Wesley, 1988.

M. Tamer Ozsu and Patrick Valduriez, *Principles of Distributed Database Systems*, Prentice Hall, 1991.

Systems analysis

Peter Checkland and Jim Scholes, *Soft Systems Methodology in Action*, John Wiley, 1990.

Rosemary Rock-Evans, *Analysis Within the Systems Development Life-Cycle*, Pergamon, 1987.
Four weighty volumes, but extremely clear and well-written.
Jeffrey L. Whitten, Lonnie D. Bentley and Thomas I. M. Ho, *Systems Analysis & Design Methods*, Time Mirror/Mosby College Publishing 1986.
Most readable and entertaining.
Edward Yourdon, *Modern Structured Analysis*, Prentice Hall, 1989.
Clear, well-written, interesting, and essential reading for the so-called structured approach.

Operating systems

Harvey M. Deitel, *An Introduction to Operating Systems*, Addison-Wesley, 1984.
A. M. Lister, *Fundamentals of Operating Systems*, 3rd edn, Macmillan, 1984.
Excellent introduction.
James L. Peterson and Abraham Silberschatz, *Operating System Concepts*, 2nd edn, Addison-Wesley, 1985.

Current trends in database development

P. Beynon-Davies, *Expert Database Systems*, McGraw-Hill, 1991.
Larry Bielawski and Robert Lewand, *Intelligent Systems Design: Integrating Expert Systems, Hypermedia, and Database Technologies*, John Wiley, 1991.
Gordon Blair, John Gallaghar, David Hutchison and Doug Shepherd (eds), *Object-Oriented Languages, Systems and Applications*, Pitman, 1991.
Kenmore S. Brathwaite, *Applications Development Using CASE Tools*, Academic Press, 1990.
A. Brown, *Object-Oriented Databases*, McGraw-Hill, 1991.
Setrag Khoshafian and Razmik Abnous, *Object Orientation: Concepts, Languages, Databases, User Interfaces*, John Wiley, 1990.
David M. W. Powers and Christopher C. R. Turk, *Machine Learning of Natural Language*, Springer-Verlag, 1989.
Stanley Y. W. Su, *Database Computers: Principles, Architectures & Techniques*, McGraw-Hill, 1988.

Articles

Since this book has not been a book of research, it has not been necessary to use articles from learned periodicals a great deal. Hence the brevity of this section.
Chris Bidmead, 'Technology, report: object oriented programming: making the right moves', *Which Computer?*, July 1991, pp. 112–14.
Rob B. Buitendijk and Harm van der Lek, 'Direct manipulation of a data dictionary with SQL', *Information Systems*, vol. 16, no. 3, pp. 323–33, 1991.

Virginia M. Doland, 'Hypermedia as an interpretive art', *Hypermedia*, vol. 1, no. 1, 1989.

Malcolm Fowles, 'Object oriented data management', *The Computer Bulletin*, vol. 2, part 10, Dec. 1990.

Timothy J. Heintz, 'Object-oriented databases and their impact on future business database applications', *Information & Management*, vol. 20, no. 2, pp. 95–103, Feb. 1991.

Jane M. Mackay and Charles W. Lamb, Jr., 'Training needs of novices and experts with referent experience and task domain knowledge', *Information & Management*, vol. 20, no. 3, March 1991, pp. 183–9.

Dave D. Straube and M. Tamer Özsu, 'Queries and query processing in object-oriented database systems', *ACM Transactions on Information Systems*, vol. 8, no. 4, pp. 387–430, Oct. 1990.

Index